Marriages and Deaths from Richmond, Virginia Newspapers

1780-1820

Published by
THE VIRGINIA GENEALOGICAL SOCIETY

Special Publication Number 8

This volume was reproduced from
A personal copy located in the
Publisher's private library

Please direct all correspondence and orders to:

www.southernhistoricalpress.com
or
SOUTHERN HISTORICAL PRESS, Inc.
PO BOX 1267
Greenville, SC   29601
southernhistoricalpress@gmail.com

Originally published: Richmond, VA   1983
Copyright 1983 by: Virginia Genealogical Society
Copyright Transferred 1986 to:
        Southern Historical Press, Inc.
ISBN #0-89308-619-3
All rights Reserved.
Printed in the United States of America

INTRODUCTION

Richmond became capitol of Virginia in 1779. In the following year The Virginia Gazette moved from Williamsburg to Richmond and began publication there. Thereafter it was published under a variety of names, some of which were published simultaneously. It is difficult to tell whether these were under the same or different management. The Virginia Gazette and American Advertiser is available for 1781-1785. The Virginia Gazette and Weekly Advertiser was published 1782-1793. The Virginia Gazette or Independent Chronicle was published 1783-1788. The Virginia Independent Chronicle appeared 1788-1789 and became the Virginia Independent Chronicle and General Advertiser 1789-1790. The Virginia Gazette and General Advertiser was published 1790-1809, The Virginia Gazette and Richmond Daily Advertiser in 1792, The Virginia Gazette and Richmond and Manchester Daily Advertiser 1793-1796, and The Virginia Gazette and Richmond Chronicle 1793-1795. The Richmond Chronicle was published 1795-1796. Files of The Virginia Argus are available for 1796-1804. A few issues were available also for: The Observatory, 1797, 98 and 1800. The Examiner 1799 and 1803, The Virginia Federalist 1799-1800, The Recorder 1802-1803, The Richmond Examiner 1803, The Impartial Observer 1807, Spirit of 76 1808-1809, The Virginian 1808, and The Visitor 1809-1810. The Richmond Enquirer began publication in 1804 and continued until late in the 19th century (in this volume carried through 1820) The Virginia Patriot, beginning in 1809 goes through 1815, and in 1816 became The Virginia Patriot and Daily Mercantile Advertiser. It is carried in this volume through 1820. The Richmond Complier began publication in 1813, and is also carried here through 1820.

It is obvious from perusal of these old newspapers that many issues are missing. Some of these can be found in other collections throughout the country. It should be emphasized that only the collection of The Virginia State Library was used in the preparation of this book. In October 1921, the Bulletin of the Virginia State Library, Vol. XIV, No. 4, carried an index of obituary notices in The Richmond Enquirer 1804-1828 and the Richmond Whig 1824-1838. This contained only the person's name and the location of the notice in the paper. It has been reprinted by The Genealogical Publishing Co. The Virginia Genealogical Society Quarterly printed the marriage and death notices from The Visitor 1809-1810, abstracted by Mrs. Anne Arritt, in Vol. 7 (1969)

Since Richmond was the state capitol and a center of commerce for a wide area, the marriage and death notices abstracted here frequently refer to persons in other states, and other areas of Virginia. Many of the notices are from the "burned counties" of Virginia. Some of the notices included were news items rather than obituaries or social notes. Many were obviously copied from out of town papers of unknown dates, and a number of these were apparently included for their humor content or strangeness.

The notices of deaths are in alphabetical order, followed by the marriage notices in alphabetical order by groom. There is a separate index of brides. The newspaper name has been indicated by initials, the key to which is at the end of this introduction.

Special thanks is due to Mr. Bernard Henley, who has the gratitude of the Virginia Genealogical Society for having abstracted all of the notices in this volume from the microfilm reels. He has graciously allowed the society the use of this material. This volume is the first in a series of approximately three volumes which will carry the project through 1860.

Finally, a word to the reader is in order to check the original if there is a question of accuracy, as errors frequently creep into works such as this. Also be warned that newspapers in the 18th and 19th centuries made just as many mistakes as they do today.

KEY:

Examiner - Examiner
IO - Impartial Observer
Observatory - Observatory
Recorder - Recorder
RC - (in 1795-96) Richmond Chronicle
RC - (1813 on) Richmond Compiler
RE - Richmond Enquirer
Richmond Examiner - Richmond Examiner
Spirit of 76 - Spirit of 76
VA - Richmond Argus
VF - Virginia Federalist
VG - Virginia Gazette
VGAA - Virginia Gazette and American Advertiser
VGGA - Virginia Gazette and General Advertiser
VGIC - Virginia Gazette and Independent Chronicle
VGRC - Virginia Gazette and Richmond Chronicle
VGRDA - Virginia Gazette and Richmond Daily Advertiser
VGRMA - Virginia Gazette and Richmond and Manchester Advertiser
VGWA - Virginia Gazette and Weekly Advertiser
VIC - Virginia Independent Chronicle
VICGA - Virginia Independent Chronicle and General Advertiser
Virginian - Virginian
VP - Virginia Patriot
VRPDMA - Virginia Patriot and Richmond Daily Mercantile Advertiser
Visitor - Visitor

Virginia Genealogical Society
P. O. Box 7469
Richmond, Virginia 23221

DEATHS

Died, MR. FLEMING ABBOTT, late one of the clerks of the Custom House of this port, at Havana on Nov. 13th
RE 3 Dec. 1811, p. 3

Died, MRS. ABBOTT, wife of Mr. Josiah Abbott of this city (No death date)
VGMA 6 April 1796, p. 3

Died on Thurs. last (Feb. 16) CAPT. MORDECAI ABRAMS of King William.
VGGA 22 Feb. 1792, p. 3

Died at Quincy, Mass., MRS. ABAGAIL ADAMS, consort of Pres. Adams, age 74. (No death date)
RE 6 Nov. 1818, p. 3, VP 5 Nov., p. 3

Died, ABIJAH ADAMS, Senior Editor of the Independent Chronicle of Boston. (No death date but notice dated May 19)
VA 29 May 1816, p. 3

Died Sunday last (Aug. 5) DR. ASHLEY ADAMS of Petersburg.
VA 8 Aug. 1804, p. 3

Died, MRS. ADAMS, consort of Col. Richard Adams. (No death date)
RE 20 Oct. 1809, p. 3; VA 24 Oct., p. 3, says, MRS. ELIZABETH ADAMS, and died on 17th Instant; Visitor 21 Oct., p. 150

Died on Monday last (Dec. 22) MRS. ADAMS, relict of Col. Richardson of this city.
VGGA 26 Dec. 1800, p. 3

Died at Haverhill, Mass. June 24th, MR. NATHANIEL G. H. ADAMS, age 24, late of firm of Adams & Spear of Richmond
RC 11 July 1820, p. 3, VPRDMA 11 July, p. 3

Died on Friday last (Aug. 1) at an advanced age, COL. RICHARD ADAMS of this city.
VA 5 Aug. 1800, p. 3; VGGA 5 Aug. p. 3

Died at his home on Richmond Hill on Jan. 9th, COL. RICHARD ADAMS, age 57.
VP 10 Jan 1817, p. 3

Died Aug. 9th in a duel near old brick church in Blandford, ROBERT C. ADAMS of Petersburg.
VPRDMA 12 Aug. 1820, p. 3

Died in this city, MRS. SALLY ADAMS, spouse of Thomas B. Adams, Esq. (No death date)
VGGA 21 May 1794, p. 2; VGRMA 15 May

Died, MRS. SARAH ADAMS, wife of Col. Richard Adams, lately married. (No death date)
RE 10 June 1815, p. 3; VA 17 June, p. 3, says died June 8th

Died, Oct. 2nd, SAMUEL ADAMS, late Gov. of Mass. age 82
VA 12 Oct. 1803, p. 3

Died on 25th Inst. at house of Mr. James Willett in Manchester, Va., MR. SAMUEL
ADAMS, age 21. He came from Tenn. in 1812
RE 30 Aug. 1815, p. 3; VA 2 Sept., p. 3 says died Aug. 27th

Died 8th July last, THOMAS ADAMS, Esq., at house of Dr. Corbin Griffin of York
IC 6 Aug. 1788, p. 3

Died Fri. last (Nov. 28) at Col. Richard Adams' in this city, THOMAS BOWLER ADAMS,
Esq.
VGGA 3 Dec. 1794, p. 3
VGRMA 1 Dec.

Died Tues. last (June 5) in this city, MR. WILLIAM ADAMS, 3rd son of Col. Richard
Adams, not more than 23 years old
VGWA 7 June, 1787, p. 3

Died lately at Pittsburg, HON. ALEXANDER ADDISON, late Pres. of Court of Common
Pleas in one of districts of Pa.
RE 15 Dec. 1807, p. 3

Died, CAPT. JOHN ADDISON, who sailed out of Richmond for many years, on the 8th,
on board the schooner Experiment
VA 29 July 1808, p. 3

On Fri. last (before Oct. 15th) (?) in Shepherdstown, a MR. AINSWORTH dropped
dead in the street
VGRDA 5 Nov. 1792, p. 3

Died Thurs. last (Aug. 4) SEIGNOR FRANCISCO ALBERTI, a native of Italy, a musician
for many years in this state
VGWA 6 Aug. 1785, p. 3

Died, _____ ALCOCK, son of Mr. John Alcock, of this city, a victim of the
theatre fire (No death date)
RE 14 Jan. 1812, p. 3; VA 16 Jan. p. 3

Killed fighting Indians in Tenn., August 8th, JOSEPH ALEXANDER
VGWA 2 Oct. 1788, p. 3

Died on Sat. last (Sept. 27th) MR. WILLIAM ALEXANDER of Campbell, murdered by
unknown persons
VGGA 3 Oct. 1800, p. 3

Died in Woodford Co., Ky., Sun. (no death date) WILLIAM ALEXANDER, age 90.
A native of Edinburgh, he later lived in France and in Richmond Va.
RC 5 Feb. 1819, p. 4

Died on 22nd Ult., MRS. JANE ALLEGRE of this city
VGGA 2 Jan. 1793, p. 3; VGWA 4 Jan 1793

Died in Prince Edward Co. on 20th Ult., JAMES ALLEN, age 69
VGGA 20 Nov. 1793, p. 3

Died in this city on 13th Inst., HON. JOHN ALLEN, Member of the Executive Council
of this State.
VA 21 May 1799, p. 3

Died, MRS. ALLEN, wife of Jedediah Allen of this city. Sat. last (Sept. 22)
VA 26 Sept. 1804, p. 3

Died on 20th Inst. at the Bowling Green, MR. WILLIAM ALLEN of New Kent Co.,
youngest son of late Col. Richard Allen of New Kent
VGGA 24 Jan. 1809, p. 3

Died, CAPT. WILLIAM G. ALLEN, on Sun. last (July 17)
VGGA 19 July 1808, p. 3

Died, MRS. FRANCES ALLISON, consort of Mr. Samuel Allison (No death date)
VGRC 30 Sept. 1794, p. 3

Died lately at James Town in James City Co., MRS. FANNY AMBLER, spouse of
Mr. John Ambler
IC 28 May 1788, p. 2

Died in this city on Wed. last (Jan. 10) JAQUELIN AMBLER, Esq., Treasurer of
this Commonwealth
VA 12 Jan. 1798, p. 3; VGGA 17 Jan., p. 3, "age 55"

Died, MRS. AMBLER of this city on Friday (Aug. 1)
VA 6 Aug. 1806, p. 3; RE 5 Aug., p. 3; VGGA 6 Aug. p. 3, says: Mrs. Rebecca
Ambler, age 61, relict of late Jacquelin Ambler

Died, MR. BENJAMIN AMES of the house of Ames & Underhill, on 15th Inst., a
member of Baptist Church in Richmond, and a deacon
RE 27 Oct. 1812, p. 3

Died, FISHER AMES, at his seat at Dedham, Mass. (No death date)
VA 15 July 1808. p. 3

Died in Richmond yesterday, MR. ISAAC AMES, age 24, formerly of Haverhill, Mass.
RC 6 Nov. 1818, p. 3; VP 6 Nov. p. 3

Died, MISS JULIA ANN AMES (No death date)
RC 18 Sept. 1818, p. 3

Died in Hanover Co., on Friday last (Aug. 8) MRS. AGNESS ANDERSON, age 93
VGGA 12 Aug. 1800, p. 3

Died, MRS. ANN ANDERSON, relict of Capt. Robert Anderson, on Fri. last (July 17)
VP 24 July 1812, p. 3

Died at his seat in Hanover, MR. BARTELOT ANDERSON (No death date)
VGGA 18 Oct. 1797. p. 2

Died in Gloucester Town on 26th July, MRS. ELIZABETH ANDERSON, consort of
Ambrose Anderson, Esq.
RC 27 Aug. 1796, p. 3

Died, GARLAND ANDERSON, Esq., at upper end of Hanover Co., age 69, on March 8th,
was a Revolutionary soldier, represented Hanover in the legislature, and was a
Magistrate in Hanover Co.
RE 15 March 1811, p. 3; VA 18 March, p. 3

Died fighting Indians in Tenn., Aug. 8th ISAAC ANDERSON
VGWA 2 Oct. 1788, p. 3

Died on 15th Inst. at The White House, New Kent Co., MR. JAMES ANDERSON, age 63
VA 17 March 1807, p. 3

Died, JAMES ANDERSON, age 29, at The White House, New Kent Co., on May 1st
VA 6 May 1813, p. 3

Died on 26th Ult. MR. JOHN ANDERSON of King William Co.
VA 7 March 1806, p. 3

Died at his seat in Chesterfield Co. on 20th Oct., DR. JORDAN ANDERSON, age 84
VGGA 9 Nov. 1805, p. 2

Died on Wed. last (Nov. 13), age 82, MRS. MARY ANDERSON, married for 57 years
to Dr. Jordan Anderson, lately dec'd
VGGA 20 Nov. 1805, p. 2

Died June 12th, MRS. MARY ANDERSON of Gloucester Co., age 71
RE 7 July 1820, p. 3

Died last Sat., (May 15) MRS. ANDERSON, spouse of Mr. George Anderson of Henrico
Co.
VGIC May 22, 1784, p. 3

Died on Sat. last (Dec. 15) CAPT. NATHANIEL ANDERSON of Caroline Co.
Observatory 20 Dec. 1798, p. 3

Died, MR. NATHANIEL ANDERSON, at his seat in Albermarle Co., for a number of years
a res. of Richmond (No death date)
RE 8 Feb. 1812, p. 3; VA 10 Feb., p. 3

Died, MR. OVERTON ANDERSON, merchant, of this city, on 19th Nov. last, at seat
of Samuel Mosby, Esq. in Hanover Co.
RE 12 Dec. 1809, p. 3; VGGA 12 Dec., p. 3; Visitor 16 Dec., p. 182

Died Aug. 15th, PETER ANDERSON, sailor on The British ship "Alligator" in Hampton Roads
RC 22 Aug. 1818, p. 3

Died Wed. last (Nov. 12) age 62, MRS. MARY BLAIR ANDREWS, late of Williamsburg, and only surviving daughter of late Judge John Blair of Williamsburg
RE 20 Jan. 1820, p. 3; RC 14 Jan., p. 3; VPRDMA 17 Jan., p. 3 says died Jan. 10th

Died Jan. 26th, MR. JOHN ANTHONY of Hanover Co., age 104
RE 13 Feb. 1817, p. 3

Died in Yorktown, MRS. ARCHER, consort of Mr. Abraham Archer of that town
(No death date)
VGGA 31 Jan. 1798, p. 2

Died, MRS. ARCHER, wife of John Archer, in Amelia, on 6th Inst.
RE 24 March 1812, p. 3

Died at his seat near Scottsville, Powhatan Co. April 25th, MAJ. PETER F. ARCHER, age 58
RE 25 May 1814, p. 3
He had married 1st Frances Tanner, dau. of Branch Tanner, Esq. of Chesterfield, and 2nd in 1797, Judith Cock, dau. of Stephen Cock, Esq. of Amelia

Died on 16th Ult. MR. RICHARD ARCHER of Amelia Co.
VGRMA 10 Sept. 1796, p. 2

Died, MR. THOMAS ARCHER, SR. of Yorktown (No death date)
VG April 7, 1781, p. 2

Died June 13th in Hampton, MR. JOHN PATRICK ARMISTEAD of that place, married only a short time.
RC 17 June 1820, p. 3

Died, MAJ. W. ARMISTEAD, on Sat. (Sept. 30) a Revolutinary Officer
RE 3 Oct. 1809, p. 3; Visitor 7 Oct, p. 142 says Majo. William Armistead

Died in Sevier Co., Tenn., MRS. NANCY ANN ARMSTRONG, formerly of Greene Co., Tenn. widow of Benjamin Armstrong, drowned in Little Pigeon River, age 59, survived by several children (No death date)
VP 3 Nov. 1818, p. 3

Died at his house in Gloucester Place, June 13th, BRIG. GEN. BENEDICT ARNOLD
VA 17 Nov. 1801, p. 3

Died yesterday, MR. CHARLES R. ARTHUR
VGGA 21 Sept. 1796, p. 2

Died, FRANCIS ASBURY, Bishop of the Methodist Episcopal Church, on March 31st. at Mr. George Arnold's in Spotsylvania Co.
RE 10 April, 1816, p. 3

Died, MR. WILLIAM FREDERICK AST, on 20th Inst., Principal Agent of Mutual
Assurance Society against Fire on Buildings
VA 23 Sept. 1807, p. 3; RE 26 Sept. p. 3, says age 41; VGGA 26 Sept. p. 3

Died on 9th Inst., MRS. PHEBE ATHERTON, wife of Capt. Daniel Atherton of this
city. Their only child died 3 weeks before
RE 14 Oct. 1806, p. 3

Died, MR. CHARLES ATKINSON of Fredericksburg age 22, in Kingston, Jamaica on
22nd Ult.
VGRMA 27 Oct. 1794, p. 3

Died on Sun. (Nov. 27th) age 26, Mr. LEWIS ATKINSON, for last 4 years a teacher
in Richmond
RC 30 Nov. 1814, p. 3

Died on 1st Inst., MR. ABNER AUSTIN of Hanover Co.
VGGA 5 Oct. 1796, p. 2; VGRMA 4 Oct. p. 3

Died Dec. 12th, JOHN AUSTIN, SR. of Hanover Co., age 90
RE 19 Dec. 1815, p. 3

Died on Sun. (Dec. 11) MR. REUBEN AUSTIN, Attorney at Law, of Manchester
VA 12 Dec., 1796, p. 3

Died on 13th Inst., MRS. SARAH AUSTIN, wife of Capt. John Austin, Jr. of Hanover
Co.
VGGA 22 Oct. 1799, p. 3

Died, MAJ. WILLIAM AUSTIN of this city on 29th Ult.
VA 1 May 1807, p. 3; RE 1 May, p. 3, says long time resident and Magis. of
Cavalry
VGGA 25 Apr., p. 3

Died Nov. 13th at Montville, King William Co., ELIZABETH H. AYLETT, 2nd dau.
of Philip Aylett, age 21.
RE 27 Nov. 1818, p. 3

Died, MR. GORDON BACCHUS, formely a merchant in Petersburg, on about 14th Inst.
in New York
RE 22 Dec. 1810, p. 3; VP 25 Dec. p. 3

Died on 5th Inst. in Philadelphia, age 34, MRS. SARAH BACHE, wife of Richard Bache,
and only dau. of late Dr. Benjamin Franklin
RE 14 Oct. 1808, p. 3

Died Jan. 8th on the Brook, Henrico Co., CAPT. IZARD BACON, age about 76
RE 11 Jan. 1816, p. 3; VP 10 Jan., p. 3

Died March 10th, HARRY BAGBY of Buckingham Co., age 77, Inspector of Tobacco
at New Canton for many years
VP 16 March 1818, p. 2

Died, MR. ADAM BAIRD, stone mason, of this city on Thurs. (Jan. 3)
VP 5 Jan. 1811, p. 3

Died in Moore Co., N.C., HON.BLAKE BAKER, a Judge of Supreme Ct. of N.C.
(No death date)
RE 20 Nov. 1818, p. 3

Died Fri. last (Aug. 31) at his seat Archers Hill in Chesterfield Co.,
JERMAN BAKER, Esq. Counsellor and Attorney at Law
VGGA 5 Sept. 1792, p. 3

Died, MR. JOHN BAKER of Goochland Co., on Sun. last (Nov. 3)
VA 6 Nov. 1805, p. 3

Died on Fri. last (Oct. 23) MR. BAKER, a native of England, lately from Guernsey
VA 30 Oct. 1801, p. 3

Died, MR. PETER BAKER of Goochland Co., on Wed. last (Oct. 15) at an advanced
age
VA 22 Oct. 1806, p. 3

Died in Washington City on 4th Inst., ABRAHAM BALDWIN, Esq., Senator from Georgia
VA 13 March 1807, p. 3

Died Jan. 4th at his seat in Amelia Co., GEORGE BALDWIN, SR., an old inhabitant
of that county
RE 13 Feb. 1817, p. 3

Died on 14th Inst. (Ult.) at his seat in Frederick Co., MAJ. THOMAS BALDWIN, age
63
Visitor 9 Sept. 1809, p. 127

Died Aug. 27th in Prince Edward Co., MR. WILLIAM BALDWIN, age 38, leaving wife
and 6 children
RC 13 Sept. 1819, p. 3

Died, COL. JAMES V. BALL, believed born in Westmoreland Co. and served in U.S. Army from 1794 (No death date)
<u>VP</u> 4 April 1818, p. 3

Died Aug. 21st at Fighting Creek, Powhatan Co., MISS CHARLOTTE BALFOUR
<u>VP</u> 26 Aug. 1815, p. 3

Died, GEORGE BALL, Esq. of Gloucester Co., on 1st Oct.
<u>RE</u> 20 Nov. 1812, p. 3

Died, MRS. LETTICE Ball of Lancaster Co., mother of late Dr. Wm. Ball (No death date)
VGWA 6 Nov. 1788, p. 3

Died, 6 year old son of Mr. Samuel Ball of Richmond, on Friday (5 Feb)
<u>RC</u> 6 Feb. 1819, p. 3

The funeral sermon of late MAJ. WILLIAM BALL will be preached on Thurs. (25 Sept.) at Brook Rock Church
<u>RE</u> Sept. 23, 1817, p. 3

Died, WILLIAM BALL, JR., Ensign of the Winchester Rifles at Fort Nelson, on May 24th
<u>RE</u> 29 May 1813, p. 2; <u>VA</u> 31 May, p. 2

Died, JOHN BALLENBERGER, formerly of Lancaster, Pa., A U.S. Soldier, killed by Indains March 28th, near Fort Armstrong, Mo.
VPRDMA 6 July 1820, p. 2

Died on 9th Inst., ABRAHAM BALLENDINE, a free mulatto, well known by gentlemen of the turf
VGRMA 15 June 1796, p. 3

Died on 1st Inst. at Ward, Mass., RUTH BANCFORT, widow, age 94
<u>Visitor</u> 23 Sept. 1809, p. 135

Died, COL. BANISTER, at his seat near Petersburg, formerly in Congress (No death date)
VGWA 16 Oct. 1788, p. 3

Died in Richmond on 10th Inst., STEWART BANKHEAD of Westmoreland Co.
<u>RE</u> 14 May 1805, p. 3

Died, ALEXANDER BANKS, merchant, of Manchester, on Sat. last (Nov. 28)
<u>RE</u> 1 Dec. 1807, p. 3

Died in this city on Sun. last (Nov. 6) MRS. CATHARINE BANKS, consort of Maj. George W. Banks of Essex Co.
<u>RE</u> 8 Nov. 1814, p. 3

Died Friday sen'night (June 15) at his seat in Stafford Co., GERRARD BANKS, Esq.
VGIC 23 June 1787, p. 3; VGWA 21 June, p. 3

Died, MR. JOHN BANKS, for some time a resident of this city (No death date)
RE 20 Oct. 1809, p. 3; VGGA 13 Oct. p. 3; Visitor 21 Oct., p. 150, says died
on 12th Inst.

Died on Mon. last (3 Dec.) MRS. MARTHA KOYALL BANKS, consort of Henry Banks of
this city
RE 6 Dec. 1804, p. 3; VA 8 Dec., p. 3; VGGA 5 Dec. p. 3 (says Mr. Banks was
an attorney)

Died lately in SC, LT. BARBOUR of the Virginia Line
VGAA Sept. 14, 1782, p. 3

Died July 4th, age 18, BENJAMIN JOHNSON BARBOUR, at home of his brother James
Barbour of Orange Co.
RE 11 July 1820, p. 2

Died on 29th Ult. in this city, COL. PHILIP BARBOUR, buried in the churchyard
VGGA 2 April 1794, p. 3; VGRMA 31 March

Died in Richmond on Sun. (Aug. 1) MISS ANN BARCLAY, dau. of Mr. David Barclay
VP 3 Aug. 1819, p. 3

Died Sat. last (April 14) a man named BARKER fell out of canoe at Rocketts
VGWA 19 April 1787, p. 3

Died yesterday at Rocketts, MRS. ELIZABETH BARKER
RC 24 March 1820, p. 3

Died this morning, CAPT. CHRISTOPHER BARMINGHAM
RC 15 Sept. 1795, p. 2

Died at Tappahannock, Essex Co., May 30th RICHARD BARNES
RE 9 June 1820, p. 3

Died in Norfolk on Sat. (Sept. 18) age 21, MRS. MARTHA BARNETT, consort of
Mr. James Barnett, of late firm of Lawson & Barnett
VP 23 Sept. 1819, p. 3

Died in Pittsburg, Pa., Dec. 1st, Commodore JOSHUA BARNEY, age 60, born
July 6, 1759
RE 12 Dec. 1818, p. 3; VP 11 Dec., p. 2

Died, CAPT. BARRE, a French gentleman, drowned in Acquia Creek
VGRMA 5 Feb. 1795, p. 3

Died, MRS. CAROLINE BARRET, wife of Mr. Charles Barret, in Williamsburg, on
the 6th this month
RE 12 April 1811, p. 3

Died Friday last (Jan 13) at Airwell in Hanover Co., WILLIAM BARRET of Richmond
VGGA 18 Jan. 1792, p. 2

Died, MR. GILES L. BARRETT, formely of the theatre, age 65, in Boston on 8th
Inst.
Visitor 16 Dec. 1809, p. 182

Died, Commodore SAMUEL BARRON, in Norfolk, on Oct. 29th
VA 6 Nov. 1810, p. 3

Died in Philadelphia on 13th Inst., Commodore JOHN BARRY
VA 21 Sept. 1803. p. 3

Died yesterday (Hanged for murder) GEORGE BARTLETT
VA 19 May, 1804, p. 2

Died lately at Marblehead, Mass., CAPT. NATHANIEL BARTLETT, age 70, served in
Navy in Revolution
VP 4 May 1819, p. 3

Died at Warren, R.I., WILLIAM BARTON, Esq., age 64 (No death date)
Visitor 9 Sept. 1809, p. 127

Died Jan. 30th, MR. THOMAS BASS, JR. of Chesterfield
RE 12 Feb. 1818, p. 3

Died, MR. BENJAMIN BATES of Hanover Co. on Sat. last (Dec. 12). He was a poet
and mathematician. A member of Society of Friends
RE 19 Dec. 1812, p. 3; VA 17 Dec., p. 3

Died, CHARLES F. BATES, Esq., Attorney at Law of Goochland Co., on Mon. last
(May 30)
VA 3 June 1808, p. 3; VGGA 3 June, p. 3; Virginian 3 June, p. 3

Died Sept. 6th, MATTHEW BATES
VA 23 Sept. 1800, p. 3

Died, MR. RICHARD BATES of Goochland Co. in Norfolk on May 3rd
VA 9 May 1811, p. 3

Died on 26th Ult. in Goochland, MR. THOMAS F. BATES, old & respected
VA 8 June 1805, p. 3

Died, TARLETON BATES, late prothonatary of (   ) county, Pa. who fell in
a duel with Thomas Stewart on 8th Inst.
VA 28 Jan. 1806, p. 3

Died Oct. 3rd, near White Chimnies, Caroline Co., MRS. DOROTHEA BAUGHN, age 108,
9 of her 10 children lived to maturity
RE 15 Oct. 1819, p. 3; VP 23 Oct., p. 2

Died, BARNABAS BAXTER of Yarmouth, Mass., knocked overboard from a ship at
Rocketts (No death date)
RC 29 May 1820, p. 3

Died on 9th Inst., MRS. FRANCES BAYLOR, relict of late Col. John Baylor of
Hay Market, Caroline Co.
VGAA July 19, 1783, p. 3

Died on 5th Inst., JOHN BAYLOR, Esq. of New Market, Caroline Co., age 47
VGGA 12 Feb. 1808, p. 3

Died on 2nd Inst., at seat of Mr. William Wyatt of Caroline, MRS. JOANNA
BAYNHAM, late of Campfields of Gloucester Co., in 80th year
RE 15 Dec. 1807, p. 3

Died, MR. JOSEPH BAYNHAM of Louisa (No death date)
VGAA 23 April 1785 p. 2

Died, MR. RICHARD BAYNHAM, at Campfield on Gloucester Co., at Mr. Wm. Wyatt's
on 1st Inst.
VGGA 6 June 1809, p. 3

Died, COL. JOHN BEALE of Botetourt Co. on 21st Inst., in Fredericksburg
RE 31 Oct. 1809, p. 3; VA 27 Oct. , p. 3; Visitor 18 Nov., p. 166

Died at New-Town Pa., SAMUEL BEALL, for many years a res. of Williamsburg
(No death date)
VGGA 8 May 1793, p. 3

Died lately ROBERT BEAN of Hawkins Co.
VGRMA 27 June 1793, p. 2

Died, MR. JOSEPH BEASLEY, printer, on 21st, leaving wife and 1 child
RE 26 May 1812, p. 3; VA 25 May, p. 3 gives his name as BERKELEY;
VP 26 May, p. 3 gives name as BEASLEY

Died on Wed. last (April 8) in Washington age 50, JOHN BECKLEY, Esq., Clerk
of the House of Representatives
VA 14 April 1807, p. 3; RE 14 Apr., p. 3

Died, BARNABAS BEEBE, of Exeter, Otswego Co., N.Y., age 18, June 9th shot
himself when rejected by girl he loved
RC 22 July 1820, p. 3

Died on 29th Ult., MR. HENRY BELCHER, a native of Boston
VGGA 3 Nov. 1801., p. 3

Died at West Hartford, Conn., MR. SIMON BELDEN, age 64, an officer in the
Quartermaster Dept. in the Revolutionary War
Visitor 23 Sept. 1809, p. 135

Died, MR. ALEXANDER BELL, merchant, of this place, on 19th Inst.
RE 24 Dec. 1812, p. 3

Died, MRS. BETSY BELL, consort of Kidder R. Bell. Funeral today
RC 8 Aug. 1820, p. 3
VPRDMA 8 Aug., p. 3, says, "people of colour"

Died on Wed. last (Nov. 5) MR. DAVID BELL, son of Henry Bell, Esq. of Buckingham
Co., age 23
VA 8 Nov. 1806, p. 3

Died, MR. NATHAN BELL, on 1st Inst., age 64, of Hanover Co.
VA 7 Oct. 1807, p. 3; VGGA 7 Oct. p. 3

Died Oct. 11th age 64, SARAH BELL, relict of Nathan Bell of Hanover Co.
RE 19 Oct. 1819, p. 3; RC 15 Oct., p. 3

Died, MRS. POLLY BELL, consort of Mr. F. Bell, in Surry, on Feb. 25th
Visitor, 17 March 1810, p. 27

Died Thurs. last (Sept. 23) in this city MR. ROBERT BELL, bookseller of Philadelphia
VGWA, 25 Sept. 1784, p. 3; (VGAA says interred in churchyard, 25 Sept.)

Died on 16th Inst. at his house in Charlottesville, COL. THOMAS BELL, a soldier
in the Revolution
VA 24 Oct. 1800, p. 3
VGGA 18 Nov. , p. 3

Died on 22nd Inst., DR. GREENBURY BELT, late of Powhatan Co.
VA 30 Oct. 1802, p. 3

Died at Garrison of New Orleans, JOHN T. BENTLEY, of 6th U.S. Regt. of Cavalry
(No death date)
Visitor 16 Dec. 1809, p. 182

Died on 15th Ult., MRS. JUDITH BENTLEY, consort of Col. William Bentley of Powhatan
VGGA 2 July 1799, p. 3

Died in Salem, Mass., Dec. 29, 1819, REV. BENTLEY, for many years Editor of the
Salem Register.
RE 8 Jan. 1820, p. 3; VPRMA 10 Jan., p. 3

Died on April 9th, CAPT. EDMUND BERKELEY, at his res. Airwell in Hanover Co.,
age 57.
RE 21 April 1820, p. 3

Died Sat. last (May 25) MRS. MARY BERKELEY, consort of Mr. Nelson Berkeley,
merchant of this city
VGGA 29 May 1793, p. 3

Died on 20th Inst. at Baltimore, REV. FRANCIS BERSTON, Rector of RC Church of
St. Peter in that city
Visitor 30 Dec. 1809, p. 190

Died on the 15th, the REV. JOHN BEUNSKILL of Amelia Co., age 90
VA 23 July 1803, p. 3

Died in Essex Co., MRS. JANE BEVERLEY, consort of Robert Beverley and dau. of
Col. John Taylor of Mount Airy (No death date)
VP 23 May 1816, p. 3; VA 22 May, p. 3

Died in Williamsburg Aug. 20th, MRS. MARIA BEVERLEY, formerly of Blandfield,
Essex Co.
VP 26 Aug. 1817, p. 3

Died at Blanfield on 12th Inst., ROBERT BEVERLEY, Esq., age 60
VGGA 18 April 1800, p. 3

Died, COL. WILDER BEVINS, at an advanced age at Lancaster, on Thurs. (Aug.
24 ?)
Visitor 26 Aug. 1809, p. 118

Died at his seat in Amherst Co., Aug. 14th, WILLIAM BIBB, Esq. age about 60,
leaving numerous offspring
VGGA 25 Sept. 1793, p. 2

Died, WILLIAM W. BIBB, Gov. of Alabama, at his seat near Fort Jackson on July
10th
RE 8 Aug. 1820, p. 3; VPRDMA 14 Aug., p. 3

Died on Sunday last (Nov. 28) MR. CHARLES BIDDLE, of the Va. Company of Comedians,
late from the Old American Co.
VGGA 1 Dec. 1790, p. 2

Died lately, MR. JOHN BIGNALL, comedian (from Norfolk paper) (No death date)
VGRMA 28 Aug. 1794, p. 2

Died April 19th in Phila. BIG TREE, one of the Indian Chiefs of the Five Nations
VGGA 2 May 1792, p. 3

Died on Feb. 22nd, MRS. ELIZABETH BILBO, consort of Mr. William Bilbo, in
Mecklenburg Co.
VA 25 March 1800, p. 3

Died on 21st Ult., MRS. FRANCES BINFORD, wife of Col. John M. Binford of
Northhampton, N.C.
RE 19 Nov. 1814, p. 3

Died on Sun. (June 30) MR. ISAAC BINGHAM, a recent resident
RC 3 July 1816, p. 3

Died at Bath, England on 6th Feb., age 53, HON. WILLIAM BINGHAM of Philadelphia, late a U.S. Senator
VGGA 28 March 1804, p. 2

Died, MRS. JUDITH BINGLEY, age 105, on 13th Inst. in Powhatan Co.
VA 16 Aug. 1806, p. 3

Died, HENRY L. BISCOE, Esq. of Manchester, on the 19th
RE 24 July 1810, p. 3; VA 27 July, p. 2, says died 17th

Died in Manchester Tues. last (June 10) MRS. BISCOE, consort of Mr. Henry L. Biscoe, merchant, of that place.
VA 12 June 1801, p. 3

Died, ROBERT BISCOE, of Powhatan Co., on the 23rd Ult., age 68
VA 4 March 1806, p. 3

Died on 31st Ult., MRS. ANN BISHOP, consort of Mr. Luman Bishop of Richmond
RE 3 Jan. 1805, p. 3

Died, WILLIAM BLACK, Esq. of Chesterfield (No death date)
VGWA Feb. 2, 1782, p. 3

Died Friday last (Oct. 8) age 33, MR. WILLIAM BLACK of Chesterfield
VGWA 16 Oct. 1784, p. 3

Died, COL. THOMAS BLACKBURN, on 17th Inst. at his seat Rippon Lodge. Fought in Revolution and wounded at Germantown
VGGA 29 Aug. 1807, p. 3

Died, MISS MARY E. BLACKWELL, age 19, at seat of Capt. Sherald Parish on 6th Inst., in Goochland Co.
VA 13 May 1813, p. 3

Died on Fri. (May 14) in Richmond, MR. THOMAS BLACKWELL, late a res. of King William Co., leaving wife and 2 children
RE 18 May, 1819. p. 3

Died Wed. (Sept. 11) REV. BENJAMIN BLAGROVE, Chaplain of the House of Delegates of this State. Interred in the churchyard
VGRC 13 Sept. 1793, p. 3

Died, MR. JAMES BLAGROVE of this city, on Wed. last (Dec. 4)
VA 11 Dec. 1805, p. 3

Died, Thursday last (Sept. 25) MRS. ANN BLAIR of this city.
VGRC 30 Sept. 1794, p. 3

Died on 14th Ult., LT. COL. JOHN BLAIR of Hawkins Co.
VGRMA 27 June 1793, p. 2

Died Aug. 31 at Williamsburg, JOHN BLAIR, Esq., age 69
VA 9 Sept. 1800, p. 3
VGGA 5 Sept., p. 3

Died Jan. 30th, MR. JACOB BLAKE of Gwynns Island, Matthews Co.
RE 16 Feb. 1819, p. 3

Died on Sun. (date ?) at New Castle, MR. SMITH BLAKEY of this city
VA 13 Oct. 1804, p. 3; VGGA 13 Oct., p. 2 (Says Monday last)

Died on Tues. last (Dec. 24) MR. THOMAS BLAKEY of Newcastle, Hanover Co.
RE 31 Dec. 1805, p. 3

Died, DR. JAMES BLAMIRE, on Wed. (Oct. 15) at his home in Portsmouth
Impartial Observer 18 Oct. 1806, p. 3

Died, MR. BAILLY BLANCHARD, cashier of Planters Bank of New Orleans. Found in
river. Missing since Fri. last (Oct. 15) (from New Orleans Gazette Oct. 21)
RE 19 Nov. 1819, p.3

Died Tues. last 8 June at his lodgings in Broad St., New York, HON.THEODORICK
BLAND, Congressman from Va., age 49. Buried in Trinity Churchyard
VICGA 16 June 1790. p. 2

Died, MRS. JANE BLEDSOE, in Franklin Co., N.C., some time ago
Visitor 6 May 1809, p. 54

Died May 10th, MRS. MARY BLOCK of Albermarle Co. relict of late Samuel Block,
age 34
RE 25 May 1819, p. 3

Died in Burlington, N.J. Nov. 28th, age 66, MRS. MARY BLOOMFIELD, wife of
Gen. Joseph Bloomfield, late Gov. of N.J.
RE 10 Dec. 1818, p. 3

Died at Knoxville, Tenn. on 26th Ult., WILLIAM BLOUNT, Esq., formerly Gov. of
Tenn., age 56
VA 18 April, 1800, p. 3

Died, CAPT. SAMUEL BLYTHE (No death date)
RE 21 Sept. 1813, p. 4

Died on Wed. last (May 30), MR. JACOB BOCKUS of this city
RE 2 June 1804, p. 3; VGGA 2 June, p. 2 (says BOCKIUS)

Died at Lamberton, N.J., JAMES BOISSEAU of Petersburg, student of Medicine at
U. of Pa. (No death date)
Visitor 7 Oct. 1809, P. 142

Died Aug. 9th in a duel near the old brick church at Blandford, JAMES B. BOISSEAU of Petersburg
VPRDMA 12 Aug. 1820, p. 3

Died, MRS. ANNA G. BOLLING, consert of Mr. John Bolling of Dinwiddie, on 1st Inst.
Visitor 17 March 1810, p. 27

Died on 9th Inst., MRS. CATHARINE BOLLING, spouse of Mr. Robert Bolling of Petersburg
VGRMA 20 Aug. 1795, p. 3

Died, daughters ages 8 and 2, of MRS. JANE S. BOLLING, relict of Robert Bolling, Esq., of Goochland
RE 12 Sept. 1804, p. 3

Died, LINNAEUS BOLLING, a student of William & Mary, and son of L. Bolling of Buckingham Co. on Sat. (1 June), drowned
RE 5 June 1816, p. 3

Died, MRS. MARY BOLLING, relict of John Bolling, Esq., at Chestnut Grove, Chesterfield Co., age 63 (No death date)
VA 28 Dec. 1803, p. 3

Died on 21st March at his seat in Buckingham, POWHATAN BOLLING, Esq., for several years a Representative in the General Assembly
VA 9 April 1803, p. 3

Died Sun. last (Oct. 2) in this city, MRS. SALLY BOLLING, spouse of Mr. Robert Bolling of Petersburg
VGGA 5 Oct. 1796, p. 2; VGRMA 4 Oct., p. 3

Died on 30th July, DR. JOSEPH BONDURANT of Buckingham Co., age 87
VA 16 Aug. 1806, p. 3

Died in Richmond on Wed. (Oct. 9), MR. ALFRED BOOKER of the House of Edward Cunningham & Co.
RE 12 Oct. 1816, p. 3; VP 10 Oct., p. 3; RC 10 Oct., p. 3

Died Nov. 15th, age 60, GEORGE BOOKER, of Elizabeth City Co.
RE 14 Dec. 1816, p. 3

Died on 15th Ult. at house of Mrs. Elizabeth Booker in Amherst, JOHN BOOKER, a brother of her late husband, Mr. William A. Booker
RE 6 Aug. 1805, p. 3; VA 31 July, p. 3

Died, in Essex Co., CAPT. LEWIS BOOKER, a soldier of the Revolution (No death date)
RE 11 Jan. 1815, p. 3

Died, RECHESON BOOKER, Esq., on 27th Oct. at his seat in Amelia Co.
VA 11 Nov. 1806, p. 3

Died at his res. in Cumberland Co., April 24th, RICHARD BOOKER, age 68
RE 1 May 1818, p. 3; VP 1 May, p. 2

Died in this city on 14th Inst., MR. WILLIAM BOOKER, tavern-keeper
VA 16 Oct. 1802, p. 3

Died March 15th, WONDER, *a negro man belonging to George Booker of Prince Edward
Co. Records show him to have been born in April 1693. Got his name because his
mother was 58 when he was born
RE 2 April 1819, p. 3
    *File under Booker

Died in Charrete, Mo., Sept. 26th, COL. DANIEL BOONE, the first settler of Ky.,
a native of Bucks Co., Pa.
RE 3 Nov. 1820, p. 3; VPRDMA 3 Nov., p. 3, says age 90

Died Sunday (Sept. 29?) MRS. FANNY BOOTH, age 49
VGGA 2 Oct. 1793, p. 3

Died, GEORGE WYTHE BOOTH, Esq. on 20th Ult., age 36, at his seat in Gloucester
Co. He was a cavalry major in Va. Militia
RE 7 Jan. 1809, p. 3

Died in Gloucester Co., Sept. 12th, MISS MARY E. BOOTH, age 18
RE 18 Sept. 1818, p. 3

Died, WILLIAM BOOTH, Esq., age 64, at his seat at Oaksell in Gloucester Co.,
Oct. 23rd
VP 13 Nov. 1812, p. 3

Died on the 18th Inst., MRS. MARIA BOSHER, wife of Mr. Charles Bosher of this
city
RE 22 March 1815, p. 3; VA 22 March, p. 3, says Mary

Died, MR. THOMAS BOTTS, Attorney at Law, late of Dumfries, killed on Wed. last
(before Nov. 7) by Mr. William Bowyer of Staunton in a duel.
VGGA 18 Nov. 1800, p. 3

Died Oct. 17th, HON. ELIAS BOUDINOT, at his res. in Newark, N.H., age 71
RE 25 Oct. 1819, p. 3

Died yesterday, MRS. CATHERINE BOWLER
VGRMA 20 Nov. 1794, p. 3; VGRC says Miss Catherine Bowles, 20 Nov.

Died on Wed. last (March 11) MR. RICHARD BOWLER, for many years inhabitant of
Richmond
VA 13 March 1807, p. 3; VGGA 14 March p. 3, says age 47

Died, MR. DANIEL BOYCE of Goochland, on 7th Inst., age 52
VA 12 Sept. 1804, p. 3

Died, ROBERT BOYD, age 62, on 17th Inst., at his seat in New Kent Co. He was a
native of Scotland and came to this country at an early age
VP   27 Nov. 1812, p. 3

Died Oct. 20th at his res. in Isle of Wight, GEN. FRANCIS M. BOYKIN, age 36
RE   28 Oct. 1817, p. 3

Died July 15th, REV. JOHN BRACKEN, Rector of Bruton Parish. A native of England,
came to Va. at early age, served in Revolution, married and raised family, and
served College of William & Mary as professor and President.
RE   24 July 1818, p. 3

Died on 30th Ult. at his seat in Amelia Co., CAPTAIN LUDWELL BRACKETT, age 53
RE   21 Dec. 1815, p. 3

Died in Phila., July 3rd, age 21, MRS. MARTHA P. BRACKETT, wife of Mr. Thomas
H. Brackett of Cumberland Co. and dau. of Mrs. Ann C. Graham of Prince William
Co.
RE   10 July 1818, p. 3

Died Aug. 23 near Phila., WILLIAM BRADFORD, Esq., Attorney General of U.S.
VGRMA   3 Sept. 1795, p. 3

Died, CAPT. JOHN BRADY, at Winchester, on the 15th (Nov.)
Visitor   2 Dec. 1809, p. 174

Died in Manchester, MR. JOHN BRAIDWOOD. His funeral this a.m. from Manchester
Exchange
RC   26 Oct. 1802, p. 3

Died at Columbia, Va., age 19, MRS. POLLY BRAINHAM, consort of Mr. James
Brainham, Merchant of Columbia (No death date)
RE   2 April, 1805, p. 3

Died on 28th Feb. at his res. in Richmond County, BENJAMIN BRAMHAM, age 86
RE   12 March 1814, p. 3

Died, MR. ARCHIBALD BRANCH, on 15th Inst., at Buckingham C.H.
VA   21 Nov. 1811, p. 3

Died Sept. 4th, age 79, MRS. JUDITH BRANCH, widow of William Branch of Chesterfield Co.
VPRDMA   20 Sept. 1820, p. 2

Died Jan. 30th at Summerville, seat of Judge Fleming, his niece, MRS. MARY FLEMING
BRANCH, age 56, leaving dau. and 2 sons
RE   13 Feb. 1817, p. 3

Died on 21st May at house of Mr. Benjamin Moseley in Buckingham, MRS. RIDLEY
BRANCH, age 69
VA   28 June 1799, p. 3

Died fighting Indians in Tenn., Aug. 8th, JOHN BRANNON
VGWA 2 Oct. 1788, p. 3

Died on Sat. last (July 27) in this city, MR. ROBERT M. BRANSFORD, formerly printer
of the Lynchburg & Farmers Gazette
Observatory 30 July 1798, p. 3; VGGA 31 July, p. 3

Died, CARTER BRAXTON, on 8th Inst. at Williamsburg, Attorney at Law
RE 14 April, 1809, p. 3; VA 14 Apirl, p. 3, says age 43, leaving widow & 7
children; VGGA 14 April, p. 3; Visitor 6 May, p. 54

Died July 5th, near Norfolk, MRS. BRAXTON, relict of Carter Braxton, age 70
VP 13 July 1814, p. 3

Died, TAYLOE BRAXTON, on 16th Inst., age 28, leaving wife and infant dau.
RE 21 Feb. 1809, p. 3; VA 17 Feb., p. 3, says "Taylor", not Tayloe;
Visitor, p. 14, 11 Feb.

Died, JOHN BRECKENRIDGE, Attorney General of the U.S. at Lexington (Ky) on
14th Ult.
RE 13 Jan. 1807, p. 3

Died, MRS. SARAH BREEDEN, wife of Mr. Moody Breeden of King William Co., age
79, on 15th Inst.
VA 28 Oct. 1808, p. 2

Died in this city Fri. last (June 21) MRS. ELIZABETH BREND, consort of
Mr. Thomas Brend, bookbinder
VA 25 June 1799, p. 3

Died on Sun. last (Dec. 22) MR. THOMAS BREND, of this city
VGGA 24 Dec. 1799, p. 3

Died April 25th, MRS. ANN FENTON BRENT, wife of Daniel Brent, Esq. of Washington
City
VA 4 May 1803, p. 3

Died Sept. 7th, ROBERT BRENT, late Paymaster General of the Army and Judge of
the Orphans Court of Washington Co.
VP 13 Sept. 1819, p. 3

Died, COL. WILLIAM BRENT of Stafford Co. (No death date)
VGWA 25 June 1785, p. 3; VGAA 25 June, p. 3 (Representative of Mat. Co. and
Col. in late Army of the State)

Died yesterday, MR. JAMES BRIDGES of late firm of Bridges & Robertson, merchant
of Richmond
VP 30 June 1818, p. 2

Died June 16th, MR. JOHN BRITT, drowned, near Bedford, Pa. Had served in
Revolution
VP 30 June 1817, p. 3

Died on Thurs. last (July 10) in a fray between soldiers, SAMUEL BRITTIN, one of the party
VGAA July 12, 1783

Murdered on 8th Inst., near his house in Spotsylvania Co., MR. JOHN BROCK, JR. leaving wife and small children
VGGA 22 Aug. 1792, p. 2

Died on 20th Ult. at his seat on banks of the Tappahannock (sic), DR. JOHN BROCKENBROUGH, physician, age 60
RE 1 Dec. 1804, p. 3

Died Aug. 18th in Bath Co., MRS. LETTICE LEE BROCKENBROUGH, consort of Dr. Austin Brockenbrough of Tappahannock. Buried in Staunton
RE 29 Aug. 1820, p. 3

Died, MRS. S. BROCKENBROUGH, relict of Dr. John Brockenbrough, Sr., at Tappahannock in Essex Co.
RE 22 June 1810, p. 3

Died at Southam Parish Glebe, Powhatan Co., age 77, MRS. SARAH BRODNAX (No death date)
VICGA 17 Feb. 1790, p. 3

Died, last Sun. (April 7) GEORGE BROOKE, Esq., late Treasurer of the Commonwealth
VGAA April 13, 1782, p. 3; VGWA April 13

Died this morning, MRS. BROOKE, spouse of Robert Brooke, Esq., Governor of this Commonwealth
RC 5 July 1796, p. 3; VGGA 6 July, p. 2; VGRMA 6 July, p. 3

Died on Thurs. last (March 24) MRS. RACHEL BROOKE, wife of Mr. Robert Brooke of this city and dau. of Gen. John Shee of Philadelphia
VA 26 March 1803, p. 3; VGGA 26 March, p. 3

Died on 27 Ult. at Fredericksburg, ROBERT BROOKE, Esq., Attorney Gen. of this state
VA 7 March 1800, p. 3; VF 5 March, p. 3; VGGA 4 March, p. 3

Died near Richmond, last Sun. (Jan. 10) MRS. URSULA BROOKE, relict of late Col. John Brooke, age 77
RC 12 Jan. 1819, p. 3

Died, MRS. FRANCES BROOKING, age 85, of King & Queen Co., on Thurs. last (Oct. 25)
VA 27 Oct. 1804, p. 3

Died on Thurs. last (before Jan. 18th) in Upper Marlborough, Md., BENJAMIN BROOKS, Esq., Major in 2nd U.S. Regt. of Artillery & Engineers
VA 24 Jan. 1800, p. 3

LT. JOHN BROOKS was buried Friday (before 17 Nov. 1817) at Fort Shelby
RE 24 Jan. 1818, p. 4

Died at the races in Manchester Fri. last (Aug. 9) MR. THOMAS BROOKS, shot by
Mr. Crawford in a dispute
VGRMA 12 Aug. 1793, p. 3

Died, MRS. BROUGH, wife of Robert Brough of Norfolk, in that city, on 15th Inst.
Impartial Observer 20 Sept. 1806, p. 3

Died on Sun. last (Dec. 13) in this city, MRS. ANNE BROWN, consort of Mr. John
Brown, Clerk to the General Court
VGGA 16 Dec. 1795, p. 5; VGRMA 16 Dec., p. 2

Died on 29th Jan. last, ELIZA R. BROWN, consort of William B. Brown, at his seat
Elsing Green, in King William Co.
RE 18 Feb. 1815, p. 3

Died at his res. in Dartmouth, N.H., July 27th, REV. FRANCIS BROWN, Pres. of
Dartmouth College, age 36
VPRDMA 14 Aug. 1820, p. 3

Died lately, JAMES BROWN, an old inhabitant of Fredericksburg
RE 6 May 1803, p. 3

Died, MR. JOHN BROWN, Clerk of Court of Appeals, in this city, on Wed. (Oct. 31)
RE 2 Nov. 1810, p. 3; VA 2 Nov., p. 3; VP 2 Nov., p. 2

Died, MR. JOHN H. BROWN of Richmond, at Savannah, on 19th Ult.
RE 2 April 1811, p. 3; VA 4 April, p. 3; VP 2 April, p. 3

Died yesterday at house of Miss Jane P. Braddock, MISS SARAH BROWN
RC 1 Nov. 1820, p. 3

Died at Cross Creek, his res. in Surry Co., MAJ. BENJAMIN EDWARDS BROWNE, age
59, a soldier of the Revolution, leaving a son and 3 daughters
RE 25 May 1819, p. 3

Died on 21st Inst., MRS. SARAH BRUCE, wife of James Bruce of Halifax Co.
RE 30 May 1806, p. 3

Died on 16th Inst. at house of Mr. George Divers of Albermarle Co., JOHN BRYAN,
Esq., of N.J., while soliciting funds to rebuild Princeton College
VA 26 Jan. 1803, p. 3

Died on Thurs. last (Jan. 30) MR. WILLIAM BRYAN, age 35, Merchant of Richmond
leaves wife and infant dau.
RE 6 Feb. 1806, p. 3

Died, ARCHIBALD BRYCE, on 29th Ult. at his house in Goochland Co.
VGGA 12 Sept. 1807, p. 3

Died Oct. 16th at Mr. Henderson's in Orange Co., MRS. MARY F. BRYCE, consort of
Rev. John Bryce.
RE 24 Oct. 1820, p. 3; RC 23 Oct., p. 3; VPRDMA 23 Oct., p. 3

Died April 21st, MRS. SOPHIA BRYCE, consort of Rev. John Bryce of Richmond, age 33, leaving husband and 5 children
RE 23 April 1819, p. 3; RC 22 April, p. 3

Died at Warm Springs, Bath Co., on 16th Inst., MR. ALEXANDER BRYDIE, merchant in Richmond
VA 25 July 1800, p. 3; VF 23 July, p. 3; VGGA 22 July, p. 3

Died, MR. ANDREW BRYSON, late merchant of this city, on Wed. last (Oct. 6)
VA 11 Oct. 1813, p. 3; RC 8 Oct., p. 3, says died yesterday (Oct. 7)

Died Oct. 10th, MR. JAMES BRYSON, practical engineer, a native of Glasgow, Scotland
VP 12 Oct. 1819, p. 3

Died on Wed. last (Oct. 20) MR. SAMUEL BRYSON of this city, leaving a wife and 2 small children
VA 23 Oct. 1802, p. 3

Died in Falmouth, Stafford Co., the wife of Andrew Buchanan, Esq. (No death date)
VGRDA 1 Oct. 1792, p. 3

Died at Brighton, England on 23rd July last, MRS. DAVID BUCHANAN, late of Petersburg Va.
VGGA 23 Sept. 1800, p. 3

Died yesterday, MR. JAMES BUCHANAN, oldest merchant in this city
VGWA 11 Oct. 1787, p. 3

Died in Caroline Co., on 19th Inst., MR. GEORGE BUCKNER
VA 28 June 1799, p. 3

Died in Manchester on Sat. (June 5) MISS JANE BUCKNER
RC 8 June 1816, p. 3

Died at Fort Johnson, Charleston Harbor, Oct. 2nd, DR. WILLIAM HORACE BUCKNER, Post Surgeon, U.S. Army
RE 17 Oct. 1820, p. 3

Died, MR. WILLIAM BULLOCK, of this city in Charleston, S.C. on 1st Inst.
RE 15 March 1808, p. 3

Died Feb. 8th, MR. JOHN BURCH of Henrico Co.of fall from horse. Had been soldier in Revolution at age 18. Leaves a wife and numerous children
RE 13 Feb. 1817, p. 3

Died at his res. in Chesterfield Co., Nov. 13th, THOMAS BURFOOT, SR. Born at Capitol Landing, Queens Creek, in York Co., and trained to be a bricklayer, he served in the Revolutionary War. He served Chesterfield as Sheriff and as Justice of the Peace.
RE 17 Nov. 1820, p. 3; RC 21 Nov., p. 3; VPRDMA 21 Nov., p. 2, says age 67

Died in Williamsburg, S.C., COL. JOHN D. BURGESS, a young man (No death date)
RE 7 Dec. 1819, p. 3

Died in Petersburg, on 11th Inst. of a wound received in a duel, JOHN D. BURK
Virginia 15 April 1808, p. 3

Died at Halifax, N.S., RT. REV. DR. BURKE, Catholic Bishop of Nova Scotia, age
77
VPRDMA 28 Dec. 1820, p. 3

Died, THOMAS BURKE of Caroline Co., on Jan 24th. He married his 3rd wife when
he was about 42, and she 14. After marriage of 2 years, he leaves 3 children
by his first wife and one by his last
RE 6 Feb. 1807, p. 3

Died yesterday, THOMAS BURLING, a native of New York City where his father still
lives. He was Supt. of Enquirer office
RE 6 Jan. 1818, p. 3; VP 6 Jan., p. 3

Died, HARDIN BURNLEY on 11th Inst. in Hanover Co., age about 47, for some years
a Member of Council of State and Lt. Gov. Left wife and 6 children
RE 17 March 1809, p. 3; Visitor 25 March, p. 31

Died at his res. in Louisa Co., July 26th MR. JAMES BURNLEY, JR., at an advanced
age
RE 30 July 1819, p. 3

Died at his res. in Louisa Co. Aug. 29th, MR. JAMES BURNLEY, age 90
RE 8 Sept. 1820, p. 3

Died on 30th Ult. MRS. BURNLEY, wife of Hardin Burnley, Esq. of this city
VGGA 8 May 1793, p. 3

Died Capt. ROBERT BURNS age 38, on 4th Inst. at Staunton
VGAA Oct. 12, 1782, p. 3

Died Dec. 25th in Washington, D.C., JAMES BURRILL, JR., Senator from R.I., age
49
VPRDMA 29 Dec. 1820, p. 3

Died, LT. WILLIAM BURROWS (No death date)
RE 21 Sept. 1813, p. 4

Died, MR. CONYNGHAM BURTON, on 29th Ult., a native of Ireland, but for many years
a citizen of Richmond
VA 5 Sept. 1807, p. 2

Died near Richmond, DANIEL BURTON (No death date)
RE 21 Sept. 1819, p. 3; VP 21 Sept., p. 3, says died Sunday (Sept. 19) in
Henrico Co.; RE 28 Sept. p. 3, says age 62, of Springfield, Henrico Co.,
leaving wife and infant

Died a few days ago, MR. MARTIN BURTON of Henrico Co., age 69
VGGA 18 April 1792, p. 3

Died on Wed. last (Feb. 12) ROBERT BURTON, Esq. of this city of the firm of
Brown, Rives & Co.
VA 18 Feb. 1806, p. 3; RE 15 Feb., p. 3; VGGA 15 Feb., p. 3

Died on Sat. (Aug. 30) age 21, MR. SAMUEL FERDINAND BURTON, eldest son of
Mr. Thomas Burton, Sr. of Henrico
RE 5 Sept. 1817, p. 3

Died lately at his seat near Richmond, WILLIAM BURTON, SR., an old inhabitant
of Henrico Co.
VPRDMA 5 Oct. 1820, p. 3

Died at Hampton, EDWIN BURWELL, Esq. of this city (No death date)
VGGA 14 March 1798, p. 3

Died Oct. 24th, MISS ELIZABETH BURWELL of Mecklenburg, Co., age 22, leaving
among her relatives a twin sister
RE 14 Nov. 1820, p. 3

Died Jan. 3rd, MR. HENRY H. BURWELL, burned to death when his home in Mecklenburg
Co. was destroyed. Was 25 years old and married 3 mos.
RE 9 Jan. 1816, p. 3; VP 10 Jan., p. 3

Died Jan 1st, infant BURWELL, child of Mr. & Mrs. Peyton R. Burwell, when fire
destroyed home of Henry H. Burwell in Mecklenburg
RE 9 Jan. 1816, p. 3; VP 10 Jan. p. 3

Died lately in Mecklenburg Co., LEWIS BURWELL, Esq., formerly of Kingsmill
VGWA 30 Oct. 1784, p. 3

Died, Jan 1st, MISS MARY BURWELL, dau. of Mr. John S. Burwell of Franklin Co.,
when fire destroyed home of Henry H. Burwell in Mecklenburg Co.
RE 9 Jan. 1816, p. 3; VP 10 Jan., p. 3

Died, Jan 2nd, MRS. BURWELL, wife of Henry H. Burwell, in fire that destroyed
their home in Mecklenburg Co.
RE 9 Jan. 1816, p. 3; VP 10 Jan. p. 3

Died last Thurs. (July 24) MRS. SUSANNAH BURWELL, consort of Nathaniel Burwell,
Esq., of Carters Grove, James City Co.
VGWA 31 July 1788, p. 3

Died, MRS. JUDITH BUSBEE, age 78, widow of Thomas Busbee, at Raleigh on the 4th
Visitor 26 Aug. 1809, p. 118

Died fighting Indians in Tenn., Aug. 8th, GEORGE BUSY
VGWA 2 Oct. 1788, p. 3

Died, MR. JOHN BUTLER, of firm of Braddock & Butler (No death date)
RE 8 May 1818, p. 3

Died on 19th Inst., MANSFIELD BUTLER of Hanover from a stab wound received at
house of James Hazlegrove
VGGA 27 Sept. 1797, p. 2

Died on Sept. 7th near New Orleans, COL. THOMAS BUTLER of U. S. Army
VA 26 Oct. 1805, p. 3

Died Sept. 2nd, COL. OTWAY BYRD, Colector of Customs in Norfolk City
VA 9 Sept. 1800, p. 3

Died at Westover in Charles City Co. (late the seat of Mrs. Byrd) RICHARD W. BYRD,
Esq., Attorney at Law, of Smithfield
RE 28 Oct. 1815, p. 3

Died in the City of Dublin, JAMES BYRNE, a citizen of Va. and resident of Petersburg,
age 73
Visitor 30 Dec. 1809, p. 190

Died, CHARLES J. CABELL, Counsellor at Law, Native of Va., in New Orleans on
Nov. 23rd last
RE 3 Jan. 1811, p. 3

Died Aug. 7th, at Montevideo, seat of Judge Cabell in Buckingham Co.,
MRS. HANNAH CABELL, widow of late Col. Nicholas Cabell and mother of
the judge, age 67, a member of the Carrington family
RE 26 Aug. 1817, p. 3

Died, DR. ROBERT B. CABELL of Chesterfield Co. on 7th Inst., age 22
RE 28 Oct. 1808, p. 3

Died July 10th, age 16, MISS SARAH S. CABELL, dau. of Mr. Frederick Cabell of
Nelson Co.
RE 18 July 1820, p. 3

Died on 9th Ult. in Frankfort, Ky., GEN. JOHN CALDWELL, Lt. Gov. of that State
VA 28 Nov. 1804, p. 3

Died in New York, March 8th, age 50, JOHN E. CALDWELL, agent for American Bible
Society. At an early age had gone to France with Lafayette for his education
VP 17 March 1819, p. 3

Died, MR. JOHN CALLAND, age 25, on 11th Ult. at his father's seat in Pittsylvania
Co.
Recorder 9 Feb. 1803, p. 3

Died, SAMUEL CALLAND, Esq., native of Scotland and long a resident of Pittsylvania
Co., on 8th Inst.
RE 18 Nov. 1808, p. 3; VGGA 2 Dec., p. 3 (says High Sheriff of Pittsylvania
Co., age 59)

Died, COL. JAMES CALLAWAY, founder of the iron works and a Rev. War Soldier
(No death date)
VA 14 Nov. 1809, p. 3; Visitor 18 Nov. p. 166, says died on 1st Inst. at his
residence in Bedford Co.

Died in Bedford Co., MR. ROBERT CALLAWAY, (No death date)
VGGA 15 Oct. 1794, p. 2; VGRMA 16 Oct.; VGRC 17 Oct., says Galloway

Died on Sun. last (July 17) JAMES THOMSON CALLENDER, drowned in James River
VA 20 July 1803, p. 3; Recorder 20 July, p. 3 (says late editor of the
Recorder)

Died yesterday, age 19, MR. HUGH CAMERON, a native of Scotland
VP 28 April 1818, p. 2

Died last night, ALEXANDER CAMPBELL, Esq., Attorney at Law
RC 19 July 1796, p. 2; VGGA 20 July says died on Mon. 18th)

Died in Washington City, GEN. DONALD CAMPBELL, who had resigned his British Com-
mission to serve in the American Army
VA 9 April 1803, p. 3

Died in Washington last St. (Nov. 11) Commodore HUGH P. CAMPBELL
RC 15 Nov., p. 3

Died on May 31st., JAMES CAMPBELL of Newark, N.J. by swallowing laudanum
VA 16 June 1804, p. 2

Died, MRS. LUCY CAMPBELL, wife of Mr. Archibald Campbell of Manchester, on Oct.
21st., leaving husband and 5 children
VA 3 Nov. 1807, p. 2

Died in Fredericksburg, MR. JOHN CAMPIONE, at an advanced age (No death date)
RE 21 July 1820, p. 3

Died Dec. 3rd, at the Glebe House, Lunenburg Co., REV. JOHN CANNON, age 71
VP 13 Dec. 1815, p. 3

Died in Salem, Mass. on 23rd Ult., MR. WILLIAM CARLETON, age 33, Editor of
The Salem Register
VA 7 Aug. 1805, p. 3

Died on 9 Feb. 1795 at Madrid, WILLIAM CARMICHAEL, Esq. late Charge d'Affaires
and one of Ministers Plenipotentiary from U.S. Court of Spain
VGRMA 16 May, 1795, p. 2

Died Oct. 14th, MR. MERIWETHER CARPENTER, eldest son of Mr. Jonathan Carpenter
of Louisa Co.
RE 20 Oct. 1820, p. 3; RC 19 Oct. , p. 3

Died, MRS. MARTHA CARR, age 64, on 3rd Inst., at Dunlora, seat of Mr. Samuel Carr
of Albermarle. She was widow of Dabney Carr and sister of Mr. Jefferson, late
Pres. of U.S.
RE 13 Sept. 1811, p. 3

Died on Feb. 17th, PETER CARR
RE 1 March 1815, p. 3

Died Oct. 21st at her res. on Richmond Hill in Richmond, age 58, MRS. ANN CARRINGTON,
relict of Col. Mayo Carrington, dec'd
RE 24 Oct. 1820, p. 3; RC 25 Oct., p. 3, says died on 22nd

Died on July 30th at his seat in Cumberland Co., age 49, CODRINGTON CARRINGTON, Esq.
VA 5 Aug., p. 3, 1815

Died, COL. EDWARD CARRINGTON, on Sun. last (Oct. 28)
RE 30 Oct. 1810, p. 3; RE 2 Nov. Obituary; VA Oct. 30, p. 3, says old Revolutionary
Officer; VP 30 Oct., p. 3

Died, GEN. GEORGE CARRINGTON, on 27th Ult. at his seat in Halifax, leaves a wife,
8 sons and 2 daus.
RE 6 June 1809, p. 3

Died on 23rd Ult. MR. NATHANIEL CARRINGTON of Cumberland Co.
VGGA 2 Nov. 1803, p. 3

Died at his seat in Charlotte Co. on Jan. 8th, PAUL CARRINGTON, JR., one of the
judges of the General Court, age 52
RE 23 Jan. 1816, p. 3; VP 24 Jan., p. 3

Died June 23rd at his seat in Charlotte Co., PAUL CARRINGTON, age 86, a veteran
of the Revolution. He represented Charlotte Co. in General Assembly and several
conventions
RE 7 July 1818, p. 3

Died on 15th Ult., MRS. PRISCILLA CARRINGTON, age 27, spouse of Mr. Paul Carrington,
the elder, of Charlotte Co., leaving aged husband and 3 small children
VGGA 1 Oct. 1803, p. 3

Died on 28th Inst. MR. ROBERT CARRINGTON of this city
VA 30 June 1801, p. 3

Died, Dec. 3rd, MOST REV. DR. JOHN CARROLL, Archbishop of Baltimore, age 80
VP 9 Dec. 1815, p. 3

Died on his res. in Cumberland Co. Oct. 10th, GEORGE CARSON, age 51, a native
of Ireland
RE 17 Oct. 1817, p. 3

Died, MRS. ANN CARTER, relict of Charles Carter, Esq., late of Shirley (No
death date)
RE 28 April 1809, p. 3; VGGA 5 May, p.3, says died on 16th Ult.; Visitor
6 May, p. 54, says died 15th

Died on 28th Ult., at Shirley, his residence in Charles City Co., CHARLES
CARTER, Esq., age 74
VA 9 July 1806, p. 3; RE 22 July, p. 3; VGGA 5 July, p. 3

Died on 11th Inst., MRS. ELIZABETH CARTER, spouse of Capt. Samuel Carter of
Prince Edward Co.
VGRMA 28 May 1795, p. 2

Died, GEORGE CARTER, Esq. of Corotman, son of Charles Carter, Esq. of Shirley
(No death date)
VGWA 6 Nov. 1788, p. 3

Died Aug. 28th in Augusta, Ga., MR. JOHN CARTER, leaving a wife and 6 children.
He had served one time in Va. State Govt. He was a druggist and moved to
Augusta some years ago
VPRDMA 26 Oct. 1820, p. 3

Died at Sabine Hall, Aug. 29th, LANDON CARTER, age 64
VPRDMA 16 Sept. 1820, p. 3

Died, MRS. MARTHA CARTER, consort of John D. Carter, 3rd dau. of Sackville King,
Esq. of Campbell Co., leaving a husband and 3 children. (No death date)
VA 14 Nov. 1806, p. 3

Died May 15th, MRS. POLLY CARTER, wife of Page Carter, near Bacon Branch
RC 20 May 1819, p. 3

Died on 14th Inst., at Shirley, the seat of Charles Carter, Esq., DR. ROBERT
CARTER, age 31
VGGA 4 Dec. 1805, p. 3

Died in this city Wed. last (June 12) DR. WILLIAM CARTER, SR., in an advanced
age
VA 14 June 1799, p. 3; VGGA 14 June, page 3, says "formerly of Williamsburg"

Died Tues. last (March 13) at his seat in Chesterfield, HON. ARCHIBALD CARY,
Speaker of the Senate
VGWA 1 March 1787, p. 2

Died in Bermuda Oct. 11th, EDWARD B.S. CARY, age 29, of Gloucester Co., Va.
He represented the county in the General Assembly
RC 27 Nov. 1819, p. 3

Died, on 6th Inst., at seat of Mrs. Ann Cary in Warwick Co., MISS ELIZABETH
CARY, age 28, 4th dau. of late Col. Richard Gary, one of the judges of the
District Court
VGGA 21 Dec. 1805, p. 3

Died at Williamsburg on 13th Inst., JANE CARY, age 14, dau. of Mrs. Jane Cary
and great grandaughter of Col. Wilson Miles Cary
RE 19 July 1805, p. 3; VGGA 24 July, p. 2

Died Friday last (Nov. 13) in this city, RICHARD CARY, Esq., one of the Judges
of the General Court of this Commonwealth
VIC 18 Nov. 1789, p. 2

Died on Thurs. last (Feb. 28) MRS. SARAH CARY, consort of Wilson Miles Cary, Esq.
of Celeys
VA 5 March 1799, p. 3; VGGA 5 March, p. 3

Died, MRS. SARAH CARY, of York Town, age 67, on Nov. 16th
RE 3 Dec. 1811, p. 3

Died on 29th Ult., WILLIAM CARY, of York Town, age 72
VGGA 10 July 1805, p. 2

Died a few days past at his seat in Fluvanna Co., COL. WILSON MILES CARY, formerly
of Hampton, age 84
RE 4 Dec. 1817, p. 3; VP 5 Dec., p. 3, says he was Collector of Port of Hampton
under Royal Governor, Member of House of Burgesses and of General Assembly

Died on 2nd Inst. at a tenement of Mr. Martin Baker's near this city, a young man,
EDMUND CASHILL, who arrived about 18 mos. ago from Ireland
VGRMA 11 July 1793, p. 3

Died in King William Co., on (   ) April, MRS. MARY CATLETT, age 89
RE 12 May 1820, p. 3

Died April 22nd at Cincinnati, Ohio, MR. THOMAS CAULFIELD, comedian, age 49
VP 13 May 1815, p. 3

Died 24 Oct. 1803, age 58, MRS. JENNY POPE CAUSIN, wife of Mr. Gerard Blakeston
Causin of Charles Co., Md.
VGGA 16 Nov. 1803, p. 3

Died in Lexington on June 20th, MR. WILLIAM CERUTHERS, merchant, of that place
RE 20 June 1817, p. 3

Died, MR. JEAN PIERRE BENJAMIN CHAIGNEAU, of this city, on June 21st.
RE 2 July 1813, p. 1

Died on 4th Inst., MR. EDWARD P. CHAMBERLAYNE of King William Co., age 48,
leaving widow and 8 children
RE 17 June 1806, p. 3

Died, MRS. ELIZABETH CHAMBERLAYNE of King William Co., age 49, leaving 5 children
VA 24 June 1807, p. 3

Died, CAPT. WILLIAM CHAMBERS in Staunton (No death date)
Visitor 27 Jan. 1810, p. 206

Died, MR. GURDEN CHAPIN, Cashier of Bank of Alexandria, age 46, June 26th
VA 1 July 1811, p. 3

Died in Williamsburg on Wed. last (Jan. 24) MR. FRANCIS CHARLTON, merchant of
that city
VGGA 31 Jan. 1798, p. 2

Died in Richmond on March 12th, DR. FRANCIS CHARLTON of Mathews Co.
VP 16 March 1813, p. 3

Died at res. of Mr. William B. Cornick in Princess Anne Co., Sept. 29th, age 26,
MR. SEYMOUR P. CHARLTON, formerly of Richmond. One of the editors of the
Norfolk American Beacon
RC 2 Oct. 1820, p. 3; VPRDMA 2 Oct., p. 3

Died, JUDGE SAMUEL CHASE of Circuit Court of U.S. (No death date)
RE 25 June 1811, p. 2; VA 24 June, p. 3, says died Thurs. last (June 20?);
VP 25 June, p. 3, days died on 20th

Died on 7th Inst. at the Navy Yard, N.Y. CATHERINE ANN CHAUNCEY, youngest dau.
of Capt. Isaac Chauncey, USN
Visitor 29 July 1809, p. 102

Died in Chesterfield Co., on Oct. 28th, COL. MATTHEW CHEATHAM, for many years a Member of Va. Legislature
RE 1 Nov. 1815, p. 3

Died, WILLIAM CHERRY, Esq., Attorney at Law, and Member of the General Assembly
Visitor 7 Oct. 1809, p. 142

Died, MR. CLAIBORNE CHEW, of firm of Stanard & Chew of Richmond, on Wed. (Jan 29)
RE 4 Feb. 1817, p. 3; RC 31 Jan., p. 3

Died July 12th, age 49, D. COLLIER CHRISTIAN of New Kent Co.
VP 20 July 1814, p. 3

Died in Buckingham Co., July 27th, MRS. MARTHA CHRISTIAN, age 72
RE 8 Sept. 1820, p. 3

Died May 19th, MRS. MARY CHRISTIAN, wife of Robert Christian of New Kent Co.
VP 29 May 1816, p. 3

Died on 4th Inst. at Norfolk, MRS. CHRISTIAN, relict of late Col. Christian, and sister to Patrick,Henry
VICGA 12 May 1790, p. 3

Died, WARREN CHRISTIAN, son of Col. John Christian of Charles City Co., on 11th Inst.
RE 19 March 1811, p. 3

Died, MR. WILLIAM CHRISTIAN of Charles City Co., age 72, on 27th Ult.
VGGA 6 May, 1808, p. 3

Died, MR. PHILIP CHULL (commonly called shoals) in 115th year of his age. Born in Germany and emigrated to America in 1721
VA 23 Dec. 1813, p. 3

Died in Nottingham, N.H., GEN. JOSEPH CILLEY, age 60 (No death date)
Va. Federalist 9 Oct. 1799, p. 3

Died at Soldiers Retreat on the Mississippi on March 22nd, GEN. FERDINAND LEIGH CLAIBORNE
VP 26 April, 1815, p. 3

Died June 11th, MRS. FRANCES CLAIBORNE, wife of William Claiborne of King William Co., age 29, leaving husband and 3 infant daughters, one a few hours old.
RE 18 June 1819, p. 2

Died, HON. DR. JOHN CLAIBORNE, late a Member of House of Representatives, age 31, on the 9th Inst. in Brunswick Co. Buried in family burying ground of late Parson Jarratt of Dinwiddie
RE 21 Oct. 1808, p. 2

Died, MRS. MARY CLAIBORNE, spouse of Mr. William Claiborne of New Kent (No death date)
VGWA April 20, 1782, p. 3

Died, MAJ. WILLIAM CLAIBORNE, an old resident of this neighborhood, and father of W. C. Claiborne, Esq., Gov. of Terr. of Orleans, on Fri. last (Sept. 29)
RE 3 Oct. 1809, p. 3; Visitor 7 October, p. 142

Died Nov. 23rd at New Orleans, WILLIAM C. C. CLAIBORNE, late Gov. of La. and Senator from La.
VP 22 Dec. 1817, p. 3

Died, WILLIAM DANDRIDGE CLAIBORNE, Esq., age 55, on the 11th, at Liberty Hall, King William Co.
RE 18 June 1811, p. 3; VA 20 June, p. 3; VP 18 June, p. 3

Died April 27th at Santa Cruz, Island of Teneriffe, DR. WILLIAM PRESLEY CLAIBORNE of King William Co.
RE 1 Aug. 1817, p. 3

Died on 17th Ult., DAVID CLARK, Esq., Senator for the Distr. of Halifax, Charlotte, etc.
VGGA 19 July 1797, p. 2

Died April 2nd in Campbell Co., MR. JOHN CLARK, SR., age 74
VP 16 April 1819, p. 2

Died June 27th at Fotheringay, the seat of George Hancock, JULIA CLARK, his only dau. wife of William Clark of Missouri, leaving husband and 5 small children
RE 1 July 1820, p. 3; RE 1 Sept., p. 3, says died June 17th

Died, MICAJAH CLARK, age 91, of Albemarle Co., on 21st Inst.
VA 29 July 1808, p. 3; RE 2 Aug. 1808, p. 3

Died on 15th Dec. at house of Nicholas Johnston, Esq., in Oglethorpe Co., Ga., GEN. ELIJAH CLARKE, late Maj-Gen. of Militia of this state.
VA 24 Jan. 1800, p. 3

Died, MRS. ELIZABETH CLARKE, late lady of Maj. John Clarke of near this city, on Fri. last (July 11)
VA 16 July 1806, p. 3; RE 15 July, p. 3; VGGA 16 July, p. 3

Died at his res. in Manchester on July 14th, MR. JAMES CLARKE, JR.
RC 10 Aug. 1816, p. 3

Died, MRS. MARY ANN CLARKE, of Powhatan on 6th Inst.
RE 12 Sept. 1807, p. 3; VGGA 12 Sept. p. 3

Died at Mr. Clausel Clusel's in Mecklenburg Co., Sat. sen'night (July 13), MR. JOHN L. CLAUSEL, a young man
VA 23 July 1799, p. 3

Died on the 7th, MR. RICHARD CLAUSEL of the District Court of Petersburg
VA 18 Feb. 1800, p. 3

Died on 10th Inst., age 22, MRS. ANN CLAY, consort of Hon. Matthew Clay of Pittsylvania
VA 19 July 1806, p. 3

Died on May 27th at Halifax, C.H., MATTHEW CLAY, Esq., Member of Congress from
Campell Distr.
RE 10 June 1815, p. 3; VA 7 June, p. 3

Died, DACRE C. CLEMENSTON, Esq. on 21st Inst., a native of Whitehaven in England
and for 20 years resident of this state
VGGA 26 Feb. 1806, p. 3

Died in Newark, N.J. on 1st Inst., the wife of Mr. Benjamin Cleveland
VGRMA 11 June 1795, p. 2

Died, GEORGE CLINTON, in Washington on April 20th
RE 24 April 1812, p. 3

Died, MRS. AGNES CLOPTON, widow of Benjamin Clopton, age 81, at her seat in
Goochland Co., on Aug. 24th
VA 3 Nov. 1809, p. 3; Visitor 4 Nov., p. 158

Died, MRS. JENNY CLOPTON on 17th this mo., age 66, consort of Mr. George Clopton,
leaving husband & 6 children
VGGA 30 Dec. 1795, p. 2

Died on Thurs. (Sept. 12) JOHN CLOPTON, Member of Congress from this district.
VP 14 Sept. 1816, p. 3; VA 21 Sept., p. 3, says died at his seat in New Kent
Co., age 64. Had also been in Revolution, a member of state legislature, and
member of Executive Council

REV. MR. REUBEN CLOPTON died on 21st this mo. at his seat in Cumberland Co.,
leaving wife and 5 children
VGGA 30 Dec. 1795, p. 2

Died in London, Mass., MR. JEREMIAH CLOUGH, merchant, age 31, in a fire on
Dec. 22nd, died Dec. 26, 1818.
RC 25 Jan. 1818, p.3

Died, MR. JOHN M. COBB, formerly of this place, at Warren in Albermarle Co.,
Sept. 27th
VA 16 Oct. 1810, p. 3

Died on 27th Ult. at New Castle in Hanover, MR. DAVID COCHRAN
VGGA 10 Oct. 1792, p. 3

Died, COL. ALLEN COCKE, for many years a representative of Surry Co., in the
legislature (No death date)
VG Dec. 16, 1780, p. 3

Died on 22nd Inst., MRS. ANN COCKE of Swanns Point, Surry Co.
VGRMA 30 May 1795, p. 3

Died, MRS. ANNE COCKE, spouse of Col. Allen Cocke, in Surry Co. (No death
date)
VG Aug. 9, 1780, p. 2

Died on Monday last (Feb. 23) JAMES COCKE, Esq. of Williamsburg
VGWA 26 Feb. 1789, p. 3

Died on 11th Inst. at Capt. William Thompson's in Halifax Co., MISS LUCY R. COCKE,
Dau. of Richard Cocke, Esq. of Greyland Surry
VGRMA 29 Sept. 1794, p. 3

Died, MRS. MARIA COCKE, wife of Bowler Cocke of Henrico Co., on 15th Ult, at age
17
VGGA 2 April 1806, p. 3

Died Dec. 28, 1816, MRS. COCKE, consort of John Hartwell Cocke of Bremo
RE 14 Jan. 1817, p. 3

Died, at Mrs. Peggy Payne's on Dec. 28th, MR. RICHARD COCKE of Fluvanna
VA 11 Jan. 1804, p. 3

Died May 17th, age 67, MR. RICHARD COCKE of Henrico Co.
RE 26 May 1820, p. 3

Died at New Castle on 28th Ult., MRS. COCKRAN, relict of David Cockran
VGGA 4 Dec. 1802, p. 3

Died Jan. 3rd, MRS. CODY, wife of James Cody of Richmond
VP 6 Jan. 1818, p. 3

Died on Sat. last (May 3) MR. NELSON COGBELL, age 22
VA 9 May 1806, p. 3; RE 9 May, p. 3 (Says Cogbill)

Died on 22nd Inst., age 60, MRS. ESTHER COHEN, wife of Mr. Jacob I. Cohen of this
city
VA 29 Aug. 1804, p. 3

Died on Friday last (July 29) MR. ISRAEL I. COHEN, merchant, of this city
VA 3 Aug. 1803, p. 3

Died at New London, HON. JOSHUA COIT, Esq., one of the Representatives in Congress
from Conn.
VA 25 Sept. 1798, p. 3

Died, MRS. LUCY COKE, consort of Capt. Richard Coke, in Williamsburg, Oct. 28th,
age 27
RE 16 Nov. 1810, p. 3

Died, DR. SAMUEL COKER, lately in Williamsburg, eldest son of Mr. John Coker
of Williamsburg
VGGA 18 April 1807, p. 3

Died in Petersburg on Sat. last (July 8) MRS. ANN COLE, relict of late Mr. William
Cole of Prince George Co.
Visitor 15 July, 1809, p. 96

Died, MR. JAMES COLE, JR., at seat of Capt. James Cole in Fluvanna, on 29th Ult.
RE 6 Feb. 1812, p. 3

Died, THOMAS LEWIS COLE, of 4th Regt. of Va. Artillery, at his seat Belle Farm
in Gloucester Co., on 9th Inst.
VA 23 Nov. 1805, p. 3

Died on 8th Ult. at his seat in Jefferson Co., DR. WALTER K. COLE
VGRMA 3 March 1794, p. 3

Died Sat. last (Dec. 9) in this city, MAJ. WYATT COLEMAN, late of Williamsburg
VGGA 13 Dec. 1797, p. 2

CAPT. LT. RICHARD COLEMAN of Spotsylvania Co., fell in defense of his country
on 29th May at Wax Saws, S.C.
VG June 28, 1780, p. 3

Died, COL. SAMUEL COLEMAN, at his house near this city, on Sat. last (March 9)
Served in Revolution. For last 25 years assistant Clerk of the Council
VA 12 March 1811, p. 3

Died on Nov. 21st, MRS. SUSANNA COLEMAN, relict of Samuel Coleman
RE 29 Nov. 1815, p. 3

Died in Williamsburg, Nov. 29th, WILLIAM COLEMAN, an old inhabitant of that city
RE 21 Dec. 1819, p. 3

Died this morning, MR. WYATT COLEMAN, SR., of this city
VGRMA 1 Aug. 1795, p. 3

Died on Feb. 9th at house of Mr. Isaac Coles in Halifax Co., ISAAC H. COLES,
age 37
RE 23 Feb. 1814, p. 3

Died Sept. 29th at his seat in Halifax Co., MR. ISAAC COLES, age 43
RE 10 Oct. 1820, p. 3

Died on 1st Inst., MRS. MILDRED COLES of Halifax Co., age 48, relict of late
Walter Coles, Esq.
VGGA 14 May 1799, p. 3

Died at his res. in Manchester on Mon. (Oct. 28) THOMAS COLLEY, age 52
RC 1 Nov. 1816, p. 3

Died, MISS ANNA COLLINS of Norfolk, killed by David Frank, who then killed
himself, on Jan. 26th
VP 5 Feb. 1811, p. 3

Died yesterday in this city, MR. JOHN COLLINS, carpenter
VGRMA 4 Sept. 1794, p. 3

Died, SIDNEY COLLINS, age 6 son of Mr. E. Collins of Cairo, N.Y., burned to death 28 Dec. 1818
RC 19 Jan. 1819, p. 3

Died in Norfolk last Sun. (Nov. 2) JOHN CONNOLLY, in blacksmith business, leaves wife and 3 children
VGWA Nov. 6, 1788, p. 3

Died at Covington, Ohio Dec. 25, 1819, S.S. CONNOR, late Lt. Col. in 16th Regt. U.S. Infantry, and Member of 14th Congress from Mass.
RE 3 Feb. 1820, p. 3

Died in Norfolk on Fri. last (Nov. 4) MRS. COMFORT COOK, wife of Capt. John Cook
VGWA 6 Nov. 1788, p. 3

Died April 13th, age 58, MR. WILLIAM COOK, funeral from his res. Falling Spring today
VPRDMA 15 April 1820, p. 2

Died, MR. SAMUEL M. COOKE of Gloucester Co., age 22 on 4 March
RE 5 April 1808, p. 3

Died Nov. 23rd, MISS ELVIRA COOPER, step-daug. of William Lemon of Cincinnati
RE 27 Dec. 1817, p. 3

Died, MRS. MARGARET COPELAND, on 26 Dec. 1811 in the fire which destroyed the Richmond Theatre
VP 7 Jan. 1812, p. 3

Died on 25th Ult., MRS. REBECCA COPLAND, consort of Mr. Charles Copland of this city
VA 5 Aug. 1800, p. 3; VGGA 29 July, p. 3

Died Dec. 8, 1815, JOHN CORBIN, son of Maj. Richard Corbin of Lanesville, Va. from a duel wound at Carlisle College
RE 11 Jan. 1816, p. 3; VA 10 Jan., p. 3

Died on Tuesday last (May 18) RICHARD CORBIN, Esq. of Lanesville, King & Queen Co., age 77
VICGA 26 May 1790, p. 2

Died at Laneville, his res. MAJ. RICHARD CORBIN, age 48, leaving wife and 4 children on June 10th
RE 18 June 1819, p. 3; RE 2 July, p. 3, days raised an artillery company in War of 1812; RC 16 June, p. 3; VP 16 June, p. 3

Died in Wilmington, N.C., MR. JAMES CORKAN, merchant, of Petersburg (No death date)
VGGA 8 Sept. 1790, p. 2

Died on Wed. last (July 18) Madame CORNILLON of this city
VGGA 21 July 1804, p. 2

Died at his res. in Louisa Co., CAPT. DUKE COSBY, leaving wife & children
(No death date)
RE 7 Sept. 1819, p. 3

Died, MR. MINOR M. COSBY of Milton, Albemarle Co., on 9th Inst.
RE 23 Feb. 1810, p. 3; Visitor 24 Feb., p. 15

Died on Sun. last (Dec. 22) SAMUEL COUCH of Goochland
VA 27 Dec. 1799, p. 2

Died on Mon. (Nov. 6) MRS. ELIZABETH COULING. Her friends and those of James
M. Couling requested to attend funeral at Methodist Old Chapel of Richmond
RC 8 Nov. 1820, p. 3

Died on 25th Ult., REV. JAMES COULING. Had lived in Richmond 9 years, and
for 5 was tutor to the old charity school in the city
VA 3 Oct. 1807, p. 3 (See VA of 26 Sept. under JAMES COWLAND. RE says
REV. JAMES COWLAND)

Died, MRS. JANE COURTNEY, age about 66, wife of Elder John Courtney, Baptist
Minister of this city, on the 19th Inst.
VA 22 March 1808, p. 3; RE 22 March, p. 3; VGGA 22 March, p. 3

Died on Aug. 18th, MRS. MILDRED COURTNEY, wife of Mr. Thomas Courtney of
Richmond
Examiner 27 Aug. 1803, p. 3

Died, MR. PHILIP COURTNEY, on 4th Inst., age 56, from King & Queen Co., drowned
in Mattapony River
RE 24 Feb. 1809, p. 3; Visitor, p. 14, 11 Feb. says survived by 5 children

Died, Aug. 29th in New Kent Co., MRS. POLLY COURTNEY, wife of Thomas Courtney,
age 22, after 13 mos. of marriage
VA 10 Sept. 1806, p. 3

Died in this city on 25th Inst., ELDER THOMAS COURTNEY, Baptist Minister of
the church of Christ, Black Creek, New Kent
VA 28 April 1797, p. 3

Died on 14th Ult. at Dr. Lockett's, MISS MARTHA E. N. COUSINS, eldest dau. of
Mr. John Cousins of Amelia
RE 4 Oct. 1815, p. 3

Died, MR. LEWIS COUTTS, on 21st
VA 26 July, 1813, p. 3

Died in this city on Mon. last (Nov. 17) MR. REUBEN COUTTS
VA 21 Nov. 1806, p. 3

38

Died Feb. 22nd, MR. ROBERT COVENTRY, a native of Scotland
RE 11 March 1817, p. 3

Died on 16th Inst. at his seat Juniper Hill, in Lunenburg, Co., MR. WILLIAN COWAN, age 56, a lawyer
VA 30 Dec. 1806, p. 2

Died, MR. JAMES COWLAND of this city, yesterday
VA 26 Sept. 1807, p. 3; RE 26 Sept., p. 3, says "Rev"

Died, MRS. ANNE COWLEY of Henrico (No death date)
VGWA March 16, 1782, p. 3

Died in Richmond Nov. 28th, ELIZA JOHNSTON COWLEY, daughter of Robert Cowley
VPRDMA 14 Dec. 1820, p. 3

Died Feb. 8th, ROBERT COWLEY, a man of color, age 125, for years had been door-keeper at the Capitol, a position given him by the governor for his services in the Revolution
RC 10 Feb. 1820, p. 3

Died, MR. CHARLES COX, Senior, an old resident, on the 2nd
RE 9 April 1811, p. 3

Died in Chesterfield on Sat. last (Dec. 20) MRS. MARTHA COX, spouse of Mr. Edward Cox
VGGA 24 Dec. 1794, p. e; VGRMA Dec. 22

Died May 3rd, MRS. SARAH COX, consort of Mr. Charles A. Cox of Richmond, leaving a husband, parents and 2 small children
RE 12 May 1820, p. 3

Died Feb. 3rd, MR. GEORGE CRADDOCK of Amelia Co., one of band of patriots who marched from Petersburg to defend the northwestern frontier
RE 20 Feb. 1816, p. 3

Died on Wed. last (May 11) MR. ADAM CRAIG, Clerk of the County Court of Henrico and of the Hustings Court of this city
VA 13 May 1808, p. 3; RE 14 May, p. 3; VGGA 13 May, p. 3

Died Wed. last (Sept. 19) age 19, MRS. ELIZABETH CRALLE, spouse of Mr. John Cralle, Jr. of Cherry Point
VGGA 26 Sept. 1792, p. 3

Died WILLIAM CRANDALL, a sailor on the brig "Eliza", fell overboard
VGGA 17 Jan. 1800, p. 3

Died yesterday, MR. JOHN CRAWFORD, at an advanced age
RC 3 Nov. 1795, p. 3; VGGA 4 Nov. 1795, p. 3; VGRMA 5 Nov. , p. 3

Died last evening, MRS. MARY ANN CRAWFORD of this city
Observatory 9 Aug. 1798, p. 3

Died March 2nd at his res. in Hanover Co., MR. JOHN CRENSHAW, age 57
RE 10 March 1818, p. 3; VP 7 March, p. 2

Died Jan. 20th in upper end of Hanover, MRS. SARAH CRENSHAW, relict of
Mr. Charles Crenshaw, and sister of late Capt. I. Bacon of Henrico, age
77
RE 3 Feb. 1816, p. 3; VP 31 Jan., p. 3; VA 31 Jan., p. 3

Died June 19th at upper end of Hanover Co., MISS SUSANNA CRENSHAW
VP 2 July 1817, p. 3

Died lately at his seat in Charles City Co., at an advanced age, JOHN CREW,
a member of Soc. of Friends
VA 7 Feb. 1800, p. 3

Died, JOHN CREW, JR. on 13th Inst., age 50, at his seat Eastrun Hill in Charles
City Co., survived by his father 81, his wife and 4 small children
VA 27 Oct. 1807, p. 3

Died, MRS. JANE CRINGHAN, spouse of Dr. John Cringhan of this city (No death
date)
VGWA 30 April 1789, p. 3

Died Mon. (Oct. 31) DR. JOHN CRINGAN, for many years physician in this city
VA 4 Nov. 1808, p. 3; VGGA 8 Nov., p. 3

Died, MRS. CRINGAN, spouse of Dr. John Cringan of this city (No death date)
VGGA 11 Dec. 1793, p. 3; VGRMA 9 Dec.

Died in this city Tues. last (March 3) MRS. Cringan, consort of Dr. Cringan
VA 6 March 1801, p. 3

Died a few days ago a man named CROSS, by drowning
VGWA April 19, 1787, p. 3

Died Aug. 21st, MRS. BETTY ANN CROSS, consort of Mr. John Cross of Hanover Co.,
age 54, leaving husband and 7 children
RE 1 Sept. 1820, p. 3

Died on 10th Inst. at Norfolk, MR. JAMES CROSS, merchant of Manchester, and a
native of Glasgow
VGWA Jan. 25, 1787, p.3

Died, MR. RICHARD CROUCH, JR., of this city, on Tues. last (Oct. 25). Left
several children
VA 28 Oct. 1808, p. 2; RE 28 Oct., p. 3

Died, MR. RICHARD CROUCH, Senior, one of the first settlers of this city, on 3rd Inst., age 80
RE 14 May 1811, p. 3; VA 16 May, p. 3

Died at Salem, CAPT. GEORGE CROWNINGSHIELD, age 51, late navigator of "Cleopatra's Barge" and son of late merchant of Salem of same name. Born in Salem May 28, 1766, he went to sea in 1790
VP 9 Dec. 1817, p. 3

Died at Marblehead, Mass., CAPT. WILLIAM CROWNINSHIELD, age 86, of that city. Was at capture of Quebec and served in both army and navy in Revolution
RC 12 Sptil 1820, p. 3

Died MAJ. ABNER CRUMP, Clerk of Powhatan Co. (No death date)
VGGA 15 Jan. 1802, p. 3

Died at Westport Sept. 7th, PAUL CUFFEE, a respectable man of color, age 59. He was a wealthy merchant and visited Sierra Leone 3 times in efforts to help negroes
RE 23 Sept. 1817, p. 3

Died, ROBERT CULPEPER, manager of a firm near Deep Creek, near Norfolk (No death date)
RC 14 Jan. 1819, p. 3

Died on 10th of last mo., MRS. MARY CUNNINGHAM, wife of John Cunningham, merchant of Cumberland
VA 22 March 1799, p. 3

Died, June 24th, MRS. CAROLINE R. CURD, wife of Dr. Thomas Curd, and dau. of James Pleasants, Jr. of Goochland Co.
RE 13 July 1816, p. 3

Died in Richmond on Tues. last (April 7), MR. ARCHIBALD CURRIE, bookbinder
VA 10 April 1801, p. 3

Died, DR. JAMES CURRIE, on Tues. last (April 21) a native of Scotland, and resident of Richmond for 40 years
VA 24 April 1807, p. 3; RE 24 April, p. 3, says died Wed.; VGGA 25 April, p. 3

Died on Thurs. last (Nov. 25) MRS. CURRIE, wife of Dr. James Currie of this city
VGGA 27 Nov. 1802, p. 3

Died, MARY CURRY, believed killed Jan. 28th in N.Y. by her husband
RC 5 Feb. 1819, p. 4

Died at Upton in Gloucester Co., res. of Mrs. Francis Wiatt, on Oct. 20th, MRS. ANN CURTIS, at an advanced age
RC 2 Nov. 1816, p. 3

Died, MAJ. CHARLES CURTIS, in Gloucester County., on Wed. last (Dec. 16)
RE 22 Dec. 1807, p. 3

Died, WILLIAM CUSHING, on Thurs. last (probably before Thurs. 20th) in Scituate, Mass., one of Justices of U.S. Court, age 77
VA 25 Sept. 1810, p. 3

Died on Thurs. (October 24), CUSTLOW, a free black man, killed by a white man not named
VP 26 Oct. 1816., p. 3

Died in Boston, MR. JAMES CUTLER, one of Editors of Boston Gazette, age 45, (No death date)
VP 9 May 1818, p. 3

Died in Fredericksburg, MRS. SALLY CARTER CUTTING, consort of John Browne Cutting, Esq., of Stafford Co. (No death date)
RE 4 May 1814, p. 3

Died on 24th May at his seat, Elmington, in Gloucester Co., BENJAMIN DABNEY, Attorney at Law, age 49
VA 19 July 1806, p. 3

Died in Hanover Co., at Capt. T. Price's, MR. GEORGE DABNEY, age 35, (No death date)
RE 25 Aug. 1818, p. 3

Died, on 24th Inst., COL. RICHARD DABNEY of King William Co., age 50
VA 30 May 1800, p. 3; VGGA 3 June, p. 3

Died on Wed. last (Jan. 15), COL. WILLIAM DAINGERFIELD of Spotsylvania Co., cut his throat
VGWA 18 Jan. 1783, p. 3

Died Jan. 17th, ALEXANDER J. DALLAS of Philadelphia
VP 24 Jan. 1817, p. 3

Died CAPT. GEORGE DANCER of Ship Marlborough at City Point (No death date)
VGWA 25 June 1785, p. 3; VGAA 25 June, says died Sun. last (June 18), native of England

Died, HON. BARTHOLOMEW DANDRIDGE of New Kent one of the Judges of the General Court (No death date)
VGAA 23 April 1785, p. 2

Died on 17th Ult. at Aux Cayes, BARTHOLOMEW DANDRIDGE, Esq. Consul of U.S. for southern part of St. Domingo. He was formerly secretary to Gen. Washington, and formerly a resident of Alexandria
VA 18 Aug. 1802, p. 3; VGGA 14 Aug., p. 3

Died on 11th at Turkey Island, seat of Bowler Cocke, Esq., in the 6 year of her age, MISS ELIZA LEWIS DANDRIDGE, eldest dau. of Francis Dandridge, Esq., lately dec'd
VGGA 20 May 1795, p. 3; VGRMA 14 May, p. 2, says age 16

Died, OCTAVIA ST. CLARIE DANDRIDGE, on Sept. 18th, age 6 years, 6 mos.
RE 24 Oct. 1806, p. 3

Died in Richmond on April 8th, MISS FRANCES G. DANIEL, dau. of Dr. John Moncure Daniel, late of Stafford Co., and niece of Peter V. Daniel
RE 14 April 1820, p. 3

Died, MRS. MARGARET DANIEL, on 9th Inst. at Falmouth, consort of Dr. John M. Daniel, eldest dau. of late Thomas Stone, Esq., of Md.
RE 17 March 1809, p. 3; Visitor 25 March, p. 31

Died at Newport, R.I. on July 17th, RICHARD F. DARRNCOAT, Esq. of Hanover Co.
VA 5 Aug. 1807, p. 3

Died Jan. 3rd, MR. JOSEPH DARMSTADT, merchant of Richmond
RE 4 Jan. 1820, p. 3; VPRDMA 4 Jan., p. 2

Died, FISHER DASHIELL, Esq., at Suffolk on Wed. (Nov. 13) for many years a Member of the Legislature, and a magistrate of Nansemond Co.
VA 21 Nov. 1811, p. 3

Died Mon. last (Nov. 25) in this city, MR. JOSEPH P. DAVENPORT, printer
VGRMA 28 Nov. 1793, p. 3

Died lately in Williamsburg, MR. WILLIAM DAVENPORT, Attorney at Law of Warwick Co.
VGGA 18 March 1795, p. 3; VGRMA 19 March, p. 3

Died in this city on Sun. last (Jan. 25) WILSON DAVENPORT, Esq. of Lynchburg, Member of General Assembly from Campbell Co.
VA 27 Jan. 1807, p. 3

Died on Mr. Harvie's Island, MR. ALEXANDER DAVIDSON. Funeral at landing on the river above Mr. Cunningham's mills (No death date)
RC 18 Oct. 1820, p. 3

Died, MR. WILLIAM DAVIDSON, native of Scotland, and for several years a resident of this city, on Sun. last (May 14)
RE 16 May 1809, p. 3; VA 19 May, p. 3, adds: leaves wife and 2 children;
Visitor 20 May, p. 62

Died at his seat in Mecklenburg Co., COL. WILLIAM DAVIES, formerly Collector of the Port of Norfolk (No death date)
VA 27 Dec. 1805, p. 6

Died Mon. last (May 20) MASTER AUGUSTINE DAVIS, second son of Augustine Davis, Printer, of this city, drowned
VGRMA 23 May 1793, p. 3

Died, MR. JOHN DAVIS, age 23, son of Mr. Augustine Davis of this city, in Hampton on 13th Inst.
VA 17 Sept. 1806, p. 3; Imp. Obs. 20 Sept., p. 3; RE 16 Sept, p. 3;
VGGA 17 Sept., p. 3, says "son of editor of this paper"

Died, MRS. MARY DAVIS, consort of Mr. Moses Davis of this city, on 24th Ult. in Baltimore
RE 4 June 1811, p. 3

Died Feb. 20th at St. Francisville, La., MR. MICAJAH DAVIS, killed by some of his slaves
VPRDMA 28 March 1820, p. 2

Died, MR. ROBERT DAVIS, on Wed. last (June 21)
VA 23 June 1809, p. 3; VGGA 23 June, p. 3; Visitor 1 July, p. 86

Died at Elysian Fields, M.T., Sept. 22nd, age 24, ROBERT PLEASANTS DAVIS, son of Micajah Davis
RE 23 Oct. 1816, p. 3

Died Dec. 3rd in Northampton Co., REV. THOMAS DAVIS, he was a native of Norfolk
Co., joined 9th Va. Regt. 1776 and was later Chaplain to Gen. Washington. Was
later rector of parishes in Alexandria, Norfolk, and lastly Hungars Parish,
where he died, age 71
RE 14 Dec. 1815, p. 3

Died, THOMAS T. DAVIS, a Judge of the Indiana Territory, formerly Congressman
from Ky
VA 1 Jan. 1808, p. 3

Died, MR. BENJAMIN DAWSON, son of Elder William Dawson, on 12th Inst., age 24
RE 16 Jan. 1808, p. 3

Died, MRS. PHILADELPHIA DAWSON, age 43, wife of Elder William Dawson of Richmond,
Aug. 31st at house of Maj. Samuel Duval in Buckingham Co.
RE 12 Sept. 1807, p. 3

Died Saturday (Nov. 14) MR. WILLIAM DAWSON, son of late Hon. Commissary Dawson.
VIC 18 Nov. 1789, p. 2

Died on Mon. last (April 2) age 77, Mr. JOHN DAY, SENR. of Hanover Co.
VGGA 4 April 1804, p. 2

Died, MR. SAMUEL DAY, age 55, in the Forks of Hanover, on 28th Ult. A soldier
in the Revolution
RE 5 Feb. 1811, p. 3; VA 8 Feb., p. 3

Died fighting Indians in Tenn., Aug. 8th, JONATHAN DEAN
VGWA 2 Oct. 1788, p. 3

Died Nov. 15th in St. Louis, age 43, REV. FELIX DeANDREIS, Vicar General of
La. and Superior of Congregation of Mo.
RC 18 Nov. 1820, p. 3

Died lately in Williamsburg, SIMEON DEANE, who was sent by U.S. to negotiate
with France and Holland
IC 9 July 1788, p. 3; VGWA says Fri last (June 30) 3 July, a res. of
Weatherfield, Conn., interred Bruton Parish Churchyard

Died at Frankfort, Philadelphia Co., Pa., STEPHEN DECATUR, late Commander of
U.S. Ship Delaware, and father of the Commodore (No death date)
VA 22 Nov. 1808, p. 3

Died March 22nd, Commodore STEPHEN DECATUR
RC 25 March 1820, p. 3; VPRDMA 25 March, p. 3

Died on Sun. last (Oct. 25), MAJ. C. C. DeKLAUMAN, age 58, served in the
Virginia Line in the Revolution
VA 30 Oct. 1801, p. 3

Died, STEPHEN DELANO, JR. of Clinton Township near Columbus, Ohio, in June
RC 14 July 1818, p. 3

Died, MRS. ELIZABETH DENHAM, consort of Mr. Richard Denham of this city, on Thurs. last (Dec. 4)
VGRMA 8 Dec. 1794, p. 3

Died on Sun. (July 6) MRS. DENNIE, consort of William Dennie of Rocketts. She was native of Philadelphia
RE 8 July 1817, p. 3

Died at Rocketts June 23rd, RICHARD DENNY, an old inhabitant of Richmond
VPRDMA 26 June 1820, p. 3

Died at New Orleans Oct. 9th, age 64, AUGUSTIN DERBIGNY, late professor at a college in Aisnex, France
RE 19 Nov. 1805, p. 3

Died at Salem, Mass., ELIAS HASKETT DERBY, age 60, merchant in that place
VA Federalist 9 Oct. 1799, p. 3

Died, HON. RICHARD DERBY, Jr., Esq., in Salem, New England (No death date)
VGWA Feb. 2, 1782, p. 3

Died on 1st Inst., MR. JAMES DeSEAR of Chesterfield, age 83
RE 12 May 1808, p. 3

Died on 30th Ult. in Williamsburg, DR.JOHN DeSEQUIRA, age 83. Had lived there 50 years.
VGGA 18 March 1795, p. 3; VGRMA 19 March, p. 3, says born in London

Died June 22nd age 54, at his res. in Buckingham Co., CAPT. ANTHONY DIBRELL, leaving widow and large family of children
RE 29 June 1816, p. 3

Died, FOUNTAINE C. DICKENSON, age 20, of Albemarle Co., in Richmond on Mon. last (Oct. 25) of wounds received at Hampton
RE 29 Oct. 1813, p. 3; VP 29 Oct., p. 3

Died on July 6th MRS. SALLY DICKERSON, consort of William W. Dickenson, late of Richmond
RE 20 July 1816, p. 3

Died in Wilmington, Del. on 14th Inst., JOHN DICKINSON, Esq., former member of Pa. lesiglature and late Gov. of that state
VA 26 Feb. 1808, p. 3

Died at his res. in Nottoway Co., on Dec. 25th, MR. ROBERT DICKINSON, age about 50, leaving wife and 6 small children
RE 23 Jan. 1819, p. 3

Died, in Williamsburg, BEVERLEY DICKSON, Esq., late Naval Officer of Lower Dist. of James Riv. (No death date)
VGWA 6 Sept. 1787, p. 3

Died, MR. JOHN DICKSON, late Editor of the <u>Petersburg Intelligencer</u> (No death date)
<u>RE</u> 20 July 1814, p. 3; <u>VP</u> 20 July, p. 3, says died July 14th

Died at his seat in Hanover Co. Feb. 25th, COL. COLE DIGGES, an old Revolutionary Soldier, age 63
<u>RE</u> 4 March 1817, p. 3

Died on 3rd Inst. at York, COL. DUDLEY DIGGES of Williamsburg
<u>VICGA</u> 12 May 1790, p. 3

Died Sat. last (Dec. 24) at Rosegill, MRS. ELIZABETH DIGGES, spouse of Dudley Digges, Esq. of Williamsburg
<u>VGWA</u> 31 Dec. 1785, p. 3; <u>WGWA</u> for 7 Jan. 1786 repeats this and still says "Sun last"

Died on 15th Inst., MRS. MARGARET DIGGES, consort of Edward Digges of Manchester
<u>RE</u> 23 July 1813, p. 3; <u>VP</u> 20 July, p. 3

Died, MR. G. DILLARD, in Petersburg (No death date)
<u>Visitor</u> 27 Jan. 1810, p. 206

Died in Prince Edward Co., at res. of his mother Oct. 30th, EDWARD D. DILLON, about 20, student at Hampton Sydney
<u>RE</u> 6 Nov. 1818, p. 3

Died, CAPT. JOHN DIX of Pittsylvania Co., age 55, on 28th Nov.
<u>VGAA</u> 3 Jan. 1784, p. 3

Died, DR. ANTHONY TUCKER DIXON of Charles City, age 52, on April 26th last
<u>VA</u> 3 May, 1808, p. 3

Died Wed. last (April 27), age 51, MR. JOHN DIXON, printer, of this state
<u>VGGA</u> 4 May 1791, p. 2

Died Wed. last (May 22) CAPT. JOHN DIXON, printer, of this city
<u>RE</u> 24 May 1805, p. 3; <u>VA</u> 25 May, p. 3; <u>VGGA</u> 25 May, p. 3

Died Monday (April 5) MRS. ROSANNA DIXON, spouse of Col. John Dixon of this city, printer
<u>VICGA</u> 7 April 1790, p. 2

Died, MRS. SARAH DIXON, relict of late Mr. John Dixon, printer of this city on Sun. last (Dec. 20)
<u>VA</u> 22 Dec. 1807, p. 3

Died in Richmond yesterday, MR. ROBERT DOBBINS
<u>RC</u> 7 Nov. 1816, p. 3

Died, MISS ANN DOBIE of Richmond (No death date)
<u>VA</u> 30 Jan. 1805, p. 3

Died on Mon. last (June 16) MR. SAMUEL DOBY of this city
VA 19 June 1801, p. 3

Died in the Penitentiary in this city on 9th Inst., RAWLEIGH DODSON from
Northumberland Co.
VA 17 Nov. 1801, p. 3

Died in Mifflin Co., Tenn. on 10th Inst., (probably Oct.) MISS MARGARET DOLTON,
age 116 years 3 mos. 10 days, a native of Ireland
VA 13 Nov. 1805, p. 3

Died, CAPT. DONAHUE, formerly of Phila. at Caracas, executed by the Spanish
Govt., in a rebellion
VA 30 Aug. 1806, p. 2

Died, MR. ALEXANDER DONALD, in Chesterfield, (No death date)
VGRMA 5 Jan. 1795, p. 3

Died in Richmond, May 10th, MRS. ELIZABETH DONALDSON, age 77
VP 14 May 1813, p. 3

Died, JOSEPH DONNISON, at his seat at Town of Tappahannock, on April 20th
RE 14 May 1808, p. 3

Died, MR. BALTAZAR DORISH, Fri. last (June 6) when brick wall fell on him
while fighting a fire
VGRMA 12 June 1794, p. 3

Died Sept. 6th, age 22, JAMES M. DOSWELL, of the Forks of Hanover, and son of
Capt. James Doswell
RE 10 Sept. 1819, p. 3; VP 10 Sept., p. 3

Died at his plantation on Horse Creek, Scriven Co. (Ga.) MR. MICHAEL DOUGHERTY,
age 125 years; on 29 May 1808
Virginian 1 July, p. 3

Died in Portland on Sun. (No death date given) MR. FRANCIS DOUGLAS, proprietor
of the Eastern Argus, age 37, accidentally shot himself
RE 19 Sept. 1820, p. 3

Died in Loudon Co., Va. on 2nd Inst., GEN. HUGH DOUGLAS, age 55
RE 12 July 1815, p. 3

Died on 19th Inst., JOHN DOUGLAS, stonecutter, from Washington, leaving wife
and 5 children
RE 21 Dec. 1815, p. 3

Died, in the Mississippi Territory, (before Nov. 10th) the great preacher,
LORENZO DOW, where he had just moved
VGGA 13 Dec. 1808, p. 3

Died Jan. 6th, near Hebran, Conn., PEGGY DOW, wife of Lorenzo Dow
RC 18 Jan. 1820, p. 3; VPRDMA 15 Jan., p. 3

Died at seat of Gen. John Blackwell in Fauquier Co., MRS. LUCY S. DOWNMAN, age
32, wife of Mr. Rawleigh Downman of Lancaster Co. (No death date)
RE 14 Oct. 1817, p. 3

Died on Tues. last (Augs. 30) in Hanover Co., age 45, MR. DAVID DOYLE
RE 3 Sept. 1814, p. 3; VP 7 Sept., p. 2

Died Feb. 3rd, at house of Peter V. Daniel, in Richmond, MASTER DAVID DOYLE,
a native of Ireland, age 12, having lived with the Daniels the past 2 years
RE 6 Feb. 1817, p. 3; RC 5 Feb., p. 3

Died lately in Westmoreland Co., RICHARD DOZIER, age 89
VGGA 1 June 1791, p. 2

Died on 24th Ult. GEN. WILLIAM DRAKE of Berkeley Co., age 66
VA 15 Dec. 1801, p. 3

Died, CARTER H. DREW, late merchant of Richmond (No death date)
RE 21 Sept. 1819, p. 3

Drowned Monday last (Aug. 25) a son of MR. DREWIDZ of West Point
VGWA 28 Aug. 1788, p. 3

Died in Vera Cruz April 6th, CAPT. CORNELIUS DRISCOLL, shipmaster out of
Baltimore
VP 10 June 1817, p. 3

Died MRS. ANNE DRUMMOND of Williamsburg. (No death date)
VGWA Jan. 26, 1782, p. 3

Died on 6th Inst., HENLEY DRUMMOND, Esq., of Amherst Co., leaving widow and 4
children
VA 16 April 1803, p. 3

Died on 23rd Ult. age 33, MRS. HANNAH DUDLEY, wife of Maj. William Dudley of
Warwick Co.
VA 2 April 1803, p. 3; VGGA 2 April, p. 3

Died, MRS. HANNAH DUDLEY, age 78, at Mr. Joseph Jenkins' in lower end of
Henrico on the 8th
VA 16 July 1806, p. 3

Died, MRS. MILDRED DUDLEY, wife of Mr. William Dudley of York Co. (No death
date)
VIC 15 July 1789, p. 2

Died, in Woodstock on 7th Inst., COL. WILLIAM H. DULANEY, for many years a
physician at that place
VA 27 Jan. 1809, p. 3; Visitor 11 Feb., p. 7

Died in Richmond on Sun. (Aug. 29) MR. CHARLES DUNBAR, formerly of Hingham, Mass.
RE 3 Sept. 1819, p. 3

Died Sun. (Aug. 22) at res. of his uncle, Capt. Jesse D. Elliott, MR. ROBERT E. DUNCAN,
Midshipman, U.S.N., age 13, at Norfolk
VP 27 Aug. 1819, p. 3

Died, MRS. MARY R. DUNLOP, wife of Mr. John Dunlop, merchant, of Petersburg, on 19th
Inst., age 26
RE 24 Jan. 1811, p. 3

Died on 27th Ult. MAJ. ANDREW DUNSCOMBE, age 45
VA 8 May 1802, p. 2 (VA of 28 April says died Mon (26th). Was "of this city")
VGGA 1 May & 8 May, p. 3 (one says died Mon. (26) and one says died 27th)

Died on 3rd Inst. in New York City, age 77, DANIEL DUNSCOMB, Esq. father to Maj.
Andrew Dunscomb, late of this city
VA 19 March 1803, p. 3; VGGA 19 March, p. 3; Examiner 19 March, p. 3

Died, MR. JOHN DUNSMORE. Funeral took place this date from his res. in rear of
the Bell Tavern in Richmond
RC 4 Oct. 1820, p.3; VPRDMA 4 Oct., p. 3

Died, BENJAMIN DONALDSON DUPREE, Esq., Delegate from Greenville Co. in this city
on Sun. last (Feb. 10)
RE 15 Feb. 1811, p. 3; VA 19 Feb., p. 3, calls him Benjamin Donald

Died on July 23rd, MR. SAMUEL DUTTON, merchant, of Richmond, formerly of Bristol,
Conn. Leaves wife and 3 children
RC 29 July 1814, p. 3

Died on 3rd Inst., ANNE, consort of Maj. William DuVal
VGGA 10 Oct. 1792, p. 3

Died on 25th Inst., MISS ANNE P. DuVAL, dau. of Maj. DuVal of this city
VGGA 27 April 1796, p. 3; VGRMA 27 April, p. 3

Died, MRS. LUCY DuVAL, wife of Mr. Francis DuVal, both of Tarborough, N.C., on 13th
Ult.
RE 6 March 1810, p. 3

Died at his seat in Gloucester Co., Sept. 23rd, WILLIAM DUVAL, age 67
RC 20 Oct. 1814, p. 3

Died Aug. 15th at his seat in Greene Co., Ga., PETER EARLY, a Senator and former Gov.
of that state
VP 6 Sept. 1817, p. 3

Died on 25th Inst., CAPT. WILLIAM EAST, on board the schooner, "Swift" in James River
VGGA 31 Aug. 1796, p. 2

Died last Sat. (June 16) in this city, MR. WILLIAM EATON of York Co.
VGIC   23 June 1787, p. 3

Died, GEN. WILLIAM EATON, at Brimfield, Mass., on June 1st.
VA   20 June 1811, p. 3

Died in this city Wed. last (July 20) CAPT. SAMUEL EDENS, one of the worthies of
'76 and an officer in the late provisional army
VGGA   23 July 1803, p. 3

Died April 4th in Hanover Co., age 13, JOSEPH EDMONDSON, son of Mr. Joseph N.
Edmondson
RE   16 April 1819, p. 3

Died, Mr. AMBROSE EDWARDS, Senior, of King William Co., on 22nd Inst.
RE   26 Jan. 1811, p. 3

Died, GEORGE WASHINGTON EDWARDS, in Woodford Co. (Ky) on 8th Inst., age 23, late
one of the Editors of The Pallidum, Frankfort, Ky
VA   30 April 1812, p. 3

Died on Wed. last (Feb. 11) MR. SAMUEL EGE, one of oldest inhabitants of this city
VA   13 Feb. 1807, p. 3

Died Aug. 2nd in Forks of Hanover, MRS. ANN C. EGGLESTON, wife of Mathew Eggleston,
age 46
RE   10 Aug. 1816, p. 3

Died, MR. EDMUND EGGLESTON of Hanover Co., on 18th Dec., age 80
RE   23 Dec. 1809, p. 3; Visitor   30 Dec., p. 190, says age 18

Died last week, JOHN EGGLESTON, son of Mr. Richard Eggleston of Powhatan Co., by
cutting his throat
VGWA   17 June 1784, p. 2

Died, MAJ. JOSEPH EGGLESTON of Amelia, on 13th Inst.
RE   22 Feb. 1811, p. 3; VA   22 Feb., p. 3

Died on 10th Inst., MRS. SARAH EGGLESTONE, consort of Joseph Egglestone, Esq. of
Amelia Co.
VGGA   17 Dec. 1794, p. 3; VGRMA 18 Dec.

Died lately in Amelia Co., RICHARD EGGLESTON, Esq.
VGRMA   2 April 1796, p. 3

Died, MR. MARCUS ELCAN, old & respected inhabitant, on Tues. last (May 3)
VA   10 May 1808, p. 3; RE   12 May, p. 3; VGGA   10 May, p. 3

Died Jan. 29th at Newport, R.I., WILLIAM ELLER, age 63, a signer of the Declaration
of Independence
RE   15 Feb. 1820, p. 3

Died at West Point, N.Y., Aug. 28th, ANDREW ELLICOTT, Prof. of Mathematics at the
Military Academy, age 67
RE 8 Sept. 1820, p. 3

Died, MR. JOHN ELLIOTT, 70, on 15th Inst., an eccentric character of this city
RE 25 June 1811, p. 3; VA 24 June, p. 3; VP 25 June, p. 3

Died on Tues. last (July 15) MISS MARY ELLIOTT, dau. of Thomas Elliott of Richmond
VA 19 July 1806, p. 3; RE 22 July, p. 3; VGGA 23 July, p. 3

Died, MR. THOMAS ELLIOTT, on 19th Inst., a native of lower part of the state & for
25 years res. of this city. For 35 years member of the Baptist Society
RE 30 July 1811, p. 3; VA 1 Aug., p. 3

Died, WILLIAM ELLIOTT of this city, yesterday, leaving a widow & child
Impartial Observer 13 Spet. 1806, p. 3

Died, MR. THOMAS ELLIS, on 15th Inst. at his seat in Henrico, age 50
VGGA 21 Oct. 1795, p. 2

Died on 12th Inst., THOMAS H. ELLIS, formerly of Amherst
RE 19 Sept. 1804, p. 3

Died, HON. OLIVER ELLSWORTH, at Windsor, Conn. on 26th Ult.
VA 11 Dec. 1807, p. 3; RE 15 Dec., p. 3

Died in Phila. on 30th Ult., age 70, SAMUEL EMLEN, an eminent Quaker minister
VA 10 Jan. 1800, p. 3

Died on 8th Inst. at Danvers, Mass., ELIZABETH ENDERS, widow, age 92
Visitor 23 Sept. 1809, p. 135

Died May 25th, MRS. ENGLE, wife of Mr. Joseph Engle of Jefferson Co., Va., in stage
accident
VP 8 June 1818, p. 3

Died fighting Indians in Tenn., Aug. 8th, WILLIAM ENGLISH
VGWA 2 Oct. 1781, p. 3

Died at Planters Town, Buckingham Co. on 20th Ult., JOHN EPPERSON, merchant
VA 5 July 1806, p. 3; RE 8 July, p. 3

Died on 3rd Ult. at Monticello, MRS. EPPES, consort of John W. Eppes
VA 2 May 1804, p. 3; VGGA 28 April, p. 2 (says dau. of Thos. Jefferson, Esq.)

Died on 6th Inst. at Cartersville, MR. GEORGE ESKRIGGE, formerly of this city
VGRMA 16 June 1794, p. 3

Died this morning, MR. NATHANIEL EUSTACE, merchant, formerly of Boston
VGGA 20 Sept. 1797, p. 3

Died on Sun. (Oct. 11) MR. JAMES EVANS, SR. of Richmond
RC 15 Oct. 1818, p. 3; VP 13 Oct., p. 3, says age 57

Died Oct. 13th, MRS. MARY EVANS, age 54, consort of Thomas R. Evans of Frazers Ferry
King William Co., leaving husband and 1 son
RE 29 Oct. 1819, p. 3

Died in N.Y. on Thurs. (April 15?) OLIVER EVANS of Phila., age 64
RC 22 April 1819, p. 3; VP 22 April, p. 3

Died, COL. WILLIAM EVANS of Murfreesboro, N.C. at Col. Brookings in Amelia Co.
(No death date)
VGRMA 5 Jan 1795, p. 3

Died on 1st Inst., JAMES EWING, in York Co., Pa.
VA 21 March 1806, p. 3

Died lately on the Eastern Shore, LITTLETON EYRE, Esq.
VGWA 21 May 1789, p. 3; VIC 10 June

Killed fighting Indians in Tenn. Aug. 8th, CAPT. JOHN FAIN
VGWA 2 Oct. 1788, p. 3

Died, MRS. JANE FAIRFAX, relict of the late Bryan, Lord Fairfax, yesterday (from
an Alexandria paper)
VA 6 July 1805, p. 3

Died 12th Dec. at his seat Greenway Court in Frederick Co., age 98, the RT. HON.
THOMAS, LORD FAIRFAX, Baron of Cameron and Proprietor of Northern Neck
VGWA Jan. 5, 1782, p. 3

Died, MRS. FARQUHARSON, spouse of Mr. John Farquharson, dec'd of Williamsburg, last
week
VGWA 6 Sept. 1787, p.3

Died 21st Nov., MRS. ELIZABETH FAUNTLEROY, spouse of Samuel Griffin Fauntleroy, Esq.
of King & Queen Co., age about 32
VGGA 3 Dec. 1794, p. 3

Died Sept. 24th at Waltham, Middlesex Co., MRS. ISABELLA FAUNTLEROY, wife of Thomas
Fauntleroy, leaving husband, 10 children and a brother
RE 24 Sept. 1819, p. 3; VP 18 Sept., p. 3, says died Sept. 4th

Died, THOMAS FEARN, in Danville, Va. on Oct. 4th. He was born Oct. 4, 1745
VA 12 Oct. 1805, p. 3

Died Oct. 15th, ARTHUR FENNER, Esq., Governor of Rhode Island
RE 8 Nov. 1805, p. 3

Died, MRS. FENWICK, spouse of William Fenwick, Esq., on Wed. last (Oct. 5)
VGGA 7 Oct. 1808, p. 3

Died on 12th Inst., MRS. JANE FERGUSON, age 27, consort of Mr. James B. Ferguson
of Goochland Co., leaving one dau.
VA 27 Feb. 1807, p. 3

Died, DR. JACOB FERRIS, in New Kent Co., on Jan. 9th
RE 23 Jan. 1812, p. 4

Died on 23rd June, MRS. FANNY FEURY, age 19, consort of Mr. Patrick Feury and dau.
of Mr. Theophilus Shannan, lately arrived from the West Indices; she leaves husband,
father, mother, sister and 4 brothers
VGGA 13 July 1796, p. 2

Died in Petersburg on Sun. last (Sept. 29) MRS. SUSAN FIELD, age 18, consort of
Mr. Thomas Field, editor of the Republican
RE 4 Oct. 1805, p. 3; VA 2 Oct., p. 3

Died at Petersburg on 9th Inst., MRS. (Susan) FIELD, consort of Mr. Thomas Field,
Editor of The Republican
VA 18 Aug. 1804, p. 3

Died, MR. GEORGE FINNELL, son of Rev. Reuben Finnell of Culpeper Co., on Aug. 1st,
age 23
RC 21 Aug. 1819, p. 3

Died, MR. JOHN FINNEY, merchant, of this city, on 2nd Inst., age 24
VA 10 Sept. 1812, p. 3

Died on 30th Ult., MRS. ELIZA FINNIE, spouse of Col. William Finnie
VGGA 8 May 1793, p. 3

Died on Fri. last (Aug. 14) MRS. FINNIE, spouse of C. William Finnie of this city
RC 18 Aug. 1795, p. 2; VGRMA 15 Aug. 3

Died, COL. WILLIAM FINNIE, age 65, at Norfolk on Thurs. last (Oct. 18)
VA 24 Oct. 1804, p. 3

Died, ALEXANDER B. FISHER, eldest son of George Fisher of Richmond, lost on Oct.
26 on his way to N.Y. on the Richmond Packet, near Smith's Inlet
RE 8 Nov. 1815, p. 3; VA 8 Nov., p. 3, says died Oct. 28th

Died at his seat in Cumberland Co., on 25th, ROBERT FITZGERALD, Esq.
RE 8 April 1815, p. 3

Died, JOHN FITZHUGH, Esq. of Belle Air, on 11th Inst., age 82
RE 19 May 1809, p. 3

Died lately in Marmion, his seat in King George Co., WILLIAM FITZHUGH, Esq.
VGGA 8 Sept. 1790, p. 2

Died, MRS. SARAH FITZWHYLSON, wife of Mr. William H. Fitzwhylson of this city,
on 6th Inst.
RE 11 March 1808, p. 3; VGGA 11 March, p. 3

Died yesterday, CASPER FLEISHER, an old and respected inhabitant of this city, for many years keeper of the Rising Sun Tavers
RE 7 Dec. 1811, p. 3; VP 10 Dec., p. 3

Died lately at Fort Washington, CAPT. TARLTON FLEMING of U.S. Cavalry
VGRMA 19 June 1794, p. 3

Died at his res. in Henrico Co., Sept. 10th, MR. ABEL FLETCHER, formerly of Mass., age 39
RC 13 Sept. 1819, p. 3

Died recently in Charleston, S.C., REV. ANDREW FLINN
VPRDMA 17 April 1820, p. 3

Died May 26th, age 59, MRS. MARY FLOOD, consort of Capt. John Flood of Buckingham Co.
VA 22 June 1816, p. 3

Died, COL. WILLIAM FONTAINE, on Sat. last (Oct. 5) at his seat in Hanover Co.
VP 12 Oct. 1810, p. 3

Died on Mon. (June 18) MRS. FORMICOLA, spouse of Mr. Serafino Formicola of this city
VGIC 23 June 1787, p. 3; VGWA 21 June, p. 3

Died on Wed. last (Oct. 6) MR. SERAFINO FORMICOLA, keeper of the Eagle Tavern in this city
VGGA 13 Oct. 1790, p. 2

Died at his res. in Chesterfield Co. on April 24th, MR. WILLIAM FORSEE, about 18, survived by mother, bro. and sis.
RE 2 May 1817, p. 3

Died, MRS. FOSTER, wife of John Foster of this city, on Tues. last (Oct. 21)
VGGA 25 Oct. 1806, p. 3

Died, MISS MARY FOSTER, dau. of A. Foster of this city on 15th Inst.
RE 26 Dec. 1809, p. 3; VA 29 Dec., p. 3

Died, DR. JOHN H. FOUSHEE, eldest son of Dr. W. Foushee of this city. Funeral this morning (No death date)
RE 17 Nov. 1812, p. 3; VA 16 Nov., p. 3; VP 17 Nov., p. 3

Died Wed. last (Nov. 2) MRS. LUCY FOUSHEE, wife of Dr. William Foushee, Jr. this city and dau. of late Mr. Lawrence, Gov. of N.J.
RE 4 Nov., 1814, p. 3; VP 5 Nov., p. 3

Died in this city Sun. last (Sept. 26) MRS. FOUSHEE, spouse of Dr. William Foushee
VA 29 Sept. 1802, p. 3; VGGA Sept. 29, p. 3

Died on Sat. last, (March 19), MISS NANCY FOUSHEE, dau. of Dr. Wm. Foushee of this city
RC 22 March 1796, p. 3; VGGA March 23, p. 3, says "Friday last"; VGRMA 23 March, p. 2, says 19th Inst.

Died on July 26th, age 66, MRS. ANNE FOX, relict of John Fox, of Greenwich, Gloucester Co.
VP 6 Aug. 1813, p. 3

Died, MR. GILBERT FOX, comedian, at Charleston, on 13th Inst.
Visitor 24 March 1810, p. 31

Died on March 5th at his seat in Louisa, CAPT. JOHN FOX
Examiner 19 March 1803, p. 3

Died on Sun. last (Dec. 9) JOHN FOX, Coach-maker
VGGA 12 Dec. 1804, p. 3

Died at Sweet Springs in Va., Oct. 30th, MRS. MARIA FOX, consort of Mr. John Fox, merchant, of Richmond
RC 11 Nov. 1819, p. 3

Died, MRS. MARY CARVER FOX, consort of Maj. Nathaniel Fox of King William Co. on 2nd March
VGGA 12 March 1806, p. 3

Died, HENRY FRANKLIN, a sailor, in Philadelphia, by a fall
VGRC 25 Nov. 1794, p. 2

Died in Norfolk on 19th Inst., CAPT. ROBERT FRANKLIN, of U.S. Army
RE 27 Aug. 1813, p. 3; VA 26 Aug., p. 3

Died, MR. ALEXANDER FRAZER, silk & woolen dyer, of this city, a native of Scotland, on 3rd Inst.
RE 13 Oct. 1809, p. 3; Visitor 21 Oct., p. 150

Died, COL. RICHARD FREAR, lately in Northampton Co.
Visitor 16 Dec. 1809, p. 182

Died on the Brig "Olympus" going from Philadelphia to Savannah, MRS. FREDERICK. (No death date)
VP 15 Oct. 1818, p. 2

Died on Tues. (Jan. 19) MRS. FREELAND, spouse of Mr. Archibald Freeland of Manchester
VP 22 Jan. 1813, p. 3

Died on Sun. (March 19) MRS. ELIZABETH FRENCH, leaving aged mother and 2 small children. She was late of Hampton
RE 22 March 1815, p. 3

Died in Richmond June 30th, ZEBEDEE FRANKLIN, killed in an argument over a game
RC 3 July 1820, p. 3; VPRDMA 3 July, p. 2

Died at Philadelphia, MRS. ESTER FULLERTON, age 90 (No death date)
Visitor 29 July 1809, p. 102

Died in London on 28th April last, age 75, JAMES GADSDEN, Esq., formerly of South
Carolina
Visitor 15 July 1809, p. 94

Died June 19th at Washington Henry Academy, age 12, THOMAS MUSE GAINES, 2nd son of
Harry Gaines of Richmond
RE 30 June 1818, p. 3

Died lately in Edinburgh, Scotland, MR. GEORGE GAIRDNER, a res. of Richmond for
20 years
RE 12 March 1805, p. 3

Died yesterday, JOSEPH GALLEGO, a native of Spain, but long a resident of Richmond
RE 3 July 1818, p. 3; RC 3 July, p. 3

Died in Island of Grenada, MR. AZEL GALT of this city (No death date)
VGGA 21 May 1794, p. 2; VGRMA 22 May

Died on 15th (Feb.) MISS FANNY GALT, youngest dau. of Dr. John M. Galt of Williamsbu
age 11
VGGA 28 Feb. 1798, p.3

Died on Sat. last (Oct. 25) MR. GABRIEL GALT of this city
VGIC 1 Nov. 1788, p. 2; IC 29 Oct.; VGWA 30 Oct.

Died on 9th Inst., MR. JAMES GALT, of Williamsburg, age 58. Keeper of the Lunatic
Hospital, since its commencement. Leaves numerous offspring.
VA 16 Dec. 1800, p. 3; VGGA 26 Dec., p. 3

Died in Williamsburg on 12th Inst., DR. JOHN M. GALT, age 64, Practiced there 40 yea
VA 24 June 1808, p. 2; VGGA 24 June, p. 3

Died on 17th Ult., WILLIAM GALT, eldest son of Mrs. Elizabeth Galt of this city.
Buried in the churchyard
VGGA 4 Oct. 1797, p. 2

Died in Richmond, some days ago, MR. FRANCIS GALVAN, a native of one of the French
West Indies Island. His br. served in our Revolution. Mr. Galvan married a sister
of Col. Ewell of Prince William Co.
VP 29 May 1816, p. 3

Died, on 30 Nov., MRS. GALVAN, wife of Francis Galvan, Post Master at the White Chi
VGGA 8 Dec., p. 3

Died, MRS. CHARLOTTE GAMBLE, wife of John Gamble, Esq. of this city on Sept. 5th on
board the Ship Powhatan on passage from London
RE 3 Nov. 1809, p. 3; VA 3 Nov., p. 3; Visitor, 4 Nov., p. 158

Died, COL. ROBERT GAMBLE of this city, last evening, of a fall from his horse
RE 13 April 1810, p. 3; VA 17 April, says was officer in Revolution

Died Oct. 21st near Rogersville, Tenn., MRS. ROBERT GAMBIL and two children
VP 18 Nov. 1818, p. 2

Died last Sat. (Sept. 25) in King & Queen Co., DR. ANTHONY GARDNER, about 75.
Had served county as magistrate.
RE 1 Oct. 1819, p. 3; VP 1 Oct., p. 3

Died in Augusta Co. a few days ago. MR. THOMAS GARDNER, a native of N.J., a pedlar
VP 25 Nov. 1817, p. 3

Died Nov. 16th at his res. in Hanover Co., MR. WILLIAM GARDNER, age 65
RE 23 Nov. 1819, p. 3; RC 23 Nov., p. 3

Died, BENJAMIN N. GARLAND, on 4th Inst., in Richmond County
RE 24 March 1812, p. 3

Died, MRS. FRANCES TAYLOR GARLAND, consort of John Garland, Esq. (No death date)
VGAA Dec. 20, 1783, p. 2

Died in Hanover, MR. THOMAS GARLAND (No death date)
VGRC 11 March 1794, p. 3

Died, MUSCOE GARNETT, on 10th Inst. at his father's in Essex Co., age 22
RE 24 March 1807, p. 3; VGGA 25 March, p. 3

Died Jan. 10th, WILLIAM GARROW, member of General Assembly from Warwick Co.,
leaving wife and 5 children
RE 13 Jan. 1816, p. 3

Died, MISS ELVEY GARTHRIGHT of Henrico Co., under 18, murdered and thrown under
Bottoms Bridge
VA 16 Sept. 1800, p. 3

Died, MR. WILLIAM GARY of City Point, on 15th Instant
Visitor 25 March, 1809, p. 31

Died Jan. 25th of Newbern, N.C., MRS. ELIZA GASTON, consort of William Gaston,
and dau. of Dr. Worthington of Georgetown, D.C.
RE 11 Feb. 1819, p. 3

Died on 2nd Ult. in Berkeley Co., MRS. ELIZABETH GATES, wife of Hon. Maj-Gen. Gates
VGAA July 19, 1783, p. 3

Died on 10th Inst., age 77, GEN. HORATIO GATES
VA 22 April 1806, p. 3; VGGA 23 April, p. 3 (says died in N.Y.)

Died, MR. ROBERT GATES of Berkely Co., only son of Gen. Gates. (No death date)
VG Nov. 4, 1780, p. 3

Died, MRS. JANE ANNE GATHRIGHT, wife of Mr. Obadiah Gathright, of this city, on
Oct. 28th
VA 4 Nov. 1813, p. 3; VP 2 Nov., p. 3

Died on Sun. (Aug. 3) MRS. FRANCES GAUTIER of this city
VA 6 Aug. 1806, p. 3; RE 5 Aug., p. 3; VGGA 6 Aug., p. 3

Died at St. Louis, Mo. Terr., Jan. 21st, MR. CHARLES C. GAY, formerly of Richmond.
RC 1 March 1820, p. 3

Died April 5th, MISS ELIZABETH GEE, of Lunenburg Co.
RE 23 April 1819, p. 3

Died, MRS. CORNELIA TAPPEN GENET, consort of E.C. Genet, Esq., on 28th Inst. (Ult.)
at Greensbush. She was dau. of George Clinton, Vice Pres. of U.S., age 35
RE 13 April 1810, p. 3

Died, MRS. HANNAH GENTRY of this city, on 17th Inst.
RE 21 May 1811, p. 3

Died, MR. ANTHONY GEOHAGAN, at an advanced age, a respected citizen of this place
(No death date)
VGGA 11 Dec. 1793, p. 3; VGRMA 9 Dec.

Died, MR. ALEXANDER GEORGE, age 22, on Sun. last (Sept. 6) at his father's seat,
a few miles from Richmond
VA 9 Sept. 1807, p. 3

Died, MR. REUBEN GEORGE, father of Alexander George, on Thurs. last (Sept. 10) at
his seat a few miles from Richmond
VA 12 Sept. 1807, p. 2

Died on 19th Nov., ELDRIDGE GERRY, Vice-Pres. of U.S.
RC 26 Nov. 1814, p. 3

Died, MR. THOMAS GHOLSON, SR., age 75, in Brunswick Co., on 10th Inst.
Visitor 25 March 1809, p. 31

Died at her seat in Richmond Co., March 31st, MRS. MARY GIBERNE, a widow of
Isaac William Giberne, formerly a clergyman of Church of England. She was
born Feb. 28, 1725
RE 12 May 1820, p. 3

Died on 25th Aug., MR. THOMAS GIBSON, SR., of Prince Edward Co., age 50
VA 4 Sept. 1801, p. 3

Died in this city Fri. last (Sept. 20) MRS. SARAH GILBERT
VA 24 Sept. 1799, p. 3; VGGA 24 Sept., p. 3, says "for many years a resident
of this city".

Died Friday last (July 16) at Port Royal, Caroline Co., ROBERT GILCHRIST, Esq.,
age 69. A native of Scotland. Was magistrate 40 yrs. and two terms representative
of his county
VICGA 21 July 1790, p. 2

Died Dec. 25, 1816, ABRAHAM B. VENABLE GILES, youngest son of William B. Giles,
age 3
RE 2 Jan. 1817, p. 3

Died on Tues. (Oct. 5) at res. of Thomas Clopton in Henrico Co., MR. KNOWLES GILES.
RC 8 Oct. 1819, p. 3

Died, MRS. GILES, consort of Hon. Wm. B. Giles, Member of Congress from this state,
on 30th Ult.
RE 23 Aug. 1808, p. 3

Died on Sat. last (Nov. 9) MRS. REBECCA WALKER GILES, consort of Capt. William Giles
of this city
VA 12 Nov. 1799, p. 3

Died, THOMAS GILES of Buckingham, age 21, on Aug. 22nd
VA 21 Sept. 1805, p. 3

Died on Tues. last (Oct. 19) MAJ. WILLIAM GILES of this city
VA 23 Oct. 1802, p. 3

Died, at Philadelphia June 10th, JAMES S. GILLIAM, age 26, son of late Dr. Gilliam
of Petersburg
RE 16 June 1820, p. 3 (Sketch of his life in RE 23 June, p. 3); RC 16 June, p. 3;
VPRDMA 16 June, p. 3 and 23 June, p. 3

Died yesterday, SIMEON GILLIAT, a man of color, celebrated as a fiddler
RC 16 Oct. 1820, p. 3; VPRDMA 16 Oct., p. 3

Died Thurs. last (Sept. 15) in this city, MRS. GILLIAT, wife of Mr. Thomas Gilliat,
merchant
VA 17 Sept. 1803, p. 3

Died in Charleston, S.C., MORDECAI GIST, late Brig-Gen. U.S. Army (No death date)
VGRDA 1 Oct. 1792, p. 2

Died, MR. THOMAS GLASS of Fredericksburg, hung himself on Sun. (Sept. 20)
RC 24 Sept. 1818, p. 3

Died Nov. 1st, age 27, MR. PARKE GLINN of Ro: R. Glinn & Co. of Richmond, and son
of Nathaniel Glinn of Hanover Co. Buried Nov. 2nd by Richmond Light Infantry Blues.
RE 10 Nov. 1820, p. 3; RC 2 Nov., p. 2

Died, MISS ANN D. GODFREY, age 16, in this city on Thurs. last (Oct. 13)
VA 18 Oct. 1808, p. 3; RE 18 Oct., p. 3

Died in Culpeper Co., March 17th, LT. THOMAS K. GODFREY, of 12th Regt., U.S. Infantry
VP 8 April 1815, p. 3

Died Aug. 16th at his res. in Amherest Co., WILLIAM B. GOOCH, age 29
RE 31 Aug. 1816, p. 3

Died Jan. 6th, COL, PARKE GOODALL of Hanover Co., age 74, in a gig accident. Was
a solider of the Revolution and had served in the State Legislature
RE 11 Jan. 1816, p. 3

Died April 23rd on board the sloop "Fanny" on his way home from Phila., COL. FRANCIS GOODE of Chesterfield Co.
VGRMA 7 May 1795, p. 2; VGRC 9 May, p. 2

Died on 7th April at his res. in Powhatan Co., FRANCIS GOODE, Esq.
RE 7 May 1814, p. 3; VP 7 May, p. 3

Died, COL. ROBERT GOODE of Whitby, on 20th Inst.
VGGA 25 April, 1809, p. 3; Visitor 6 May, p. 54

Died, MRS. S. GOODE, on 13th Inst., a consort of Col. Robert Goode of Whitby
VGGA 27 May 1807, p. 3

Died, MR. THEODRICK GOODE, on 3rd Inst., at his place in Chesterfield Co., youngest son of Col. Robert Goode of Whitby
RE 8 May, 1810, p. 3; VA 8 May, p. 3

Died, JOHN GOODRICH, Esq., for many years Senator from Isle of Wight Co. in the Va. Legislature, on 1st Inst.
VA 10 June 1808, p. 2; RE 14 June, p. 3

Died Sun. last (Augs. 12) MISS ANN G.C. GOODSON of Richmond
VA 18 Aug. 1804, p. 3; VGGA 18 Aug., p. 3 (says died at house of Mrs. Whitaker and was age 29)

Died MRS. MARY GOODSON of Williamsburg. (No death date)
VGWA 5 Jan 1792, p. 3

Died Mon. last (Dec. 8) in Petersburg, MR. THOMAS GOODSON, Member of General Assembly from Isle of Wight Co.
VGRMA 11 Dec. 1794, p. 3

Died Sat. (July 2) at Rocketts, MRS. ELIZABETH GOODWIN, consort of Capt. Wm. Goodwin
RC 5 July 1796, p. 3; VGGA 13 July, p. 2, says "Sunday, 3rd"

Died, MR. REUBEN GOODWIN, on 5th Inst., and old inhabitant of Hanover
RE 22 June 1813, p. 3

Died at Rocketts on Sat. (June 15), CAPT. WILLIAM GOODWIN
RE 19 June 1816, p. 3; RC 18 June, p. 3, says long time resident, leaves wife & children

Died Feb. 21st, COL. PETERSON GOODWYN, Congressman from Petersburg District
RE 26 Feb. 1818, p. 3; VP 26 Feb., p. 3

Died in Albermarle Co., March 22nd, MR. WILLIAM GOOLSBY, age 108, leaving a wife to whom he had been married 80 years
RE 17 April 1818, p. 3

Died lately in Suffolk, MRS. MARY GOOSLEY, consort of George Goosley, Esq. and eldest dau. of Martin Mims, Esq. of this city, age 21
VA 17 March 1804, p. 3; VGGA 17 March, p. 3 (says: died on 7th Inst.)

Died, MRS. GOOSELEY, in this city, formerly of York-town, on Wed. (Aug. 25)
VA 26 Aug. 1813, p. 3

Died on Sun. last (Sept. 2) age 19, MRS. MARTHA GORDAN, relict of Mr. Jacob Gordan
of Manchester
VA 5 Sept. 1804, p. 3

Died, MR. DANIEL GORDON, on Dec. 27, 1812, at Hartford, N.C., age 63, formerly an
inhabitant of Manchester, Va.
RE 21 Jan. 1813, p. 3; VA 25 Jan., p. 3

Died, MR. JOHN GORDON of Petersburg (No death date)
VGWA April 20, 1782, p. 3

Died at Derby, Conn., March 9th, CAPT. EBENEZER GRACIE, for 60 years inhabitant
of that place
RC 22 March 1820, p. 3

Died in Petersburg on Thurs. (June 10) MRS. ELIZA GRAHAM, wife of Robert Graham
of Manchester
RE 11 June 1819, p. 3; VP 4 June, p. 3, says died Thurs. (June 3) and in Richmond

Died yesterday, MR. GEORGE H. GRAHAM of this city
VGRMA 11 Aug. 1794, p. 3

Died Aug. 6th at house of Andrew Ramsay in Washington, D.C., JOHN GRAHAM, late
Minister of the Court of the Brazils in Rio de Janeiro
VPRDMA 9 Aug. 1820, p. 3

Died Sun.(Sept. 24) in Richmond, CAPT. JOHN GRAHAM, buried at his coal pits outside
this city
RE 26 Sept. 1820, p. 3; RC 26 Sept., p. 3; VPRDMA 26 Sept., p. 3

Died in this city last Sat. (June 8), the REV. WILLIAM GRAHAM of Kanawha Co., a
Presb. Minister. He established the Academy in Rockbridge Co., which later
developed into Liberty Hall College
VA 11 June 1799, p. 3; VF 12 June, p. 3; VGGA 11 June, p. 3

Died in this city Sat. last (June 7) REV. WILLIAM GRAHAM of Kanawha Co.
VF 12 June 1800

Died, FLEMING GRANTLAND, Junior Editor of the Georgia Journal, in Milledgeville, Ga.
A Virginia native, he moved there several years ago and had been elected to Ga.
Senate (No death date)
RE 11 Feb. 1819, p. 3; RC 10 Feb., p. 3, says died Jan. 28th

Died, MICHAEL GRANTLAND of Richmond on Tues. (Aug. 1) at Mountain Top, near
Waynesboro in Augusta Co., age 56, leaving wife and son
RE ' 8 Aug. 1820, p. 3; RC 8 Aug., p. 3; VPRDMA 8 Aug., p. 3

Died April 17th, MRS. MARY GRAVES of Richmond
VPRDMA 18 April 1820, p. 3

Died yesterday in this city, MR. FRANCIS GRAVES
VGGA 20 Dec. 1797, p. 3

Died on Sat. (Sept. 26) MR. EDWARD GRAY, dyer, a native of Scotland
VGRMA 1 Oct. 1795, p. 3

Died, MR. FRENCH GRAY, merchant, age 23, in Fredericksburg (No death date)
VGGA 22 Aug. 1792, p. 2

Died at res. of Charles Scott in Halifax Co., Va., in Sept., HUGH GRAY, a native
of Scotland, believed to have married dau. in Richmond
VP 21 Dec. 1818, p. 3

Died, MRS. PHEBE GRAY, consort of Henry Gray of Goochland, on 5th Inst.
RE 14 Oct. 1808, p. 3

Died on 12th Inst. at Dumfries, Va., on his way to Congress, HON. COL. WILLIAM
GRAYSON, U.S. Senator. Remains deposited in family vault at Rev. Mr. Spence
Grayson's
VICGA 24 March 1790, p. 3

Died, PETER GRAVES, on Nov. 28, 1794, killed by Indians 20 miles north of Knoxville
VGRMA 15 Jan. 1795, p. 3

Died, MR. AMBROSE GREEN of Sandy Point, Charles City Co., murdered on Sat. last
(Feb. 6)
RE 11 Feb. 1808, p. 3

Died Nov. 12th, at Farm Hill, Amelia Co., MRS. ELIZABETH AUBIN GREEN, consort of
Mr. A. A. Green, age 20, leaving husband & infant. dau.
RE 23 Nov. 1819, p. 3

Died in St. Louis, Mo., Oct. 13th, MR. JOHN GREEN, age 22, son of Gen. Moses Green
of Culpeper Co. and nephew of Mr. John W. Green, present Chancellor of the Frederick
burg District
RE 29 Oct. 1819, p. 3

Died Dec. 26, 1815, in Philadelphia, DR. JAMES GREENHOW of Richmond
VP 3 Jan. 1816, p. 3; RE 30 Dec. 1815, p. 3

Died July 22nd in Charleston, S.C., JAMES GREENWOOD, a free man of color, drowned
RC 30 July 1818, p. 3

Died, in Williamsburg, last week, MR. JOHN GREENHOW, merchant of that city
VGWA 6 Sept. 1787, p. 3

Died on Sun. (Sept. 27) MR. JOHN GREENHOW, merchant
VGRMA 1 Oct. 1795, p. 3

Died on 14th, SAMUEL GREENHOW, Esq., age 43
RE 18 Feb. 1815, p. 3

Died, MRS. CATHERINE S. GREENUP, consort of Christopher Greenup, Esq., present Gov. of Ky., at Frankfort on Nov.16th
VGGA 4 Dec. 1807, p. 3

Died fighting Indians in Tenn., Aug. 8th, HERMON GREGG
VGWA 2 Oct. 1788, p. 3

Died March 27th, WILLIAM A. GREGORY, a lawyer of Fredericksburg
RE 4 April 1820, p. 3

Died, CAPT. ARCHIBALD GREIG, oldest commander of Va. and Md. trade and a near relation in Admiral Greig in the Russian service (No death date)
VGIC 1 Nov. 1788, p. 2; IC 29 Oct.

Died, LADY C. STUART GRIFFIN, eldest dau. of John, Earl of Traquair in Williamsburg
VGGA 17 Oct. 1807, p. 3

Died at York-town on Sept. 20th, DR. CORBIN GRIFFIN, age 74
VP 5 Oct. 1813, p. 3

Died, CYRUS GRIFFIN, Esq., Federal District Judge in this State, at York, Va. on Friday last (Dec. 14)
RE 18 Dec. 1810, p. 3; VA 28 Dec., p. 3 (with biographical sketch); VP 1 Jan. 1811, p. 3

Died on Sept. 30th, LLEWELLYN GRIFFIN, only son of Maj. Thomas Griffin, age 14, at Lewisville, Gloucester Co.
VP 5 Oct. 1813, p. 3

Died, COL. SAMUEL GRIFFIN, of Williamsburg, in New York on 23rd Nov. A Revolutionary solider
VA 18 Dec. 1810, p. 3; VP 11 Dec., p. 3

Died in Hospital for Lunatics in Williamsburg, SARAH GRIFFIN, from Augusta (No death date)
VGGA 6 Oct. 1790, p. 2

Died, REV. DAVID GRIFFITH, late of Fairfax Co., Bishop-Elect of Va., in Phila. Aug. 3rd
VGWA 27 Aug. 1789, p. 3; VIC 19 Aug.

Died yesterday MR. DAVID GRINLY, a native of Scotland, detained as a hostage in this state for several years
VGWA 25 Oct. 1783, p. 3

Died, ROGER GRISWOLD, Esq., Gov. of Conn., on 25th (Oct.?) at New Haven
VA 2 Nov. 1812, p. 3

Died at seat of Judge Hanson in Md., THOMAS P. GROSVENOR, Member of late House of Representatives (No death date)
RE 29 April 1817, p. 3

Died Dec. 14th at Col. John S. Farrar's in Albemarle Co., MR. MATTHEW GRUBBS of Louisa Co., age 19
RE 28 Dec. 1820, p.3

Died, BENEDICT GRUM, age 72 at his res. in New Kent Co. on 20th Inst.
VA 26 Aug. 1811, p. 3; VP 27 Aug., p. 3 gives the name as CRUMP (which is most likely correct)

Died on April 15th, MR. CHARLES W. GRYMES, shot in a duel with Mr. Keeling Tyrrel on April 14th
Examiner 23 April 1803, p. 3

Died Oct. 25th at Brandon in Middlesex Co., MRS. JUDITH GRYMES, widow of late Philip Ludwell Grymes
RE 30 Oct. 1816, p. 3; VP 29 Oct., p. 3

Died, WYNDHAM GRYMES of Richmond (No death date)
Examiner 20 April 1803, p. 3

Died, MRS. BETSEY GUERRANT, consort of Maj. Daniel Guerrant, on 4th Inst. in Goochland
VA 28 Aug. 1810, p. 3

Died, JOHN GUERRANT, SR., age 80, in Goochland on 25th Ult. was 2nd (?) generation of French refugees that settled in Manakin, Powhatan Co.
VA 18 Jan. 1813, p. 3

Died on 22nd Inst., MRS. MARY GUERRANT, consort of Mr. Peter Guerrant of Buckingham, age 66
VA 3 Aug. 1805, p. 3

Died, MR. ROBERT GUERRANT, eldest son of Gen. John Guerrant of Goochland, on 19th Inst.
VA 29 July, 1808, p. 3; RE 26 July, p. 3; Virginian 22 July, p. 2

Died Sept. 2nd in New Kent Co., MRS. ANN ELIZA GUNN, wife of Mr. John S. Gunn, and eldest dau. of Mr. Samuel McCraw of City of Richmond, age 29, leaving husband and 3 infants
RE 10 Sept. 1819, p. 3; RC 8 Sept., p. 3

Died lately in Louisville, Ga., GEN. GUNN, Senator from that state
VGGA 14 Aug. 1801, p. 3

MR. JOSEPH GUNN died in Savannah Ga., on March 26th, lately of this city
VA 12 April 1808, p. 3

Died in Caroline Co., on 24th Inst., MRS. ANN GUY, age 90
RE 27 Sept. 1815, p. 3

Died on 25th Inst., CAPT. GEORGE GUY of Caroline Co., age 70
VA 30 Oct. 1801, p. 3

Died in Caroline Co., June 25th, MRS. MARY GUY, wife of Mr. James Guy of the White
Chimnies, leaving children
RE   29 June 1819, p. 3

Died Sun. last (Nov. 15) MR. THOMAS T. GUY of Caroline Co.
VGRMA   21 Nov. 1795, p. 3

Died, MR. WILLIAM GUY, on 11th Inst. at his seat in Caroline Co.
RE   17 March 1807, p. 3

Died Sept. 29th, age 25, MRS. ANN MARIE GWATHMEY, wife of Mr. Temple Gwathmey of
Richmond
RE   1 Oct. 1819, p. 3

Died Oct. 25th, age 69, CAPT. JOSEPH HADEN of Fluvanna Co., a soldier in the Revolution,
Member of the Virginia Convention, and for many years in the legislature from his
county
RE   10 Nov. 1820, p. 3

Died Sun. last (June 21) age 58, MR. JOHN HAGUE
RC   23 June 1795, p. 2; VGGA   1 July; VGRMA   25 June, p. 2

Died at Tappahannock, JOHN HAILE, Collector of Customs for Fredericksburg District
(No death date)
RE   31 Dec. 1818, p. 3

Died, CONSTANTINE HAIRSTON, 8th son of Col. George & Mrs. Elizabeth Hairston, on
Feb. 12th, shortly after death of his mother. His home was in Patrick Co. Was 21
RE   27 Feb. 1819, p. 3

Died, age 60, MRS. ELIZABETH HAIRSTON, wife of Col. George Hairston of Henry Co.,
in Richmond (No death date)
RE   27 Feb. 1819, p. 3

Died at his house in lower Goochland Co. on 3rd Inst., DR. WILLIAM HALE
VGGA   20 Dec. 1797, p. 3

Died, MRS. MARGARET HALL, wife of Mr. Smith Hall, and eldest dau. of William Lane,
Esq. of Mathews Co., on 28th Sept. in Glouchester Co.
RE   5 Nov. 1811, p. 3

Died in Wakefield, N.H., Mrs. PATIENCE HALL, age 79. She is supposed to have
assisted at the birth of over 1000 children
Visitor   12 Aug. 1809, p. 110

Died, age 75, LEWIS HALLAM, father of the American Theatre(No death date)
VA   8 Nov. 1808, p. 3

Died last week in Williamsburg, Mrs. HALLAM, spouse of Mr. Hallam, comedian of
Phila.
VGGA   12 Dec. 1792, p. 3

Died, MRS. HALLAM, wife of Mr. N. Hallam of this city, on Mon. last (Nov. 1)
VA 4 Nov. 1813, p. 3

Died Aug. 10th at White Sulphur Springs, MR. NICHOLAS HALLAM, age 49, leaving wife
and 5 children
RE 31 Aug. 1816, p. 3

Died on 27th Ult. in Hanover Town, MR. ALEXANDER HALLOM, age 22 (Sat. was 28th-Ed)
VGGA 8 May 1798, p. 3

Died Dec. 19, 1816, GEORGE HALLOWELL of Poughkeepsie, N.Y. by drowning
VP 2 May 1817, p. 3

Died, MRS. CHRISTIAN HAMELIN, on 23rd. Ult., age 18, a dau. of Lewis Burwell, Esq.
of Mecklenburg
VGGA 16 Sept. 1795, p. 3

Died on July 12th, GEN. ALEXANDER HAMILTON, wounded in a duel with Aaron Burr on
the 11th
VGGA 21 July 1804, p. 2

Died yesterday, MRS. MARGARET HAMILTON
RC 20 Oct. 1819, p. 3

Died at Beaufort,S.C., June 30th, HON. PAUL HAMILTON, late Sec. of Navy
RE 17 July 1816, p. 3

Died, CAPT. THOMAS HAMILTON of the State Legion, on 15th at Yorktown
VGAA Sept. 28, 1782, p. 3

Died at Detroit on 11th Ult., JOHN F. HAMTRAMCK, Esq., Col. of 1st Regt. U.S. Army.
A native of Canada, he joined U.S. Army in 1777
VGGA 14 May 1803, p. 3

Died July 18th at Fotheringay, his late res., COL. GEORGE HANCOCK, age 66. Had
served in Revolutionary Army and later in U.S. Congress
RE 8 Aug. 1820, p. 3

Died, A.C. HANSON, Chancellor of State of Md. (No date date)
VA 28 Jan. 1806, p. 3

Died at Belmont, near Baltimore, age 33, Hon. ALEXANDER C. HANSON, U.S. Senator
from Md.. (No date date)
RE 27 April 1819, p. 3

Died, MR. COLLIER HANSON, on Thurs. last (Nov. 23 or 16) at his seat on James River
in Charles City Co., leaving wife & 3 children
VA 24 Nov. 1809, p. 3; Visitor 2 Dec., p. 174, says Collier Harrison

Died lately JOHN HANSON, Esq. late Pres. of United States in Congress, assembled,
at his seat in Frederick Co., Md. (No death date)
VGAA April 12, 1783, p. 3; VGAA Dec. 6, p. 3, says age 63 and died in Prince
George Co., Md.

Died at Beacons Castle, Surry Co., MRS. CATHARINE HARE, wife of Thomas M. Hare of Elizabeth City Co.
VGGA 8 Feb. 1804, p. 3

Died June 28th, DR. WILLIAM B. HARE, age 50, at his seat in Nelson Co.
RE 1 September 1818, p. 3

Died in Powhatan Co., Sept. 6th, age 16, MISS MAHALA HARDIN, dau. of Mr. George Hardin
RE 22 Sept. 1820, p. 3

Died Jan. 5th in Richmond, WILLIAM HARDING, age 34, leaves wife & 2 infant children
VP 11 Jan. 1819, p. 3

Died yesterday, WILLIAM HARDY, Esq. late a member of the General Assembly of this state from Isle of Wight Co.
VGGA 31 Dec. 1794, p. 3; VGRMA 1 Jan, 1795, p. 3

Died in Charleston, S.C. Jan 9th, MRS. STARR HARRETT, age 120, born 1699 in one of the Barbary States
VPRDMA 1 Feb. 1820, p. 3

Died on Wed. last (Dec. 15) MR. ELDRIDGE HARRIS of this city, a teacher for nearly 20 years
VA 18 Dec. 1802, p. 3

Died, MR. JOHN HARRIS, age 57, in Hanover Co., on Dec. 30, 1808
VA 7 Feb. 1809, p. 3; Visitor 11 Feb., p. 7

Died on 4th Inst., at his seat in Chesterfield, MAJ. JOHN HARRIS, age 58, leaving wife & numerous offspring
RE 21 Dec. 1815, p. 3

Died on Mon. (Feb. 10) MRS. MARY HARRIS, an old inhabitant of Richmond
RE 13 Feb. 1817, p. 3; RC 11 Feb., p. 3, says was 67

Died Feb. 4th, MRS. MARY HARRIS, widow of James Harris, late of Albermarle Co., age 88 years 10 mos. 22 days. Her nephew was Sec. of Treas.
RE 4 Feb. 1819, p. 3

Died in Halifax Co., Jan. 24th, MISS MILDRED C. HARRIS, eldest dau. of Thomas Harris
RE 10 Feb. 1816, p. 3

Died on Sept. 7th at his seat in Hanover Co., MR. OVERTON HARRIS, age 46, leaving widow and children
VP 15 Oct. 1813, p. 3

Died Oct. 2nd in St. Louis, Mo., MRS. SARAH HARRIS, consort of Mr. Benjamin James Harris, Merchant of Richmond, leaving husband and 5 small children
RE 28 Nov. 1817, p. 3

Died lately in Charles City Co., MR. WILLIAM HARRIS
VA 30 March 1803, p. 3; VGGA 26 March, p. 3

Died Feb. 22nd at his res. in Hanover Co., WILLIAM L. HARRIS, SR., age 48, leaving
wife and 7 children
RE 11 March 1817, p. 3

Died on 11th Inst., BENJAMIN HARRISON, Esq. of Berkeley on James River
VA 20 Aug. 1799, p. 3; VGGA 20 Aug., p. 3

Died lately in western part of Ga., MR. BENJAMIN HARRISON, age 44, a native of Va.
but resident of Ga.
RE 19 May 1818, p. 3

Died, BRAXTON HARRISON, in his 44th yr. lately, at his seat in Charles City Co.
RE 15 May 1809, p. 3; Visitor 20 May, p. 62; Visitor 6 May, p. 54, says died
on 14th, Ult.

Died CARTER B. HARRISON, Esq. of Maycon of James River, on 14th Inst. He was for
several years a member of State and National Legislatures
VA 19 April 1808, p. 3; RE 19 April, p. 3

Died July 10th, MR. EDMUND HARRISON, son of Edmund Harrison of Amelia Co., age 20
RE 18 July 1820, p. 3

Died, May 13th MR. JACOB HARRISON, age 51, for 26 years an inhabitant of Richmond
VP 20 May 1817, p. 3; RC 20 May, p. 2

Died on 18th Inst. (Ult.) MRS. MARY HARRISON, consort of Emund Harrison, Esq. of
Amelia
VA 1 Feb. 1804, p. 3

Died, MATTHEW HARRISON, late of Dumfries (No death date)
RE 12 Sept. 1807, p. 3

Died, MRS. HARRISON, spouse of Benjamin Harrison, Jr., Esq. of this city (No death
date)
VGWA 30 Aug. 1787, p. 3

Died on Sun. last (Nov. 3) MRS. HARRISON, wife of Mr. Jacob Harrison of this city
RE 5 Nov. 1805, p. 3; VA 6 Nov., p. 3 (says Mrs. Martha Harrison); VGGA 6 Nov.,
p. 3

Died Tues. (June 8) at house of William Cook in Richmond, MISS POLLY HARRISON,
eldest dau. of Mr. Jacob Harrison, dec'd, age 21
RE 11 June 1819, p. 3; RC 11 June, says Wednesday

Died in Yorktown, Pa., Dec. 21st, THOMAS HARTLEY, age 52, Member of Congress from Pa
VA 2 Jan. 1801, p. 3

Died, the celebrated ALBINESS (formerly MISS HARVEY) at Havana Cuba several weeks
since
VPRDMA 23 March 1820, p. 3

Died, EDWIN JAMES HARVIE, from effects of the theatre fire (No death date)
RE 18 Jan. 1812, p. 3

Died on Friday last (Feb. 6) COL. JOHN HARVIE, near this city
VA 10 Feb. 1807, p. 3; RE 10 Feb., p. 3, adds "at Belvidere"; VGGA 11 Feb., p. 3

Died, LEWIS HARVIE of Richmond, eldest son of Col. John Harvie, Dec'd, on Tues. the
14th Inst. at the Exchange in Norfolk. He was a Member of the Executive Council
of State
Impartial Observer 25 April 1806, p. 3

Died on Tues. last (April 14) LEWIS HARVIE, Member of the Council of State (Editorial)
VA 21 April 1807, p. 3; Impartial Observer 25 April, p. 3, says "eldest son of Col.
John Harvie, dec'd, died on 14th Inst. at the Exchange in Norfolk"; RE 21 April, p.
3; VGGA 18 April, p. 3

Died Sat., last MR. CHRISTOPHER HARWOOD, (March 30) in King & Queen Co.
VGRC 6 April 1793, p. 3

Died on Sun. last (Nov. 23) CAPT. HUMPHREY HARWOOD of Williamsburg. Leaves wid.
& 6 children
VGWA 27 Nov. 1788, p. 3; VIC 3 Dec.

Died lately, MR. HARWOOD, comedian, near Phila.
Visitor 7 Oct. 1809, p. 142

Died Sunday (Feb. 15) MRS. HARWOOD, widow of Humphrey Harwood, late of Williamsburg
VGWA 19 Feb. 1789, p. 3

Died on Sat. last (Aug. 9) MR. SAMUEL HARWOOD of this city
VA 12 Aug. 1800, p. 3

Died Tues. last (July 7) at his seat near Richmond, MR. THOMAS HARWOOD
VGRMA 11 July 1795, p. 3

Died, COL. WILLIAM HARWOOD of Warwick Co., (No death date)
VG Oct. 4, 1780, p. 3

Died, MR. WILLIAM HARWOOD, age 31, at King & Queen C.H., leaving widow and infant
VIC 26 Aug. 1789, p. 2

Died Nov. 19th, MRS. MARTHA HASKINS of Powhatan Co., age 56
VA 2 Dec. 1800, p. 3

Died in Goochland Co. on 15th Inst., MR. JOSIAH HATCHER, age 26
VGGA 22 Sept. 1804, p. 1

Died Oct. 24th at home of his father in Powhatan Co., DR. HARDAWAY HATCHER, age 30,
son of Mr. Seth Hatcher
RE 5 Nov. 1819, p. 3

Died in Lunenburg Co., Aug. 11th, DR. ARCHIBALD HATCHETT
RE 1 Sept. 1820, p. 3

Died on 25th Ult. at his seat on Shelter Island, N.Y., JONATHAN N. HAVENS, Esq.,
Member of Congress from Long & Staten Islands
VGGA 12 Nov. 1799, p. 3

Died Nov. 2nd, MISS AMANDA MALVINA FITZALLEN HAWKINS, dau. of Mrs. Harriet Hawkins
of Richmond, age 11
RE 13 Nov. 1818, p. 3

Died in Richmond, yesterday, MRS. ELIZABETH HAWKINS, wife of Mr. Samuel Hawkins
RE 23 March 1816, p. 3

Died at Springfield, Henrico Co., res. of Mr. Samuel Burton, MR. MARTIN HAWKINS
of Fayette Co., Ky., age 68 (No death date)
RE 25 July 1820, p. 3

Died on 21st Inst., CHARLES HAY, Esq. of this city, for several years Clerk of
the State House of Delegates
RC 28 July 1795, p. 2; VGGA 29 July, says died on 20th at seat of Sampson Mathews
in Augusta Co.

Died, MISS ELIZABETH HAY, dau. of William Hay of Richmond, on Friday last (March 27)
VA 3 April 1807, p. 3; VGGA 1 April, p. 3, says "only dau."

Died, on 1st Inst., age 2, JOHN HAY, son of Mr. John Hay, dec'd, late a merchant
of this city
VGWA Sept. 7, 1792, p. 3

Died about 1st of Oct. last at St. Marys Ga., MR. JOHN HAY, late merchant of Richmond
VGGA 26 Jan. 1802, p. 3

Died at Chambersburg, DR. JOHN HAY, formerly Pastor of the Independent Tabernacle in
Phila.
Visitor 23 Sept. 1809, p. 135

Died on Sat. last (March 21) MRS. HAY, wife of Mr. George Hay of this city
VA 24 March 1807, p. 3; RE 24 March, p. 3, says "Mrs. Rebecca Hay, age 35, leaving
husband and 2 children"
VGGA 25 March, p. 3

Died on 10th Inst., MRS. HAY, consort of Mr. William Hay, of this city
VGGA 14 Dec. 1796, p. 3; VA 12 Dec., p. 3

Died, MR. PETER HAY, merchant of this town (No death date)
VGWA Feb. 16, 1782, p. 3

Died, MRS. POLLY HAY, on Sun. last (Nov. 1)
RC 3 Nov. 1795, p. 3; VGGA 4 Nov., says "sister of Mr. Charles Hay, dec'd"
VGRMA 5 Nov. , p. 3

Died on 6th Inst., JAMES HAYES, Esq., age 44
RE 10 Oct. 1804, p. 3; VA 13 Oct., p. 3 (says age 48); VGGA 10 Oct., p. 2 (says
age 44)

Died at Maj. John Price's at upper end of Henrico Co., on 5th Inst., man who called himself THOMAS P. HAYS
VA 4 Oct. 1808, p. 3; RE 7 Oct., p. 3

Died on 6th Inst., MR. WILLIAM HAYWOOD, at Blacwell's Neck in Hanover
VGWA 17 April 1788, p. 3

Died at Troy, N.Y., GEN. MOSES HAZEN, age 69, who commanded "Congress's Own Reginent" in the Revolutionary War
VA 12 March 1803, p. 3

Died in Fredericksburg on Fri. last (April 5) MR. GEORGE HAZLETON of Norfolk, age 28
VA 12 April 1799, p. 3

Died, MRS. FANNY C. HEATH, at Dumfries, on Jan. 31st, age 17, wife of James C. Heath, Esq. and dau., eldest, of Rev. M. L. Weems
VA 4 March 1813, p. 3

Died, HON. JOHN HEATH, a member of Privy Council, in this city, on 13th Inst. Former member of state legislature and of House of Representatives
RE 16 Oct. 1810, p. 3; VA 16 Oct., p. 3, says was from Northern Neck and was in Revolution

Died lately at his Glebe, near Urbanna, Middlesex Co., REV. HENRY HEFFERMAN, a Minister of Church of England. A native of Ireland, came to Va. 20 years ago
RE 12 March 1814, p. 3

Died Nov. 8th at his seat in Nottoway Co., MR. JAMES HENDERSON, a native of Scotland, age 80
RE 18 Nov. 1817, p. 3; VP Nov. 17, p. 3

Died Dec. 1st, JAMES HENDERSON, a native of Scotland, for more than 20 years a resident of Williamsburg
VP 15 Dec. 1818, p. 2

Died on Friday last (Dec. 19) MRS. JANE HENDERSON, wife of James Henderson, and dau. of late John Blair, Esq.
VGGA 26 Dec. 1800, p. 3

Died on Oct. 6th, of pains of childbirth, MRS. HENDERSON, wife of Mr. James Henderson
VP 12 Oct. 1813, p. 3

Died in Williamsburg, July 16th, THOMAS H. HENDERSON, son of James Henderson by his first wife Jane, dau. of late Judge John Blair, age 17
VP 23 July 1814, p. 3

Died Nov. 6th, MRS. ALICE E. HENDREN, consort of Patrick Hendren of Charles City Co., leaving husband and 6 infant children
RE 21 Nov. 1820, p. 3; VPRDMA 22 Nov., p. 2

Died, MRS. MARTHA HENLEY, age 18, consort of B.D. Henley, of Smithfield, on 8th Inst.
RE 24 Sept. 1811, p. 3

Died, MRS. ANN HENRY, consort of Lafayette Henry, Esq. and dau. of Mr. Lion Elcan, at Red Hill, in Charlotte Co., on 1st of this month
VA 10 May 1808, p. 3; RE 12 May, p. 3; VGGA 10 May, p. 3

Died on Wed. (Sept. 13) MR. DANIEL HENRY, merchant of Baltimore
VGGA 20 Sept. 1797, p. 3

Died, FAYETTE HENRY of Campbell Co., son of late Patrick Henry, on 15th Inst. at home of Mr. William Moncure, near this city
VA 18 March 1813, p. 3

Died on Dec. 9th (1804) at his seat Fleetbay, Northumberland Co., JAMES HENRY, Esq. formerly a congressman and a Judge of the Va. General Court
RE 18 Jan. 1805, p. 3; VA 19 Jan., p. 3 (says age 73)

Died, MR. JOHN HENRY, merchant, of this place, drowned on Sun. last (Aug. 23)
VGGA 26 Aug. 1807, p. 3

Died at his seat in Charlotte Co. on 4th Inst., PATRICK HENRY, esq.
VA 18 June 1799, p. 3; VA 25 June, p. 3, says 6th Inst.; VGGA 14 June, p. 3, says 6th Inst.

Died on 22nd Ult., PATRICK HENRY of Amherst Co., age 22
VA 13 Oct. 1804, p. 3; VGGA 24 Oct., p. 3 (says son of Patrick Henry, dec'd, of Charlotte Co. Leaves a widow)

Died on Thurs. last (Dec. 4) CAPT. THOMAS HERBERT of Norfolk
VGRMA 11 Dec. 1794, p. 3

Died on Tues. last (Sept. 29) MR. JAMES HERON, merchant, of this city
VA 2 Oct. 1801, p. 3; VGGA 2 Oct., p. 3

Died on 4th Inst. at Norfolk City, MR. AMBROSE HERRON, age 23, of the house of Cunningham & Herron of Cartersville
VA 15 Aug. 1800, p. 3; VGGA 8 Aug., p. 3

Died, HENRY G. HETH, drowned in James River, Oct. 7th
RE 16 Oct. 1816, p. 3; VA 9 Oct., p. 3; RC 15 Oct., p. 3

Died, CAPT. JOHN HETH, in this city on Friday last (Nov. 15). A soldier in the Revolution and Member of Society of the Cincinnati
RE 20 Nov. 1810, p. 3; VA 20 Nov., p. 3; VP 20 Nov., p. 3

Died, COL. WILLIAM HETH, at his seat near Curles, on Sun. last (March 29)
VA 3 April 1807, p. 3; VGGA 1 Apr., p. 3

Died on 9th Inst. at Falmouth, MAJ. HEWITT
RC 28 Nov. 1795, p. 3

Died Sat. (Nov. 18) at his res. in Powhatan Co., MR. WILLIAM HICKMAN, age 77
RE 21 Nov. 1820, p. 3 (also Nov. 24, p. 3); VPRDMA 22 Nov., p. 2

Died yesterday, MRS. ANN H. HICKS, consort of Mr. John Hicks, merchant of this city
VGGA 30 Dec. 1795, p. 2

Died on 23rd Ult., MRS. SARAH HICKS, consort of Mr. John Hicks, merchant of this
city
VGGA 2 April 1794, p. 3; VGRMA 27 March

Died Jan. 15th, MR. EDWARD HILL, of King & Queen Co., age 70
RE 23 Jan. 1816, p. 3

Died Feb. 21st at res. of Mrs. Ann L. Meredith in Hanover Co., MISS ELIZA C. HILL
RE 4 March 1815, p. 3

Died Dec. 13th at Oak Grove in King William Co., age 54, MRS. ELIZABETH HILL,
consort of Maj. Thomas Hill, leaving husband, son and 4 daughters
RE 28 Dec. 1820, p. 3; RC 23 Dec., p. 2

Died at his seat in Greenville Co., Va. FRANCIS HILL, Esq., eminent lawyer and
member of state legislature
RE 22 Nov. 1805, p. 3

Died in Manchester Oct. 21st, MISS JEMINA HILL, dau. of Mr. James Hill
VP 25 Oct. 1817, p. 3

Died, MR. ROBERT HILL, at his seat in King William Co., on Dec. 22nd (1813) leaving
widow and 6 children
RE 1 Jan. 1814, p. 3

Died, SAMUEL HILL of Caroline Co., hanged in Fredericksburg, on Aug. 8th for murder
of William Summerson of Caroline
VA 16 Aug. 1808, p. 3

Died Wed. (Sept. 15) at Baltimore, MR. THOMAS H. HILL, age 29, formerly one of
proprietors of Baltimore Telegraph
VP 21 Sept. 1819, p. 3

Died, MR. TARLTON HINES, age 45, on 15th Inst. at his res. in Goochland Co.,
leaving wife and 3 small daughters
VP 26 Oct. 1810, p. 2

Died June 28th from bite of a mad dog, MR. LEWIS HIPKINS, in Alexandria
VGRMA 4 Aug. 1794, p. 3

Died, CAPT. LEROY HIPKINS of U.S. Navy on Oct. 1st, age 35
VA 14 Oct. 1808, p. 3; RE 14 Oct., p. 3

Died at Green Springs on 19th Oct., REV. JOHN HIRT
VA 23 Oct. 1801, p. 3

Died on April 1st, MR. JOSEPH HOBSON, merchant, of Manchester
RC 2 April 1817, p. 3

Died Fri. last (Nov. 25) at Mrs. Timberlake's in Hanover, MRS. MARTHA HOBSON, wife
of Matthew Hobson of Buckingham
VA 29 Nov. 1808, p. 3; VGGA 29 Nov., p. 3

Died a few days ago, MRS. MARY HOCKADAY, consort of Col. John Hockaday of New Kent
Co.
VGGA 20 Nov. 1793, p. 3

Died, MR. JOHN HODGES, age 59, at Fairfield, Norfolk Co., on 4th Inst.
Visitor 17 March 1810, p. 27

Died in Wasnington, MR. HODGKINSON, one of the most distinguished theathrical
performers on the continent
RE 24 Sept. 1805, p. 3

Died, MR. WILLIAM P. HODGSEN on 18th, at Manchester, thrown from a horse
RE 29 June 1813, p. 3

Died, REV. MOSES HOGE, Pres. of Hampden-Sydney College, and Prof. of Divinity,
in Philadelphia July 5th
RE 11 July 1820, p. 3

Died at his late seat in Spotsylvania Co., at an advanced age, Oct. 29th,
MAJ. LEWIS HOLLADAY, a soldier in the Revolution, and for many years a county
magistrate
RE 3 Nov. 1820, p. 3

Died, MRS. JULIA HOLLOWAY, on 6th Inst., age 32, consort of Maj. David Holloway
of this city
VGGA 11 March 1807, p. 3

Died Sept. 3rd, MR. WILLIAM HOLLOWAY, age 35
RC 7 Sept. 1818, p. 3

Died in Cumberland Co., July 20th, JOHN HOLMAN, almost 87, had been a Justice of
Peace of the County
RE 4 August 1818, p. 3

Died at Rockaway, Long Island, N.Y., on Aug. 24th, JOSEPH GEORGE HOLMAN, 53. A
native of England, he was a descendant of Sir. George Holman, Bart., of Warkworth
Castle. An actor, he appeared in London 1784, and later in U.S.
RE 2 Sept. 1817, p. 3

Died on 14th Inst. at his seat in Goochland, CAPT. WILLIAM HOLMAN, age 74
VGGA 24 Aug. 1796, p. 3

Died, MR. DANIEL HOLT of Williamsburg in Petersburg (No death date)
VGRMA 5 Jan. 1795, p. 3

Died, MR. HENRY HOLT, of New Kent Co., in Richmond on 11th Ult.
RE 16 Feb. 1813, p. 3

Died, MR. JOHN HOLT, Printer to State of N.Y. on 30th Jan., age 64
VGAA 21 Feb. 1784, p. 2

Died in Orange Co., N.C. July 11th, MR. LEWIS HOLT, age 26, by lightning
VP 12 Aug. 1819, p. 3

Died, MRS. ELIZABETH HOLTZ, wife of Mr. P. Holtz of this city, on Wed. (Dec. 8)
RE 11 Dec. 1813, p. 3

Died last Sunday sen' (April 1) MR. JAMES HONEY, a native of Perth in Scotland,
for many years a res. of Williamsburg
VGWA 12 April 1787, p. 3

Died at Berry Hill, his res. in Fauquier Co., on Oct. 16th, MR. JOHN HOOE, age
64
RE 22 Oct. 1819, p. 3

Died, MRS. ANN C. HOOMES, wife of Armistead Hoomes, Esq. of Caroline Co., age 22
RE 27 March 1810, p. 3; VA 27 March, p. 3

Died on 22nd Inst., in Williamsburg, MR. GEORGE WASHINGTON HOOMES, 2nd son of Col.
John Hoomes of the Bowling Green, age 23, leaving wife and infant son
VA 31 July 1802, p. 3; VGGA 28 July, p. 3

Died, JOHN HOOMES of Bowling Green in Caroline Co., on 15th Inst.
RE 27 Dec. 1805, p. 3; VA 24 Dec., p. 3; VGGA 21 Dec., p. 3

Died at his seat in Caroline Co., Feb. 26th, DR. WILLIAM HOOMES, 2nd son of late
Col. John Hoomes of Bowling Green
RE 9 March 1819, p. 3

Died, (   ) HOPKINS, age 7, on Sept. 11th believed killed by his mother near
Poplar Springs
RC 18 Sept. 1820, p. 3

Died in Washington, MR. C. D. HOPKINS, comedian, on 26th Ult.
RE 5 Nov. 1805, p. 3; VA 6 Nov., p. 3; VGGA 6 Nov., p. 3

Died, GEORGE HOPKINS, of Charles City, drowned, Sat. last (before May 16) son of
Mr. Benskin Hopkins
VGGA 26 May, 1809, p. 3

Died on Mon. last (Dec. 8) MRS. LUCY HOPKINS, spouse of John Hopkins of this city
VA 12 Dec. 1800, p. 3

Died, LT. HOPKINS, killed in duel near Bladensburg, Md., by Lt. Hall, both of
Col. Carberry's Regt.
RE 19 March 1814, p. 3

Died at his res. in Henderson Co., Ky., GEN. SAMUEL HOPKINS, a Revolutionary soldier
(No death date)
RE 7 Dec. 1819, p. 3

Died Oct. 31st, DR. BERNARD HORNET of New Kent Co., a native of Burgundy in France
VA 15 Nov. 1799, p. 3

Died on 19th Inst., at his seat in King & Queen Co., age 63, COL. JOHN HOSKINS
RE 26 Nov. 1813, p. 3

Died Nov. 19th at his res. in King William Co., DR. JOHN HOSKINS
RE 21 Nov. 1820, p. 3; VPRDMA 22 Nov., p. 2

Died in Richmond City Tues. last (April 28) MRS. HOVEY, wife of Mr. Henry Hovey
VA 1 May 1801, p. 3

Died at St. Louis, Mo., Sept. 18th, GEN. BENJAMIN HOWARD of U.S. Army, late Gov.
of the territory, and formerly Congressman from Ky.
RE 18 Oct. 1814, p. 3

Died lately at house of Gen. Clarke near Wilmington, N.C., ROBERT HOWE, Esq., late
General in service of U.S.
VGWA 22 Feb. 1787, p. 2

Died Feb. 24th, MRS. MARY HOWLETT, age 68, for many years an inhabitant of Richmond
VPRDMA 28 Feb. 1820, p. 3; RC 29 Feb., p. 3

Died in this city Mon. last (Feb. 27) MISS MARY HOYE, a young lady
VGGA 29 Feb. 1804, p. 3

Died, MARTIN HOYLE, a native of Ireland, but for years a res. of Petersburg, on
Tues. last (before May 20)
VA 27 May 1808, p. 3

Died in Williston Township, near Westchester, Pa., April 14th, MR. BENJAMIN HUBBARD,
age 79, in a fire
RC 3 May 1819, p. 3

Died, DR. JAMES T. HUBBARD, formerly of Petersburg, on Sept. 7th
RE 18 Sept. 1812, p. 3

Died Aug. 30th, age 28, at his father's in Charles City Co., JOHN K. HUBBARD,
eldest son of George Hubbard
RE 10 Sept. 1819, p. 3

Died, MR. JOHN C. HUBNER, merchant, of this city, a native of Germany, on 26th
Inst.
RE 28 Dec. 1813, p. 3; VA 27 Dec., p. 3; VP 31 Dec., p. 3, says died Dec. 20th

Died, MR. GEORGE HUGELEY, on Sat. last (July 27) suicide
VA 1 Aug. 1811, p. 1

Died, MR. LEANDER HUGHES, on 28th March at house of Archelaus Hughes, in this city
RE 13 April 1813, p. 3; VA 26 April, p. 3, says died on 26th, age 30

Died Aug. 25th, MRS. MARGARET J. HUGHES, consort of Madison R. Hughes of Patrick Co., leaving husband and an infant
RE 24 Sept. 1819, p. 3

Died in Williamsburg, MR. CHALRES HUNT, Oct. 11th
VGGA 15 Oct. 1794, p. 2; VGRMA 16 Oct;VGRC 17 Oct.

Died near Charlotte C.H. June 9th, DR. JAMES W. HUNT
RE 17 June 1817, p. 3

Died Monday (Sept. 3) MR. ICHABOD HUNTER, merchant of this city
Observatory 6 Sept. 1798, p. 2; VGGA 4 Sept., p. 2

Died in Oct. 1812, JAMES HUNTER, late a judge of State of Ky.
VP 21 May 1813, p. 3

Died, MRS. MARGARET HUNTER, in Williamsburg (No death date)
VGIC 6 Oct. 1787, p. 3; VGWA 4 Oct. 1787, p. 3

Died, Friday last (Dec. 12) MR. MILES HUNTER, printer of Petersburg.
VGWA 18 Dec. 1788, p. 3; VIC 17 Dec. 1788

Died in Williamsburg, June 28th, MR. MUSCOE GARNET HUNTER, eldest son of James Hunter of Essex Co.; a student at William & Mary, age 18
RE 4 July 1817, p. 3

Died lately near Savannah, Ga., WILLIAM HUNTER, killed in a duel by David B. Mitchell
VA 15 Sept. 1802, p. 3

Died on Tues. (before Jan. 8) at his seat in Norwich, Conn., age 64, SAMUEL HUNTINGDON, Gov. of Conn.
VGRMA 6 Feb. 1796, p. 3

Died in New London, Conn., GEN. JEDEDIAH HUNTINGTON, age about 80 (No death date)
RE 2 Oct. 1818, p. 3

Died, REV. RICHARD HURST, Baptist Minister on 15th, taken sick in pulpit at Four Mile Creek
VA 22 Nov. 1813, p. 3

Died on 6th Inst., POLLY W. HURT, wife of Rev. Robert Hurt of Halifax Co., Va.
RE 21 Dec. 1815, p. 3

Died fighting Indians in Tenn. Aug. 8th, ROBERT HUSTON
VGWA 2 Oct. 1788, p. 3

Died Oct. 15th, MRS. ANNA HUTCHESON, consort of Mr. James Hutcheson of Richmond, age 34, leaving husband and 5 young children
VP 19 Oct. 1813, p. 3

Died Jan. 4th at house of Robert Wilson, East Windsor, Middlesex Co., N.J.
ANN HUTCHINSON, widow of William Hutchinson, age 101. Mother of 13 children
VA 6 Feb. 1801, p. 3

Died on Thurs. last (before Dec. 22) on Long Island, N.Y., JOHN STRANGEWAYS HUTTON, born on the island in 1682
VGRDA 31 Dec. 1792, p. 3

Died in Richmond on Sept. 8th, MR. PELEG HYDE, at an advanced age
VP 12 Sept. 1816, p. 3

Died, DANIEL L. HYLTON, Esq., Clerk of the Executive Council, on Sat. last (Jan. 19) in this city (Obituary Jan. 24)
RE 22 Jan. 1811, p. 3

Died on 28th Ult. in Manchester, MR. RALPH HYLTON, Attorney at Law
VGGA 7 March 1792, p. 3

Died, REV. DR. JAMES INGLIS, pastor of First Presb. Ch. of Baltimore, on Sun. (Aug. 15)
RC 21 Aug. 1819, p. 3

Died lately in Phila, COL. JAMES INNES of this city
Observatory 9 Aug. 1798, p. 3

Died on 20th Ult. at Edenton, N.C., the HON. JAMES IREDELL, Esq. one of the Assoc. Justices of the U.S.
VA 12 Nov. 1799, p. 3

Died, at Mr. Gilley Lewis's in Cumberland Co., on 13th Inst., MR. WALTER IRVINE, merchant, of New Canton, survived by wife and 2 small children
VA 24 April 1807, p. 3; VGGA 25 Apr., p. 3

Died in Charlottesville on Wed. last (April 2) MR. ISAIAH ISAACS, formerly of this city
VA 8 April 1806, p. 3; VGGA 9 April, p. 3

Died on May 30th at his house on South Bay, South Carolina, RALPH IZARD, Esq., late Senator from S.C.
VA 30 June 1804, p. 3

Died at Corinth, Me., COL. ABEL JACKMAN, age 58
VPRDMA 18 Aug. 1820, p. 3

Died on 20th Inst., MARTHA JACQUELIN, age 82
VGGA 26 Dec. 1792, p. 2

Died on 26th Jan., COL. RICHARD JAMES of Cumberland
VA 9 Feb. 1802, p. 3

Died Sun. (Sept. 6) in Williamsburg, MR. GEORGE B. JACKSON of that place
RC 11 Sept. 1818, p. 3

Died, GEN. JAMES JACKSON, a Senator from Ga. (No death date)
VA 28 March 1806, p. 3

Died on Tues. last (June 2) JOSEPH O.B. JACKSON
RC 6 June 1795, p. 3; VGGA 3 June, "in this city"; VGRMA 4 June, p. 3

Died MR. WILLIAM JACKSON and 2 of his daughters when home destroyed by fire July
26th in Shenandoah Co.
VP 20 Aug. 1817, p. 3

Died, ROBERT B. JAMES, in this city on 16th Jan. last, formerly of Phila, Principal
Survyor of North American Land Co. for this state
Virginian 14 June 1808, p. 3

Died on 10th Inst., DAVID JAMESON, Esq. of Yorktown
VGGA 24 July 1793, p. 3; VGRMA 25 July

Died, the spouse of Mr. Edmund Jameson of Charlotte Co., on 12th Inst.
VA 25 April 1806, p. 3

Died Thurs. last (May 30) at Raleigh, near Four Mile Creek, MRS. MARGARET JANEY
VA 4 June 1799, p. 3

Died on Friday last (April 24) ABEL JANNEY, a Member of Society of Friends
VA 28 April 1801, p. 3

Died, MR. GEORGE JEFFERSON, at sea, on July 20th. He was late American Consul
at Lisbon, a relation of the late president, and formerly a merchant in Richmond
RE 4 Aug. 1812, p. 3; VA 3 Aug., p. 3; VP 4 Aug., p. 3

Died in Manchester, July 2nd, JOHN JENKINS, resident for many years there
RE 11 July 1817, p. 3

Died, MR. JOSEPH JENKINS of Henrico, on 26th Ult., age 65
VA 1 June 1812, p. 3

Died Nov. 10th, ROBERT JENKINS, Mayor of Hudson, N.Y.
RE 19 Nov. 1819, p. 3

Died, MR. WILLIAM JENKINS, in Fredericksburg (No death date)
VGRMA 5 Jan. 1795, p. 3

Died on 27th Ult., CAPT. ROBERT JENNINGS of Charlotte Co., age 61
VA 8 Nov. 1806, p. 3; RE 7 Nov., p. 3

Died last week in Petersburg, MR. ANDREW JOHNSON, merchant of that place
VGWA 14 May 1785, p. 3

Died in Louisa Co. April 20th, MRS. ANN C.H. JOHNSON, wife of Thomas Johnson, age 33,
leaving husband and 8 children
RE 28 April 1820, 1820, p. 3

Died at Cincinnati, Ohio, Aug. 16th, age 26, MR. ARCHIBALD JOHNSON, late student of
Divinity under Dr. Wilie of Phila. Leaves a wife
RC 16 Sept. 1819, p. 3

Died in Canton, Mass., Oct. 10th, DANIEL JOHNSON, age 12, son of Nathaniel Johnson of Bridgewater, accidentally in the cotton factory
RC 31 Oct. 1816, p. 3

Died, EDWARD JOHNSON, of N.C. at William & Mary College (No death date)
VA 16 Oct. 1805, p. 3

Died Lexington, Ky., Sept. 7th, JACOB JOHNSON of Philadelphia, a Quaker and book-seller
RE 1 Oct. 1819, p. 3; RC 1 Oct., p. 3

Died, COL. JAMES JOHNSON of Isle of Wight Co. (No death date)
VA 16 March 1805, p. 3

Died at his res. in Fluvanna Co., April 19th, MR. JOHN JOHNSON, age 42, leaving wife and 4 children
RE 23 April 1819, p. 3

Died Sept. 22nd, age 33, MRS. MARY JOHNSON, consort of Mr. David Johnson of House of Galt & Johnson
RE 28 Sept. 1819, p. 3; VP 24 Sept., p. 3

Died on Aug. 26th, MISS MILDRED M. JOHNSON, only dau. of Francis Johnson of Louisa Co.
RE 4 Sept. 1816, p. 3

Died Oct. 12th, MR. REUBEN JOHNSON, leaving wife and 6 children
RC 13 Oct. 1820, p. 3; VPRDMA 16 Oct., p. 3

Died May 13th in Old Town, King & Queen Co., ROBERT JOHNSON, son of late James Johnson
RC 25 May 1816, p. 3

Died in Charleston, S.C., March 21st, age 77, MR. WILLIAM JOHNSON, for over 50 years, a resident of Charleston
VP 25 April 1818, p. 3

Died Dec. 10, 1818, at res. of his father near Abingdon, DR. JOHN W. JOHNSTON, age 28
RE 9 Jan. 1819, p. 4

Died fighting Indians in Tenn., Aug. 8th, LUTHER JOHNSTON
VGWA 2 Oct. 1788, p. 3

Died on 12th June, age 67, MRS. MARTHA JOHNSTON, relict of late Peter Johnston, Esq. of Prince Edward Co.
VA 25 June 1799, p. 3

Died Sat. (Jan. 29) MRS. JOHNSTON, wife of Charles Johnston, merchant of this city
VA 5 Feb. 1803, p. 3; VGGA 1 Feb., p. 3

Died, on 15th Inst., MR. PHILIP JOHNSTON, of James City County
VGWA 19 March 1789, p.3

Died on 9th Ult. in Phila. MR. SAMUEL JOHNSTON, printer
<u>VGGA</u> 2 Oct. 1793, p. 3

Died on 30th June, MISS ANN JONES, dau. of Mrs. Mary Jones of Hanover
<u>VGGA</u> 6 July 1796, p. 2; <u>VGRMA</u> 2 July, p. 3

Died, MRS. BARBARA O. JONES, for many years a resident of Hanover C.H., on 17th
Inst.
<u>RE</u> 25 Aug. 1812, p. 4

Died BATHURST JONES, Esq. on 2nd Inst., for some years a representative of Hanover
Co., in the Va. House of Delegates
<u>RE</u> 6 April 1810, p. 3

Killed fighting Indians in Tenn. on Aug. 8th, CALEB JONES
<u>VGWA</u> 2 Oct. 1788, p. 3

Died, a few days since, MAJ. CATESBY JONES of Mount Sion, Northumberland Co.
<u>VA</u> 30 Sept. 1800, p. 3; <u>VGGA</u> 26 Sept., p. 3

Died, age 81, at his farm in Chester Co., Pa., Feb. 5th, REV. DAVID JONES, Chaplain
of the Revolutionary Army
<u>RE</u> 15 Feb. 1820, p. 3

Died at Mr. Lund Hopkins in Powhatan Co. on the 21st Inst., MRS. ELIZABETH JONES,
consort of Paul G. G. Jones of Cartersville
<u>VA</u> 28 Feb. 1806, p. 2

Died, FREDERICK JONES, Esq. age 45, at his seat in Cumberland Co., on Feb. 11th
<u>VA</u> 15 March 1813, p. 3

Died on 18th Ult. at his seat in Rockingham Co., GABRIEL JONES, lawyer, in his 85th
year
<u>VA</u> 8 Nov. 1806, p. 3; <u>RE</u> 31 Oct., p. 3

Died on 2nd Inst. age 14, MISS HARRIOT JONES, dau. of Capt. Nathan Jones
<u>Visitor</u> 16 Dec. 1809, p. 182

Died on 5th Inst. MR. HENRY JONES of Caroline Co. of a fall from a horse
<u>VGRMA</u> 15 April 1793, p. 3

Died in Richmond on 31st Ult., JEKYLL JONES, Attorney at Law
<u>RE</u> 2 Aug. 1815, p. 3

Died in Richmond, JOHN R. JONES, Attorney at Law (No death date)
<u>RE</u> 21 Sept. 1819, p. 3; <u>VP</u> 21 Sept. says died Sun. (Sept. 19)

Died, JOSEPH JONES, one of the Judges of the General Court of Va., in Fredericksburg
on Oct. 20
<u>RE</u> 5 Nov. 1805, p. 3; <u>VA</u> 2 Nov., p. 3; <u>VGGA</u> 2 Nov., p. 2

Died April 18th, MRS. MARY JONES of Gloucester Co., age 70
RE 19 May 1820, p. 3

Died on 9th Inst., near Sweet Springs, MERRIWETHER JONES, Esq., Commissioner of
Loans
VA 20 Aug. 1806, p. 3; Imp. Obs. 23 Aug., p. 3 (says age 41), and that he died at
Warm Springs, Bath Co.; RE 19 Aug., p. 3; VGGA 23 Aug, p. 3 (says also former
Editor of The Richmond Examiner)

Died at Capt. Peter Foster's in Hanover Co., Oct. 9th, age 51, MRS. PAULINA JONES,
dau. of Col. Turner Southall, dec'd, of Henrico Co.
RE 29 Oct. 1819, p. 3

Died, MR. SKELTON JONES, in this city on Wed. last (Oct. 28). He was Editor of
The Examiner, and also worked on the History of Va., begun by Mr. Burk
RE 30 Oct. 1812, p. 3; VP 30 Oct., p. 3 says died Tues. last (Oct. 27)

Died, DR. WALTER JONES of Northumberland Co. on Jan. 31st in 70th year. Had served
in Va. Senate and in Congress
RE 13 Feb. 1816, p. 3

Died on Sun. last (June 3) WILLIAM JONES of Buckingham Co., commonly called
"Uncle Bill the great tobacco maker"
VA 9 June 1804, p. 3

Died on Wed. (June 23) DR. WILLIAM P. JONES, physician to the penitentiary and
Public Guard
RE 25 June 1819, p. 3; RC 25 June, p. 3; VP 25 June, p. 3

Died on 24th Ult. THOMAS JOPLING, the Elder of Amherst Co. at advanced age
VIC 9 Sept. 1789, p. 3

Died, MR. AUGUSTUS C. JORDAN, Printer, of Norfolk, on Wed. last (March 28)
Visitor 31 March 1810, p. 35

Died, MRS. MARY JORDAN, age 17, wife of Mr. Edward Jordan of Caswell Co., S.C.
on June 6th
VA 19 June 1805, p. 3

Died at his res. on March 9th, MR. NOBLE JORDAN of Henrico Co., age 76, member of
Baptist Church for 46 years
RE 24 March 1820, p.3

Died Nov. 22nd, MR. LAZARUS JOSEPH, a native of Germany, age 53, and res. of
Richmond for 18 years, leaving wife and 2 sons
VP 24 Nov. 1817, p.3

Died on June 5th, COL. ROBERT JOUETT of Charlottesville
VGGA 22 June 1796, p. 3

Died in this city Thurs. (Oct. 23) MR. JOHN JOY, merchant
VA 28 Oct. 1800, p. 3

Died, MR. ABRAHAM JUDAH, formerly of Richmond, in Essex Co., on 6th Inst.
VA 20 Nov. 1810, p. 3

Died Sun. last (Oct. 9) MR. HILLEL JUDAH of Richmond, formerly a resident of Newport,
R.I.
VA 15 Oct. 1803, p. 3

Died on 3rd Inst., in Charleston, S.C., MICHAEL KALTELSEN, Esq., Commandant of
Fort Johnson in U.S. Regt. of Artillerists and Engineers, age 85
RE 20 Nov. 1807, p. 3

Died Feb. 15th, MRS. KITTY KEAN, wife of Dr. A. Kean of Louisa Co., leaving husband
and two boys
VA 12 March 1803, p. 3

Died on Dec. 15th, NEVIN KEARINES, age 43
RE 21 Dec. 1816, p. 3

Died on 14th Inst., MR. WILLIAM KEENE of James City, at an advanced age
VGGA 28 Feb. 1798, p. 3

Died Feb. 11th, MR. CHARLES KEESEE, age 24
RE 20 Feb. 1817, p. 3

Died Oct. 4th, HENRY KEFFER, son of Mr. Henry Keffer of Lancaster, age 5 years 6 mo.
18 days
RC 21 Oct. 1820, p. 3; VPRDMA 21 Oct., p. 3, says age 6 yr, 6 mo., 18 days

Died last week a man named KELL, living in Williamsburg, a native of Great Britain
VGWA 28 Feb. 1784, p. 3

Died lately in Southampton Co., RICHARD KELLO, Esq.
VGWA 4 June 1789, p. 3; VIC 3 June

Died Dec. 24th, MR. JOHN KELSO, proprietor of the Bell Tavern in Richmond
RE 28 Dec. 1820, p. 3; RC 27 Dec., p. 3; VPRDMA 27 Dec., p. 3

Died at Norfolk, GEORGE KELLY, age 33 (No death date)
RE 28 April 1820, p. 3

Died yesterday in this city, MR. JAMES KEMP
VGGA 16 Dec. 1795, p. 5; VGRMA 16 Dec., p. 3, says "for many years a resident of
Richmond"

Died, PETER KEMP, son of Mr. Matthew Kemp, in Gloucester Co., on 29th Ult.
RE 30 Dec. 1809, p. 3

Died, COL. PETER KEMP, of this city, age 53, a Revolutionary soldier, on Tues.
(July 21)
VP 24 July 1812, p. 3

Died Aug. 3rd, at Huntington, in Middlesex Co., MR. PETER KEMP, age 56, leaving a sister
RE 13 Aug. 1819, p. 3; VP 13 Aug., p. 3

Died, at the Great Bridge, Norfolk Co. on 2nd Inst., MR. JOHN KENNEDY, merchant
VGGA 15 Oct. 1794, p. 2

Died at Norfolk on 19th Ult., MRS. RUTH KER, wife of Mr. James Ker, formerly of this city
VGGA 12 Oct. 1796, p. 6

Died, MR. WILLIAM KERNOHAN, merchant of Charlotte Co. by fall from his horse on 18th July
VIC 5 Aug. 1789, p. 3

Died, MR. JAMES KERR of this city (No death date)
VGIC 25 Oct. 1788, p. 3

Died, MAJ. WILLIAM KERSEY, of 3rd U.S. Regt. in a duel with Lt. Marks of same regt. at Ntchez on March 11th
VGGA 16 May 1800, p. 3

Died Sunday last (Aug. 19) MR. JESSE KEY of Albemarle Co., but for some time past a res. of this city
VGWA 23 Aug. 1787, p. 2

Died Friday last (Nov. 28), MR. ROBERT KIBBLE of this city
VGGA 3 Dec. 1794, p. 3; VGRMA 1 Dec.

Died on Thurs. (Oct. 15) in Richmond, MR. SPOTSWOOD KILBY, 19, son of Capt. John Kilby of Hanovertown
RC 17 Oct. 1818, p. 3

Died Oct. 29th, at the Vauxhall Garden, near Richmond, THOMAS BARNES KIMBERLY, age 14, leaving mother and 2 sisters
VPRDMA 1 Nov. 1820, p. 3

Died, MR. ROBERT KINCAID, at his seat in Buckingham Co. on May 19th, survived by 2 children
VP 28 May 1811, p. 3

Died, MRS. BARBARA KING, wife of Mr. Miles King of Hampton (No death date)
VG June 28, 1780, p. 3

Died at Saco, Me., April 25th, MAJ-GEN. CYRUS KING, age 41, late Member of Congress
RE 6 May 1817, p. 3

Died, MISS ELIZA KING of Norfolk, on Mon. last (Sept. 16) by taking laudanum
VA 19 Sept. 1811, p. 3

Died Sun. (June 19) age 70, MILES KING, SR., had served as Burgess, Member of General Assembly and JP for Elizabeth City Co. 14 years ago moved to Norfolk. Served there as Alderman
VP   25 June 1814, p. 3

Died in Abingdon on 12th Ult., WILLIAM KING, Esq., merchant
VA   8 Nov. 1808, p. 2; RE   8 Nov., p. 3 (says died 13th Ult.)

Died at Burlington on 4th Inst., JAMES KINSEY, Esq., LLD, Chief Justice of State of N.J., age 70
VA   22 Jan. 1802, p. 3

Died in Richmond last Wed. (April 22) MRS. ELIZABETH KIRBY
RE   28 April 1818, p. 3

Died at Fort Stoddert Oct. 20th, EPHRAIM KIRBY, late of Litchfield, Conn. Judge of U.S. District Court of New Orleans
VA   29 Dec. 1804, p. 3

Died July 14th, 10 year old dau. of MRS. KIRK. Injured by a horse
VICGA   21 July 1790, p. 2

Died, JOHN KIRKE, on 12th Inst. at Maj. Peter F. Archer's at Scotsville, Powhatan Co. He was from near Nashville, Tenn., returning to Dinwiddie Co. where his father resides, and was age 24
RE   20 March 1810, p. 3; VA   23 March, p. 3

Died, MR. GEORGE KIRKLAND, at Carcasas, executed by Spanish Gov't in a rebellion
VA   30 Aug. 1806, p. 2

Died, MR. JOHN KNOTT, in this city, on Tues. last (Oct. 6). Lately from Norfolk, he was a printer at The Virginia Argus
VA   10 Oct. 1807, p. 3; VGGA   10 Oct., says died Wed.

Died, MR. JOHN KNOX, printer, on Wed. last (Oct. 7)
VGGA   10 Oct. 1807, p. 3

Died in Savannah, Ga., Dec. 29th, 1819, REV. H. KOLLOCK, Pastor of Presbyterian Society
VPRDMA   10 Jan. 1820, p. 3

Died, Capt. JOHN LACKLAND, merchant, of Claira, Cumberland Co., Va., in Rockingham Co., N.C. on April 30th
RE   16 May 1809, p. 3; Visitor   20 May, p. 62

Died Oct. 1st, age 24, MRS. MARY C. LACKLAND, consort of Mr. Matthew C. Lackland, merchant, of Richmond
RE   20 Oct. 1820, p. 3; RC   2 Oct., p. 3, says infant dau. also died

Died, MR. ELLIOTT LACY, age 73, on Thurs. last (Dec. 1) for nearly 50 years an inhabitant of Goochland
Spirit of 76, 9 Dec. 1808, p.

Died a few days ago, MR. JOHN LACY of New Kent Co., at an advanced age
VA 18 May 1803, p. 3

Died on 6th Inst., age 69, SARAH LADD of Charles City Co.
RE 12 March 1814, p. 3

Died at his res. in Chesterfield Co. on Sept. 16th, REV. THOMAS LAFON, age 63, a Baptist Minister
RE 2 Oct. 1816, p. 3

Died on Tues. last (May 17) MRS. LAFOREST, consort of Mr. Aubin Laforest of this city
VA 20 May 1808, p. 3

Died, MRS. ELIZABETH P. LAKENAN, consort of James Lakenan of this city, on the 18th
RE 31 July 1812, p. 3

Died on Wed. (May 7), COL. DAVID LAMBERT, age 67, for last 48 years inhabitant of Richmond
RE 13 May 1817, p. 3; RC 9 May, p. 2

Died on 28th Inst., MRS. LAMBERT, wife of Col. David Lambert of this city
VA 30 June 1801, p. 3

Died Sat. (date ?) in New York, PETER LANDAIS, age 87, known as "Admiral Landais". He had been a Captain in the squadron of Paul Jones
RE 29 Spet. 1820, p. 3

Died April 30th in Amelia Co., JOHN LANE, leaving a widow and 3 children
RE 5 May 1820, p. 3

Died, MR. ARCHIBALD LANG of Manchester, age 30 yrs, 1 mo, 8 das (No death date)
VA 6 Feb. 1805, p. 3

Died fighting Indians in Tenn. Aug. 8th, WILLIAM LAND
VGWA 2 Oct. 1788, p. 3

Died Sept. 18th at his mansion in Portsmouth, N.H., JOHN LANGDON, formerly Senator, and recently Gov. of N.H.
RE 1 Oct. 1819, p. 3; VP 30 Sept., p. 3

Died at Callaway's in Bedford Co., Aug. 5th, age 60, MRS. ELIZABETH LANGHORNE, relict of Mr. John Langhorne, formerly of Warwick Co.
RE 18 Aug. 1818, p. 3

Died Dec. 12, 1798 in the wilderness on the way to Ky.,MR. THOMAS LANKFORD of
Pittsylvania Co.
VGGA 22 Jan. 1799, p. 3

Died, MRS. LUCY LATIL, consort of Joseph Latil, Esq. of this city, on Sat. last
(Jan. 16)
VICGA 20 Jan. 1790, p. 3

Died on Friday last (Nov. 26) MRS. ELIZABETH W. LAUGHLIN, consort of Mr. Edmund
Laughlin of this city
VA 1 Dec. 1802, p. 3

Died on Wed. (April 29), MR. GEORGE LAUGHLIN
VA 1 May 1801, p. 3

Died lately at the Green Springs, MR. JAMES LAWRENCE, formerly of this city
VGRMA 26 Jan.1795, p. 3

Died, CAPT. JAMES LAWRENCE (No death date)
RE 31 Aug. 1813, p. 2

Died, MR. WILLIAM LAWRENCE, formerly of this city, (No death date)
VGGA 28 Jan. 1795, p. 3

Died on Nov. 13th at Louisa C.H., age 51, MR. WILLIAM LAWRENCE
VA 21 Nov. 1806, p. 3; RE 21 Nov., p. 3 (says died on 12th); VGGA 22 Nov., p. 3
(says 13th)

Died on Sat. last (Feb. 14), MR. JOHN LAYPOLD of Rocketts
VGGA 18 Feb. 1795, p. 3

Died on 27th Ult., MR. JOHN LEA of Louisa Co., between 70 and 80 years old, leaving
widow and 5 children
VA 11 Jan. 1815, p. 3

Died, CAPT. ELISHA LEAKE of Goochland Co., on 19th Inst.
VA 29 Oct. 1806, p. 3

Died on 31st Ult. at house of Josiah Leake in Goochland Co., DR. SAMUEL D. LEAKE,
age 25
VA 8 Nov. 1808, p. 3

Died Aug. 24th at her father's res. in Goochland Co., MISS SARAH H. LEAKE, age 18
RE 21 Sept. 1819, p. 3

Died Wed. last (Dec. 12) at Urbanna in Middlesex Co., ARTHUR LEE, Esq.
VGGA 19 Dec. 1792, p. 2; VGRDA 21 Dec.

Died June 24th, age 58, at his res. in Fauquier Co., CHARLES LEE, long a res. of
Alexandria, Va., graduate of Princeton, lawyer, and Attorney General of the U.S.
VP 12 July 1815, p. 3

Died, FRANCIS LIGHTFOOT LEE, Esq., at his seat in Richmond Co., on 18th Ult.,
age 63
VGGA 8 Feb. 1797, p. 3

Died JAMES LEE, at Eagle Tavern on 24th Inst., on his way from Savannah to Baltimore
RE 29 Sept. 1812, p. 3

Died on 13th Inst., MRS. JANE LEE, consort of William Lee, Esq., of Goochland
VA 24 March 1797, p. 3

Died, MRS. LEE, wife of Richard E. Lee, Esq., age 55, of Norfolk, on July 14th
Virginian 22 July 1808, p. 2

Died on 17th Inst. in this city, MASTER PHILIP LEE, eldest son of Henry Lee, Esq.,
Gov. of this state
VGGA 25 July 1792, p. 3

Died on 21st. Ult. at Lee Hall, RICHARD LEE, only son of Richard Lee, Esq. of
Westmoreland
VGRMA 1 Aug. 1793, p. 3

Died on 10th Inst., RICHARD LEE, Esq., of Lee Hall, Westmoreland Co., age 71
VGRMA 16 Oct. 1794, p. 3; VGRC 17 Oct., says for 36 years a Rep. of his co. in
State Legislature

Died on June 8th, RICHARD E. LEE, Pres. of Bank of Va. at Norfolk. Was at one time
in General Assembly
RC 16 June 1814, p. 3

Died, age 34, RICHARD HENRY LEE, Attorney at Law in this Borough (Norfolk).(No
death date)
RE 21 Oct. 1815, p. 3

Died in Manchester Friday last (June 20), MR. WILLIAM LEE of Cumberland Co.
VGRMA 23 June 1794, p. 3

Died near Bladensburg, Md., LT. WILLIAM ARTHUR LEE, son of late Charles Lee of Va.,
age 21. Shot by person unknown on June 15th and died July 10th
VP 18 July 1817, p. 3

Died at his seat near Williamsburg on Mon. last (Jan. 24), WILLIAM LUDWELL LEE, Esq.
VGGA 29 Jan. 1803, p. 3

Died on Fri. last (Jan 12), MISS POLLY LEEDS, 2nd dau. of Jedediah Leeds of this
city
VGGA 17 Jan. 1798, p. 3

Died, LT. LEFTWICH of the Bedford Artillery, on 15th Inst. at Fort Norfolk
VA 21 Sept. 1812, p. 3

Died at Pittsylvania C.H. Sept. 30th, DR. WILLIAM LEFTWICH, age 28, leaving wife
and 2 small children
RE 13 Oct. 1818, p. 3

Died, MRS. LEIGHIE, age 42, mother of Mrs. William Wallace.(No death date)
RC 30 Aug. 1820, p. 3

Died, JOHN LEONARD of Henrico Co. (No death date)
VG Oct. 4, 1780, p. 3

Died on Fri. last (Feb. 7), MR. PRICE LEONARD of this county
VGRMA 10 Feb. 1794, p. 2; VGRC 11 Feb., says Feb. 6

Died, JAMES LESLIE of Phila., at Caracas, executed by order of Spanish Gov't
VA 30 Aug. 1806, p. 2

Died Dec. 21st, MR. JOHN LESSLIE of Richmond
RE 24 Dec. 1818, p. 3; VP 23 Dec., p. 2, says age 46

Died Dec. 19th at Rocketts, CAPT. JOHN LESTER, born in Saul, Surry, England in 1748
RE 22 Dec. 1804, p. 3; VGGA 22 Dec., p. 3

Died yesterday, JOHN LeTELLIER, late Keeper of the City Poor and Workhouse
RC 17 May 1819, p. 3

Died, MR. EZEKIEL LEVY, at his mansion house near Farnham Church in Richmond Co.,
on 11th Inst., a merchant at that place
VA 28 Dec. 1812, p. 3

Died on 28th Jan. in Farnham, Richmond Co., age 32, MRS. FANNY LEVY, consort of
Mr. Ezekiel Levy
VA 21 Feb. 1800, p. 3

Died a few days age 14 yr. old son of Mr. Thomas Lewis, near Reading, Pa. He
swallowed a bee and was stung and died in 15 min.
VA 25 Nov. 1800, p. 3

Died yesterday, MR. BENJAMIN LEWIS of this city
VGGA 19 Sept. 1800, p. 3

Died yesterday at his seat near this city, MR. CHARLES LEWIS
VGRMA 22 Aug. 1793, p. 3

Died at Bellefonte, Pa., DAVID LEWIS, age 30
VPRDMA 28 July 1820, p. 2

Died on 13th Inst., at his seat near Richmond, MR. FRANCIS LEWIS of Henrico
VA 21 Nov. 1800, p. 3

Died Feb. 15th, age 76, MRS. JANE LEWIS, widow of Col. Robert Lewis, at her seat,
The Byrd, in Goochland Co.
RE 21 Feb. 1818, p. 3; VP 20 Feb., p. 3

Died, MISS JANE ELIZABETH LEWIS, on 28th Ult., at seat of her father, Capt. Howel
Lewis, North Garden, Albemarle Co., age 19
RE 12 July 1811, p. 3

Died, JOHN LEWIS, Esq. of Spotsylvania, one of first lawyers in American.(No death
date)
VG Oct. 4, 1780, p. 3

Died, JOSEPH W. LEWIS of Powhatan Co., on 14th Inst. at house of Mr. J. Shields
of this city, a student at Academy of L.H. Girardin
Visitor 17 Feb. 1810, p. 11

Died in this city on 4th Inst., MRS. MARTHA LEWIS, relict of late Benjamin Lewis.
Funeral by Rev. John Buchanan
VA 16 Jan. 1801, p. 3

Died in Fredericksburg on Fri. last (Apr. 5), MRS. MARY ANNE LEWIS, consort of
Mr. John Lewis
VA 12 April 1799, p. 3

Died Oct. 24th, age 17, MATILDA B. LEWIS, youngest daug. of Capt. H. Lewis of
Albemarle Co.
RE 2 Nov. 1819, p. 3

Died at his seat in Goochland Co. on 10th Inst., COL. ROBERT LEWIS, aged about 68
VA 26 Jan. 1803, p. 3

Died at Marrins Hill, near this city, yesterday, MISS SALLY LEWIS, dau. of Mr.
Charles Lewis
VGRMA 25 July 1793, p. 3

Died on 15th Inst., MAJ. THOMAS LEWIS of Greenbrier Co.
VA 26 Sept. 1804, p. 3

Died, THOMAS LEWIS, of Christiansburg, Montgomery Co., on May 16th, killed in a
duel with John McHenry
RE 31 May 1808, p. 2

Died yesterday at his seat in Henrico, COL. WILLIAM LEWIS
VGRMA 28 Nov. 1793, p. 3

Died Aug. 16th, WILLIAM LEWIS, Senior Counsellor of the Pa. Bar
RE 3 Sept. 1819, p. 3

Died, MRS. ANN LIGHTFOOT, spouse of Mr. William Lightfoot of Sandy Point, on 25th
Ult.
VA 1 June 1805, p. 4; VGGA 29 May, p. 3

Died yesterday in Richmond, MR. FRANCIS LIGHTFOOT, 2nd son of late William Lightfoot
of Sandy Point
VP 2 Nov. 1813, p. 3

Died in Richmond Oct. 28th, HENRY BENSKIN LIGHTFOOT, about 58, late of Island of Antigua
RE 19 Nov. 1805, p. 3

Died a few days ago at an advanced age at Teddington, MRS. LIGHTFOOT, relict of late Mr. Wm. Lightfoot
VGIC 22 Nov. 1793, p. 3

Died, MAJ. WILLIAM LIGHTFOOT, for many years a member of General Assembly, on 6th Inst., at his seat near Williamsburg
RE 10 March 1809, p. 3

Died, MR. WILLIAM LIGHTFOOT, Esq. of Sandy Point, on 17th Inst.
RE 25 July 1809, p. 3

Died, BENJAMIN LINCOLN, an officer in the Revolution, Collector of the Ports of Boston and Charleston, at Hingham, Mass. on 9th Inst.
VA 25 May 1810, p. 3

Died at Worcester, Mass., LEVI LINCOLN, formerly Attorney General of U.S., and later Lt. Gov. of Mass. (No death date)
RE 28 April 1820, p. 3

Died in Albemarle Co., WILLIAM LINDSAY, only son of Col. Lindsay.(No death date)
RE 19 Sept. 1820, p. 3

Died, MR. LIPPINCOTT, formerly of Phila. at Caracas, executed by the Spanish Gov't, in a rebellion
VA 30 Aug. 1806, p. 2

Died 21st Oct., AMBROSE LIPSCOMB of Hanover Co.
VGGA 29 Oct. 1794, p. 3

Died lately at Hanover, MRS. ELIZABETH LIPSCOMBE, wife of Mr. Ambrose Lipscombe
VGAA 14 May 1785, p. 2

Died Friday (Feb. 28), age 28, MRS. HARRIET LIPSCOMB, wife of Mr. John Lipscomb of Richmond
RE 5 March 1817, p. 3

Died, MRS. LUCY LIPSCOMB, a relict of Pemperton Lipscomb, of King William Co., age 57, on 17th Inst.
RE 20 Aug. 1811, p. 3

Died in Hanover Co., Fri. last (May 29), MRS. PEGGY LIPSCOMB, wife of Nathaniel C. Lipscomb, Esq.
RC 6 June 1795, p. 3; VGRMA 4 June, p. 3

Died at Mr. Joseph Brand's at Albemarle on 17th Inst., MR. ROSCOE LIPSCOMBE of this city, age 32
VA 22 June 1803, p. 3

Died, MR. LITCHFIELD, of Richmond.(No death date)
Visitor 27 Jan. 1810, p. 206

Died at New Orleans on 19th Ult., LT. WILLIAM LITHGOU of 2nd Regt., U.S. Infantry
Visitor 26 Aug. 1809, p. 118

Died in Boston July 29th, MR. EBENEZER LITTLE, of lockjaw
RC 14 Aug. 1818, p. 3

Died on 8th Inst. by bite of a mad dog, MR. EDMUND LITTLEPAGE of Newcastle
VGGA 24 Nov. 1790, p. 3

Died, ISAAC BURNLEY LITTLEPAGE, on 3rd Inst., at his seat in King William Co.,
age 23
RE 13 Jan. 1814, p. 3

Died in Fredericksburg on Mon. last (July 19), GEN. LEWIS LITTLEPAGE, age 40
VGGA 24 July 1802, p. 2

Died, MR. JOHN LOCKHEART, on Sept. 18th, in Richmond, age 39. He was born in Antrim
Ireland Nov. 17, 1774. Leaves widow and one son
RC 22 Sept. 1813, p. 3

Died on Sat. last (April 27) at his seat in Powhatan Co., MR. EDMOND LOCKWOOD
VA 3 May 1799, p. 3

Died in Richmond yesterday, MR. H.C. LOFTIN, age 24
RE 7 June 1815, p. 3; VA 7 June, p. 3, says Herbert C.; VA 10 June, p. 3, says
he served with a Petersburg Company during the war

Died Thurs. last (July 3) at his seat in Powhatan Co., MR. CHARLES LOGAN
VGRMA 10 July 1794, p. 3

Died in Phila. Sept. 25th, MR. JAMES LOGAN, an aged inhabitant, and son of James
Logan, one of first settlers of that state
VA 1 Oct. 1803, p. 3

Died, MRS. MARY LOGAN, consort of Mr. Logan of this city on Wed. last (March 8)
Visitor 11 March 1809, p. 23

Died Oct. 15th in Chesterfield Co., age 72, WILLIAM LOGWOOD
RE 26 Oct. 1819, p. 3

Died, MR. JOHN LOMAX of Alexandria, for many years a noted tavernkeeper of that
town.(No death date)
VGWA 1 Feb. 1787, p. 3

Died at Fredericksburg on 29th May, THOMAS LUNSFORD LOMAX, Esq., age 25
RE 7 June 1805, p. 3

Died on Sun. (July 14), MISS MARY LONG
RC 19 July 1816, p. 3

Died July 15th, at his res. in Henrico Co., MR. ROBINSON LORD, age 55, for many
years Sergeant at Arms for the Senate of Va.
RE 23 July 1819, p. 3

Died in Halifax Co., Feb. 13th, ALLEN LOVE, Attorney at Law, leaving wife and 1
child
RE 22 Feb. 1817, p. 3

Died at his res. in Northumberland Co. on 3rd Inst., REV. SAMUEL LOW, Minister of
Prot. Episcopal Church
RE 16 July 1814, p. 3

Died at Raleigh, N.C., Dec. 21st, ALEXANDER LUCAS, Senior Editor of the Minerva,
age 33
VPRDMA 27 Dec. 1820, p. 3

Died, LT. LUDLOW. (No death date)
RE 31 Aug. 1813, p. 2

Died, REV. THOMAS W. LUMPKIN, on 6th Inst., at Charlottesville
VA 15 Sept. 1809, p. 3

Died, JAMES LYLE, on Sun. last (26 Jan.) an inhabitant of Manchester, age 88
VP 28 Jan. 1812, p. 3

Died on the 29th Ult., JAMES LYLE, Jr. Esq., of Manchester
VA 6 Aug. 1806, p. 3; VGGA 2 Aug., p. 3

Died on Wed. last (July 18), MRS. FRANCES LYNCH, relict of Mr. James Head Lynch,
dec'd
VGGA 21 July 1804, p. 2

Died on Wed. last (Oct. 17) in the bloom of youth, MR. HASTINGS LYNCH of this city
VGGA 20 Oct. 1804, p. 2

Died on 17th Ut., DR. JAMES LYNCH, Physician and Director General of all military
militia hospitals in S.C., age 72
Visitor, 18 Nov. 1809, p. 166

Died, DR. JOHN LYNCH, in Lynchburg, on 5th Inst.
Visitor 17 Feb. 1810, p. 11

Died lately, COL. GEORGE LYNE in King & Queen Co.
VGAA 31 Jan 1784, p. 3

Died Tues. last (Jan. 15) JOHN LYNE, Esq. of this city, old and respected citizen
VA 18 Jan 1799, p. 3

Died, COL. WILLIAM LYNE, age 71, on 10th Inst., on way to his seat in King & Queen Co.
RE   27 Sept. 1808, p. 3

Died last night, MR. LYON of Alexandria
VGGA   20 Sept. 1797, p. 3

Died, MRS. LYON, on Wed. (Feb. 7), wife of Mr. Jacob Lyon of this city, left husband and 4 small children
VA   9 Feb. 1810, p. 3

Died, Aug. 21st, MRS. NANCY LYON, wife of Mr. Jacob Lyon, merchant, of Richmond
RC   24 Aug. 1814, p. 3

Died April 1st. at Studley, Hanover Co., JOHN LYONS, age 58
RC   8 April 1819, p. 3

Died Thurs. (March 3) at Sutdley, in Hanover Co., MRS. JUDITH LYONS, wife of Judge Lyons
VA   9 March 1803, p. 3; VGGA   9 March (says age 63 and wife of Judge Peter Lyons)

Died in this city on Sun. last (Dec. 21) PETER LYONS, JR., Esq.
VGGA   24 Dec. 1794, p. 3; VGRMA   22 Dec.

Died, PEYTON LYONS, President of the Court of Appeals, on 30th Ult. at his seat in Hanover Co., age 75
RE   4 Aug. 1809, p. 3; VA   4 Aug., p. 3, says PETER LYONS; VGGA   4 Aug., p. 3, says Peter; Visitor   12 Aug. 1809, p. 110, says Peter

Died on 6th in Petersburg, MR. JOHN MABIN, saddler
VA   18 Feb. 1800, p. 3

Died, MR. JAMES MABON, formerly Captain in American Army. (No death date)
VGWA   28 Aug. 1794, p. 2; VGAA   28 Aug., 1784, says he died Aug. 26)

Died on Sat. (April 11), MR. ROBERT MACARTNEY, of this city, merchant
VGGA   15 April 1795, p. 2; VGRC   14 April, p. 2

Died, FRANCIS MACAULEY, age 19, at York Town on Sept. 30th
RE   22 Oct. 1811, p. 3; VP   22 Oct., p. 2

Died on 3rd Inst. at Norfolk, MR. PATRICK MACAULEY
VICGA   13 Jan. 1790, p. 3

Died April 16th, MRS. JULIA MACLIN, consort of Maj. Thomas Maclin of Brunswick Co.
RE   24 April 1818, p. 3

Died, at Wakefield in New Hampshire on 4th Inst., MR. ROBERT MACLIN, baker, formerly of Portsmouth, age 115
VGWA   March 29, 1787, p. 2

Died, MR. JOHN H. MACOMB, late a merchant of this city, at Falmouth, on British Packet, Princess Charlotte
RE 29 Jan. 1811, p. 3

Died on Sept. 18th, MRS. HANNAH MACON, spouse of William H. Macon of Mount Prospect, New Kent Co.
VP 28 Sept. 1813, p. 3

Died lately, MR. JOHN MACON of Cumberland Co., one of Representative of that County in the General Assembly
VGGA 27 Nov. 1793, p. 3

Died, CAPT. WILLIAM MACON, age 88, on 25th Ult., at his seat in Hanover
RE 3 Dec. 1813, p. 3; VP 26 Nov., p. 3

Died on Oct. 14th at Paris, Bourbon Co., Ky., GEORGE MADISON, Gov. of Kentucky
RC 25 Oct. 1816, p. 3

Died, Bishop JAMES MADISON, in Williamsburg, on March 6th
RE 10 March 1812, p. 3; VA 12 March, p. 3

Died, MR. JOHN MADISON, on 23rd Ult., in Orange Co.
Visitor 8 April 1809, p. 38

Died, MISS PAMELA MADISON, on 24th Inst. at res. of her father in Louisa Co.
RE 29 Dec. 1810, p. 3

Died at Williamsburg on 14th Inst., MRS. SARAH MADISON, relict of late Bishop of Virginia
RE 26 Aug. 1815, p. 3

Died, WILLIAM F. MADISON, son of Gen. W. Madison of this state, and nephew of President of U.S., at Woodberry Forest in Madison Co., on ____ Ult.
RE 25 Aug. 1812, p. 4

Died Jan. 11th in New York, MARGARET MAGEE, age 60, a native of Ireland
VP 24 Jan. 1817, p. 3

Died in Washington March 31st, MRS. MARTHA MAGRUDER, consort of Patrick Magruder, and dau. of P. Goodwyn, a Congressman from Va.
VA 6 April 1816, p. 3

Died Tues. last (Feb. 1) near Williamsburg, MR. SAMUEL MAJOR, a printer
VGAA 5 Feb. 1785, p. 2

Died, MR. FRANCIS MALBONE, a Senator from Rhode Island, in Washington. (No death date)
Visitor 17 June 1809, p. 78

Died at Blair Park, Albemarle Co., on June 23rd, JAMES MALLOCH, a native of Scotland
VP 30 June 1818, p. 3; RE 3 July, p. 3, says "James Malcoce"

Died July 10th, MR. CHARLES MALLORY at his house on Eagle Cr., Scott Co., Ky., murdered by Perell Davenport
RC 16 Aug. 1819, p. 3

Died on Sat. (April 15) in Norfolk, CHARLES K. MALLORY, a native of Elizabeth City Co. He represented his county in the General Assembly a number of years. He served on the Council of State and as Lt. Gov. In 1813 he became Collector of Customs for Norfolk District
RE 21 April 1820, p. 3; RC 22 April, p. 3, says age 39

Died, MR. MINOR MALLORY of Nottoway Co., murdered by party unknown on 19th
RE 30 Jan. 1813, p. 3

Died in Hanover on 25th U.t, THOMAS MALLORY, age 91
VGGA 17 Jan. 1798, p. 3

Died on 19th Ult., at his seat in Essex Co., MR. ROBERT MANN, age 73
VGGA 6 Dec. 1797, p. 3

Died on Sun. last (Feb. 12), MR. MARCHAND of this city
VA 14 Feb. 1797, p. 3

Died on 13th Inst. at his seat near Manchester, COL. BERNARD MARKHAM
VA 21 July 1802, p. 3; VGGA 17 July, p. 3

Died Nov. 23rd at New Orleans, CAVETANO MARIOTINI, Manager of Olympic Circus
VP 22 Dec. 1817, p. 3

Died, MR. HENRY MARKS, age 83, on 10th Inst., formerly of Phila. but for years a resident of Richmond
RE 17 March 1809, p. 3; VA 17 March, p. 3; Visitor 11 March, p. 23

Died at Capt. James Winston's in Louisa, on the 23rd (Jan.), SAMUEL MARRS
VA 1 Feb. 1804, p. 3

Died, CHARLES MARSHALL, Esq., Attorney at Law, in Fauquier Co. (No death date)
VGGA 13 Aug. 1806, p. 3

Died, JOHN MARSHALL, Commander of Gun Vessel #20, age 22. (No death date)
Visitor 16 Dec. 1809, p. 182

Died, WILLIAM MARSHALL, whose funeral was last Wed. (May 29)
RE 1 June 1816, p. 3; VP 29 May, p. 3, says died yesterday, was Commonwealth Attorney for the city, Clerk of Federal District Court; VA 29 May, says died May 27th; RC 28 May, p. 3, says died yesterday

Died Friday last (April 16), MRS. MARSHALL, consort of William Marshall, Esq. of this city
VA 21 April 1802, p. 3; VGGA 24 April, p. 3 (says 17th and Mrs. Alice Marshall)

Died on 16th Inst. at house of John Anderson, Esq., in King William Co., DR. WILLIAM
MARSHALL of Gloucester Co.
VGRMA 21 May 1796, p. 3

Died, MRS. MARY MARSHALL, spouse of William Marshall, Esq., of this city, on Sun.
last (Jan. 5)
RE 7 Jan. 1812, p. 3; VP 7 Jan., p. 3

Died, BRIG.-GEN. JOSEPH MARTIN, in Henry Co., Dec. 18,1808, age 69
RE 10 Jan. 1809, p. 3

Died Jan. 18th, MAJ. THOMAS MARTIN, age 68
RE 11 Feb. 1819, p. 3

Died Friday (July 9), MRS. FANNY MARX, an old inhabitant of Richmond. Buried from
home of her son, Mr. Joseph Marx
RE 13 July 1819, p. 3; RC 9 July, p. 3

Died, GEN. ARMISTEAD T. MASON, on Feb. 6th, killed by John M'Carty in a duel near
Bladensburg, Md., leaving wife & child
RE 9 Feb. 1819, p. 3; RC 11 Feb., p. 3; VP 8 Feb., p. 3

Died at New Orleans on 19th Ult., LT. EDWARD MASON of 3rd Regt., U.S. Infantry
Visitor 26 Aug. 1809, p. 118

Died in New York, Jan. 9th, ELIZA MASON, age 20, from opium
VP 24 Jan. 1817, p. 3

Died in Rhode Island, Aug. 31st, JAMES BROWN MASON, late Congressman from R.I.
VP 13 Sept. 1819, p. 3

Died May 9th in Phila., GEN. STEVENS THOMSON MASON, Senator from Va. in Congress
VA 14 May 1803, p. 3; VGGA 18 May, p. 3(spells it Thompson)

Died on 18th Inst., THOMAS MASON, Esq., one of Delegates in the Assembly from Prince
William Co.
VA 30 Sept. 1800, p. 3

Died at his seat in this county (Wake Co., N.C.?) near the falls of the Neuse, on
7th Inst., DR. CARGILL MASSENBURG
Visitor 2 Dec. 1809, p. 174

Died fighting Indians in Tenn., Aug. 8th, GEORGE MATTHEWS
VGWA 2 Oct. 1788, p. 3

Died in Hanover Co., Sept. 20th, JAMES MATTHEWS, age 99, good husband, master &
parent
RE 1 Oct. 1819, p. 3

Died on 8th Inst., MR. RICHARD MATTHEWS of Louisa of a fall from a horse
VGRMA 15 April 1793, p. 3

Died, GEN. THOMAS MATHEWS, yesterday in Norfolk (20 Feb.)
VA 24 Feb. 1812, p. 3

Died on Wed. last (Dec. 4) EBENEZER MAULE, of this city
VA 6 Dec. 1799, p. 3

Died on 20th Ult. at his seat in Albemarle, DANIEL MAUPIN, who was born 25 March
1700, survived by his wife about same age and about 200 descendants
IC 22 Oct. 1788, p. 3

Died on 11th Inst., age 36, REV. WALKER MAURY, Rector of Elizabeth River Church &
Master of Norfolk Academy
VGIC 25 Oct. 1788, p. 3

Died June 4th at his res. in S.C. College at Columbia, S.C., DR. JONATHAN MAXEY,
Pres. of that institution for 16 years
RE 16 June 1820, p. 3; VPRDMA 17 June, p. 2, says MACY

Died Sun. last (Sept. 2), age 28, GEORGE MAYO, Esq., late a representative of
Chesterfield Co., in the legislature
Observatory 6 Sept. 1798, p. 2; VGGA 4 Sept., p. 2

Died a few days ago in Phila., JOHN MAYO
VGRMA 14 Oct. 1793, p. 3

Died on 18th Ult., DR. JOHN MAYO, son of Joseph Mayo of Powhatan Co., during his
attendance on the medical lectures in Phila.
VA 5 April 1799, p. 3; VGGA 5 April, p. 3

Died, COL. JOHN MAYO, on Wed. (May 27) builder of 1st bridge over James River at
Richmond
RE 29 May, 1818, p. 3; VP 29 May, p. 3, says died yesterday (May 28)

Died Oct. 2nd at his res. in Richmond, MAJ. JOSEPH MAYO, age 50
RC 3 Oct. 1820, p. 3; VPRDMA 3 Oct., p. 3

Died Oct. 13th in Richmond, MR. ALEXANDER M'BRIDE, upholsterer
RC 17 Oct. 1818, p. 3

Died in Richmond on Sat. last (Oct. 29), ARCHIBALD McCALL, Esq. at advanced age.
Lived most of life at Tappahannock, but last 5 in Richmond
RE 1 Nov. 1814, p. 3; VP 2 Nov., p. 3

Died, GEORGE McCARTY, age 22, 2nd son of MRS. Sarah McCarty of Fairfax Co. and
grandson of late venerable George Mason, in Williamsburg on Aug. 7th
RE 27 Sept. 1808, p. 3

Died this morning, MR. JOPSEH M'CAUGHEY, blacksmith, of this city
VGRMA 4 July 1795, p. 3

Died Tues. last (July 17) at Yorktown, MR. ALEXANDER M'CAULEY, a merchant of that town, leaves wife & child
Observatory 23 July 1798, p. 2; VGGA 24 July, p. 3

Died in Fluvanna Co., Sept. 14th, MR. WILLIAM M'CHESNEY, merchant, age 31, formerly of Philadelphia
RE 19 Oct. 1816, p. 3

Died Sat. last (June 9) a man named M'CLOUD, a native of north Scotland, by cutting his throat
VGWA 14 June 1787, p. 3

Died on Thurs. (June 29) MRS. McCLURG, wife of Dr. McClurg, in a carriage accident
VP 1 July 1815, p. 3

Died yesterday at res. of her son-in-law, James Smith, MRS. RACHEL M'CLURG, age 66
VP 29 Oct. 1817, p. 3

Died, WALTER M'CLURG, Esq., only son of Dr. James M'Clurg of this city, on 7th Inst. at Fincastle
VGGA 22 Aug. 1809, p. 3; Visitor 26 Aug., p. 118

Died, CAPT. ANDREW M'COMBE, on 16th Inst.
VA 25 Sept. 1805, p. 3

Died, MRS. EMILY McCRAW, wife of Samuel McCraw and 2nd aug. late Col. John Harvie
RE 29 March 1808, p. 3; Virginian 29 March, p. 3 (says Fri. last March 25)

Died on Friday (Dec. 19), MRS. EMILY FOWLER McCRAW, consort of Dr. Frederick McCraw of Richmond
RE 23 Dec. 1817, p. 3; VP 19 Dec., p. 3, says died Friday last (Dec. 12)

Died on 25th Ult., MRS. M'CRAW, wife of Samuel M'Craw, Esq.
VA 3 Oct. 1804, p. 3; VGGA 10 Oct., p. 2

Died in Richmond City on Thurs. last (July 8), MR. MILLER W. M'CRAW, merchant
VA 10 July 1802, p. 3

Died, MR. GEORGE M'CREDIE, merchant, of Manchester, on Sun. last (June 28)
VA 4 July 1807, p. 2

Died, JOHN M'CREDIE, a member of the fire brigade, shot accidentally by a sentinel
VA 6 Feb. 1807, p. 3; RE 6 Feb, p. 3, says "died last Wed" (Feb. 4); VGGA 7 Feb., p. 3

Died Feb. 5th, age 20, MRS. MARY W. McCULLOCH, wife of William H. McCulloch, res. in Amherst Co.
RE 18 Feb. 1819, p. 3

Died on last Sabbath (Sept. 27) REV. JOHN McCUE of Spotsylvania Co., leaves wife and children. Buried at Tinkling Spring
RE 2 Oct. 1818, p. 3

Died in Norfolk on Sat. last (before June 29) at the Marine Hospital, ROBERT MacDONAl one of the seamen wounded on the frigate Chesapeake
VA 4 July 1807, p. 3; RE 3 July, p. 2; VGGA 4 July, p. 1

Died on 11th Ult. in Burke Co., N.C., GEN. JSOEPH McDOWELL, late a Member of Congres: from that state
VA 25 Aug. 1801, p. 3

Died near Danville, Ky., Oct. 25th, COL. SAMUEL McDOWELL, age 85, an early settler of Ky. and Judge of District Court
RE 18 Nov. 1817, p. 3

Died in the Creek Country, COL. ALEXANDER M'GILLIVRAY, cebebrated Chief of that Nation and Ally of the U.S.
VGGA 30 May 1792, p. 3

Died, in Richmond on Sun. (Oct. 30) JOHN McHENRY (or M'ENERY), Esq., a native of Ireland
RE 1 Nov. 1814, p. 3; VP 2 Nov., p. 3, says M'ENERY; RC 1 Nov., p. 3

Died in Darien, Ga., MR. M'QUEEN M'INTOSH on March 26th, killed on street by Col. John L. Hopkins
VP 6 April 1819, p. 3

Died on Sunday last (April 29), MR. JOHN M'KEAND of this city.
VGGA 2 May 1792, p. 3

Died in Charlotte Co., June 25th, age 29, MRS. MARTHA P. M'KENNEY, spouse of William M'Kenney of that county.
RE 9 July 1819, p. 3

Died Friday last (May 31) in Manchester, DR. WILLIAM M'KENZIE of that town
VGRMA 3 June 1793, p. 3

Died at sea on July 1st, CAPT. JOHN McKOON of the Schooner Slinington. A native of Ronney, R.I., he had married a Virginian and resided here
RE 25 July 1817, p. 3

Died, MRS. M'LANE of this city on 8th Instant
Visitor 11 Feb. 1809, p. 7

Died on 7th Inst., in Powhatan Co., MRS. ELIZABETH M'LAURINE, relict of late Rev. Robert M'Laurine
VA 13 Aug. 1803, p. 3

Died June 14th, MISS HENRIETTA McLAURINE, only dau. of William LcMaurine of Powhatan Co.
RE 27 June 1820, p. 3

Died on 18th Inst., age 32, MR. JOHN M'LEAN, Printer, at Norfolk, a native of Glasgow
VGWA 28 May 1789, p. 3; VIC 27 May

Died in Xenia, Ohio, April 18th, MR. WILLIAM M'LELLAN, age 60. Struck by lightning
VP 30 May 1817, p. 3

Died Aug. 31st in New York City, CHRISTOPHER McPHERSON, 55, a man of color noted for
his eccentricities and acts of benevolence and charity
VP 8 Sept. 1817, p. 3

Died at Orono, Me., April 13th, MR. JAMES McPHETRES, age 28, drowned
VPRDMA 6 May 1820, p. 2

Died yesterday, MR. JAMES McQUEEN, funeral from his late res. at the Old Academy
RC 18 Oct. 1820, p. 3

Died, MR. E. M'QUILLAN on 30th Ult.
Visitor 7 Oct. 1809, p. 142

Died, REV. CHRISTOPHER McRAE of Powhatan Co. (No death date)
RE 31 Dec. 1808, p. 3

Died Oct. 18th, MR. CHRISTOPHER M'RAE
RC 19 Oct. 1818, p. 3

Died in Richmond City on 12th Inst., MRS. HARRIET M'RAE, wife of Alexander M'Rae, Esq.
VA 14 Aug. 1802, p. 3; VGGA 18 Aug., p. 3

Died on Aug. 7th, MRS. HYPATIA McRAE, late consort of Colin McRae of Manchester, and
dau. of Maj. John Harris, late of Powhatan Co.
RE 15 Aug. 1817, p. 3

Died in Richmond City, MR. JOHN M'RAE. (No death date)
VGGA 15 Oct. 1794, p. 2

Died, MAJ. JOHN M'RAE of Petersburg, yesterday
VA 23 June 1809, p. 3; Visitor, says died Mon. last (June 12), 17 June 1809, p. 78

Died on board ship Indian Queen, on passage from London to City Point, MRS. McRAE,
consort of Colin McRae of Manchester. (No death date)
VP 18 Oct. 1815, p. 3

Died, MR. PHILIP M'RAE, in this city, at a very advanced age
VGRMA 16 Oct. 1794, p. 3; VGRC 17 Oct.

Died, REV. ARCHIBALD M'ROBERT, on 8th Inst., at Providence in Prince Edward Co.
He was 71 on Sept. 20th last
VA 16 Oct. 1807, p. 3

Hanged in Charlottesville Friday last (Dec. 9) for the murder of Dr. James Hopkins
of Amherst Co., last April, LEWIS McWAINE
VA 14 Dec. 1803, p. 3

Died at his seat in Amelia Co., MAJ-GEN. EVERARD MEADE. (no death date)
VA 29 Sept. 1802, p. 3

Died on Sun. last (May 15) MR. ROBERT MEANS of this city
VGGA 17 May 1808, p. 3; Virginian 17 May, p. 3

Died fighting Indians in Tenn. Aug. 8th, JOHN MEDLOCK
VGWA 2 Oct. 1788, p. 3

Died, MR. ALEXANDER MELVIN of Georgetown on Aug. 21st, hunting accident
RC 28 Aug. 1818, p. 3

Died Wed. last (Oct. 30) in this city, JAMES MERCER, Esq., for many years a Judge
of the General Court
VGGA 6 Nov. 1793, p. 3

Died at Warm Springs, Bath Co., on Sept. 30th, COL. JOHN MERCER of Fredericksburg
RE 14 Oct. 1817, p. 3

Died Sept. 3rd at her seat in Hanover Co., MRS. ANNE L. MEREDITH, widow of Col.
Elisha Meredith, age 59
RE 11 Sept. 1816, p. 3

Died in Hanover Co., June 5th, MRS. ELIZABETH K. MERIDETH, wife of Dr. R. Merideth,
age 19, leaving husband and an infant
RE 20 June 1817, p. 3

Died, COL. SAMUEL MEREDITH, on 22nd Ult., at his seat in Amherst Co., age 77
RE 19 Jan. 1809, p. 2; VA 13 Jan., p. 3, "was soldier in Revolution"

Died, CAPT. WILLIAM MEREDITH, an old inhabitant of Richmond, at home of Thomas
Pulling in this city, on March 4th
RE 6 March 1812, p. 3

Died at Sandfield, April 24th, MRS. ELIZABETH MERRILL, age 100 (from Hampshire,
Mass., newspaper)
VP 2 May 1817, p. 3

Died Sat. (Nov. 11) in Harrisburg, Pa., MR. BARNEY MERKLE, painter, age 65. In
Revolution he served on the Hyder Ally at capture of Gen. Monk
RC 18 Nov. 1820, p. 3

Died Wed. last (Feb. 2) in this city, CAPT. WILLIAM MESTON of Phila.
VGAA Feb. 5, 1785, p. 2

Died in Buckingham Co., Aug. 11th, MRS. JUDITH ANDERSON MICHAUX, wife of Mr. Joseph
Michaux, leaving husband and several small children
RE 15 Aug. 1817, p. 3

Died at Lancaster, Pa. on 20th Ult., age 57, GEN. THOMAS MIFFLIN, late Gov. of
that state
VA 4 Feb. 1800, p. 3; VGGA 31 Jan., p. 3

Died Aug. 5th, MRS. ANN MILLER, consort of Mr. William Miller of Goochland, leaving husband & 6 children
VA 14 Aug. 1802, p. 3

Died Thurs. last (July 19), MR. DAVID MILLER, in Williamsburg
Observatory 23 July 1798, p. 2; VGGA 24 July, p. 3

Died, DR. EDWARD MILLER, one of the Editors of The Medical Repository, in New York, on 17th Inst.
RE 31 March 1812, p. 3

Died in Ky., at res. of Mrs. Scott, relict of late Gen. Charles Scott, on July 16th, MRS. ELIZA L. MILLER, wife to Mr. Maurice L. Miller, who moved from Va. last autumn. Infant child died 11 days before.
VP 23 Aug. 1816, p. 3

Died at Wakefield, his res. in Goochland Co., on Feb. 1st, COL. HEATH J. MILLER, age 57
RE 14 Feb. 1818, p. 3

Died lately, MR. HENRY MILLER of Bethlehem in Northampton Co., Pa., formerly an eminent printer of Phila., age 80
VGAA May 11, 1782, p. 3

Died, MRS. HESTER MILLER of this city, on Mon. last (April 22) at an advanced age
VA 25 April 1811, p. 3

Died near New Haven, Conn., MR. JOEL B. MILLER, son of Hezekiah Miller, age 31, while hunting, leaves wife and 2 small children
RC 25 Jan. 1820, p. 3

Died, JOHN MILLER, Esq., on 1st Inst. in Northumberland Co. He was Member of the Legislature last session
VA 19 Sept. 1807, p. 2

Died Oct. 23rd in Baltimore, age 58, MRS. PHEBE MILLER, wife of Peter Miller of Richmond, Va.
VP 30 Oct. 1818, p. 3

Died a few weeks ago, ROBERT MILLER of Smithfield, Capt. of Schooner "Betsy" of drowning in James River
VA 15 Jan. 1803, p. 3

Died in LaValle, his res. in Goochland Co., April 27th, CAPT. THOMAS MILLER, age 66, leaving wife and children
RE 7 May 1819, p. 3; VP 6 May, p. 3, says died April 26th

Died on 25th Ult. at his res. in Goochland Co., age 66, MR. WILLIAM HEATH MILLER, leaving widow, dau. with 4 children, and 2 orphan grandaughters
RE 10 June 1815, p. 3

Died yesterday (date unknown), MR. JOSEPH MILLET, Jr. son of Capt. Joseph Millet of Salem, Mass., age 24
RC 28 Aug. 1819, p. 3

Died, in Mountjoy in Township, Lancaster Co., Pa., Brig-Gen. BENJAMIN MILLS
VA 26 Sept. 1804, p. 3

Died on Sat. (Sept. 25) MR. MARTIN MIMMS, age 66. A native of Goochland Co.,
he served in the Revolution in the first volunteer company raised.
RE 28 Sept. 1819, p. 3; RC 29 Sept., p. 3

Died, MRS. SARAH MINGE, consort of John Minge of Weanoak, Charles City Co., on
27th Feb.
VP 10 March 1812, p. 3

Died June 3rd, MRS. MINIS the elder, age 74, drowned near Santee, S.C.
RC 19 June 1819, p. 3

Died on 25th Ult. in Louisa Co., COL. GARRITT MINOR
VGGA 12 July 1799, p. 3

Died in Richmond June 8th, GEN. JOHN MINOR of Fredericksburg
RE 12 June 1816, p. 3; VP 12 June, p. 3, says died June 3rd; VA 12 June, p. 3,
says died Sat. last (June 8); RC 11 June, p. 3, says died Sat. (June 8)

Died in Richmond on Wed. last (Oct. 15), MR. WILLIAM MINOR
VGRC 17 Oct. 1794, p. 3

Died on 4th Inst., MR. ANDREW MITCHELL of New Castle
VGGA 17 Dec. 1794, p. 3; VGRMA 15 Dec.

Died, MRS. ANN MITCHELL, on Thurs. last (June 10), age 23, at Mr. J. Cunliffe's
in Chesterfield Co., wife of Mr. Wm. Mitchell of Richmond
VA 14 June 1813, p. 3

Died, MRS. JUDITH MITCHELL, wife of Capt. Robert Mitchell, of this city on 24th
Inst., age 63
VA 25 March 1808, p. 3

Died, CAPT. ROBERT MITCHELL, in this city, on Tues. last (Jan. 1)
RE 3 Jan. 1811, p. 3; VP 5 Jan., p. 3

Died at Sweet Springs Aug. 25th, MR. THOMAS MITCHELL of Louisa Co., age 79. A
native of Scotland, he had lived in Va. for the past 50 years.
VP 5 Sept. 1816, p. 3; VP 6 Sept., says age 70

Died last Monday (Nov. 10) in this city, MR. MOFFAT, merchant, late from Ireland
VGIC 15 Nov. 1783, p. 3

Died, HENRY MOLLESTON, Governor-elect of Del. (No death date)
RE 26 Nov. 1819, p. 3

Died on 16th Inst. at dwelling of Mrs. Moore in Prince Edward Co., MR. THOMAS MOLLO
Attorney at Law, and a member of General Assembly
VGRMA 27 Aug. 1795, p. 3

Died at Yorktown Oct. 29th, MR. JOSEPH MONNET
RC 2 Nov. 1820, p. 2

Died on Feb. 18th at Col. Gordon's in Northumberland, SARAH MONROE, wife of Joseph
J. Monroe, Attorney at Law in Westmoreland
Examiner 12 March 1803, p. 3

Died, MR. WILLIAM MONROE, merchant of Boston, in Richmond on Sun. last (May 30)
RE 1 June 1813, p. 3; VA 3 June, p. 3; VP 1 June, p. 3, says left widow and 3
children

Died Sept. 9th, age 58, MRS. ELIZABETH POPE MOODY, wife of Capt. John Moody, late
of Richmond, in Cartersville
RE 26 Sept. 1820, p. 3; RC 22 Sept., p. 3, says leaves husband & dau.

Died at Lexington, Ky., MRS. HARRIET MOODY, wife of Mr. Burgess S. Moody, and dau.
of late David Corey of Middlesex Co., Va.
VP 21 Sept. 1816, p. 3

Died, MR. PHILIP MOODY, at Williamsburg, Proprietor of Mail Stages from Hampton
to Richmond, and for many years keeper of the Raleigh Tavern in Williamsburg.
(No death date)
VA 10 Oct. 1807, p. 3

Died, MASTER ROBERT MOODY, age 15, only son of John Moody, a Revolutionary Soldier,
in this city, Sat. week last (either Sept. 5 or Aug. 29)
RE 8 Sept. 1812, p. 3

Died in vicinity of Burton's Spring on Mon. last (Sept. 4) MR. ARCHIBALD MOORE,
Member of Richmond Light Infantry Blues
Visitor 9 Sept. 1809, p.127

Died, on Sat. last (March 5), MR. CURTIS R. MOORE, late keeper of the Washington
Tavern in Richmond
RE 9 March 1814, p. 3

Died, GEN. DANIEL MORGAN. (No death date)
VGGA 17 July 1802, p. 3

Died, MRS. SARAH MORGAN, in Petersburg, on Tues. (Dec. 26)
Visitor 30 Dec. 1809, p. 190

Died, MRS. HARDENIA MORRIS, age 18, in Richmond, wife of James M. Morris of
Hanover Co. (No death date)
RE 22 Nov. 1811, p. 3

Died, JOHN MOSBY MORRIS, on Oct. 1, son of Austin Morris, late of Hanover Co.
RE 6 Oct. 1812, p. 3

Died on 30th July, MRS. MARY MORRIS, spouse of Mr. John Morris of Cumberland Co.
VA 16 Aug. 1806, p. 3

Died on Thurs. last (before May 15) ROBERT MORRIS, Esq. (Rev. War. Financier)
VGGA 17 May 1806, p. 3

Died Sept. 17th at house of Mr. John West in Louisa Co., MR. WILLIAM O. MORRIS,
eldest son of Col. Richard Morris of Louisa Co.
RE 28 Sept. 1819, p. 3

Died April 26th at his seat on Taylors Creek in Hanover Co., MR. WILLIAM MORRIS, SR.,
age 80
RE 2 May 1820, p. 3

Died in Goochland Co., Nov. 14th, MR. BECKWITH B. MORRISON of Richmond
RC 16 Dec. 1816, p. 3

Died, MR. HENRY MORRISS, aged inhabitant of Gloucester, on 22nd Ult.
RE 9 Oct. 1810, p. 3

Died between 1st & 3rd of Oct., MRS. MATILDA MORRISS and SAMUEL C. MORRISS, wife
and son of Mr. Christopher Morriss of Gloucester Co.
RE 12 Nov. 1819, p. 3

Died March 17th, CAPT. JOHN MORTON of Charlotte Co., leaving wife and 8 children
RE 3 April 1818, p. 3

Died at his seat in Charlotte Co., MR. QUIN MORTON, age 55, on Tues. (Feb. 12)
VA 16 Feb. 1805, p. 3

Died at his res. on Staunton River in Charlotte Co., Nov. 29th., COL. WILLIAM MORTON
age 78, a soldier in the Revolution
RE 21 Dec. 1820, p. 3

Died in Powhatan Co., on 1st Inst., MR. JACOB MOSBY
VA 9 Oct. 1802, p. 3

Died JOSEPH MOSBY, Esq., in Powhatan on March 19th
VA 5 April 1808, p. 3

Died, COL. LITTLEBERRY MOSBY, age 80, on 14th Inst., at his seat in Powhatan Co.
VA 20 Jan. 1809, p. 3

Died, MRS. MARY MOSBY, wife of Capt. Benjamin Mosby of this city, on 5th Inst.,
at White Sulfur Springs, Greenbrier Co.
VA 21 Oct. 1813, p. 3

Died on 27th Ult. COL. EDWARD H. MOSELEY, of Princess Anne Co., age 66, for years
a magistrate and representative of his co. and officer of customs in lower district
of James River
VGWA Nov. 16, 1782, p. 3

Died, MR. PETER MOSELEY, of this city, on Mon. last (Jan. 11)
RE 14 Jan. 1813, p. 3

Died yesterday in Manchester at res. of Mr. Allen McRae, MRS. SUSANNA MOSELEY
RC 1 June 1820, p. 3

Died, GEN. WILLIAM MOSELEY, Treasurer of the Commonwealth, at Fincastle. (No death date)
VA 7 Oct. 1808, p. 3; RE 7 Oct., p. 3 (says died on 28th Ult.); VGGA 11 Oct., p. 3

Died, MAJ. HENRY MOSS, on June 14th, of Pittsylvania Co., age 72, at res. of Col. Wm. Bently. He served in Revolution and for several years past was Sergeant at Arms of HOuse of Delegates
RE 6 July 1810, p. 3

Died on Dec. 14th, CAPT. JOHN MOSS of Richmond, age 64
VP 21 Dec. 1813, p. 3

Died on Thurs. last (May 15) MRS. MOSS, consort of Mr. Sheldon Moss of this city
VGGA 20 May 1800, p. 3

Died, COL. ALEXANDER MOULTRIE, age 57, on the 28th Ult., a Soldier of the Revolution
VA 15 Aug. 1807, p. 2

Died on Sept. 27th, MAJ.-GEN. WILLIAM MOULTRIE, in Charleston, S.C.
VA 9 Oct. 1805, p. 3

Died, JOSEPH MOXLEY, formerly a Midshipman in U.S. Navy. Testified at trial of Aaron Burr, for U.S. Took overdose of Laudanum on Wed. last (Oct. 21)
VGGA 24 Oct. 1807, p. 3

Died, GEN. MUHLENBERG, Collector of the Port of Philadelphia. (No death date)
RE 7 Oct. 1807, p. 3

Died July 18th at Belle Air, res. of Jonathan Swift, REV. JAMES MUIR, Sr., Pastor of First Presbyterian Church in Alexandria, Va.
VPRDMA 14 Aug. 1820, p. 3

Died at Rehoboth, MRS. HANNAH MUNRO, age 98, relict of late John Munro and grandau. of the celebrated Col. Church
Visitor 12 Aug. 1809, p. 110

Died on Sun. last (Aug. 14) MR. MATTHEW MURCHIE of Manchester
VGRMA 17 Aug. 1796, p. 3

Died on Feb. 11th, age 81, MRS. ANNE MURRAY of Petersburg
VA 18 Feb. 1800, p. 3

Died, HON. JOHN MURRAY, EARL OF DUNMORE, Gov. of Va. previous to the Revolution, at Ramsgate, England. (No death date)
Visitor 1 July, 1809, p. 86

Died Sun. last (March 2) MR. ROBERT MURRAY, merchant, for several years a res. of
Manchester
VGWA 6 March 1788, p. 3

Died on 11th Inst. at his seat in Dorchester Co., Md., WILLIAM VANS MURRAY, Esq.,
late Minister of the U.S. at the Hague, and Minister Plenipotentiary to the
French Republic
VA 24 Dec. 1803, p. 3

Died, MRS. JANE MUSE, wife of Lawrence Muse at Tappahannock, on 17th Inst.
RE 24 Nov. 1807, p. 3

Died, COL. GEORGE MUTER on 9th Inst., at Thomas Todd's in Woodford Co., Ky.,
former Chief Justice of Kentucky
VA 27 May 1811, p. 3

Died on 18th Inst., At Baltimore, MRS. MUTTER, wife of John Mutter, Esq., merchant,
at Richmond
RE 22 Oct. 1814, p. 3

Died in this city Tues. last (May 27) MR. JOSEPH MYERS, SR.
VA 29 May 1801, p. 3

Died in Manchester on Wed. (Sept. 10), age 60, MR. JOSEPH M. MYERS
VP 12 Sept. 1817, p. 3

Died in Richmond City on Mon. last (Feb. 24), MR. LEWIS MYERS
VA 28 Feb. 1800, p. 3

Died in New York on 4th Inst., MR. SAMPSON MYERS, merchant, of this city
VA 13 Aug. 1803, p. 3

Died in Petersburg on Mon. last (Oct. 12) MRS. SARAH MYERS, consort of Mr. Samuel
Myers, merchant of that place
VGRMA 15 Oct. 1795, p. 2

Died on 11th Inst. at Columbia, age 64, CAPT. JOHN NAPIER of Fluvanna. He had been
a magistrate of the co. and a member of the legislature
VA 18 Feb. 1806, p. 3; RE 18 Feb., p. 3

Died, MRS. LUCY NELSON, age 57, wife of late Col. William Nelson of King William Co.
on 13th Inst.
RE 20 April 1810, p. 3

Died in Williamsburg July 9th, age 40, Chancellor ROBERT NELSON
RE 14 July 1818, p. 3

Died on Aug. 4th, ROBERT NELSON of Malvern Hills, age 66, was last of 5 bros.,
one being Gov. Nelson
RE 11 Aug. 1818, p. 3

Died, GEN. THOMAS NELSON, at his seat in Hanover, on Jan. 4. He served in House
of Burgesses and in U.S. Congress
VGWA 15 Jan. 1789, p. 3

Died lately, at his seat in York, Brig. Gen. William Nelson, son of late Gen.
Thomas Nelson, age 38
VA 16 Jan. 1801, p. 3

Died at his seat in King William Co., on 25th Ult., COL. WILLIAM NELSON, age 61
VGGA 1 Dec. 1807, p. 3

Died, WILLIAM NELSON, one of the Judges of the General Court of this state, in
Williamsburg, on the 8th, age 54
RE 16 March 1813, p. 3; VA 18 March, p. 3

Died on June 18th, age 71, the Most Rev. LEONARD NEALE, Archbishop of Baltimore
RE 27 June 1817, p. 3

Died in the south of Ireland, where she had gone for her health, MISS ELIZA NEILSON,
sister of Messrs. Robert and Hall Neilson of this city.(No death date)
RE 9 Aug. 1815, p. 3

Died in Poughkeepsie, N.Y. on Aug. 29th, MR. SAMUEL NEILSON, a native of Ireland,
lately from that country
VA 28 Sept. 1803, p. 3

Died in Charleston, S.C., JOHN NEURVILLE, Esq., Commissioner of the Continental
Loan Office of that state
VA 22 Aug. 1804, p. 3

Died, JOHN NEWELL, JR. of Havana. A native of Md., and lately res. of Norfolk.
(No death date)
RE 23 Jan. 1812, p. 4

Died Tues. last (Feb. 4) at seat of Wm. Alexander, Esq., near this city, on way
from Balt. to Charleston, MR. LEWIS NEWHOUSE, a native of Sweden and had served
in Swiss Guards under Louis XVI
VGRMA 10 Feb. 1794, p. 2

Died lately at Northampton Ferry, MR. THOMAS NEWMAN, merchant of Yorktown
VGGA 28 Feb. 1798, p. 3

Died at Norfolk on 13th Inst., THOMAS NEWTON, SR., Esq., age 82
VGGA 24 Dec. 1794, p. 3; VGRMA 22 Dec.

Died Sept. 11th in Norfolk, THOMAS NEWTON, SR., Collector of the Port of Norfolk
VA 16 Sept. 1807, p. 3

Died on Oct. 15th in Laurens Distr., S.C., MR. SOLOMON NIBLETT, age 143. Born in England, he came to Md. at age 19.
RE 11 Nov. 1815, p. 3

Died, DR. JAMES NIBLOCK, of Brunswick Co., a native of Ireland, shot to death by person unknown, on July 5th
RE 20 July 1810, p. 3

Died on Wed. last (April 27), MR. WILLIAM NICE, for years respectable inhabitant of this city
VA 29 April 1808, p. 3

Died on 25th July in Lexington, Va., COL. GEORGE NICHOLAS
VA 30 Aug. 1799, p. 3; VF 17 Aug., p. 3, says "in Kentucky"; VGGA 20 Aug., p. 3, says "Kentucky"

Died, GEORGE W. NICHOLAS of Va. on 3rd Inst., at New York, age 16, Midshipman on U.S. Frigate Essex
RE 12 Sept. 1809, p. 3; Visitor 7 Oct., p. 142

Died, JOHN NICHOLAS, the elder, on 4th Nov. age 75, at his seat on James River in Buckingham Co.
VGGA 11 Nov. 1795, p. 3; VGRMA 12 Nov., p. 3

Died Sunday (Feb. 22), COL. JOHN NICHOLAS, of Dinwiddie Co.
VP 26 Feb. 1818, p. 3

Died Jan. 1st at his res. in Geneva, N.Y., JOHN NICHOLAS, for many years a congressman from Va.
RE 15 Jan. 1820, p. 3; RC 18 Jan., p. 3, says, age 56

Died Nov. 8th at Slate River in Buckingham Co., MRS. LOUISA H. NICHOLAS, consort of Capt. John Nicholas, late of Charlottesville, leaving husband and children
VP 18 Nov. 1816, p. 3

Died, MRS. NICHOLAS, consort of Philip Norborne Nicholas of Richmond, on Wed. (April 26)
RE 28 April 1820, p. 3; RC 28 April, p. 3, says MRS. MARY NICHOLAS; VPRDMA 28 April, p. 3

Died, ROBERT C. NICHOLAS of Hanover Co., was interred last Sunday in church yard in Richmond. (No death date). Date of burial Sept. 10
VG Sept. 13, 1780, p. 3

Died, MISS SALLY NICHOLAS, at Maj. Butler's in Surry Co., on 24th Ult.
RE 13 July 1810, p. 3

Died Oct. 10th at res. of Mr. Thomas J. Randolph in Albemarle Co., WILSON C. NICHOLA late Gov. of Va.
RC 17 Oct. 1820, p. 3; VRPDMA 16 Oct., p. 3

Died at New Market, Caroline Co., Oct. 11th, MRS. CAROLINE NICHOLSON, age 57
VP 28 Oct. 1815, p. 3

Died in New York City Sun. last (date ?), COMM. JAMES NICHOLSON, age 69
VA 12 Sept. 1804, p. 3

Died in Manchester, MR. ANDREW NICHOLSON, of house of Nicholson & Heth of that
place. (No death date)
VA 24 Aug. 1810, p. 3

Died lately on his passage to Maddra, GEORGE NICHOLSON, Esq. of this city
VGGA 19 June 1802, p. 3

Died on the 17th (Feb.) MR. HENRY NICOLSON of Williamsburg
VGGA 28 Feb. 1798, p. 3

Died yesterday, MRS. NICOLSON, consort of Mr. William Nicolson
VA 25 June 1799, p. 3; VGGA 25 June, p.3, says Mon. last, MRS. MARTHA NICOLSON

Died last Friday (July 14) MR. ROBERT NICOLSON, an old citizen of Williamsburg
VGGA 19 July 1797, p. 2

Died on Wed. last (Aug. 9) MR. ROBERT NICOLSON of Petersburg
Visitor 12 Aug. 1809, p. 110

Died on 10th Inst., MR. THOMAS NICOLSON, printer, of this city
RE 18 Nov. 1808, p. 3; VGGA 15 Nov., p. 3

Died lately on his passage from Maddra, MR. WILLIAM NICOLSON of this city
VGGA 19 June 1802, p. 3

Died on Thurs. last (June 14) MR. WILLIAM NIMMO of this city
VGGA 16 June 1804, p. 2

Died, MR. ROBERT NISBET, age 66, on 14th Inst., a native of Scotland and res. of
Richmond
VA 20 Aug. 1812, p. 3

Died at Norfolk, age 61, COL. JOHN NIVISON, late recorded of that borough and
eminent lawyer. (No death date)
RE 26 May 1820, p. 3

Died Dec. 3rd, ROBERT S. NIXON, age 38.
RE 8 Dec. 1818, p. 3; VP 7 Dec., p. 3

Died yesterday at house of Capt. Otis on Mayo's Bridge, MR. SOLOMON NORTON, age 17
RC 14 Oct. 1820, p. 3

Died Sept. 27, MR. THOMAS NORVELL of Richmond, age 45
RE 30 Sept., 1817, p. 3; VP 29 Sept., p. 3

Died on 22nd Nov., MR. WILLIAM NORVELL of James City Co., age 77
VGGA 1 Dec. 1802, p. 2 (also 27 Nov., p. 3)

Died in George Town on the 5th Inst., JAMES OAXLEY, Esq., Collector of that port
VGGA 10 May 1806, p. 3

Died, MRS. ELIZA O'CONNOR, consort of Mr. James O'Connor, Editor of the Norfolk
Herald, on 12th Inst., age 37
VA 20 June 1811, p. 3

Died, MR. JAMES O'CONNOR, co-editor of the Norfolk Herald, on July 3rd, age 60
VP 9 July 1819, p. 3

Died in Baltimore Dec. 18th, CAPT. JOHN OERSTEDT, a native of Sweden, about 40
years old
VP 30 Dec. 1817, p. 3

Died in Chester-town on Sat. last (before Oct. 1) the REV. JOHN COUSINS OGDEN
VA 7 Oct. 1800, p. 3

Died in Annapolis on 6th Inst., BENJAMIN OGLE, Esq. late Gov. of Maryland, age 61
Visitor 29 July 1809, p. 102

Died at King George Court House Sept. 10th, CAPT. DANIEL OLINSTED, late of Albany,
N.Y., age 26
VP 18 Sept. 1817, p. 3

Died Dec. 20th, MR. BENJAMIN OLIVER, SR. of Hanover Co., age 89
RE 24 Dec. 1818, p. 3; VP 25 Dec., p. 2, says age 80

Died at his summer res. in Albemarle Co., Sept. 9th, BENJAMIN OLIVER of Hanover Co.,
leaving a wife and children
RE 19 Sept. 1820, p. 3; VPRDMA 20 Sept., p. 2

Died, MR. JOHN O'LYNCH, printer, of this city, age 24, on 21st Inst.
RE 28 Aug. 1812, p. 3; VA 27 Aug., p. 3, says a native of Londonderry, Ireland

Died at King & Queen C.H. on 25th Sept., MR. JOHN O'MEALY
VGGA 10 Oct. 1800, p. 3

Died, MR. GREGORY O'NEALE, Sr. of King William Co., age 68, on 10th Inst.
VA 26 Aug. 1808, p. 3

Died, JOHN ORD, Esq. of Phila. (No death date)
VGWA Feb. 2, 1782, p. 3

Died on Aug. 20th, DAVID ORGAN, a native of Ireland, but for many years an inhabitan
in the vicinity of Petersburg
Visitor 9 Sept. 1809, p. 127

Died lately in Williamsburg, MRS. ORR, widow of Capt. Hugh Orr, age 79
VGWA   4 Dec. 1788, p. 3

Died 13th Inst. at Chestnut Hill in Chesterfield Co., MISS NANCY OSBORNE
VGGA   22 Feb. 1792, p. 3

Died, MR. JAMES OTEY, SR., age 66, at his residence in New Kent Co., on 31st Ult.,
survived by wife and 9 children
VA   10 June 1807, p. 3

Died in Kentucky on 20th February, JAMES OVERTON, JR., Attorney at Law
VGWA   20 May 1790, p. 3; VICGA   19 May

Died Nov. 24th, CHRISTOPHER OWEN, husband of Mrs. Martha Owen, dec'd, age 52
RE   7 Dec. 1820, p. 3

Died Thurs. last (Aug. 4) MR. HOBSON OWEN of Henrico Co., for many years Inspector
of Tobacco at Shockoe Warehouse
RC   6 Aug. 1796, p. 2; VGGA   10 Aug., p. 2; VGRMA   6 Aug., p. 3

Died Nov. 22nd, MRS. MARTHA OWEN, consort of Mr. Chris'r Owen of Urbanna, age 47
RE   7 Dec. 1820, p. 3

Died in Halifax Co., Jan. 22nd, age 64, MR. ROBERTSON OWEN, Sr.
RE   23 Feb. 1819, p. 3

Died March 29 at his home in Charlestown, Va., age 29, LT. JOHN PACKETT, U.S.N.
RE   18 April 1820, p. 3

Died, MRS. JANE PAGE, on 29th, wife of Mr. William Byrd Page of this city
VP   31 July 1812, p. 3

Died, JOHN PAGE of Caroline, on Thursday last (April 30)
VIC   6 May 1789, p. 3

Died, COL. JOHN PAGE, Commissioner of Loans, and late Gov. of this Commonwealth,
on Tues. last (Oct. 11). He had been a soldier in the Revolution and for several
years a Member of Congress
VA   14 Oct. 1808, p. 3; RE   14 Oct., p. 3; VGGA   14 Oct., p. 3

Died lately at Mannsfield in Spotsylvania Co., MANN PAGE
Examiner   6 April 1803, p. 3

Died, MRS. MARY PAGE, consort of Mr. Robert Page. (No death date)
VGRC   11 March 1794, p. 3

Died, MRS. PAGE, spouse of John Page, Esq. of Rosewell, Gloucester Co.
VGWA   1 Feb. 1787, p. 3

Died on 27th Inst. at Presque Isle, the seat of David M. Randolph, Esq., MRS. PAGE,
wife of Carter Page, Esq. of Cumberland Co.
VA   31 Jan. 1797, p. 3

Died, OCTAVIUS AUGUSTUS, PAGE, Lt., U.S.N., son of late J. Page, Esq. of Gloucester, on 4th Inst. at Boston, had served on the Chesapeake. Buried in Boston in North Church
VA 14 June 1813, p. 3; VP 15 June, p. 3

Died on Aug. 2nd, MRS. POLLY PAGE, relict of Mr. Mann Page, near Hanover Town, leaving 3 children
VP 6 Aug. 1813, p. 3

Died Sat. last (Nov. 15) in Hanover Co., ROBERT PAGE, Esq.
VGRC 21 Nov. 1794, p. 2

Died, MRS. MARGARET PAINE, on Sat. last (Oct. 5), consort of Mr. Orris Paine of this city
RE 8 Oct. 1805, p. 2; VA 5 Oct., p. 3; VGGA 2 Oct., p. 2

Died Tues. (Nov. 2), MRS. MARY PAINE, consort of Mr. Samuel Paine of Richmond
RE 26 Nov. 1819, p. 3

Died, MRS. PAINE, wife of Thomas Paine, author of "The Rights of Man" at her brother's house, age 68
RE 30 Sept. 1808, p. 3

Died, ROBERT TREAT PAINE, JR., Esq., poet, at Boston on 13th Inst.
RE 22 Nov. 1811, p. 3

Died lately, the celebrated THOMAS PAINE, at house of the American Minister in Paris
RC 19 Jan. 1796, p. 3

Died, THOMAS PAINE, June 8th, in N.Y.
RE 16 June 1809, p. 3; Visitor 17 June, p. 78, says author of "The Rights of Man"

Died on Wed. (July 15), CAPT. HENRY PALMER of the British brig "Lee"
RC 17 July 1818, p. 3

Died on 6th Inst., MRS. SUSANNA C. PALMER, wife of Mr. Charles Palmer of King and Queen Co.
VA 16 Oct. 1807, p. 3

Died at Williamsburg, April 24th, MISS LUCY LUDWELL PARADISE, an unfortunate lady of wealth and family
RC 29 April 1814, p. 3

Died in Standish, Mass., January 29th, MR. ELEAZAR H. PARKER, 44, of hydrophobia
RC 8 March 1814, p. 3

Died on 20th Ult., MRS. ELIZABETH PARKER, consort of Richard Parker, Esq., Judge of the Court of Appeals, age 66
VGGA 31 Jan. 1798, p. 2

Died, COL. JOSIAH PARKER, on Wed. (March 21) at his seat in Isle of Wight Co. He was an officer in the Revolution and for many years a Representative in Congress
RE   27 March 1810, p. 3; VA   23 March, p. 3, says age 59 and died on 15th Inst.; Visitor   24 March, p. 31

Died, MRS. MARY PARKER, age 53, in Westmoreland Co., Nov. 3rd
RE   20 Nov. 1810, p. 3

Died, Hon. RICHARD PARKER, one of the Judges of the General Court, age 84, on 4th of this month at his seat in Westmoreland
RE   13 April 1813, p. 3; VA   3 May, p. 3

Died at Boston, MR. THOMAS PARKER, age 50, a naval officer during the Revolution
VA   11 July 1800, p. 3

Died in late Nov. 1819, COL. THOMAS PARKER of Accomac Co., a Revolutionary Soldier
RE   20 Jan. 1820, p. 3

Died in Loudon Co., WILLIAM H. PARKER, son of Judge Parker of Westmoreland Co. (No death date)
RE   16 Dec. 1815, p. 3

Died, MR. EDWARD PARKS, of this place, tanner. (No death date)
VG   Aug. 2, 1780, p. 2

Died yesterday, SAMUEL PARSONS, an old and respectable member of the Society of Friends
RC   25 March 1820, p. 3

Died Sat. last (June 18) in Williamsburg, DR. WILLIAM PASTEUR
VGGA   22 June 1791, p. 3

Died, MR. JOHN B. PATTERSON, age 24, on 22nd Ult. at res. of his father in Mathews Co.
RE   7 Dec. 1811, p. 3

Died March 1, MRS. MARY PATTERSON of Henrico Co., age 58
VP   8 March 1815, p. 3

Died lately in Mecklenburg Co., MR. SAMUEL PATTERSON, a young man
VGWA   25 Sept. 1784, p. 3

Died in Albany on 9th Inst. at mansion of Stephen Van Renselear, Esq., the HON. WILLIAM PATTERSON, Esq., an Associate Judge of the U. S. Supreme Court
VGGA   27 Sept. 1806, p. 3

Died, REV. DAVID PATTESON, of Buckingham Co. on 24th Ult. at an old age
VA   14 March 1806, p. 3

Died on 15th Ult., MR. DAVID PATTESON, JR., Attorney at Law, of Manchester. Buried at home of his father Col. D. Patteson
RE   2 Jan. 1806, p. 3

Died, CAPT. JOHN PATTESON, Inspector at Horsleys Warehouse in Town of Diuguidsville, Buckingham Co., murdered by a slave
VA 5 Sept. 1800, p. 3

Died at Wilmington, N.C., on 9th Inst. (Ult.), MR. ALEXANDER PATTON, merchant
Visitor 2 Dec. 1809, p. 174

Died on Friday last (Jan. 22), MR. HUGH PATTON, merchant of this city
VICGA 27 Jan. 1790, p. 3

Died lately in New Kent Co., MR. WILLIAM PATTON, a native of Ireland
VGGA 22 May 1798, p. 2

Died fighting Indians in Tenn., Aug. 8th, CHARLES PAYNE
VGWA 2 Oct. 1788, p. 3

Died, MR. FLEMMING PAYNE of Goochland Co. (No death date)
RE 3 Nov. 1809, p. 3

Died Dec. 6th, MRS. FRANCES M. PAYNE, consort of Col. Charles Payne of Fluvanna Co.
RE 14 Dec. 1816, p. 3

Died, MRS. MARGARET B. PAYNE, consort of Smith Payne, Esq. of Buckingham, on 11th Inst., leaving husband and 11 children
VA 8 May 1810, p. 3

Died July 7th, MR. JOHN PEATROSS of Richmond, robbed and killed
VP 9 July 1817, p. 3

Died on 11th Inst., MRS. LETITIA PECK, wife of Mr. Simon Peck of Manchester
VGGA 14 Dec. 1796, p. 3

Died MISS PRISCILLA PECK on Thurs. last (July 31) dau. of Mr. Simeon Peck of Manchester. Interred in churchyard in Richmond
VGWA 7 Aug. 1788, p. 3

Died, MR. J. L. PEERS, in Goochland, on Oct. 11th, age 25
RE 7 Nov. 1809, p. 3; VGGA 7 Nov., p. 3, says died on 10th; Visitor 18 Nov., p. 166, says John L. Peers, age 27 and died on Oct. 21

Died, MR. THOMAS PEERS, yesterday. For some years keeper of the upper lock gates
RE 22 Oct. 1811, p. 3

Died Wed. Last (Oct. 26), EDMUND PENDLETON, President of Virginia Court of Appeals, age 83
VA 29 Oct. 1803, p. 3

Died, JOHN PENDLETON, Esq., last Sat. (Aug. 9)
VGGA 13 Aug. 1806, p. 3

Died lately in Clifton, Hanover Co., MRS. MARY PENDLETON, spouse of Mr. John
Pendleton of this city
VGWA 6 Nov. 1784, p. 3

Died Sept. 4th at her res. in King & Queen Co., MRS. MARY ANN PENDLETON, relict of
late Col. Philip Pendleton
RE 29 Sept. 1820, p. 3

Died at his seat near Bath a few days ago, COL. PHILIP PENDLETON of Martinsburg
VA 15 Dec. 1801, p. 3

Died 31 Dec. 1803, COL. PHILIP PENDLETON of King & Queen Co.
RE 8 Aug. 1804, p. 3; VGGA 8 Aug., p. 3, says died July 31 and was Major)

Died on 8th Inst., age 57, at his seat in Amherst Co., COL. GABRIEL PENN
VGGA 24 Jan. 1798, p. 2

Died, JOHN PENN, Esq. of North Carolina, for years a Member of Congress. (No
death date)
IC 24 Sept. 1788, p. 3; VGWA 25 Sept.

Died at Norfolk, MR. WILLIAM PENNOCK, one of its oldest citizens. (No death date)
RE 15 May 1816, p. 3

Died at New York on 5th Inst., DR. PERKINS, inventor of the Metanic Tractor
VA 17 Sept. 1799, p. 3

Died at Providence, on 18 Aug., CAPT. NATHANIEL PERKINS, age 80
Visitor 9 Sept. 1809, p. 127

Died on 7th Inst., MRS. ELIZABETH PERRY, wife of Mr. James Perry of Chesterfield
VA 15 Aug. 1800, p. 3

Died Aug. 23rd, in Port of Spain, Trinidad, OLVIER H. PERRY of U.S. Navy
RC 30 Sept. 1819, p. 3

Died Sat. last (April 10), MRS. ELIZABETH PESCUD, wife of Edward Pescud, Editor
of The Petersburg Republican
RE 16 April 1819, p. 3; VP 14 April, p. 3

Died Nov. 10th at his res. in Warwick Co., MR. THOMAS PESCUD, age 49. He was a
Delegate from Warwick and York, and Justice of the Peace for Warwick. Leaves
wife and 2 daughters
RE 17 Nov. 1820, p. 3; VPRDMA 18 Nov., p. 3

Died in Woodford, Co., Ky. NATHANIEL PETERS, killed on July 5th
VPRDMA 2 Aug. 1820, p. 2

Died March 17th, in Lunenburg Co., MRS. JANE C. PETINS, wife of Mr. William C. Petins and dau. of Col. Peter Lamkin of Lunenburg
RE 11 April 1817, p. 3

Died Dec. 7th at Mount Eagle, Albemarle Co., MRS. JANE PEYTON, age 43
RE 21 Dec. 1820, p. 3

Died at Natchez, MR. JOHN PEYTON, of Milton, age 33. (No death date)
Visitor 9 Sept. 1809, p. 127

Died, MRS. SALLY PEYTON, wife of John Peyton, Esq. of Mathews on 26th Ult. at seat of her father, Charles Carter of Frederick, age 18
RE 10 Oct. 1807, p. 2; VGGA 10 Oct., p. 3

Died July 15th, MRS. SUSANNAH PEYTON, wife of John H. Peyton of Staunton
RE 24 July 1820, p. 3

Died lately, MRS. ANN PHILLIPS, consort of Capt. Richard Phillips of Louisa Co., and dau. of Col. William Johnston
VGAA 25 Sept. 1784, p. 3

Died in Curracoa (Curacao?) on 11th of March, age 47, BENJAMIN HAMMETT PHILLIPS, Esq., U.S. Consul to that island
VA 25 May 1803, p. 3

Died, MR. FRANCIS PIATTI, a native of Italy, but res. of this state for many years, yesterday
VA 11 Oct. 1813, p. 3; RC 11 Oct., p. 3

Died May 4th in Tewksbury, near Germantown, N.J., FREDERICK PICKLE, age 100, leaving a widow 90, married 70 years
RC 11 May 1820, p. 3

Died, MRS. SUSANNA PIERCE, wife of Mr. Godwin Pierce, formerly of Philadelphia, in this city, on Tues. last (Oct. 16)
VA 19 Oct. 1810, p. 3

Died fighting Indians at Tenn. on Aug. 8th, VAN PIERCEFIELD
VGWA 2 Oct. 1788, p. 3

Died on 29th Ult. in Norfolk at house of Otway Burd, Esq., MRS. ANNE C. PINCKARD of Williamsburg
VGGA 12 June 1798, p. 2

Died on 10th Inst. in Williamsburg, age 42, MRS. ELEANOR PITT, relict of late Wm. Pitt, merchant
RC 21 Nov. 1795, p. 2

Died on 10th Inst. in City of Annapolis, His Excellency GEORGE PLATER, Esq.
VGGA 29 Feb. 1792, p. 3

Died May 3rd, age 18, MRS. ANN ELIZA PLEASANTS, dau. of late Samuel Irvine and wife of John H. Pleasants of Lynchburg
RE 21 May 1819, p. 3

Died Tues. last (Dec. 17) at Four Mile Creek in this county, COL. JOHN PLEASANTS
VGRMA 19 Dec. 1793, p. 3

Died, JOHN SCOTT PLEASANTS, formerly a merchant in Richmond, in Charles City Co., on Tues. last (Aug. 31)
VA 2 Sept. 1813, p. 3

Died in Bell-Mead in Powhatan Co., on 13th Inst., MRS. MARY PLEASANTS, consort of Mr. Robert C. Pleasants
VA 26 Feb. 1799, p. 3

Died July 8th, MR. RICHARD S. PLEASANTS, employed in Chancery District Court, Williamsburg
VA 16 July 1806, p. 3

Died in this city on 4th Inst., age 70, ROBERT PLEASANTS
VA 6 March 1801, p. 3

Died, SAMUEL PLEASANTS, Esq., Editor of the Virginia Argus, yesterday
RE 5 Oct. 1814, p. 3; VP 5 Oct., p. 3, says Samuel Pleasants, Jr. ; RC 5 Oct., p. 2

Died on 4th Inst., age 78, THOMAS PLEASANTS of Beaverdam, Goochland Co.
VA 9 May 1804, p. 3

Died on 10th Inst. at house of Dr. Cringan, in this city, THOMAS PLEASANTS, JR. of Four Mile Creek
VGGA 13 Jan. 1796, p. 3; VGRMA 13 Jan., p. 3

Died on Sun. last (Dec. 8) MRS. POE, one of the actresses of the company at present playing on the Richmond Boards
RE 10 Dec. 1811, p. 3; VP 10 Dec., p. 3, says MRS. ELIZABETH POE

Died April 13th, MR. JAMES POINDEXTER, Clerk of the Courts of Powhatan Co., age 47
RE 17 April 1816, p. 3

Died at his res. in Goochland Co., July 18th, WILLIAM GREEN POINDEXTER, lawyer and former Member of General Assembly, leaving wife and numerous children
RE 24 Sept. 1819, p. 3

Died, MR. SAMUEL POINTER of this city, on 12th Inst.
RE 19 July 1808, p. 3; VGGA 19 July, p. 3

Died, MR. WILLIAM POINTER of this city on 25th Feb.
VGGA 1 March 1808, p. 3

Died, MRS. ELIZABETH POLLARD, consort of William Pollard, Esq., Clerk of Hanover Co. on 5th Inst.
VA 7 Nov. 1811, p. 3

Died lately in Goochland Co., MR. JOSEPH POLLARD, age 91, leaves wid., age 87, married 68 years, 7 children survive
VGGA 11 Jan. 1792, p. 2

Died in King William Co., Jan. 19th, MRS. MARY ELLEN POLLARD, age 23, wife of John Camm Pollard, leaving husb. and 1 child
RE 26 Feb. 1818, p. 3

Died, MR. RICHARD POLLARD, age 53, in King & Queen Co., on 4th Inst.
RE 18 Aug. 1809, p. 3

Died at Zoar, his res. on April 29th, MR. ROBERT POLLARD, Clerk of the Court of King William Co., age 63, leaving wife & children
RE 18 May 1819, p. 3; VP 4 May, p. 3

Died in Shelby Co., Ky., Jan. 29th, age 76, MR. THOMAS POLLARD, SR., formerly of Fairfax Co., Va.
RE 27 March 1818, p. 3

Died at Chelsea, near Richmond, on Mon. (Jan. 29) ALLAN POLLOK, 36. Came to this country age 13 and lived in Va. ever since
VP 31 Jan. 1816, p. 3

Died at his seat in Largs, Scotland on March 20th, ALLAN POLLOK, age 75, leaving widow and 4 sons. He was father of Allan Pollok of Chelsea and Robert Pollok who died lately (VP 31 Jan., says Allan, not Robert, died lately)
VP 22 May 1816, p. 3

Died at Col. Yancey's in Albemarle Co., April 26th, JOHN POLLOK, age 34
RE 2 May 1817, p. 3; VP 1 May, p.3, came from Scotland 15 mos. ago. Brother, father and mother all died recently.

Died, MR. ROBERT POLLOK, merchant, of Petersburg, on Sun. last (May 19)
VA 23 May 1811, p. 3

Died, JOHN S. PONTER, son of Henry Ponter, drowned Sat. last (beofre May 16)
VGGA 26 May 1809, p. 3

Died, MR. ALEXANDER POPE, age 18, 3rd son of Nathaniel Pope, Esq., of Hanover, at seat of Philip Duval, Esq. in Buckingham. (No death date)
VA 28 Oct. 1808, p. 2; RE 25 Oct., p. 3

Died at his plantation in Wilkes Co., Ga., on 14th Inst. (Ult.), MR. JOHN POPE, late from Dumfries, Va., leaving wife and 5 children
VGGA 1 Sept. 1802, p. 3

Died on 23rd Ult., MRS. LUCY POPE, consort of Nathaniel Pope, Esq. of Louisa Co.
VIC 5 Aug. 1789, p. 3

Died lately near Richmond, MRS. MARY POPE, consort of Dr. Matthew Pope
VG or AA Jan 12, 1782, p. 3; VGWA Jan. 12

Died on 24th Ult. at Montpelier in Powhatan Co., CAPT. NATHANIEL POPE, age 77
VA 2 Dec. 1806, p. 2; RE 2 Dec, p. 3

Died, NATHANIEL POPE of Hanover Co. (No death date)
RE 24 March 1809, p. 3; RE 23 May, p. 3, says age 49 and died March 13th;
VGGA 17 March, p. 3, at Chiltern Farm, Hanover, on Tues. last (March 14);
Visitor 25 March, p. 31

Died at Natchez, in July last, CAPT. PIERCY SMITH POPE of U.S. Artillery
Examiner 27 Dec. 1799, p. 3; VA 13 Dec., p. 3; VGGA 10 Dec., p. 3

Died on 17th Ult. at the Lunatic Hospital in Williamsburg, MR. WILLIAM PORROCK
of Amherst Co.
VGWA 26 Aug. 1790, p. 3

Died, LT. CHARLES PORTERFIELD, in Staunton. (No death date)
Visitor 27 Jan. 1810, p. 206

Died on 3rd Inst., MRS. REBECCAH PORTERFIELD, consort of Gen. Robert Porterfield
in Augusta Co.
Observatory 23 July 1798, p. 2; VGGA 24 July, p. 3

Died in Wilmington, N.C. Sept. 17th, age 29, COL. THORNTON A. POSEY, late of
U.S. Army. A native of Va., he was son of Gov. Posey, a veteran of the Revolution
RE 30 Sept. 1817, p. 3. (Also see RE 26 Sept. p3)

Died, MRS. ANN POTTER, spouse of Mr. Walter Potter of this city, on Thurs. last
(Feb. 28)
RE 5 March 1811, p. 3; VP 1 March, p. 3

Died in this city Thurs. last (June 30), CAPT. EDMUND POTTER
VA 2 July 1803, p. 3

Died at South Kingstown on 26th Ult., SAMUEL J. POTTER, one of the Senators from
Rhode Island
VA 20 Oct. 1804, p. 3

Died on Sun. (Nov. 23) MR. WALTER POTTER, of late firm of Fitzwhylson and Potter
VP 25 Nov. 1817, p. 3

Died, HANNAH POTTS in Norfolk, June 23rd
VP 27 June 1817, p. 3

Died in Washington City, MR. JOSEPH POUMEYROI, formerly of French Corps of
Engineers, an adopted citizen of this country. (No death date)
RE 1 Sept. 1820, p. 3

Died at his farm near Williamsburg on 20th Ult., MR. BENJAMIN POWELL, age 65
VGGA 1 Dec. 1790, p. 2

Died, MRS. POWELL, spouse of Benjamin Powell, Esq. of Williamsburg. (No death
date)
VGWA Jan 12, 1782, p. 2

Died a few days ago in Phila., SAMUEL POWELL
VGRMA 14 Oct. 1793, p. 3

Died, LT. THOMAS POWELL of State Artillery, at his father's in Yorktown. (No
death date)
VG Oct. 4, 1780, p. 3

Died on Sat. last (May 10) WILLIAM POWELL of Cumberland, leaving 4 children
VA 16 May 1806, p. 3

Died on May 25th, MR. WILLIAM POWELL, SR. of Goochland Co., age 80. A native of
England, he had resided in this country 60 years
RE 30 May 1817, p. 3

Died in res. of Mr. Alexander Fallow, MR. FRANCIS POWER, a native of Waterford,
Ireland.   (No death date)
RC 30 Sept. 1820, p. 3

Died on 23rd Inst. in James City Co., MR. EDWARD POWERS
VGRC 30 Sept. 1794, p. 3

Died, WILLIAM POWERS and his wife JUDITH POWERS, both on 28th July, in Goochland,
after a marriage of 57 years
VA 6 Aug. 1806, p. 3

Died in Salem, Mass., a black man, CESAR PRATT, age 65, remarkable for his instincti-
ability with numbers
VA 20 June 1804, p. 3

Died, EDWARD PRESBLE, Commodore in U.S. Navy in Washington on Sept. 2nd
RE 9 Sept. 1807, p. 3

Died in Richmond on Sun. (April 13) EBENEZER PREBLE of Boston, brother of Commodore
Preble
RE 15 April 1817, p. 3; VP 15 April, p. 3; RC 15 April, p. 2

Died, JOSEPH PRENTIS, ESQ., Senior Judge of the General Court of this Commonwealth,
on 18th Inst. at his home in Williamsburg, age 57
RE 23 June 1809, p. 3; VGGA 27 June, p. 3; Visitor 1 July, p. 86

Died on 24th Ult. in Williamsburg, MRS. PRENTIS, wife of Judge Prentis of that city
VA 1 Sept. 1801, p. 3

Died in Brimfield, Mass, CHARLES PRENTISS, formerly known by his literary production
in poetry and prose, and his editorial labors in Washington, Richmond and Baltimore
VPRDMA 9 Nov. 1820, p. 3

Died, MRS. PRESTON, consort of Gen. John Preston, Treasurer of this Commonwealth,
on Mon. last (March 26)
RE 30 March 1810, p. 3; Visitor 31 March, p. 35

123

Died, THOMAS L. PRESTON, Esq., at Lexington on 11th Inst. (also see RE 25 Aug., p. 4)
·RE 18 Aug. 1812, p. 3; VA 20 Aug., p. 3

Died lately in New Orleans, MRS. FRANCES PREVOST, dau. of Rev. Stanhope Smith of
Princeton, and consort of Hon. J. B. Trevosi, late Recorder of New York
RE 15 Dec. 1807, p. 3

Died on 4th Inst. at Mr. John Moody's in Richmond, MR. ALEXANDER POPE PRICE of
Petersburg and Fluvanna, age 30, leaving mother, 2 bros. and 5 sis.
RE 19 July 1805, p. 3; VA 24 July, p. 3

Died on 20th Inst., near Richmond, MRS. ANNIE PRICE, consort of Elisha Price, Esq.,
of Henrico
VA 26 Feb. 1802, p. 3; VGGA 26 Feb., p. 3 (says Ann)

Died Thurs. last (Sept. 4), CAPT. BARRET PRICE of Henrico
VGRMA 8 Sept. 1794, p. 3

Died April 19th in Goochland Co., MRS. E. PRICE, relict of Capt. Meredith Price,
age 76
RE 4 May 1814, p. 3; VP 30 April, p. 3; RC 2 May, p. 3, says Mrs. ELIZABETH Price

Died on Tues. last (April 4), CAPT. ELISHA PRICE of this city
Visitor 8 April 1809, p. 38

Died Aug. 29th, MRS. ELIZABETH G. PRICE, consort of Mr. Nathaniel W. Price of
Henrico Co.
VP 9 Sept. 1815, p. 3

Died on 30th Ult. at his house in Henrico, MR. JAMES PRICE, an old citizen. He
was Inspector of Tobacco at Byrd's Warehouse for 20 years
VA 1 May 1802, p. 3; Recorder 19 May, p.3 (says died 29th, age 60, at his seat
"Westwood"); VGGA 8 May, p. 3 (says died 29th)

Died MRS. JANE PRICE, consort of Maj. John Price of Henrico Co., on Sat. last
(Feb. 27)
VA 1 March 1808, p. 3

Died Feb. 18th, MR. JOHN PRICE of Henrico Co., age 65
RE 24 Feb. 1816, p. 3

Died, CAPT. JOHN F. PRICE, age 36, at his house in this city, this morning
VA 15 Feb. 1813, p. 3; VP 19 Feb., p.2, says Capt. John Fleming Price

Died, JOHN LEWIS PRICE, only child of Maj. William Price of this city, on Mon.
last (Oct. 6), age 18
VA 11 Oct. 1806, p. 3; Imp. Obs. (says Sun. last); RE Oct. 10th, p. 3

Died on 11th Inst., MR. JOHN W. PRICE on Henrico Co.
VGGA 20 July, 1791, p. 3

Died on Mon. last (March 7) CAPT. JOSEPH PRICE of Henrico Co.
VA 9 March 1803, p. 3

Died Sept. 14th at the Hot Springs, MR. MARRIN PRICE, a res. of Richmond. He had lost his last child 6 wks ago
RC 6 Oct. 1820, p. 3

Died on 7th Inst., MRS. MARTHA PRICE, wife of Marrin Price of this city
VA 14 Jan. 1815, p. 3

Died, MRS.MARY PRICE, relict of Capt. John Price, a few days since, age 86
VA 14 March 1806, p. 3; RE 18 March, p. 3; VGGA 15 March, p. 3 (says left 181 descendants)

Died on 31st Ult., MRS. MILLISENT PRICE, widow of Thomas Price, age 23, a native of Md., in Powhatan at Woodburg Mills
VA 8 June 1805, p. 3

Died Sat. last (March 26) MRS. PRICE, consort of Mr. Nathaniel Price, merchant of this city
RC 29 March 1796, p. 3; VGGA 30 March, p. 3, Mrs. Jane Price; VGRM 30 March, p. 3, Mrs. Jane Price

Died in Richmond on Sun. (Aug. 25), MR. NATHANIEL WEST PRICE, age 49
VP 27 Aug. 1816, p. 3

Died, MR. PETER PRICE of this city, on Wed. (Oct. 11)
VGGA 13 Oct. 1809, p. 3; Visitor 21 Oct., p. 150, says died on 14th Ult.

Died in Powhatan at Woodbury Mills on April 23rd, MR. THOMAS PRICE, age 26, a native of Maryland
VA 8 June 1805, p. 3

Died, MR. WILLIAM PRICE, Register of the Land Office of this Commonwealth, at house of Maj. Wm. Duval in Buckingham. (No death date)
VA 18 Oct. 1808, p. 3; RE 18 Oct., p. 3

Died, MR. WILLIAM PRICE, 3rd son of Capt. Thomas Price of Hanover Co., on Sun. last (Aug. 2) age 24 or 25
VP 14 Aug. 1812, p. 3

Died, DR. WILSON PRICE, age 31, of New Canton on Nov. 24th
VA 11 Dec. 1807, p. 3

Died October 6th, MRS. FRANCES PRICHARD, wife of Mr. Richard Prichard of Warwick
RC 8 Oct. 1818, p. 3

Died in Richmond, MR. WILLIAM PRICHARD, bookseller, at advanced age. (No death date)
RE 1 March 1815, p. 3; VA 4 March says died Mon. (Feb. 27th), age 65

Died at Northumberland, Pa., MRS. PRIESTLEY, relict of Rev. Dr. Priestley
VGRMA 8 Oct. 1796, p. 2

Died March 8th at Bremo, seat of Mr. William Prosser in lower Henrico Co., his
wife, MRS. LETITIA PROSSER, age 33
RE 14 March 1817, p. 3; RC 14 March, p. 3, says leaves infant 2 weeks old

Died, on the Brook in this county, on Sun. last (Oct. 2), MRS. PROSSER, consort
of Maj. Thomas Prosser
VGRMA 4 Oct. 1796, p. 3

Died, MR. JOHN PROSSER of house of Prosser & Moncure, age 38, on Thurs. last
(Oct. 25). Left wife and 4 children
RE 30 Oct. 1810, p. 3; VA 30 Oct., p. 3; VP 30 Oct., p. 3

Died in New York on April 11th, PETER PULLIS, suicide
VP 2 May 1817, p. 3

Died, MASTER JAMES PURDIE, eldest son of late Mr. Alexander Purdie, Printer.
(No death date)
VG Aug. 2, 1780, p. 2

Died at her res. in Goochland Co. on Oct. 28th, MRS. ANN PURYEAR, age 62
RE 15 Nov. 1815, p. 3

Died yesterday in Goochland Co., MRS. JANE PURYEAR, wife of Mr. Hugh Puryear,
leaving 4 small children
VGGA 4 Dec. 1801, p. 3

Died, MR. THOMAS PURYEAR, age 24, of Goochland, on 23rd Inst.
RE 2 July 1813, p. 1

Died, MRS. FRANCES PYNES, on 22 June, of King & Queen Co., age 78
VGGA 4 July, 1807, p. 3

Died, MRS. ELIZABETH QUARLES, wife of Maj. Isaac Quarles, in King William Co.,
on 19th Ult.
RE 3 July 1810, p. 3; VA 3 July says of "Woodberry" and mother of 24 children;
VP 3 July, p. 2

Died in Fluvanna Co., July 28th, MAJ. JOHN QUARLES, age 47, leaving wife and 6
children
VP 31 July 1816, p. 3

Died in Fluvanna Co., Dec. 1st, MRS. MARY QUARLES, consort of James Quarles, age
73
RE 10 Dec. 1816, p. 3

Died on 10th Inst. in this city, WILLIAM H. QUARLES
Visitor 18 Nov. 1809, p. 166

Died on Thurs. last (Sept. 21) MRS. ELIZABETH QUARRIER, consort of Maj. Alexander
Quarrier of this city
VGGA Sept. 27, 1797, p. 2

Died, COL. RICHARD QUINCE, lately, in vicinity of Wilmington, N.C.
Visitor 4 Nov. 1809, p. 158

Died, Gov. RABUN of Ga. at his res. in Hancock Co. (No death date)
RE 9 Nov. 1819, p. 3

Died at his res. in Powhatan Co., Nov. 19th, MR. GEORGE RADFORD, age 90
RE 1 Dec. 1820, p. 3

Died at house of her son William Radford in Bedford Co., MRS. REBECCA RADFORD of
Richmond, on Aug. 6th
RE 22 Aug. 1820, p. 3; RC 21 Aug., p.3

Died on Sun. last (April 3) MR. WILLIAM RADFORD, merchant of this city
VA 6 April 1803, p. 3; VGGA 6 April, p. 3

Died on 1st Inst., MAJ. DRURY MRGSDALE of King William Co., age 55
VGGA 14 March 1804, p. 2

Died, DR. GEORGE RAINE, at Norfolk, on Fri. last (Oct. 8) surgeons mate to Col.
Read's Artillery Regt.
VA 11 Oct. 1813, p. 3

Died on 13th Inst., MR. JOHN RAINE of Cumberland Co., leaving wife & children
RE 24 May 1815, p. 3

Died at his res. in Giles Co., Tenn., July 12th, WILLIAM RAINEY, age 67. Had lived
in Caswell Co., N.C. for 60 years. In Caswell Co. had been member of country court
and sheriff
RE 17 Sept. 1819, p. 3

Died, COL. DENNIS RAMSAY, at Alexandria, on Friday last (Sept. 7), age 56
VA 11 Sept. 1810, p. 2

Died in Norfolk on Mon. last (Nov. 3) age 23, MRS. MARGARET RAMSAY, consort of
Dr. James Ramsay, and dau. of James Taylor, Esq. of Norfolk
VGWA 6 Nov. 1788, p. 3

Died Oct. 24th, COL. NATHANIEL RAMSAY of Baltimore, an officer in the Revolution
VP 6 Nov. 1817, p. 3

Died Mon. (Sept. 3), MR. SAMUEL RAMSAY, a native of Scotland. Buried in the Churchyard
Observatory 6 Sept. 1798, p. 2; VGGA 11 Sept., p. 2

Died, MRS. ANN RANDOLPH, spouse of Thomas M. Randolph, Esq. of Tuckahoe. (No death date)
VGWA 12 March 1789, p. 2

Died on Tues. last (Oct. 30) at Powhatan Seat, near this city, MRS. ANN RANDOLPH of the Bloombury stock, age 48
VA 3 Nov. 1804, p. 2; VGGA 3 Nov., p.3

Died on 9th Ult., MRS. ANNE RANDOLPH, relict of Col. Richard Randolph, late of Curles, Henrico Co., in Powhatan
VA 28 Jan. 1815, p. 3

Died Jan. 20th, age 56, MRS. ANN RANDOLPH, consort of Mr. Brett Randolph of Powhatan Co.
RE 25 Jan. 1820, p. 3

Died, COL. ARCHIBALD RANDOLPH, a few days since, in Frederick Co.
RE 3 Dec. 1813, p. 3; VP 26 Nov., p.3, says died in Brunswick Co.)

Died on 7th Inst. at his res. on Green Cr. in Cumberland Co., COL. BEVERLY RANDOLPH, age 43
VA 17 Feb. 1797, p. 2; VGGA 15 Feb., p. 3

Died Sept. 24th at res. of his father in Powhatan Co., BRETT N. RANDOLPH, age 29
RE 5 Oct. 1819, p. 3; RC 6 Oct., p. 3, says died Sept. 26th

Died, MRS. CAROLINE MATILDA RANDOLPH, wife of Henry Randolph, age 20, on 25th Inst.
RE 30 Sept. 1808, p. 3; VGGA 30 Sept., p. 3

Died, MRS. ELIZABETH RANDOLPH, consort of Edmund Randolph, in this city, last Tuesday (March 6)
RE 9 March 1810, p. 3; Visitor 10 March, p. 23, says died Thurs.

Died on Tues. last (either Dec. 27th or Jan. 3), MR. JOHN RANDOLPH of Chesterfield Co., murdered
VA 4 Jan. 1804, p. 3

Died at Fort Montgomery, Alabama Terr., JOHN T. RANDOLPH, 4th son of Brett Randolph of Culpeper Co., age 20. Died Aug. 23rd
RE 15 Oct. 1819, p. 3

Died, MRS. LAVINIA RANDOLPH, spouse of Beverley Randolph, and eldest dau. of Col. Harry Heth. (No death date)
VP 22 March 1815, p. 3

Died on 16th Inst., MRS. MARY R. RANDOLPH, wife of Thomas Randolph, Esq. of Morven
VA 25 April 1806, p. 3; RE 22 April, p. 3; VGGA 26 April, p. 3

Died, MRS. RANDOLPH of Chatsworth. (No death date)
VGWA April 27, 1782, p. 3

Died on Wed. last (April 8) at Capt. joseph Weisiger's in Prince George Co., MISS NANCY KENNON RANDOLPH, dau. of William Randolph, Esq. of Charles City
VGRMA 11 April 1795, p. 2

Died on Sat. last (Nov. 16) MR. PETER S. RANDOLPH of this county
VA 19 Nov. 1799, p. 3

Died, Midshipman PETER B. RANDOLPH, on board USS Macedonia. (No death date)
RC 18 March 1819, p. 3

Died on 15th Inst. at his seat near this city, PEYTON RANDOLPH, Esq.
VGIC 22 May 1784, p. 3

Died Mon. last (March 25), age 42, RICHARD RANDOLPH, eldest son of Richard Randolph, dec'd, of Curles. Interred in burial grounds of this city
VGGA 26 March 1799, p. 3

Died on 16th Inst., MR. RICHARD RANDOLPH, Jr., of Cumberland Co.
VGRMA 22 June 1796, p. 2

Died in New York, RYLAND RANDOLPH, Esq., late of this city. (No death date)
RE 18 Oct. 1815, p. 3; VA 18 Oct., p. 3, says died Oct. 10th and was 4th son of Richard and Ann Randolph, formerly of Curles, Henrico Co.

Died yesterday, MRS. SARAH RANDOLPH, late wife of Mr. William Randolph of Chatsworth
RE 9 April 1819, p. 3; RE 16 April says she was 23 yrs. old, and left infant dau. and parents; VP 10 and 13 April, p. 3

Died Wed. last (Nov. 20) in this city, COL. THOMAS MANN RANDOLPH
VGGA 27 Nov. 1793, p. 3; VGRMA 25 Nov.

Died, MR. WILLIAM RANDOLPH of Wilton, near Richmond. (No death date)
VP 22 March 1815, p. 3

Died May 15th, MR. ROBERT RANSONE of Gloucester C.H., age 61, a tavern keeper
RE 22 June 1819, p. 3; RC 21 June, p. 3

Died on 5th Inst., MRS. ANN RAVENSCROFT, consort of John S. Ravenscroft, Esq. of Lunenburg Co.
RE 23 Aug. 1815, p. 3; VA 23 Aug., p. 3

Died on 25th Inst. (Ult.), MRS. PATSEY RAWLEIGH, consort of Mr. William Rawleigh of this city
VGGA 2 Aug. 1797, p. 3

Died, MR. WILLIAM RAWLEIGH, on 8th Inst., for years a respected mechanic in this city
RE 14 June 1811, p. 3

Died, MR. ROBERT RAWLINGS of Richmond. (No death date)
VGWA 24 Sept. 1789, p. 3

Died on 4th Inst., DAVID RAWN, Esq., principal clerk in office of the Comptroller of the Treasury, age 35, at Staunton, Va.
VA 17 July 1805, p. 3

Died in Richmond, MR. LEWIS RAYMOND, age 25, a native of Mass. (No death date)
RE 7 Sept. 1819, p. 3; VP 6 Sept., p. 3, days died Friday (Sept. 3), was from Shutesbury, Mass.

Died Mon. last (Sept. 18) MR. ASHTON REA, late of Hampton
VGGA 20 Sept. 1797, p. 3

Died, BENJAMIN FRANKLIN READ, Lt. USN, in New Orleans on Jan. 27th last, a native of Va.
VA 12 March 1812, p. 3

Died on 7th Inst., MRS. FRANCES READ, wife of Dr. Read of Hanover Town
VIC 17 Dec. 1788, p. 2

Died (No death date), DR. JOHN K. READ, Sr. of Norfolk, age 50
VA 16 Feb. 1805, p. 3

Died on Thurs. last (Feb. 28) at Goochland C.H. DR. JOHN K. READ, eldest son of Dr. K. Read, Sr., who died at Norfolk on 10th Ult. and of Mrs. Martha Bowles who was called to the tomb on 3rd Dec. last. Dr. Read, Jr. had married, Miss Maxwell, 9 mos. ago
RE 5 March 1805, p. 3; VA 6 March, p. 3

Died at Hampden-Sydney Sept. 12th, SAMUEL V. READ, age 17
RE 29 Sept. 1820, p. 3

Died last Sat. (Feb. 18) MR. JAMES REAT, age 33
RE 25 Feb. 1815, p. 3; RC 23 Feb., says leaves wife and father, p. 3

Died, GEORGE W. REDD, on 16th (Dec. 1812) at Mr. Thomas Redd's in Prince Edward Co.
RE 2 Jan. 1813, p. 3

Died at his seat in Mecklenburg Co., Aug. 20th, age 67, GEORGE REDD, leaving 7 children
RE 4 September 1818, p. 3

Died July 26th at seat of Maj. Redd in Henry Co., MRS. KEZIAH C. REDD, consort of Waller Redd, and dau. of Col. Samuel Staples of Patrick Co., age 27
RE 11 Aug. 1818, p. 3

Died, ANDREW REID, Esq., on 2nd Inst., at seat of Dr. Hare in Nelson. He was member of the Privy Council of Va. Was taken sick on his way from Richmond to Lexington where his parents reside
RE 13 Sept. 1811, p. 3; VA 12 Sept., p. 3

Died at Norfolk on Thurs. last (Aug. 13) MR. JAMES REID, merchant
VGRMA 20 Aug. 1795, p. 3

Died Jan. 18th, at his father's seat in Bedford Co., MAJ. JOHN REID of U.S. Army
RE 3 Feb. 1816, p. 3; VA 3 Feb., p. 3

Died 20th March last, CAPT. THOMAS REYNOLDS, on his way from Slate Creek Iron Works
to Morgans Station, Ky
VGGA 29 June 1791, p. 3

Died at Yorktown, Friday last (July 11) DR. THOMAS REYNOLDS, Surgeon of U.S. Brig.
"Richmond"
VA 18 July 1800, p. 3

Died, MRS. RICAUD, wife of Mr. Francis Ricaud, of this city. (No death date)
VGRMA 20 Nov. 1794, p.3; VGRC 21 Nov., says died Nov. 19th

Died, Capt. CHARLES RICE of Prince Edward Co., on April 24th, age 56, a solider
of the Revolutionary War
VP 8 May 1816, p. 3; VA 8 May, p. 3

Died June 13th, MRS. JOANNA RICE, late wife of Matthew Rice of Richmond, leaving
husband and 6 children
VP 14 June 1817, p. 3

Died, in Alexandria, in the prime of life, MR. GEORGE RICHARDS, Printer, and one
of the Editors of the Virginia Journal. (No death date)
VGWA 16 July 1789, p. 3

Died Feb. 3rd, age 39, MR. JONATHAN RICHARDS, formerly of Ipswich, Mass., but long
a res. of Richmond
RE 9 Feb. 1819, p. 3

Died yesterday at an advanced age, MRS. ABIGAIL RICHARDSON
VGRC 9 May 1795, p. 2

Died on 11th Inst. at his seat Turkey Hill, in Hanover Co., MAJ. GEORGE RICHARDSON,
long a res. of this city
RE 18 Oct. 1805, p. 3

Died, MR. JOHN RICHARDSON, age 23, in New Kent Co., on 1st Inst., until recently
a res. of Richmond City
RE 18 Dec. 1813, p. 3; VP 14 Dec., p. 3, says age 21

Died on 29th Ult. at his seat in Henrico Co., COL. SAMUEL RICHARDSON, age 56
RE 7 April 1807, p. 3

Died in Wingfield's Tavern in Hanover Co., June 9th, SAMUEL RICHARDSON, Common-
wealths Attorney for the county, leaving one son
RE 16 June 1820, p. 3; RC 16 June, p. 3

Died on Sun. (June 11) CAPT. WILLIAM RICHARDSON, Capt. of Light Infantry Blues
and Master of Police of this city
RE 13 June 1809, p. 3; VA 13 June, p. 3; VGGA 13 June, p. 3; Visitor 17 June,
p. 78

Died at res. of his uncle, Mr. John Payne, near Craney Island, Norfolk Co., on
Sept. 4th, WILLIAM T. RICHARDSON, eldest son of Capt. William Richardson of
Norfolk City, age 19
RE 14 Sept. 1816, p. 3

Died at his res. in King William Co. on Nov. 7th, MR. FRANCIS WEST RICHESON, of
fall from horse, age 39, leaving wife and children
RC 14 Nov. 1816, p. 3

Died, MRS. SUSANNA RICHESON, wife of Col. Holt Richeson of King William Co. (No
death date)
VG Dec. 16 1780, p. 3

Died lately in Williamsburg, MRS. SUSANNAH RIDDEL
VGWA 10 Dec. 1785, p. 3

Died lately at Rocky Mills, MRS. ANNA MARIA RIDDICK
RE 29 Aug. 1804, p. 3; VA 29 Aug., p. 3; VGGA 29 Aug., p. s (says "Fork Mills")

Died, LEMUEL RIDDICK, Esq. on the 18th at Suffolk, Representative in General Assembly
from Nansemond Co.
VA 26 Feb. 1811, p. 3

Died on 12th Inst. at his seat near Suffolk, WILLIS RIDDICK, Esq., who long represented
Nansemond Co. in the Assembly
VA 24 Oct. 1800, p. 3

Died, ATLEE RIGGS, a U.S. Soldier, formerly of Lancaster, Pa., killed by Indians
near Fort Armstrong, Mo. (No death date)
VPRDMA 6 July 1820, p. 3

Died, MR. ADOLPHUS RIESS, a native of Berlin in Prussia, a passenger on the sloop
Superior, going from Richmond to New York, drowned in James River while bathing,
age 22. (No death date)
RE 25 July 1820, p. 3; RC 25 July, p. 3; VPRDMA 22 July, p. 3

Died, age 45, on 19th Inst., MRS. MARGARET RIVES, dau. of late Col. William Cabell,
and consort of Mr. Robert Rives of Nelson Co.
RE 30 Aug. 1815, p. 3

Died, MRS. AGNES ROANE of King & Queen Co., on Jan. 13th, murdered by her husband,
John Roane, Jr.
VA 6 Feb. 1810, p. 3

Died on 22nd Inst. at house of Mr. P. Aylett in King William, MRS. ANNE ROANE,
consort of Hon. Spencer Roane
VA 28 May 1799, p. 3

Died Oct. 25th, age 18, MISS CHARLOTTE N. ROANE, dau. of late Thomas Roane of
King & Queen Co.
RE 1 Nov. 1815, p. 3

Died, JOHN ROANE, JR. on 15th Inst. in jail of King & Queen Co., having confessed
to murder of his wife
RE 24 April 1810, p. 3

Died, MR. JOHN ROANE of Middlesex Co., age 48, on 26 Nov.
RE 6 Dec. 1810, p.3

Died, MRS. MARTHA ROANE, consort of Mr. William Roane at home of her father, Mr.
M. Selden, on Friday last (Aug. 10)
RE 14 Aug. 1810, p. 3; RE 17 Aug. gives her father as Col. Miles Selden; VP
17 Aug., p. 3

Died on Tues. last (Feb. 1) at his father's in Richmond, MR. PATRICK H. ROANE,
youngest son of Judge Roane. Buried in King & Queen
RE 3 Feb. 1814, p. 3

Died, MR. SAMUEL ROANE, age 32, at Mrs. Roanes in King & Queen Co. on 22nd Inst.
RE 27 Feb. 1807, p. 3

Died, THOMAS ROANE, late Member of Va. Senate, at his seat in King & Queen Co.,
near Dunkirk. (No death date)
RE 23 Jan. 1808, p. 3

Died, WILLIAM ROANE of King & Queen Co., a magistrate of the co. (No death date)
RC 6 June 1795, p. 3; VGRMA 4 June, p. 3

Died in Richmond last Sat. (May 3), MR. JASPER ROBBINS, saddler, inhabitant of
city for many years
RE 6 May 1817, p. 3

Died in New York, Nov. 13th, MR. HOPKINS ROBERTSON, Comedian, age 38
RE 23 Nov. 1819, p. 3; RC 24 Nov., p. 3

Died Sept. 29th at Mr. Philip Slaughter's in Culpeper Co., age 50, JOHN ROBERTSON,
a native of Glasgow, Scotland, a teacher
RE 20 Oct. 1818, p. 3

Died April 22nd, MRS. MARY E. ROBERTSON, consort of Col. James Robertson, leaving
husband and 2 children
RE 1 May 1818, p. 3

Died Oct. 18th, MR. POWHATAN ROBERTSON, a son of William Robertson, now a member
of Executive Council of Va. He was a brother to recently elected Gov. of La.
Age 22, dec'd moved to La. 6 mos. ago
RE 28 Nov. 1820, p. 3

Executed yesterday near Richmond, JAMES ROBINSON for burglary
VGAA Jan. 26, 1782, p. 3; VGWA Jan. 26

Died in Alexandria on 31st Ult., JOHN COTTON ROBINSON, by hanging himself
VGWA 12 June 1784, p. 3 and 19 June

Died in Bennington, Vt., Nov. 3rd, JONATHAN ROBINSON, 64, late Senator
RE 19 Nov. 1819, p. 3

Died yesterday in Richmond, CAPT. CHARLES ROCKE
RC 20 June 1820, p. 3

Died, MR. BALDWIN ROCKET of Henrico. (No death date)
VGWA March 16, 1782, p. 3

Died at Havre de Grace, Md., Sept. 19th, MRS. ELIZABETH RODGERS, relict of John
Rodgers, and mother of Commodore Rodgers
RC 16 Oct. 1816, p. 3

Died on Feb. 10th, MRS. ROE, wife of Mr. Thomas Roe of Petersburg
VA 18 Feb. 1800, p. 3

Died last Wed. (April 16) in this city, MAJ. JOHN ROGERS of Caroline Co. Buried
in the churchyard
VGGA 23 April 1794, p. 3; VGRMA 21 April

Died on Sat. (June 1) in this city, ANDREW RONALD, Attorney at Law
VA 4 June 1799, p. 3; VGGA 4 June, p. 3

Died last Wed. (May 21) MRS. SARAH RONALD, spouse of Andrew Ronald, Esq. of this
city
IC 28 May 1788, p. 2; VGWA 29 May

Died on Tues. last (May 14) at Martinsburg, Berkeley Co., MRS. ELIZABETH ROOTES,
consort of George Rootes, dec'd
VGRMA 23 May 1793, p. 3

Died Wed. last (July 6) MRS. ELIZABETH ROOTES, wife of Mr. Edmund W. Rootes,
merchant of this city
VA 9 July 1803, p. 3; VGGA July 9, p. 3 (says age 24); Examiner 9 July, p. 3
(says leaves parents, husband and 1 child)

Died on 7th Inst. at Martinsburg, Berkeley Co., GEORGE ROOTES, Esq., late of this
city
VGRMA 23 May 1793, p. 3

Died on May 18th, age 20, at res. of Mrs. Ann Sharp, at lower end of Henrico Co.,
MRS. ANNA ROPER, consort of Mr. George Roper, formerly of Richmond
RC 28 May 1814, p. 3

Died Monday last (Sept. 16) at Rocketts, MR. JOHN ROPER
VGGA 18 Sept. 1793, p. 3

Died on Wed. (July 5) MR. JOHN ROPER, a young man, resident of Henrico
RC 7 July 1820, p. 3

Died last Tues. (March 20) MRS. ROPER, spouse of Mr. Jesse Roper of this city
VGWA March 22, 1787, p. 2

Died, MRS. CATHERINE ROSE, relict of late Col. John Ross of Amherst, on 1st Inst.,
in Alexandria
VGGA 19 Jan. 1808, p. 3

Died on Sun. (July 6) WILLIAM ROSE, one of Richmond's oldest inhabitants, and long
time Public Jailor for Richmond
RE 8 July 1817, p. 3

Died, DAVID ROSS of Richmond, last Sun. (May 4) over 80, served Commonwealth during
the Revolution
RE 6 May 1817, p. 3; VP 5 May, p. 3, says was native of Scotland

Died, COL. HUGH ROSS (or ROSE), age 52, on 18th Oct. in Amherst Co.
VGRMA 6 Nov. 1794, p. 2

Died a few days ago in Phila., JOHN ROSS
VGRMA 14 Oct. 1793, p. 3

Died June 9th, MRS. JULIANA ROSS, consort of Mr. David Ross of Mt. Ida
VP 17 June 1818, p. 3

Died on 18th Inst. at Cobham, seat of his father, David Ross, Esq., WILLIAM ROSS, Es
of Mt. Ida
VA 26 Sept. 1804, p. 3; VGGA 26 Sept., p. 2

Died on 10th Inst., MR. CHARLES ROTHERY, printer, of this city
VGGA 18 March 1795, p. 3; VGRMA 19 March, p. 3

Died, MISS LAVINIA ROULSTONE, killed by lightning in Morristown. (No death date)
VA 23 Sept. 1811, p. 3

Died, MRS. MARGARET ROWLAND, on 7th Inst.
VA 10 Aug. 1805, p. 3

Died yesterday, MR. ZACHARIAH ROWLAND of this city
VGGA 29 May 1802, p. 3

Died, MRS. ELIZABETH ROY, wife of James Roy of Green Palms, Mathews Co., on 12th
Inst.
RE 30 April 1813, p. 3; VP 4 May, p. 3, days lived at Green Plains

Died on Sat. (Sept. 16) at Locust Hill, his seat in Caroline Co., MUNGO ROY, age 73
VP 23 Sept., 1815, p. 3

Died at his res. in King & Queen Co., Oct. 22nd, DR. WILEY ROY, leaving wife and 2
daughters
RE 7 Nov. 1817, p. 3; VP 3 Nov., p. 3

Died, a few days ago, at his house in Port Royal, age 46, MR. WILLIAM ROY, merchant
of that place
VP 22 April 1815, p. 3; VP 19 April, says Ray

Died June 24th, WILLIAM ROYAL of Lynchburg
RE 1 July 1817, p. 3

Died at his seat in Amelia, on 9th Inst., COL. JOHN ROYALL, age 51
VA 28 Aug. 1805, p. 3

Died, MR. ANDERSON ROYSTER of Goochland Co., on Sun. last (May 29)
VA 3 June 1808, p. 3; Virginian 3 June, p. 3

Died on 16th Inst. in Goochland Co., MR. HENRY ROYSTER, age 28
VA 31 March 1804, p. 3

Died on Sun. (Feb. 2) MR. JOHN H. ROYSTER, a firm of Royster & Walls of Richmond
RE 4 Feb. 1817, p. 3; VP 5 Feb., p. 3

Died, MRS. NANCY ROYSTER, wife of Littleburg Royster, of Henrico Co., on Sept. 27th
VA 7 Oct. 1808, p. 3

Died May 12th REV. JAMES RUCK of Chesterfield Co., age 67, leaves wife and 3 children
RE 22 May 1818, p. 3

Died at Hobbs Hole, May 2nd, MARIA RUFFIN, eldest dau. of Mr. Wm. Ruffin of Brunswick Co., age 10
VA 22 May 1801, p. 3

Died Jan. 10th in Dunkirk, DR. THOMAS RUFFIN
RE 3 Feb. 1816, p. 3

Died April 20th, some miles from Montreal, MR. GEORGE RULE
VP 14 May 1818, p. 3

Died Jan. 5th, age 74, JACOB RUSH, Pres. of Court of Common Pleas of County of Philadelphia
VPRDMA 15 Jan. 1820, p. 3

Died in Goochland on 1st Inst., BENJAMIN RUSSELL, Member of Soc. of Friends
VA 10 Feb. 1801, p. 3

Died June 15th at res. of Mrs. Smith in York Co., DR. BENJAMIN D. RUSSELL
RE 27 June 1817, p. 3; VP 19 June says died June 12th, and was son of Mr. Russell of Richmond

Died Jan. 28th in N.Y., JAMES RUSSELL, age 9, run over by a carriage
RC 5 Feb. 1819, p. 3

Died, MRS. JANET RUSSELL, a native of Stirlingshire, Scotland, age 68, in this city
VA 28 Sept. 1805, p. 3

Died in Charleston, S.C., April 11th, NATHANIEL RUSSELL, late Tres.of the Bible Society of S.C. A native of Rhode Island. Was age 87
VPRDMA 6 May 1820, p. 2

Died, MR. WILLIAM RUSSELL, in Williamsburg, and old inhabitant of that city. (No death date)
RE   28 April 1812, p. 3

Died Sept. 16th, at her res. in Charlotte Co., age 44, MRS. ELIZABETH RUTHERFOORD, widow of John A. H. Rutherfoord, formerly of Charlotte C.H.
RE   10 Oct. 1820, p. 3

Died on 11th Ult., Gov. RUTLEDGE of South Carolina, at Charleston
VA   4 Feb. 1800, p. 3; VGGA   31 Jan., p. 3

Died in Philadelphia, GEN. JOHN RUTLEDGE of S.C. (No death date)
RE   7 Sept. 1819, p. 3; VP   8 Sept., p. 3, says died Sept. 1, age 53

Died on Sun. (Oct. 5) THOMAS RUTTER, Marshall of Md. District, age 55
VP   10 Oct. 1817, p. 3

Died, Mrs. MARY SACKRIDER, consort of Dr. Sackrider of this city. Left husband and 4 childre. (No death date)
RE   17 Aug. 1810, p. 3; VA   10 Aug., p. 3, says died Aug. 6th; VP   14 Aug., p. 3, sayd died on 7th

Died Feb. 27th, REV. W.H. SALTER of Yorktown, leaving widow and 2 children
VP   4 March 1815, p.3

Died in this city on 23rd Inst., MR. JESSE SANDERSON, formerly of New York
VA   31 March 1797, p. 2

Died, MISS GULIAN A. ELMOES SANDS, on 2nd Inst., in New York
VA   17 Jan. 1800, p. 2

Died last Fri. (May 17) in Manchester, CAPT. LEWIS SARANO, Master of the Schooner "Betsy" from North Carolina
VA   21 May 1799, p. 3

Died in New Orleans May 31st, COL. WINTHROP SARGENT, former Gov. of Miss. Terr.
RE   11 July 1820, p. 3

Died at his father's res. in King & Queen Co., July 11th, MR. GEORGE SANDERS
RE   18 July 1820, p. 3

Died, MAJ. JOHN SAUNDERS, res. of Norfolk for 18-20 years, on 15th Inst. (Ult.) in Command at Fort Nelson
RE   6 April 1810, p. 2; VA   23 March, p. 3; Visitor   24 March, p. 31

Died at his res. in Powhatan Co., June 24th, REV. JOHN H. SAUNDERS, age 76
RE   25 July 1817, p. 3

Died, MRS. JUDITH SAUNDERS, consort of Col. Robert Saunders of Goochland, on July 21st
Visitor 29 July 1809, p. 102

Died, MRS. MARIANNE SAUNDERS, consort of R. Saunders, Esq. of Williamsburg. (No death date)
RE 28 Dec. 1809, p. 3

Died, MRS. MARY SAUNDERS on 24th Ult., the consort of Col. Robert H. Saunders of Goochland
RE 10 Feb. 1809, p. 3; Visitor 11 Feb., p. 7

Died on Tues. (Jan. 30) MRS. SAUNDERS, consort of Mr. Tarlton Saunders of Whitby, near Manchester
VP 31 Jan. 1816, p. 3

Died on 12th Inst. at house of Mr. Lipscomb Wash in Powhatan Co., SAMUEL SAUNDERS, a youth, son of Mr. Jesse Saunders of Lunenburg Co.
VGGA 18 Oct. 1799, p. 3

Died yesterday, MR. WILLIAM SAUNDERS, bricklayer, of Richmond, leaving wife and three small children
RC 19 Aug. 1819, p. 3

Died at Phila. PATRICK SAVAGE, British Consul for Va. (No death date)
RE 14 Aug. 1818, p. 3; RC 14 Aug., p. 3, days Mon. last (Aug. 10)

Died, MRS. JANE SAYRE, wife of Samuel William Sayre, Esq., and dau. of late Philip Ludwell Grymes, Esq. of Middlesex Co. on 1 Jan, at Brandon in said co.
VGGA 18 Jan. 1806, p. 3

Died at res. of his son in Va. Sept. 27th, STEPHEN SAYRE, a native of Long Island, age 85, and on the next day his wife died
RE 10 Dec. 1818, p. 3

Died in Hanover Co., MR. SAMUEL SCHERER, formerly of this city. (No death date)
VA 26 Sept. 1804, p. 3; VGGA 26 Sept, p. 2, says Thurs. last (Sept. 20)

Died on 18th Inst., MR. SIMON SCHULTZ, painter, of this city
VA 20 July 1803, p. 3; Examiner 20 July, p. 3

Died at Albany, Nov. 18th, GEN. PHILIP SCHUYLER, age 73
VA 1 Dec. 1804, p. 3

Died on Fri. last (Oct. 25) at the seat of George Mayo, Esq. in Chesterfield, MR. DANIEL SCOTT of Cumberland Co., and eldest son of Gen. Charles Scott of Ky.
VGRMA 28 Oct. 1793, p. 3

Died Wed. (March 8) in Manchester, ELIZABETH SCOTT, consort of William Scott, a free woman of colour.
RC 10 March 1820, p. 3; VPRDMA 10 March, p. 3

Died on 6th Inst. MRS. FRANCES SCOTT, consort of Gen. Charles Scott of Woodford
Co., Ky.
VA 24 Oct. 1804, p. 3

Died in Albemarle on 8th Inst., MISS FRANCES SCOTT
VA 29 May 1805, p. 3

Died, GUSTAVUS SCOTT, in Washington (before Dec. 16)
VA 2 Jan. 1801, p. 3

Died, MAJ. JAMES SCOTT, Marshal of Virginia District, on Friday last (Nov. 30)
RE 4 Dec. 1810, p. 3; RE 8 Dec., says name is Joseph Scott, age 67, of Amelia,
& died on 20th; VA 4 Dec., p. 3, says Joseph, an old Revolutionary Soldier;
VP 4 Dec., p. 2

Died in Amelia Co., Feb. 28th, MRS. LUCY SCOTT, consort of Mr. John Scott, age 57,
leaving husband and 6 children
RE 10 March 1818, p.3

Died on 1st Inst., age 28, MRS. MARTHA C. SCOTT, consort of Mr. James Scott, Jr.,
merchant of Richmond
RE 7 May 1814, p. 3; VP 7 May, p. 3

Died, MRS. MARY COLES SCOTT, wife of Joseph W. Scott of Halifax Co., and eldest
dau. of late Gen. Carrington, age 26, on 16th Aug.
RE 28 Aug. 1810, p. 3

Died on Thurs. last (Nov. 24) MRS. SCOTT, consort of Mr. Thomas Scott of this city
VA 26 Nov. 1796, p. 3

Died, MRS. SCOTT, wife of Richard M. Scott, Delegate from Fairfax Co., a victim
of the theatre fire (Dec. 26, 1811)
RE 14 Jan. 1812, p. 3; VA 16 Jan, p. 3; VP 21 Jan, p. 2, says MRS. MARY M. SCOTT,
says died 13 Lan.

Died, MRS. PATSEY SCOTT, age 48, on 12th Inst., 2nd dau. of Robert Woolfolk of
Caroline Co.
RE 26 Jan. 1813, p. 3

Died Wed. last (Nov. 2) MRS. MARY SEABROOK, age 66
VA 4 Nov. 1808, p. 3

Died Monday last (June 28) in this city, CAPT. NICHOLAS B. SEABROOKE
VICGA 30 June 1790, p. 2

Died on Sat. (18 Sept.) on board the packet "Ariadne" at Newport News, CAPT. ISAAC
SEAMAN, SR., master of the schooner
VP 23 Sept. 1819, p.3

Died, JOHN SEAMAN, drowned in James River, Oct. 7th
RE 16 Oct. 1816, p. 3; RC 15 Oct., p. 3

Died on 9th Inst. at house of Capt. George Guy in Caroline Co., MISS MARY SEARS, about 16
VGRMA 16 May 1795, p. 2

Died, MR. JOHN SEATON, of this city, yesterday
RE 19 July 1808, p. 3; Virginian 22 July, p. 2

Died at Cartersville on Friday (July 16), MRS. JUDITH SEAYERS, wife of Mr. Thomas Seayers of that place
VA 24 July 1802, p. 3

Died in Havana Oct. 5th, MR. FRANCIS SEIGNE, late of the Equestrian Co. of Perpin & Breschard
VP 18 Nov. 1815, p; 3

Died, JOSEPH SELDEN, at his seat in Henrico Co., on 1st Inst.
RE 31 Jan. 1807, p. 3

Died, COL. MILES SELDEN of Tree Hill, near this city, on Sat. last (May 18). Held various political offices
RE 24 May 1811, p. 3

Died, MRS. SELDEN, consort of Nathaniel Selden, Esq., of this county, on Sun. last (June 23)
RE 28 June 1811, p. 3; VA 24 June, p. 3

Died at Mr. Miles Selden's on 12th Inst., MR. SAMUEL SELDEN
VA 25 June 1799, p. 3

Died Feb. 22nd in Williamsburg, MR. PETER SEMON, age 68
RE 11 March 1817, p. 3

Died on 12th Ult. at Green Way, seat of Judge Tyler, his dau., ANN COUNTES SEMPLE, wife of James Semple, Attorney at Law, age 26
VA 6 July 1803, p. 3

Died on 22nd Ult., JOHN SHACKLEFORD, Esq., Attorney at Law in King & Queen
VGWA 19 Feb. 1789, p. 3

Died on Wed. last (May 14), LYNE SHACKELFORD, a member of the Privy Council
VA 16 May 1806, p. 3; RE 20 May, p. 3

Died at his seat in Richmond Co., Feb. 12th, COL. VINCENT SHACKLEFORD, of the artillery; fought in late war
RE 17 Feb. 1820, p. 3

Died yesterday, MRS. ELIZABETH H. SHAPARD, consort of Mr. William Shapard of Richmond
RC 8 July 1818, p. 3

Died, MR. MICHAEL SHARKEY, merchant of this city. (No death date)
VGWA 28 Aug. 1784, p. 2; VGAA 28 Aug., says died Sun. last (Aug. 15) and was from
Ireland

Died, ALEXANDER SHELTON, of this city, on Sat. last (Jan. 11)
VGGA 15 Jan. 1806, p. 3

Died on Thurs. (Sept. 21) in Richmond, SAMUEL SHEPARD, late Auditor of Va. A native
of Boston, he had lived in Va. 29 years
RE 23 Sept. 1815, p. 3; VA Sept. 23rd, p. 3

Died, JORDON SHEPHERD, age 57, res. of Greensville, Pitt Co., N.C. for 30 years,
but a native of Nansemond Co., Va., on Dec. 15th last (1811)
VA 23 March 1812, p. 3

Died on 11th July in upper end of Fluvanna Co., MRS. MARY SHEPHERD, wife of Abraham
Shepherd, and dau. to Col. James Payne, leaving husband and 4 children
RE 22 July 1815, p. 3

Died on Wed. last (March 29) MRS. ANN SHEPPARD, spouse of Nathaniel Sheppard of
this city
VA 31 March 1797, p. 2

Died April 7th, age 55, MR. JOHN M. SHEPPARD of Scotchtown, Hanover Co.
VP 11 April 1817, p. 3; RC 11 April, p. 2

Died Fri. last (Jan. 17) MR. JOSEPH SHEPPEARD of this city
VGRMA 20 Jan. 1794, p. 3

Died lately in York Co., SAMUEL SHIELD, Esq., for many years a member of the General
Assembly
VA 2 March 1803, p. 3

Died on 17th April, CAPT. SAMUEL SHIELD of York Co., served in war of 1812 and was
in State Senate
RE 7 May 1814, p. 3

Died, MRS. ANNE SHIELDS, wife of Mr. David Shields of Lexington, Rockbridge Co.,
on 11th Inst.
VA 19 Oct. 1805, p. 3

Died, MR. JAMES SHIELDS of this city, age 45, on Sat. last (March 15)
VGGA 19 March 1806, p. 3

Died, MRS. PHEBE SHIELDS, on 7th Inst.(Ult.) wife of Maj. Alexander Shields, and
only dau. of Capt. John Carruthers
RE 7 Feb. 1809, p. 3

Died on April 15th, EDWARD SHIPPEN, Judge of the Supreme Court of Pa., age 78
VA 25 April 1806, p. 3

Died at Philadelphia, DR. WILLIAM SHIPPEN, age 90. (No death date)
VGGA 20 Nov. 1801, p. 3

Died Thurs. last (May 19) MRS. SHORE, wife of Mr. Henry S. Shore of this city
VA 21 May 1803, p. 3; VGGA 21 & 25 May, p. 3 (says Martha Shore, 25 May)

Died at Halifax, N.C. on 4th Inst., JOHN SILGREAVES, Esq., Judge of U.S. Court for
Distr. of N.C.
VA 23 March 1802, p. 3

Died at Alexandria, COL. CHARLES SIMMS, Collector of the Port of Alexandria. (No
death date)
RE 7 Sept. 1819, p. 3

Died on Wed. last (Dec. 4) in this city, JAMES SIMMS, tailor
VGRC 6 Dec. 1793, p. 3

Died March 25th, age 52, MRS. SUSANNA SIMPSON of Chesterfield Co., Member of the
Baptist Church, leaving 7 children
RC 29 March 1820, p. 3

Died, MRS. MARY SIMS, age 76, in Cumberland Co., on 9th Inst.
VA 3 Feb. 1809, p. 3

Died on 9th Inst., a preacher named DAVID SINCLAIR, by hanging himself, near
Averasborough, N.C.
VA 20 July 1805, p. 3

Died lately at Newport, R.I., CAPT. ANTHONY SINGLETON of this city
VGGA 21 Oct. 1795, p. 2

Died on Tues. week (Feb. 21) GEN. JAMES SINGLETON, Pres. of Winchester Bank,
leaving wife & 7 children
RE 1 March 1815, p. 3

Died, MRS. LUCY SINGLETON, age 31, of Richmond, lately, in Staunton at home of
Capt. George Turner
Visitor 7 Oct. 1809, p. 142

Died at Dunkirk, King & Queen Co., on 12th Inst., MR. ROBERT SINGLETON, JR.
VGGA 24 July, 1798, p. 3

Died in Richmond on Sat. (Oct. 19), MR. EDWARD SKATTS, age 33, formerly of N.Y.
VP 21 Oct. 1816, p. 3; RC 21 Oct., p.3, says SKAATS

Died Friday last (Nov. 12) DR. ALEXANDER SKINNER, age 49, buried in the churchyard
IC 19 Nov. 1788, p. 3; VGWA, says age 45, 20 Nov.

Died, MR. JOHN SKINNER of King George Co., on Mon. last (June 26), murdered by
persons unknown
RE 30 June 1809, p. 2

Died on 19th Inst., MISS ELIZABETH SKIPWITH, eldest dau. of Col. Henry Skipwith
VA 23 March 1802, p. 3; VGGA 26 March, p. 3

Died in Williamsburg, Aug. 6th, MRS. ELIZABETH H. SKIPWITH, an old lady, dau. of
late Col. William Byrd
VP 10 Aug. 1819, p. 3

Died, SIR PEYTON SKIPWITH, on 8th Inst. at his seat in Mecklenburg Co.
VA 19 Oct. 1805, p. 3; VGGA 26 Oct., p. 3

Died at his res. in Amelia Co., March 9th, REV. JOHN SKORRY, for 30 years a Baptist
Minister, and pastor at Sandy Creek Meeting House
RE 20 March 1818, p. 3; VP 21 March, p. 3

Died, MRS. CATHERINE SLAUGHTER, wife of Mr. George Slaughter of Lexington, on April
30th
RE 14 June 1811, p. 3

Died lately in Woodward in Prince Georges Co. (Md.), GEN. WILLIAM SMALLWOOD, former
Gov. of Md.
VGGA 29 Feb. 1792, p. 3

Died in Augusta, Ga., Oct. 22nd, DR. DENNIS SMELT, age 55. A native of Va., had
lived in Ga. 20 yrs. and had been Congressman from Ga.
RE 13 Nov. 1818, p. 3

Died, MRS. ANN SMITH, consort of Larkin Smith, Esq., Collector of this Port, on
Fri. last (Dec. 18)
VA 24 Dec. 1812, p. 3

Died in Louisa Co., on Sat. last (Oct. 14), MR. CHARLES SMITH, a young man
RE 14 Oct. 1815, p. 3

Died in Richmond on Thurs. last (Sept. 20), MR. CHRISTOPHER L. SMITH
VGGA 22 Sept. 1804, p. 1

Died at home of Mr. Colter, St. Louis, Missouri Terr., Aug. 17th, Prof. EDWARD D. SM
of College of S.C. at Columbia
RC 15 Oct. 1819, p. 3

Died on 16th Inst., MRS. ELIZABETH SMITH of Hanover Co., age 85
VA 25 Oct. 1799, p. 3

Died July 18th, age 64, MRS. ELIZABETH SMITH, wife of Capt. Francis Smith of Chester
field
RE 24 July, 1816, p. 3

Died on 17th Inst., MRS. ELIZABETH GARLAND SMITH, consort of Mr. Jesse Smith of
Henrico
VGRMA 20 Aug. 1796, p. 3

Died, MR. JAMES SMITH, (no death date), funeral today from his res. on Church Hill
VP 19 March 1818, p. 3

Died, DR. JOHN SMITH, at his residence in King & Queen C.H., on 12th Inst.
RE 22 Dec. 1807, p. 3

Died at Mastic, L.I., N.Y., June 25th, age 61, GEN. JOHN SMITH, Marshal for Dist.
of N.Y.
RE 3 July 1816, p. 3

Died, COL. LARKIN SMITH, Collector for Port of Norfolk, at Fredericksburg, on 28th
Ult.
RE 8 Oct. 1813, p. 3

Died, MRS. MARY E. SMITH, consort of Col. Larkin Smith of King & Queen Co., on 10th
Ult.
VGGA 1 March 1797, p. 2

Died, MAJ. OBADIAH SMITH, age 53, on 23rd Inst., at his seat in Chesterfield Co.
VA 3 Feb. 1808, p. 3

Died, REV. PERO G. SMITH, age 28, late of Massachusetts, on 11th Inst. at house of
Mr. John Bryce in Goochland Co.
RE 31 July 1807, p. 3

Died, MR. PEYTON SMITH, son of Gen. John Smith of Frederick Co., killed in a duel.
(No death date)
VA 8 Dec. 1809, p. 3

Died in Pohite, on Sunday (Sept. 17), MR. REUBEN SMITH, age 49
RE 22 Sept. 1820, p. 3; VPRDMA 20 Sept., p. 2

Died, MR. RICHARD SMITH, in this city on 18th Inst., late of N.Y., formerly an
inhabitant of this city
RE 23 June 1809, p. 3; VA 23 June, p.3, says "SMYTH" and died on 19th; VGGA
23 June, p. 3, days Smyth & June 19th; Visitor 1 July, p. 86

Died at Charleston, S.C., ROBERT SMITH, Bishop of S.C., age 73, for 47 years
Minister at Philp's Church
VA 17 Nov. 1801, p. 3

Died, MR. ROBERT SMITH, of Princess Anne, at Norfolk, on 14th Inst.
Visitor 17 March 1810, p. 27

Died at Princeton, N.J., REV. SAMUEL STANHOPE SMITH, late Pres. of College of
N.J. (No death date)
RE 3 Sept. 1819, p. 3

Died, MRS. SARAH SMITH, wife of George William Smith, Esq., of this city. (No
death date)
VA 4 Oct. 1806, p. 3; Imp. Obs. 11 Oct., p. 3; RE 10 Oct., p. 3 (says died on
1st. Inst.)

Died, MRS. SARAH G. SMITH, consort of Thomas L. Smith of Louisa Co., and eldest
dau. of Matthew Clay of Va.
RE 24 May 1811, p. 3; VA 23 May, p. 3, days died on 23rd Inst.

Died yesterday, MR. THOMAS SMITH, printer, of this city
VGRMA 20 Jan. 1794, p. 3

Died on 12th Inst., THOMAS SMITH, Esq. of Louisa Co.
VA 23 Dec. 1796, p. 2

Died, THOMAS SMITH, Esq. one of the Judges of the Supreme Court of Pa., on 31 March, in Phila.
Visitor 6 May 1809, p. 54

Died, THOMAS L. SMITH, in Charleston, S.C., Nov. 26th
VP 16 Dec. 1817, p. 3

Died April 29th at his seat in Kent Co., Md., THOMAS S. SMITH, age 89. Had helped write state constitution, and on Committee of Safety during the Revolution
VP 4 May 1819, p. 3

Died on 14th Inst., age 76, REV. DR. WILLIAM SMITH, writer, preacher & for many years provost of the College of Philadelphia
VA 25 May 1803, p. 3

Died on 16th Inst. at an advanced age, WILLIAM SMITH, SR., Esq. of Powhatan
VICGA 27 Jan. 1790, p. 3

Died on 4th Inst. in Powhatan Co., MAJ. WILLIAM STERLING SMITH
VA 13 Oct. 1802, p. 3

Died at his farm near Washington, Culpeper, on 18th last month, COL. GABRIEL SMITHER age 39, leaving wife & 6 children
RE 22 March 1815, p. 3

Died in Hosp. for Lunatics in Williamsburg, HYMAN SNOW, from Norfolk Borough. (No death date)
VGGA 6 Oct. 1790, p. 2

Died at Selina Grove, Pa., Nov. 9th, SIMON SNYDER, late Gov. of Pa.
RE 16 Nov. 1819, p. 3; VP 15 Nov., p. 3

Died Oct. 8th at Bush Hill, Charles City Co., MISS ANN BOLLING SOUTHALL
RE 27 Oct. 1820, p. 3

Died last evening in this city, MR. PLEASANT SOUTHALL, a young man
VGGA 7 March 1798, p. 2

Died on Sat. last (March 2) in this city, MAJ. STEPHEN SOUTHALL
VA 5 March 1799, p. 3

Died at Bermuda 22nd Jan., MR. W. SOUTHALL, merchant of this city
RC 12 Feb. 1796, p. 3

Died, MR. JOHN SOUTHGATE, merchant at King & Queen C.H., on 21st Ult., age 49
RE 2 May 1809, p. 3

Died at Mecklenburg C.H., Aug. 26th, JOHN H. SPEED, age 30, leaving wife & children
RE 11 Sept. 1818, p. 3

Died at the garrison at New Orleans, KEITH SPENCER, Esq. Navy agent. (No death
date)
Visitor 16 Dec. 1809, p. 182

Died, at Mr. William Patterson's in Richmond, WILLIAM A. SPOONER of Frederickburg.
(No death date)
RE 29 Sept. 1818, p. 3

Died on Sun. (Dec. 27) at Nottingham, his seat in Spotsylvania Co., GEN. ALEXANDER
SPOTTSWOOD, a distinguished officer of Revolutionary Army
RE 31 Dec. 1818, p. 3

Died, MAJ. MELCHIZADEK SPRAGINS, age 47, of Halifax Co., age 47, on 10th Inst.
(Ult). Just elected to General Assembly. Leave wife and 5 children
VA 8 May 1810, p. 3

Died on Feb. 22nd, age 27, MR. JOHN SPRATT, a native of Ireland, same to N.Y., as
infant, and to Va. in 1805 to Petersburg. Served with Petersburg Volunteers in War
of 1812
RC 27 Feb. 1815, p. 3

Died on 11th Inst. at seat of William Stanard of Spotsylvania Co., MR. BEVERLEY STANARD
of Albemarle
RE 19 Nov. 1805, p. 3

Died, EDWARD CARTER STANARD, Esq. Editor of The Spirit of '76 on 8th Inst. at Leesburg
RE 15 Dec. 1810, p. 3; VA 18 Dec., p. 3; VP 15 Dec., p. 3

Died on Tues. last (March 12) at Summerville, seat of Judge Fleming in Chesterfield,
his 2nd dau., MRS. JANE W. STANARD, consort of Mr. Beverley Stanard of Orange Co.
VA 19 March 1799, p. 3

Died, MRS. MARY B. STANARD, consort to Bev. C. Stanard, Esq., and dau. of Judge
Fleming, at Summerville in Chesterfield Co., on Tues. (Jan. 28)
RE 30 Jan. 1812, p. 3; VA 3 Feb., p. 3

Died Jan. 4th, MRS. NANCY STANBACK, wife of Mr. George H. Stanback of Richmond, age 38,
leaving husband and 2 children
RC 7 Jan. 1815, p. 3

Died in Richmond, Oct. 2nd, MR. WILLIAM STANHOPE, a native of England
VP 5 Oct. 1819, p. 2

Died, MRS. GRISELLA STANTON, consort of Mr. Thomas Stanton of Richmond, on July 15th,
age 27
RE 21 July 1818, p. 3

146

Died Dec. 17th, MAJ. THOMAS STARKE of Hanover Co.
RE 22 Dec. 1818, p. 3

Died in Richmond Sat. (June 6) MR. THOMAS STAUNTON, a native of Conn., who had come
to visit his children
VP 10 June 1818, p. 3

Died Sept. 18th at Chestnut Ridge, near Greensburgh, Pa., MRS. ST. CLAIR, relict of
late Maj-Gen. Arthur St. Clair
RE 6 Oct. 1818, p. 3; VP 2 Oct., p. 3

Died Jan. 9th near Natchez, Miss., COL. JOHN STEELE, a patriot of the Revolution
RE 11 Feb. 1819, p. 3

Died July 18th, ELIZABETH STEGER, dau. of William Steger of Buckingham Co.
RE 8 Aug. 1820, p. 3

Died May 20th, MRS. SUSAN G. STEGER, wife of Mr. John H. Stegner of Powhatan Co.,
dau. of Col. Overton of Louisa Co.
RC 27 May 1819, p. 3

Died on 16th Ult., at Martinsburg, Berkeley Co., at advanced age, GEN. ADAM STEPHEN
A native of Scotland, he was an officer under Braddock at his defeat. He served
in Continental Army in the Revolution
VGGA 10 Aug. 1791, p. 2

Died on 27th Ult. at his seat Steubenville, BARON FREDERICK de STEUBEN, Maj-Gen in
late U.S. Army
VGGA 31 Dec. 1794, p. 3

Died at Culpeper C.H. Aug. 17th GEN. EDWARD STEVENS, an officer in the Revolutionar
Army
RE 1 Sept. 1820, p. 3; VPRDMA 1 Sept., p. 2 (with details of his army record)

Died at Culpeper C.H. Dec. 3rd, MRS. GILLY STEVENS, relict of Gen. Edward Stevens,
age 75
VPRDMA 27 Dec. 1820, p. 3

Died in Havana, June 11th, GEORGE P. STEVENSON, late of Richmond. His father-in-la
was late Peter Carr. He leaves wife and 4 children
RE 6 July 1819, p. 3

Died in New Orleans last August, DR. JAMES STEVENSON, formerly of Fredericksburg
RE 14 Oct. 1817, p. 3

Died, MRS. M. STEVENSON, consort of Andrew Stevenson of this city, on 4th Inst.
VA 14 May 1812, p. 3

Died in Paris, March 29th, MRS. ANNA MARIA CAMPBELL STEWART, wife of Frederick Camp
Stewart of this state
RE 28 May 1819, p. 3; RC 27 May, p. 3

Died, MR. ARTHUR STEWART, merchant of this city. (No death date)
VICGA 13 Jan. 1790, p. 3

Died, MR. CHARLES STEWART of this city. Interred in churchyard Sat. last (Sept. 20)
VGWA 25 Sept. 1788, p. 3

Died in Ohio, JOHN STEWART, Esq. of York, Pa., late a member of U.S. House of
Representatives. (No death date)
Visitor 23 Sept. 1809, p. 135

Died in Alexandria on Thurs. (Jan. 19th) MR. WILLIAM STEWART, for many years an
inhabitant there
RE 26 Feb. 1818, p. 3

Died yesterday, MR. BARTLETT STILL, an old inhabitant of Richmond
RC 16 June 1819, p. 3; VP 16 June, p. 3, days died yesterday

Died lately, in North Caroline, COL. BASSETT STITH, formerly of Va.
VP 23 Sept. 1816, p. 3

Died Sunday last (before Oct. 9) age 64, in Halifax N.C., MRS. JOANNA STITH,
widow of Anderson Stith, Esq. of Hampstead in King William Co.
VGRMA 14 Oct. 1793, p. 3

Died, COL. JOHN STITH, a veteran of the Revolution, on 10th Inst., at his seat in
Brunswick Co.
RE 2 March 1810, p. 3; Visitor 24 Feb., p. 15

Died on Sat. last (March 31) MRS. REBECCA STITH, spouse of Maj. John Stith, Westbury,
Charles City Co.
VGWA 5 April 1787, p. 2

Died on 13th Inst. in Henrico Co., MR. J. STOCKDELL
Observatory 23 July 1798, p. 2; VGGA 24 July, p. 3

Died Friday last (Oct. 12 or 19), age 54, GEN. JOHN HOSKINS STONE
VA 20 Oct. 1804, p. 3

Died at seat of Col. Bailey Washington in Stafford Co., on 14th Inst., MISS CATHERINE
STORKE, dau. of William Storke of Belle Isle in King George Co.
RE 2 Aug. 1805, p. 3

Died on Thurs. last (Dec. 12) at Contention the seat of Mr. James Pleasants in
Goochland Co., MRS. SUSANNA R. STORRS, consort of Mr. Gervas Storrs
VGRMA 16 Dec. 1793, p. 3

Died in Raleigh on 27th Ult., MR. CHARLES STORY, comedian, for some time attached
to the Virginia Company
VA 9 Dec. 1806, p. 3

Died, JOHN STOTT, drowned in James River Oct. 7th, buried at Curles
RE 16 Oct. 1816, p. 3; VA 9 Oct., p. 3, days Capt. Stott; RC 15 Oct., p. 3

Died Thurs. last (Feb. 19) DR. ALEXANDER STRACHAN, of this city at an advanced age
VGWA 26 Feb. 1789, p. 3

Died at Brodie, his res. in Spotsylvania Co., May 14th, THOMAS STRACHAN, age 74
RE 25 May 1819, p. 3

Died, MR. JAMES STRANGE, a native of Scotland, & for many years resident of
Petersburg, on Sun. last (May 14)
RE 19 May 1809, p. 3; VA 19 May, p. 3

Died, MR. GEORGE F. STRAS, on Sat. last (Jan. 19)
RE 22 Jan. 1811, p. 3

Died on Tues. last (June 11) MRS. STRAS, consort of Mr. George Stras of this city
VA 18 June 1799, p. 3

Died, MRS. PATSY PERKINS STREET, consort of Capt. Parke Street, and dau. of Col.
Goodall, at her res. in Hanover Co. on 1st Inst.
RE 19 May 1809, p. 3

Died in Richmond, MR. FRANCIS STROBIA, an officer in the Va. Bank. (No death date)
RE 1 March 1815, p. 3; RC 1 March, p. 3, says died Tues. (Feb. 28), age 28, first
teller in Bank of Va.

Died, MR. JOHN STROBIA, on Fri. last (March 10) for 28 years a citizen of Richmond,
age 67
RE 17 March 1809, p. 3; VA 14 March, p. 3; VGGA 14 March, p. 3; Visitor 11 March
p. 23

Died, MR. JOHN STROBIA, on Fri. last (March 10) for 28 years a citizen of Richmond,
age 67
RE 17 March 1809, p. 3; VA 14 March, p. 3; VGGA 14 March, p. 3; Visitor 11 March
p. 23

Died on Sun. last (May 24) MRS. MARY STROBIA, consort of Mr. John Strobia of this
city
RC 26 May 1795, p. 3; VGRMA 28 May, p. 2

Died at Southampton, Mass., Nov. 7th, CALEB STRONG, late Gov. of Mass.
RE 16 Nov. 1819, p. 3; VP 15 Nov., p. 3

Died Sat. last (febore Dec. 12), JAMES SULLIVAN, Gov. of Mass., in Boston
VA 20 Dec. 1808, p. 3; RE 20 Dec. 1808, p. 3(says died on 10th Inst.);
Spirit of 76 20 Dec., p. 3; VGGA 20 Dec., says died 10th Inst.)

Died, MR. SULLY, formerly of the Charleston Theatre, on Tues. last (April 7).
For past few weeks a resident of this city (Augusta, April 9)
RE 24 April 1812, p. 3; VA 23 April, p. 2

Died, GOV. INCREASE SUMNER of Mass. at his seat near Boston, on 7th Inst.
VA 21 June 1799, p. 3

Died Jan. 10th, GEORGE SUMMERS OF Kanawha Co., age 59
RE 31 Jan. 1818, p. 3

Died Friday (Oct. 1) at res. of Mr. Richard Prichard, Warwick Co., CAPT. DANIEL
H. SWAIN of the ship "Maria"
RC 5 Oct. 1819, p. 3

Died, MR. MATTHEW SWAIN, SR., yesterday, a res. of Richmond formerly of Ky.
RC 16 April 1819, p. 3; VP 16 April, p. 2

Died on 28th Ult., MR. JAMES SWAINE of Charles City Co.
VGWA 11 June 1789, p. 3

Died in Washington City on 29 Nov. CALEB SWAN, Esq., late Paymaster General of
U.S. Army
Visitor 16 Dec. 1809, p. 182

Died, JOHN SWANN, SR., at his seat in Powhatan, on 11th Inst.
VGGA 21 Nov. 1809, p. 3; Visitor, 2 Dec., p. 174

Died, MRS. MARY SWANN, wife of John Swann of Powhatan, on Nov. 13th, leaving husband
and 7 children
VP 30 Nov. 1810, p. 3

Died July 31st, JOHN SWANWICK, representative from Phila. to the Federal Councils
Observatory 9 Aug. 1798, p. 3

Died Aug. 15th, MRS. ANNA SWINTON, relict of late Mr. George Swinton of Caroline Co.,
age about 90
RE 1 Sept. 1820, p. 3

Died, MR. FORTUNATUS SYDNOR, on the 10th, at West Wood
RE 26 July 1811, p. 3

Died on 21st Inst., MR. ROBERT SYDNOR of this city
VGGA 28 March 1804, p. 2

Died, CAPT. WILLIAM SYDNOR, Aug. 4th at his res. in Nottoway Co., a veteran of the
Revolution
RE 13 Aug. 1819, p. 3; RC 13 Aug., p. 3, says age 67

Died on Fri. last (July 15) in this city, MR. SAMUEL J. SYKES, a native of England
RC 19 July 1796, p. 2; VGGA 20 July, p. 3

Died, MRS. ELIZABETH SYME, on 14th Inst. (Ult.), wife of Mr. Nicholas Syme of
Hanover Co.
RE 7 Aug. 1807, p. 2

Died at Rocky Mills, Hanover Co., on 25th Inst. (Ult.), COL. JOHN SYME, age 77 years
11 months. He was State Senator, was in the French & Indian War in 1755 and in the
Revolution
VA 4 Dec. 1805, p. 3

Died, MRS. SARAH SYME, at Rocky Mills, on 20th Inst.
RE 23 Nov. 1810, p. 3; VX VP 23 Nov., p. 3

Died Dec. 18 at his res. in Powhatan Co., THOMAS TABB
RE 10 Jan. 1818, p. 3

Died Aug. 17th on board the ship "Philip Tabb" en route from Liverpool to Norfolk,
MR. THOMAS T. TABB, a farmer, of Matthews Co., age 28
VP 20 Sept. 1819, p. 3

Died in this city on Sun. last (Aug. 2), MR. BENJAMIN TALIAFERRO of Williamsburg
VA 4 Aug. 1801, p. 3

Died March 25th at res. of her mother in Henrico Co., MRS. MARTHA TALIAFERRO, consor
of Mr. James Taliaferro of Lynchburg
RC 28 March 1820, p. 3

Died, MRS. REBECCA TALIAFERRO, consort of late Col. Richard Taliferro of James City
Co., on 24th Inst.
VP 30 Oct. 1810, p. 3

Died, MR. ROBERT H. TALIAFERRO, age 23, at his seat near Williamsburg, on 17th Ult.
RE 1 July 1807, p. 3

Died at his father's res. in Hanover Co., PETER TALLEY, son of Rev. Charles Talley,
age 15
RE 22 Aug. 1820, p. 3

Died, MRS. MARY TALLY, consort of Mr. William Tally, and only dau. of Capt. Samuel
Grantland, on 22nd Inst., near New Castle
RE 30 June 1812, p. 3

Died, MR. WILLIAM TALMAN of New Kent Co., age 85, on Wed. last (Feb. 15)
VA 17 Feb. 1809, p. 3

Died yesterday, COL. WILLIAM TATHAM (stepped in front of a cannon in Capitol Square
as a salute was fired)
VP 23 Feb. 1819, p. 2

Died lately in King William Co. at an advanced age, MRS. ANN TAYLOR, wife of
Richard S. Taylor, Esq.
VA 16 Oct. 1802, p. 3

Died, BEVERLEY C. TAYLOR, eldest son of Mrs. S. Taylor, formerly of New Kent, now
of this city, on Sat. last (April 30)
RE 3 May 1808, p. 3

Died on Thurs. (May 18) MR. FRANCIS TAYLOR, age 52 of Richmond
VP 20 May 1815, p. 3

Died at Petersburg Nov. 9th, GEORGE KEITH TAYLOR, Counsellor at Law
RE 18 Nov. 1815, p. 3; VA 15 Nov., p. 3

Died, MR. JOHN TAYLOR, of this city, on Wed. last (June 13). Was a brassfounder.
VP 15 June 1810, p. 3

Died on Thurs. last (July 29) MRS. JUDITH TAYLOR, consort of Mr. Thomas Taylor,
and eldest dau. of John Brown, Esq. of this city
VGGA 31 July 1802, p. 3

Died, MRS. MARTHA TAYLOR, consort of Samuel Taylor, Esq., of Manchester. (No
death date)
Visitor 10 Feb. 1810, p. 6

Died, MRS. TAYLOR, spouse of Col. John Taylor of Richmond Co.
VGWA 1 Feb. 1787, p. 3

Died on 14th Inst. at house of Mr. James Herron, merchant, MRS. TAYLOR
VGGA 22 Feb. 1792, p. 3

Died, NATHANIEL G. TAYLOR, 3rd son of Mrs. Susanna Taylor of this city, on Wed.
(Nov. 25), age 16
RE 27 Nov. 1807, p. 3

Died on 1st this mo. in Halifax Co., MRS. OBEDIENCE TAYLOR, wife of Dr. Thomas
Taylor, age 20, leaving a husband and father
RE 28 Oct. 1815, p. 3

Died, MISS PATSEY TAYLOR of Williamsburg. (No death date)
VGGA 31 Jan. 1798, p. 2

Died Nov. 27th, MRS. SARAH TAYLOR, consort of Mr. William D. Taylor, of Hanover Co.,
leaving husband and 6 small children
RE 9 Dec. 1815, p. 3

Died, CAPT. WILLIAM TAYLOR, drowned on 29th Ult.
RE 13 Oct. 1809, p. 3

Died Sept. 11th at his res. in Lunenburg Co., age 82, WILLIAM TAYLOR, at one time
a member of the House of Burgesses. Leaves a widow and numerous offspring
RE 22 Sept. 1820, p. 3

Died March 8th, WILLIAM ROSCOW TAYLOR, of New Kent, age 31
RE 13 March 1818, p. 3

Died in Phila, on the ____ Ult., HENRY TAZEWELL, Esq., Senator of this state in
U.S. Congress
VGGA 29 Jan. 1799, p. 3

Died, JOHN TAZEWELL, Esq. of Williamsburg. (No death date)
VG April 7, 1781, p. 2

Died on 27th Ult., MRS. FANNY TEMPLE, relict of Col. Samuel Temple of Caroline
VA 5 May, 1801, p. 3

Died on Mon. last (Oct. 8) MR. LISTON TEMPLE of this city
VA 13 Oct. 1804, p. 3; VGGA 13 Oct., p. 2 (says Thurs. last)

Died Aug. 7th, age 72, MRS. MOLLY TEMPLE, widow of Capt. Benjamin Temple of King
William Co.
RE 18 Aug. 1820, p. 3

Died on Sun. last (Aug. 5) MRS. TEMPLE, consort of Mr. Liston Temple of this city
Observatory 9 Aug. 1798, p. 3

Died on Tues. 23rd (24th) July at his seat in Caroline Co., COL. SAMUEL TEMPLE
Observatory 30 July 1798, p. 3

Died Dec. 12th, MAJ. GEORGE TERRELL of Caroline Co., an officer in the Revolution
VP 19 Dec. 1817, p. 3

Died, MR. S. Q. TERRY, age 25, son of MRS. MARY RAINS of King William Co., in
Richmond. (No death date)
RE 12 May 1809, p. 3

Died, STEPHEN TERRY, on 1st Inst. in King William Co., at an advanced age. His
Bible gave his birth date as July 4, 1711
VP 26 Jan. 1811, p. 3

Died, COL. WILLIAM TERRY, Delegate from Halifax on Friday last (Dec. 21)
RE 25 Dec. 1810, p. 3

Died on 2nd Inst. at Saratoga Springs, MR. ALEXANDER THOMAS of Walpole, proprietor
and editor of The Farmer's Museum
Visitor 12 Aug. 1809, p. 110

Died in Tattnal Co., Ga., on 11th April last, JAMES THOMAS, age 134
VA 21 Nov. 1804, p. 3

Died in Frederick Co., Md., May 2nd, JOHN HANSON THOMAS, age 39
VP 13 May 1815, p. 3

Died on 4th November, MRS. ANN T. THOMPSON, wife of Mr. Thomas Thompson of Fair Hil
VGGA 21 Dec. 1791, p. 3

Died, MR. BELFOUR THOMPSON, merchant of this city, age 47, at Yorktown, on 29th Ult
RE 11 Sept. 1812, p. 3

Died in Petersburg on Thurs. last (Jan. 24), JOHN THOMPSON, Esq., Attorney at Law.
Buried in family burying ground 7 miles from town
VGGA 29 Jan. 1799, p. 3

Died in Philadelphia, MR. JOHN THOMPSON, printer, celebrated for his edition of
The Bible
VA 21 Aug. 1805, p. 3

Died on Mon. last (Aug. 12) at his seat in Hanover Co., age 75, MR. NATHANIEL
THOMPSON, Sr.
RE 16 Aug. 1805, p. 3; VA 17 Aug., p. 3; VGGA 17 Aug, p. 2

Died on 25th Inst., age 44, MR. ROBERT THOMPSON, wheelwright, of this city
VA 26 Nov. 1803, p. 3

Died at Rocky Mills on 5th Inst., THOMAS THOMPSON, a native of Ireland
VA 15 Nov. 1799, p. 3; VGGA 15 Nov., p. 3, "says formerly wine merchant in
Madeira"

Died on Sat. last (Aug. 20) MR. JESSE THORNTON, hatter, of this city
RC 27 Aug. 1796, p. 3; VGRMA 24 Aug., p. 3

Died lately at his seat in Orange Co., GEN. WASHINGTON THORNTON, in prime of life
RE 19 Dec. 1816, p. 3

Died May 22nd at his res. in Fredericksburg, COL. WILLIAM THORNTON, age 73
RE 26 May 1818, p. 3

Died on Wed. (before Aug. 5) in Charleston, S.C., MR. WILLIAM THROCKMORTON, printer
VGRMA 20 Aug. 1796, p. 3

Died in the Penitentiary in this city, 29 Nov., BLUMER TILMAN, from Brunswick
VA 4 Dec. 1801, p. 3

Died on Mon. last (April 25) MR. ARCHIBALD TIMBERLAKE, age 20, an apprentice in
the newspaper office
VGGA 30 April 1803, p. 3; Examiner 30 April, p. 3

Died, MR. FRANCIS TIMBERLAKE of Hanover Co., on 7th Inst. Leaves wife and 7 children
RE 15 March 1808, p. 3; VGGA 15 March, p. 3; Virginian 15 March, p. 2

Died, MR. MATTHEW TIMBERLAKE, in Hanover Co., Friday last (Feb. 5)
RE 11 Feb. 1808, p. 3

Died, MRS. MILDRED TIMBERLAKE, on 25th Inst. in Hanover Co.
RE 30 Jan. 1810, p. 3

Died, MRS. SARAH TIMBERLAKE, consort of Capt. David Timberlake of Hanover, on Thurs.
last (A pril 2 or 9)
RE 10 April 1812, p. 3

Died, PETER TINSLEY, Esq., Clerk of the High Court of Chancery, on 21st Inst., at
his house in this town
RE 24 July 1810, p. 3; VA 24 July, p. 2; VP 24 July, p. 3

Died at New Orleans Oct. 11th, MR. WILLIAM TISDALE, formerly of Petersburg, Va., who served as Lt. in Petersburg Volunteers in late war.
RE 27 Nov. 1818, p. 3

Died at Newburyport, Mass., MR. WILLIAM TITCOMB, trying to cure rheumatism by fire
VA 13 Feb. 1801, p. 3

Died June 9th, MRS. FRANCES S. TODD, consort of Rev. William Todd of King & Queen Co. and eldest dau. of Mr. Joseph Gwathmey of King William Co.
RE 20 June 1820, p. 3

Died on 10th Inst., age 19, HENRY TODD, son of Mr. B. Todd of Charlotte Co.
VGGA 27 Nov. 1801, p. 3

Died yesterday, MR. MILES TODD, a blacksmith
VP 24 Nov. 1817, p. 3

Died, MRS. MARY TOLER, on 15th Inst. at her res. in Caroline Co.
RE 26 Nov. 1813, p. 3

Died, Jan. 16th, MORGAN TOMKIES, U.S. military storekeeper, and former delegate from Gloucester Co. in the Assembly
RC 18 Jan. 1815, p. 3

Died on 6th Inst. at Clay Hill in Amelia Co., age 27, MRS. ELIZABETH C. TOMPKINS, wife of Maj. Christopher Tompkins of Matthews Co.
RE 14 Sept. 1814, p. 3

Died at Lynchburg on 20th Ult., the REV. JAMES TOMPKINS
RE 1 Aug. 1806, p. 3

Died in Fauquier Co. June 28th, MR. JOHN TOMPKINS, late of this city, leaving an amiable consort
VA 28 July 1802, p. 3; VGGA 21 July, p. 3

Died on 13th Ult. at his seat in Lancaster Co., COL. HENRY TOWLES, age 53
VGGA 6 Dec. 1799, p. 3

Died Feb. 2nd at his res. in Chesterfield Co., MR. DANIEL TRABUE, age 68
RE 13 Feb. 1819, p. 3

Died at home of his father in Georgetown, D.C., GEORGE TRAVERS, Attorney at Law, suicide. (no death date)
RC 15 March 1819, p. 3

Died, COL. CHAMPION TRAVIS of Williamsburg, on 22nd Inst. (Ult.), one of the owners of Jamestown Island, a former member of the legislature
RE 4 Sept. 1810, p. 3

Died on Mon. last (Dec. 10) CAPT. FRANCIS TRAVIS, employed by American Gov't in
the Revolution
VGGA 12 Dec. 1804, p. 3

Died Feb. 3rd in Williamsburg, MR. FRANCIS B. TRAVIS, only son of Capt. Samuel
Travis now of House of Delegates
RE 12 Feb. 1818, p. 3

Died in Weston, Conn, July 19th, MR. BRADLEY TREADWELL, age 31
VPRDMA 3 Aug. 1820, p. 3

Died, MRS. SARAH TREBELL, consort of Mr. Wm. Trebell, at his seat in Martins
Hundred, James River. (No death date)
VGWA 12 Feb. 1789, p. 3

Died on Sunday last (Oct. 11) at his seat near Williamsburg, MR. WILLIAM TREBELL,
age 68
VGWA 15 Oct. 1789, p. 3

Died, MRS. JANE TREDWAY, wife of Thomas Tredway, age 23, on 15th Ult. at Mr. James
MacFarland's in Lunenburg
VGGA 1 Nov. 1806, p. 3

Died, MR. MOSES TREDWAY of Prince Edward Co., on 14th Inst.
VA 27 Nov. 1805, p. 3

Died, MASTER ALEXANDER TRENT, eldest son of Peterfield Trent, Esq. of Chesterfield
Co., age 13, on 13th Ult.
VGAA 7 Aug. 1784, p. 2

Died Wed. (May 20th) MR. EDWARD W. TRENT of Manchester
RE 22 May 1818, p. 3; VP 22 May, p. 2

Died, DR. JOHN TRENT, at Camden, S.C. on 9th Inst.
Visitor 16 Dec. 1809, p. 182

Died on 16th Inst., MRS. TRENT, spouse of Alexander Trent, Esq. of Cumberland Co.
VGGA 24 Dec. 1794, p. 3

Died Dec. 15th PETER F. TRENT, Esq. eldest son of Peter Field Trent, age 18 of
this city
VGGA 15 Jan. 1794, p. 3

Died, PETERFIELD TRENT, at an advanced age. (No death date)
VGRMA 20 Nov. 1794, p. 3; VGRC 21 Nov., says died Nov. 19th

Died in Sadsburg Township, Pa., Chester Co., July 21st, MR. JOHN TREVILLA, age 50
VPRDMA 3 Aug. 1820, p. 3

Died, COL. JOHN TRIGG, in Bedford Co., a Member of Congress. (No death date)
VA 14 July 1804, p. 3

Died in Richmond, MR. DANIEL TRIPLETT, a venerable inhabitant. (No death date)
RE 8 May 1818, p. 3

Died in New York, Nov. 10th, MISS LAETITIA ANN TRIPLETT, youngest dau. of Daniel
Triplett of Richmond, age 19
RE 21 Nov. 1817, p. 3; VP 17 Nov., p. 3, days died Nov. 11th, age 18

Died in Westport, Mass, April 13th, PELEG TRIPP, age 20, of drinking too much at
one time
VP 26 April 1819, p. 3

Died at New Orleans 29 Aug., GORE BROWSE TRIST, Collector of the Port
RE 13 Oct. 1804, p. 3; VA Oct. 17, p. 3 (says Bore)

Died Thurs. (Aug. 29) MR. JOHN TROWER, an old inhabitant of Richmond, leaving wife
and several infant children
RE 31 Aug. 1816, p. 3; VP 31 Aug., p. 3

Died Nov. 17th, MRS. ELIZABETH TRUEHEART, wife of Mr. H. Trueheart of Powhatan Co.,
dau. of late Gen. L. Mosby, and granddau. of late Gen. Charles Scott of Ky
RE 14 Dec. 1816, p. 3

Died Jan. 28th, MRS. ELIZABETH TRUEHEART, consort of Col. William Trueheart of
Hanover Co.
RE 2 Feb. 1819, p. 3; RC 30 Jan, p. 3; VP 1 Feb., p. 3

Died on 24th Inst., MRS. ELIZABETH H. TRUEHEART, consort of Maj. William Trueheart
of Hanover Co.
VA 29 Jan. 1799, p. 3

Died Aug. 17th, MRS. MARIA D. TRUEHEART, consort of Mr. Daniel Trueheart of Richmond
leaving an infant, age 1 mo.
RE 19 Aug. 1817, p. 3; VP 19 Aug., p. 3

Died on Wed. last (Dec. 2) MRS. TRUEHEART, wife of Daniel Trueheart, Esq. of Hanover
VA 4 Dec. 1801, p. 3

Died on Wed. last (May 11) MRS. POLLY TRUEHEART, consort of Mr. Bartholomew Truehear
VGRMA 18 May 1796, p. 3; RC 14 May, p. 2

Died, JONATHAN TRUMBULL, Gov. of Conn. at his seat in Lebanon, on 7th Inst., age 69
RE 18 Aug. 1809, p. 3; Visitor 26 Aug., p. 118 says died on 31st Ult.

Died at Coxsackie, N.Y., MR. THOMAS TRYON, aged at least 110, some say 120
VA 20 Aug. 1803, p. 3

Died, on the 8th Inst., MR. JOEL TUCKER of this city
VA 17 Sept. 1806, p. 3

Died on Wed. last in this city (Feb. 27) MR. JOHN TUCKER, Chief Asst. in the land
office. Interred in the churchyard
VGGA 1 March 1799, p. 3

Died at G. Anderson's of Newington, on 16th Inst., MRS. REBECCA E. TUCKER, age 77
VA 31 March 1804, p. 3

Died, MR. GEORGE TURBERVILLE of Peckatone in Westmoreland Co. (No death date)
VGWA 4 Jan. 1793, p. 3

Died, MRS. ANN TURNER, consort of Capt. George Turner of Staunton, on 17th
RE 24 April 1810, p. 3; VA 24 April, p. 3

Died April 5th, CAPT. ANTHONY TURNER of Richmond, age 40, leaving wife and 3 small
children
RC 6 April 1819, p. 3

Died, MRS. ELIZABETH TURNER, consort of Mr. Martin Turner, of this city, on 18th
Inst.
VA 26 Feb. 1811, p. 3

Died on 19th Ult., MR. JEDEDIAH TURNER of Hanover Co., age 29
VA 16 March 1803, p. 3

Died Tues. (Sept. 8) MRS. MARY TURNER, age 80. Lived in Richmond for last 23 years
RC 10 Sept. 1818, p. 3

Died in D.C., MISS MARY C. TURNER, age 17, eldest dau. of Samuel Turner of Georgetown. (No death date)
RE 7 Sept. 1819, p. 3

Died, MR. REUBEN TURNER, age 67, at Warm Springs in Bath Co., on 8th Inst.
VA 16 May 1807, p. 3

Died in Richmond on March 23rd, MISS SALLY TURNER, dau. of Mr. Nathaniel Turner,
late of Hanover Co.
RE 30 March 1816, p. 3

Died Wed. last (Nov. 20) at Salisbury in Chesterfield Co., MRS. CAROLINE M. TURPIN,
wife of Dr. Philip Turpin of that place
VGGA 27 Nov. 1793, p. 3; VGRMA 25 Nov.

Died on 20th Inst. at his house in Powhatan, CAPT. THOMAS TURPIN, age 81
VICGA 30 June 1790, p. 2

Died on ____ Inst. at his seat in Powhatan Co., MR. THOMAS TURPIN
VA 31 March 1797, p. 2; VGGA 29 March, p. 3, says Thomas Turpin, Sen.

Died last Fri. (May 3) MRS. TWINING, spouse of Mr. Nathaniel Twining of this city
VGRMA 6 May 1793, p. 3

Died in Mass., JAMES TYLER, age 58, late of Scotland, where he was distinguished
surgeon & geographer
VA 11 Feb. 1804, p. 3

Died, JOHN TYLER, Judge of Federal Court of District of Va., at his home in Charles
City Co., on 5th Inst.
RE 12 Jan. 1813, p. 3; VA 14 Jan., p. 3, days died on 9th

Died on 22nd Inst., MRS. MARY TYLER, spouse of Judge Tyler, leaving many children
VA 31 March 1797, p. 2; VGGA 29 March, p. 3

Died, SAMUEL TYLER, (Chancellor) in Williamsburg on Mon. last (March 23)
RE 31 March 1812, p. 3; VA 30 March, p. 3, says late Chancellor of Williamsburg
District, age 47, died on 24th, leaving wife and 4 children

Died, MR. THOMAS UNDERWOOD, age 75, in Hanover Co. (No death date)
RE 4 Feb. 1815, p. 3

Died on Thurs. last (Aug. 4) in this city, MR. WILLIAM UNDERWOOD of Goochland, a
young man
RC 6 Aug. 1796, p. 2

Died at his seat in Caroline Co. on 16th Ult, COL. JAMES UPSHAW
VA 12 July 1806, p. 3; RE 22 July, p. 3, says age 76

Died at his seat in Essex 23rd July, JOHN UPSHAW, Esq., age 86
VA 7 Aug. 1801, p. 3

Died on Aug. 27th at White Hall, seat of late John Upshaw, Esq., MRS. MARY UPSHAW,
in her 64th yr.
VA 16 Sept. 1807, p. 3

Died on 22nd Aug., MRS. MOLLY UPSHAW, 41, wife of Maj. James Upshaw of Essex Co.
VA 17 Sept. 1803, p. 3

Died, DR. JOHN UPSHUR of Northampton Co., age 26, leaving aged mother. (No death
date)
RE 26 May 1818, p. 3

Died on Mon. (Sept. 12), age 9, CHRISTOPHER ROGERS VAIL, eldest son of Mr. I. Vail,
of Richmond
RC 21 Sept. 1816, p. 3

Died Sept. 29th at his res. near Vevay, Ind., MR. JEAN PIERRE VAIRIN, leaving
widow and 3 sons
RE 31 Oct. 1817, p. 3

Died on Sun. last (June 12) MARKS VANDEWALL, Post Master of this city
VA 14 June 1808, p. 3; RE 14 June, p. 3; VGGA 14 June, p. 3; Virginian 14 June,
p. 3

Died yesterday, MRS. SUSANNA VANDEWALL, consort of Col. Marks Vandewall of this
city
VGRMA 26 June 1794, p. 3

Died Jan. 13th in Ky., CAPT. HENRY VanSWEARINGEN, a native of Berkeley Co., Va.
RE 15 Feb. 1820, p. 3

Died at his res. in Amelia Co. May 31st, ASA VAUGHAN, leaving wife and numerous
children
RE 9 June 1820, p.3

Died in Powhatan Co., Oct. 19th, at Capt. M. Montague's, MRS. ELIZABETH VAUGHAN,
age 86, formerly of Mecklenburg Co.
RE 27 Oct. 1820, p. 3

Died at Amelia C.H. Sat. last (May 30) MR. JAMES VAUGHAN, JR., formerly of this
city
RC 6 June 1795, p. 3; VGRMA 4 June, p. 3

Died Jan. 5th at her res. in Goochland Co., MRS. MARY VAUGHAN
RE 11 Jan. 1820, p. 3

Died on the 8th last, at Rising Sun Tavern, MISS FANNY VENABLE of Prince Edward
VA 18 June 1799, p. 3

Died, JAMES VEST, executed last Friday in Chesterfield Co., for murder (17 Dec.)
RE 25 Dec. 1819, p. 3; RC 23 Dec., p. 3, for murdering this wife

Died, CAPT. ELI VICKERY late of Phila, at Old Point Comfort, recently
Visitor 26 Aug. 1809, p. 118

Died, ROBERT BROOKE VOSS, Esq. on 12th Inst. of a fall from his horse
VA 17 Oct. 1811, p. 3

Died, REV. JAMES WADDELL of Albemarle. (No death date)
RE 4 Oct. 1805, p. 3; VA 9 Oct., p. 3

Died Oct. 7th, at Mrs. Waddy's in Louisa Co., age 40, MR. JOHN WADDY, one of the
first accountants in Va. Leaves mother, brothers and sisters
RE 22 Oct. 1819, p. 3

Died at Hartford on April 30th, HON. JEREMIAH WADSWORTH, age 61, a Colonel in the
Revolution and a Member of Congress
VA 19 May 1804, p. 3

Died on 9th Ut., age 107, MRS. ELIZABETH WAGNER, born and died within a few miles of Gloucester
VA 6 March 1807, p. 3

Died, MRS. ANN WALFORD, consort of Mr. Edward Walford, on May 13th, at Mr. John Wile in Amelia, leaving husband and three children
RE 29 May 1812, p. 3; VA 21 May, p. 3

Died on 11th Inst., MRS. SUSANNA WALFORD, consort of Mr. Edward Walford of this city
RE 18 March 1806, p. 3

Died Mon. last (Dec. 9) at Eppington in Chesterfield Co., MRS. ELIZABETH WALKER, consort of Dr. David Walker of Petersburg
VA 14 Dec. 1805, p. 3

Died, in Petersburg, DR. WALKER, an eminent physician and first Member of House of Delegates from Borough of Petersburg
RE 20 July 1816, p. 3

Died, MRS. JANE B. WALKER, widow of late Col. Francis Walker, at her seat Castle Hill in Albemarle Co. on 6th Ult.
VA 1 March 1808, p. 3

Died, JOHN WALKER, Esq. of Belvoir at his seat in Albemarle Co. (No death date)
RE 2 Jan. 1810, p. 3

Died Aug. 13th, MRS. MARY WALTHALL, consort of Mr. Francis Walthall of Buckingham Co., age 69
RE 27 Aug. 1819, p. 2

Died at Castle Hill on 7th Nov., age 81, DR. THOMAS WALKER
VGGA 12 Nov. 1794, p. 3

Died last evening, MR. THOMAS WALKER of this city, tailor
RC 25 June 1796, p. 3; VGRMA 25 June, p. 2

Died, THOMAS WALKER of Indian Fields, Charles City Co., on 18th Ult., the date of his birth, age 29
RE 6 Feb. 1808, p. 3

Died at Norfolk on 12th Inst., WILLIAM WALKER, Esq. of this city, late of Warren and Albemarle Counties, age 33
VA 21 March 1804, p. 3

Died in Huntington Co., Pa., Nov. 4, 5 year old dau. of William WALKER of Alexandri
VP 19 Nov. 1817, p. 3

Died Oct. 23rd, BENJAMIN CARTER WALLER, Attorney at Law, of Williamsburg, age 62
RC 31 Oct. 1820, p. 3

Died, JOHN WALKER WALLER, on 22nd Inst., in King William Co., at seat of Mrs. Mártha Williams. Had lived in York Co.
RE 29 May 1813, p. 3

Died on Friday last (Aug. 4), MRS. MARTHA WALLER, spouse of Hon. Benjamin Waller, Esq., in Williamsburg
VG Aug. 9, 1780, p. 2

Died, MRS. ELIZABETH WALTON, consort of Mr. Thomas Walton or Prince Edward, on 13th Inst., age 39
VA 28 Jan. 1815, p. 3

Died on 2nd Ult. near Augusta, Ga., HON. GEORGE WALTON, a Judge of the Superior Court and a Patriot of the Revolution
VA 7 March 1804, p. 3

Died March 3rd, at her res. in Cumberland Co., MRS. JANNETTE WALTON, wife of Mr. Edward Walton of that co., and eldest dau. of Mr. William McLaurine of Powhatan Co.
RE 17 March 1818, p. 4

Died on Thurs. last (Nov. 4), MR. EDWARD WANTON, watchmaker, age 40
VA 8 Nov. 1813, p. 3

Died, MR. GIDEON WANTON of this city, on 8th Inst., age 85, formerly inhabitant of Newport, R.I.
VA 11 April 1809, p. 3; Visitor 6 May, p. 54

Died at Salem, Mass., Nov. 26th, SAMUEL CORWEN WARD
VP 6 Dec. 1817, p. 3

Died, MR. HUGH WARDEN, in this city, on Fri. last (March 29)
RE 2 April 1811, p. 3; VA 4 April, p. 3; VP 2 April, p. 3

Died on Thurs. last (July 28) MRS. WARDEN, wife of Mr. Hugh Warden of this city
VA 3 Aug. 1803, p. 3

Died on 30th Ult., age 109, SUSSANAH WARDER, formerly wife of William Warder. A negro, she was one of the house servants of William Penn, proprietor of Pa. She was born in Pennsburg Manor in March 1701
Visitor 29 July 1809, p. 102

Died, MRS. SARAH WARDLAW, consort of Dr. William Wardlaw of this city, on 22nd Inst.
VA 26 April 1808, p. 3; RE 26 April, p. 3; VGGA 26 April, p. 3, says Wardlow

Died yesterday, DR. WILLIAM WARDLAW, at his res. in Manchester
RC 13 Oct. 1819, p. 3

Died Thursday last (Feb. 17) MR. DANIEL WARDROP of Manchester, merchant, age 29. Interred at Ampthill, seat of his bro., James Wardrop, Esq.
VGGA 23 Feb. 1791, p. 3

Died on 10th Inst., MRS. WARDROP of Ampthill, near Richmond, a native of Scotland
VGRC 13 Sept. 1793, p. 3

Died about 3 weeks since, MRS. HANNAH CLARKE WARE, consort of Robert S. Ware of
New Kent Co.
RE 3 Dec. 1805, p. 3

Died at his res. in Goochland Co., July 1st, MR. JAMES WARE, age 62, veteran of the
Revolution
RE 14 July 1818, p. 3

Died in March last, MR. JOHN WARE of King & Queen Co.
VGGA 19 June 1793, p. 3

Died in Dumfries on 17th Inst., MR. JOHN WARE
RE 23 Aug. 1805, p. 3

Died, FRANCIS F. WARING, killed in a duel near Frankford, KY
RE 10 Aug. 1819, p. 2

Died Feb. 13th, HORATIO, eldest son of Mr. James Warrell of Richmond
RC 15 Feb. 1820, p. 3

Died, WILLIAM WARROCK, of this city, on Thurs. last (Sept. 19)
VA 21 Sept. 1805, p. 3

Died on Sat. last (Dec. 14) GEN. GEORGE WASHINGTON
VA 20 Dec. 1799, p. 3; VF 18 Dec., p. 3, "age 68"

Died, COL. JOHN WASHINGTON, on 16th Ult. at Sandy Hill, S.C.
RE 2 April 1810, p. 4

Died at Mount Vernon Sat. last (May 22) MRS. MARTHA WASHINGTON, widow of late
illustrious Gen. George Washington
VA 29 May 1802, p. 3; VGGA 29 May, p. 3

Died at Harwood on 2nd Inst., MRS. MARY WASHINGTON, age 30, consort of Col. Wm. A.
Washington, and eldest dau. of Richard Henry Lee, dec'd
RC 28 Nov. 1795, p. 3

Died Tuesday (Sept. 1) at her seat near Fredericksburg, at an advanced age,
MRS. WASHINGTON, mother of our President
VGWA 3 Sept. 1789, p. 3; VIC 2 Sept.

Died Oct. 27th, JOEL WATKINS of Boydton
RE 24 Nov. 1818, p. 3

Died at his seat in Charlotte County, Jan. 3rd, COL. JOEL WATKINS
RE 11 Jan. 1820, p. 3; VPRDMA 10 Jan., p. 3

Died on 9th Inst. near Rockfish Gap, COL. JOSEPH WATKINS of Goochland
VA 26 Sept. 1804, p. 3

Died, DR. MAYO C. WATKINS of Goochland Co., on 17th Ult., age 25
RE 8 June 1813, p. 3; VA 3 June, p. 3

Died, THOMAS WATKINS, SR., of Chesterfield on 4th Inst. He was for over 30 years
Clerk of the Chesterfield County Court
RE 11 Jan. 1812, p. 3; VA 13 Jan., p. 3

Died at his res. in Halifax Co., July 28th, MR. THOMAS WATKINS, SR., age 68,
for many years a member of the Va. Legislature
RE 21 Aug. 1816, p. 3; VA 21 Aug., p. 3

Died Feb. 25th, WILLIAM WATKINS, of Hanover Co., age 40, formerly of King & Queen
Co., leaving wife and 5 small children
RE 28 Feb. 1817, p. 3

Died, COL. ARMISTEAD WATLINGTON, of Halifax Co., age 80
VA 13 June 1807, p. 3

Died, LT.-COL. AUGUSTUS WATSON of 7th Regt., at Camp Carter, on Jan. 26th, was of
Prince Edward Co.
RE 4 Feb. 1815, p. 3

Died, JOSEPH SHELTON WATSON, age 26, at his father's home in Louisa on Sept. 23rd.
He was a lawyer, educated at William & Mary
RE 8 Oct. 1805, p. 2; VA 5 Oct., p. 3

Died yesterday, MRS. SARAH WATSON, age 57
VP 15 Feb. 1819, p. 3

Died, MR. THOMAS WATSON, SR., age 61, on 17th Inst. inhabitant of Richmond for
many years
RE 19 Oct. 1813, p. 3; VP 19 Oct., p. 3; RC 18 Oct., p. 3

Died, MR. HENRY WATTERS, lately, in vicinity of Wilmington, N.C.
Visitor 4 Nov. 1809, p. 158

Died, DR. WATTS, in Manchester, on Thurs. last (Nov. 16)
VA 20 Nov. 1810, p. 3

Died, MR. WILLIAM WATTS, Sheriff of Dinwiddie, in that county. (No death date
VGRMA 5 Jan. 1795, p. 3

Died, REV. ABNER WAUGH, Protestant Episcopal Minister, at seat of Col. John Taylor
in Caroline Co., on 13th Inst.
VA 20 Sept. 1806, p. 3

Died Sept. 8th, age 38, at Oxford, N.C., VICTOR WAUHOP, a native of Ireland, former resident of Richmond
RE 12 Oct. 1819, p. 3; RC 11 Oct., p. 3

Died on 15th Dec. at Presque Isle, his excellency, ANTHONY WAYNE, Commander in Chief of the Federal Army
VA 6 Jan. 1797, p. 2

Died, MRS. CATHERINE WEBB, age 62, on 12th this month, at Studley, seat of John Lyon, Esq. in Hanover Co. Buried at family burial ground, Chemocking, in New Kent Co.
RE 17 Sept. 1811, p. 3; VP 17 Sept., p. 3

Died on 15th April, MR. FOSTER WEBB of New Kent Co., age 59, leaving wife & 8 children
VGGA 22 April 1795, p. 3

Died Dec. 9th at his seat in New Kent Co., FOSTER WEBB, age 58
VP 22 Dec. 1812, p. 3

Died on Sun. (Jan. 28) MRS. LUCY WEBB, consort of Conrad Webb of Hamstead, New Kent Co.
VP 31 Jan. 1816, p. 3

Died on Tues. last (Jan. 9) age 28, MRS. MARY SHORE WEBB, consort of James P. Webb, of River Edge in Hanover Co., leaving husband & infant child
VP 17 Jan. 1816, p. 3

Died at Hampstead in New Kent Co., May 4th, age 16, OSBORNE WEBB, son and only child of Conrad Webb
RE 9 May 1820, p. 3

Died on 17th Ult. at Epping Forest, Essex Co., MRS. SARAH ROWSEY WEBB, age 20, wife of Dr. William Webb of Tappahannock
VGGA 26 Feb. 1802, p. 3

Died on 4th Inst. only child (not named) of Dr. William WEBB
VGGA 26 Feb. 1802, p. 3

Died, CAPT. WILLIAM WEBB, on Sat. last (April 27) in this city
VA 1 May 1805, p. 3

Died, ELDER WILLIAM WEBBER of Goochland Co., the 1st of last month, age 61. Pastor of Dover Baptist Church of Christ for 30 years
VA 5 April 1808, p. 3

Died March 4th at his res. in Chesterfield Co., age 42, ISAAC WEBSTER, leaving widow and 8 children
RE 9 March 1816, p. 3

Died, MR. WILLIAM WEBSTER of this city, on Mon. last (Oct. 28)
VA 30 Oct. 1805, p. 3

Died at Boston, Mass., Feb. 2nd, CPL. WEDD of Fort Independence, of exposure
VPRDMA 14 Feb. 1820, p. 3

Died, JOSEPH WEIGLEY, Attorney at Law of Westmoreland Co., Pa., on Jan. 3rd, by
cutting his throat
RC 25 Jan. 1819, p. 3

Died, LT. THOMAS WELLER of Roxbury, Conn., an officer in U.S. Army, stationed at
New Milford. (No death date)
VP 28 May 1814, p. 3

Died in Fredericksburg Aug. 17th, MRS. BETTY BURWELL WELLFORD, wife of Dr. Beverley
Wellford, and eldest dau. of Charles C. Page of King William Co., age 20, leaving
husband and infant daughter
RE 3 Sept. 1819, p. 3

Died at Southwark on 28th Ult., GODFREY WELLSER, SR., aged about 98
VA 16 March 1803, p. 3

Died, MR. LOUIS WERCQ, merchant tailor, of this city, on Mon. last (Dec. 7).
A native of France, a res. of Richmond for 20 years
VA 10 Dec. 1812, p. 3

Died on 28th June, FRANCIS WEST, Esq., of King William, age 94
VGGA 6 July 1796, p. 2

Died Jan. 28th in Essex Co., age 47, MRS. LUCY DAINGERFIELD QUARLES WEST, widow of
Francis West, Jr., dec'd and daughter of Col. Meriwether Smith, dec'd
RE 15 Feb. 1820, p. 3

Died, MRS. MARGARET WEST, on 6th Inst. formerly an actress of the Virginia Company
of Comedians, and late proprietor of the Norfolk and Richmond Theatres
VA 15 June 1810, p. 3; RE 15 June, p. 3, says relict of Thos. West

Died on Sun. (Jan. 20) MRS. WEST, JR., the most distinguished ornament of the
Virginia Stage
RE 22 Jan. 1805, p. 3

Died at Alexandria Feb. 13th, ROGER WEST, Esq. of Fairfax Co.
VA 24 Feb. 1801, p. 3

Died at Freetown, Mass. on 11th Inst. (Not March) THOMAS WEST, age 100
VA 12 March 1803, p. 3

Died July 28th in Alexandria, THOMAS WADE WEST, Esq. age 54
VA 2 Aug. 1799, p. 3

Died yesterday, MR. WILLIAM WEST, apothecary and druggist, age 36
VA 1 May 1816, p. 3

Died Sept. 20th, age 20, ELIZA WESTMORE, wife of Dr. William H. Westmore of Dunkirk and eldest dau. of Mr. George Watt of Richmond
RE 17 Sept. 1819, p. 3

Capt. WILLIAM W. WEYMOUTH of schooner "Cyane" buried last Sat. (Dec. 27, 1817)
RE 3 Jan. 1818, p. 3

Died at Greenville, Culpeper Co., MRS. SARAH WHARTON, consort of Mr. John Wharton. (No death date)
RE 14 Oct. 1817, p. 3

Died, MR. JACOB WHEATON, coppersmith of this city, on 8th Inst., at New London, Conn., leaving wife, 2 children and an aged father
VA 21 July 1804, p. 3

Died in Richmond Oct. 1st, MR. BENJAMIN T. WHEELER, about 30, native of New York state
RE 27 Oct. 1818, p. 3

Died, EPHRAIM WHEELER of Lenox, Mass., Feb. 20th, hanged from rape of his daughter, Betsy Wheeler
VA 25 March 1806, p. 3

Executed yesterday near Richmond, MAURICE WHEELER, for murder
VGAA Nov. 30, 1782, p. 3

Died on Wed. last (Sept. 7) MR. RICHARD WHEELIN of this city
VGRMA 10 Sept. 1796, p. 2

Died, WILLIAM WHITAKER of this city on 6th Inst., leaving wife & 2 children. Buried with honors by the Society of the Cincinati
VGGA 11 Oct. 1806, p. 3

Died on Tues. last (date unknown) at Woodville, near Winchester, Va., ALEXANDER WHITE, age 65, lawyer and congressman
RE 17 Oct. 1804, p. 3; VA 17 Oct., p. 3 (says 2nd Inst.)

Died near Winchester on 24th Ult., MRS. ELIZABETH WHITE, wife of Alexander White, a Delegate to Assembly
VGAA Nov. 9, 1782, p. 3

Died on 14th Inst., MRS. ELIZABETH WHITE of Hanover Co., age 80
RE 21 Dec. 1815, p. 3

Died, COL. JOHN WHITE, at his plantation in Henrico, on 17th last mo., a Rev. Solider, a former member of the legislature and of the executive council
VGGA 18 July 1809, p. 3

Died Thurs. last (March 29) MRS. WHITE, spouse of William White, merchant of this city
VGWA April 5, 1787, p. 2

Died Oct. 21st, age 44, MR. RICHARD WHITE, a native of England, and for 26 years a
res. of Richmond. Leaves wife, son, and dau.
RC 25 Oct. 1820, p. 3

Died on Thurs. (March 4) MR. THOMAS WHITE, at home of his brother in Richmond
RE 6 March 1819, p. 3; VP 6 March, p. 3, says brother is Isaac White

Died Sept. 10th on Richmond Hill, CAPT. WILLIAM WHITE, late resident in Hanover
Co., age 48, Buried in Hanover on 11th
RC 16 Sept. 1820, p. 3

Died in Richmond July 22nd, MR. DENNIS WHITEHURST, a native of Princess Anne Co.,
age 40
VP 23 July 1814, p. 3

Died, COL. JOHN WHITING, yesterday, about 54, of 5th Regt. of U.S. Infantry
VA 11 Sept. 1810, p. 2

Died on 28th Ult. PETER BEVERLEY WHITING, Esq. of Gloucester
VGAA 21 Dec., 1781, p. 3

Died Sept. 20th, COL. SKAFE WHITINGE of Gloucester Co.
RE 31 Oct. 1817, p. 3

Died, MRS. WHITLOCK, consort of Mr. Charles Whitlock of this city, on March 30th
RE 2 April 1811, p. 3; VA 1 April, p. 3

Died Aug. 24th, CHARLES WHITLOCKE, merchant of Fredericksburg
RE 25 Aug. 1820, p. 3; RC 25 Aug., p. 2; VPRDMA 26 Aug., p. 3, says "of Richmond"

Died, MRS. HARRIET WHITLOCKE, wife of John Whitlocke of Beaverdam in Hanover Co.
on Sun. last (Nov. 22)
VGGA 24 Nov. 1807, p. 3

Died March 9th, MRS. MARTHA B. WHITLOCKE, consort of Izard B. Whitlocke, leaving 7
small children
RE 20 March 1818, p. 3

Died in Fredericksburg, WILLIAM WIATT, Esq., Postmaster
VGGA 22 APRIL 1800, p. 3

Died on Sat. last (Sept. 7) in this city, MR. JOHN WIGHT of Connecticut
VGRC 13 Sept. 1793, p. 3

Died, MRS. NANCY CALL WILDER, wife of Mr. John Wilder, Cashier of Bank at Petersburg,
in that city, on 9th Inst.
Visitor 21 Oct. 1809, p. 150

Died at Pittsburg on 11th Inst., JOHN WILKINS, Esq.
Visitor 30 Dec. 1809, p. 190

Died at New Orleans on Feb. 23rd, MRS. ANNE WILKINSON, consort of Gen. Wilkinson
VA 3 April 1807, p. 3

Died, COL. NATHANIEL WILKINSON, a Member of the Present General Assembly from this
county, at an advanced age, Fri. last (Dec. 18)
VA 22 Dec. 1807, p. 3

Died, DR. WILLIAM WILKINSON, at Ca Ira, Cumberland Co., on 12th Inst.
VA 23 Nov. 1805, p. 3

Died in Halifax Co., Nov. 5th, age 32, MRS. ANN WILLIAMS, consort of Mr. Samuel
Williams, Clerk of Halifax Co., leaving husband & children
RE 16 Dec. 1819, p. 3 (See RE of 3 Dec.)

Died, MRS. JANE WILLIAMS, consort of Capt. Thomas Williams of this city. (No death
date)
VGIC 6 Oct. 1787, p. 3; VGWA 4 Oct. 1787, p. 3

Died in Woodford Co., Ohio, March 20th, MR. JOHN WILLIAMS, of wound received from his
son, Milton Williams
VP 22 April 1818, p. 2

Died at Brooklyn,N.Y., MR. JOHN WILLIAMS, better known as ANTHONY PASQUIN, poet.
(No death date)
RE 27 Oct. 1818, p. 3

Died Nov. 5th, MRS. MARY WILLIAMS, wife of Samuel Williams, Clerk of Halifax Co.,
age 28
RE 3 Dec. 1819, p. 3

Died, MR. MONTAGUE WILLIAMS, merchant, in King William Co., on 7th Inst.
RE 14 Aug. 1812, p. 3

Died at his seat in Annapolis, Md., Dec. 27, 1819, GEN. OSBORN WILLIAMS, a Revolutior.
Solider
RE 20 Jan. 1820, p. 1

Died Oct. 1st, MRS. SARAH WILLIAMS, consort of Mr. Thomas Williams, leaving husband
and two infant children
RC 3 Oct. 1820, p. 3

Died at Lexington, Ky., MR. THOMAS JASPER WILLIAMS of Halifax Co., Va., age 52.
Leaves wife and children. (No death date)
RE 4 September 1818, p. 3

Died Oct.   at Woodstock, Va., WILLIAM C. WILLIAMS of Richmond, Attorney at Law
VP 21 Oct. 1817, p. 3

Died at Charleston, S.C. on Tues. last (before Sept. 18) ARGYLE WILLIAMSON, a
gunsmith, a native of Richmond, Va.
VA 3 Oct. 1807, p. 3

Died on 11th Inst. at his seat in Henrico, JOHN WILLIAMSON, Sr.
VA 19 July 1806, p. 3; VGGA 16 July, p. 3

Died Nov. 10th at his res. in Henrico, DR. JOHN WILLIAMSON, age 41
RE 14 Nov. 1817, p. 3

Died Jan. 14th, MR. MADISON WILLIAMSON, son of Mr. George Williamson, age 27,
leaving parents, sisters & brothers
RC 16 Jan., 1817, p. 3

Died on 5th Inst., MRS. WILLIAMSON, consort of Thomas Williamson, Esq., Cashier
of Office of Discount and Deposit of the Bank of Virginia, at Norfolk
VA April 14, 1807, p. 3

Died on 28th Ult., MR. SAMUEL WILLIAMSON of Henrico Co.
VGGA 9 July 1799, p. 3

Died a few days ago in Phila,,THOMAS WILLING
VGRMA 14 Oct. 1793, p. 3

Died MR. ELIAS WILLIS, age 75, at Capt. Matthew Willis' in Fluvanna on 3rd Inst.
RE 8 Oct. 1805, p. 2; VA 9 Oct., p. 3

Died lately, near Portsmouth, CAPT. JOHN WILLIS, formerly of Bermuda
VG Nov. 4, 1780, p. 3

Cied Sun. (June 6), MAJ. JOHN WILLIS of Spotsylvania. Interred in the churchyard
VGGA 9 June 1802, p. 3

Died on 21st Ult. at his res. in Fluvanna, DR. JOHN WILLIS, a physician there for
over 20 years
RE 4 Oct. 1815, p. 3

Died on 16th Inst., in Fluvanna Co., MRS. LUCY WILLS, consort of Dr. John Wills
Observatory 24 Dec. 1798, p. 3

Died in Manchester on 22nd Inst., JAMES WILSON, member of Soc. of Friends, and
late resident of Yorkshire, England
VGGA 25 Sept. 1798, p. 3

Died at his mansion house in Rockbridge on 20th Inst. (Ult.) JAMES WILSON, SEN.,
age 94
Visitor 9 Sept. 1809, p. 127

Died on 11th Inst. in this city, MR. JOHN WILSON, watchmaker from London. Interred
in the churchyard
VGGA 18 March 1795, p. 3; VGRMA says "Captain" 12 March, p. 3; VGRC 13 March,
p. 3, says "Captain"

Died at his res. at Danshill, Pittsylvania Co., May 21st, COL. JOHN WILSON, age 70,
leaving wife, 3 sons, 3 daughters
RE 9 June 1820, p. 3

Died on 28th Ult. at seat of his father in Halifax Co., MR. LEONARD WILSON, youngest son of Daniel Wilson, survived by parents and a bro. and sis.
RE 19 Nov. 1805, p. 3; VA 13 Nov., p. 3; VGGA 13 Nov., p. 3

Died at Wilmington, Del. on 4th Inst. (Ult.) SAMUEL WILSON, Esq., Senator of the U.S
Visitor 2 Dec. 1809, p. 174

Died lately at Smithfield, MR. SOLOMON WILSON, formerly of this city
VA 18 Jan. 1799, p. 3

Died in Richmond, THOMAS WILSON, Mayor of the city, on Sun. (May 3)
RE 5 May 1818, p. 3; VP 4 May, p. 3

Died Dec. 25, 1818, MAJ. JOHN WIMBISH, Clerk of Halifax Co., age 67, leaving wife and children. Served in Revolution
RE 9 Jan. 1819, p. 4

Died in Halifax Co., Jan. 11th, MISS SARAH C. WIMBISH, eldest dau. of Maj. John Wimbish
RE 23 Jan. 1816, p. 3

Died, GEN. LEVIN WINDER, late Gov. of Md., and Past Grand Master of Grand Lodge of Md., on July 1st, age 63
RE 6 July 1819, p. 3

Died at his res. last Sat. (June 21) MR. CHARLES WINEGARDNER, at an advanced age. Was a native of Germany, but res. of Richmond for 35 years. Left widow & children
RE 27 June 1817, p. 3; VP 24 June, p. 3, says left 7 children

Died, MRS. ANNE WINSTON, spouse of Col. John Winston of Hanover Co., on 6th Inst., age 32
VIC 11 Nov. 1789, p. 3 and 18 Nov., p. 2, *more detailed

Died, MRS. ANN K. WINSTON, consort of Col. William O. Winston of Hanover Co., on July 4th
RE 10 July 1812, p. 3

Died, MRS. WINSTON, wife of Capt. Isaac Winston, on Tues. last (Aug. 14), of Henrico
VA 17 Aug. 1810, p. 3; VP 17 Aug., p. 3, says MRS. ELIZABETH WINSTON, at house of her father, Mr. William Burton, in Henrico. Was his 2nd dau.

Died yesterday, GEDDES WINSTON, Esq. of this city, age 63
VGGA 4 June 1794, p. 3; VGRMA 12 June

Died at his seat in Hanover on 11th Inst., COL. JOHN WINSTON
VGGA 22 Nov. 1797, p. 3

Died, MRS. MARY WINSTON, of this city, on 9th Inst., age 69. Funeral sermon by Rev. Buchanan at the Capitol
RE 17 Dec. 1811, p. 3

Died on May 23rd, age 29, MRS. NANCY C. WINSTON, wife of Mr. Peter Winston of Hanover Co.
RE 1 June 1816, p. 3

Died on 24th Ult., age 66, MR. WILLIAM WINSTON, of Amelia Co.
RE 19 April 1805, p. 3; VA 20 April, p. 3

Died at Gloucester, a few days ago, at the house of Mr. John Seawell, MR. WILLIAM WISEMAN of this city
VGGA 7 Aug. 1805, p. 3; VA 10 Aug., p. 3, says Wischam

Died on 4th Feb. last, in Bucks Co., Pa., JABOB WISMER, a native of Germany. He emigrated to N.C. in Queen Anne's reign and lived 10 years, then to Pa. where he married his 3rd wife with whom he lived 67 years. His widow is about 87
VGWA 22 March 1787, p. 2

Died, REV. JOHN WITHERSPOON, Pres. of Princeton College on 16th Nov. at Princeton
VGRMA 1 Dec. 1794, p. 4

Died on Sat. (Feb. 1) MR. BENJAMIN WOLFE, an old resident of Richmond
RE 4 Feb. 1817, p. 3; VP 5 Feb., p. 3

Died Sat. (Nov. 4) age 42, MRS. SOPHIA WOLFE, relict of late Benjamin Wolfe, leaving 8 children
RE 10 Nov. 1820, p. 3; RC 9 Nov., p. 2

Died yesterday, at res. of Mr. Robert M'Kim, MR. DAVID J. WOOD, of Richmond, a young man
RC 8 Sept. 1818, p. 3

Died on Sept. 25th, age 22, MR. EDMUND WOOD, 3rd son of Maj. William Wood of Amelia Co.
RE 16 Oct. 1818, p. 3

Died, GEN. JAMES WOOD, on Wed. (June 16), a member of the Executive Council, and soldier of the Revolution (Obit. 29 June, p. 3)
RE 18 June 1813, p. 3; VA 17 June, p. 3

Died, MISS JANE WOOD, dau. of Mrs. Lucy Wood, on Oct. 16th at Buck Island, Albemarle Co.
RE 9 Nov. 1810, p. 3

Died, MR. LEIGHTON WOOD of this city, on Thurs. (March 24) at Mr. Mathias Sims' in Hanover
VA 29 March 1808, p. 3

Died on 1st Inst. at age 80, at seat of Mr. Robert Wood near Winchester, MRS. MARY WOOD, mother of his Exc. James Wood, Esq., Gov. of Va.
VGGA 17 Jan. 1798, p. 3

Died May 24th at his res. in Albemarle Co., MAJ. WILLIAM WOOD, age 55, an old solider of the Revolution
RE 4 June 1819, p. 3

Died on 2nd Inst., MR. THOMAS WOODFIN of Henrico Co.
VA 6 Nov. 1802, p. 3

Died near end of Nov., JOHN WOODGERS of Louisa Co., almost 90
VA 22 Dec. 1804, p. 3

Died at Philadelphia, DR. JAMES WOODHOUSE, late Prof. of Chemistry of U. of Pa.
Visitor 17 June 1809, p. 78

Died at Fayette, N.Y., MR. JAMES WOODRUFF. (No death date)
VPRDMA 18 Aug. 1820, p. 3

Died at his seat in Powhatan Co., on the 10th Inst., age 85, CHARLES WOODSON
VGGA 17 Feb. 1796, p. 2; VGRMA 17 Feb., p. 3

Died on 30th Jan. at her house in Goochland, ELIZABETH WOODSON
VA 14 Feb. 1797, p. 3

Died July 21st at Maj. Charles Woodson's in Prince Edward Co., MAJ. FREDERICK WOODSO
of Powhatan Co., an old Revolutionary officer. He represented Powhatan in the Gene:
Assembly
RE 1 Aug. 1817, p. 3

Died Nov. 18th at his father's in Cumberland Co., FREDERICK A. WOODSON, youngest so
of Charles Woodson, age 17
RE 28 Nov. 1817, p. 3; VP 25 Nov., p. 3

Died on July 23rd at his father's house in Goochland Co., JOHN P. WOODSON, age 20
RE 16 Aug. 1815, p. 3

Died, MAJ. JOSEPH WOODSON at his res. in Goochland Co., on 31st Jan.
RE 8 Feb. 1810, p. 3

Died in Woodford Co., Ky., MRS. MARY WOODSON, wife of Philip Woodson, Jr., of
Goochland Co., Va., age 25, leaving husband and 2 children. (No death date)
RE 10 June 1817, p. 3

Died on 10th Inst., ROBERT H. WOODSON of Goochland, age 27
VA 18 March 1806, p. 3; RE 18 March, p. 3 (says died on 11th); VGGA 15 March, p.

Died, CAPT. SAMUEL WOODSON, age 58, on 13th Inst., survived by wife & children
RE 25 May 1810, p. 3

Died Jan. 24th in Norfolk, DR. EDWARD WOODWARD, late surgeon of the Frigate United
States, age 26, native of Delaware Co., Pa.
VP 29 Jan. 1818, p. 3

Died, MRS. HENRY T. WOODDY of Oglethorpe, Ga., in Chesterfield, on 15th Ult.
RE 3 Dec. 1812, p. 3; VA 3 Dec., p. 3, says HENRY T. WOODY, and that he died
at Capt. Haley Cole's in Chesterfield, leaving a wife

Died at the canal mills on Fir. last (Nov. 24) MAGOR WOOLEN, principal superintendant
of the mill
VGGA 29 Nov. 1797, p. 3

Died at his res. near Bowling Green, Caroline Co., JOHN G. WOOLFOLK, on April 15th
RE 23 April 1819, p. 3; VP 22 April, p.3, says died 16th, was 70

Died, at his seat in Caroline Co. on 4th Inst., MR. PAUL WOOLFOLK
VA 8 Feb. 1804, p. 3

Died at his father's res. in Caroline Co., on Wed. (May 24) MR. RICHARD WOOLFOLK of
firm of Coleman & Woolfolk of Richmond, leaving wife and infant daughter
RE 30 May 1820, p. 3; RC 27 May, p. 3

Died in New Haven, Conn., on Sat. last (before June), MRS. MARY WOOSTER, age 78,
widow of Gen. David Wooster, who was killed in the Revolution
VA 24 June 1807, p. 3

Died 21st Oct., MRS. JANE WORMELEY, age 67, widow of Ralph Wormeley, Esq.
VGGA 6 Nov. 1793, p. 3

Died on 19th Inst., age 75, RALPH WORMELEY, Esq. of Rosegill
VGGA 25 Aug. 1790, p. 2; VGWA 26 Aug.

Died, RALPH WORMELEY, Esq. of Rosegill, age 62, on 19th Ult.
VGGA 1 Feb. 1806, p. 3

Died, MRS. WORRALL, consort of Dr. James Worrall, of this city, on Sat. last
(Aug. 28)
VA 30 Aug. 1813, p. 3

Died, DR. WRAY, an old inhabitant of this city, on Fri. last (July 6)
VA 11 July 1804, p. 3

Died, MRS. ELIZABETH WREN, an old res. of this city, on 24 Oct.
RE 1 Nov. 1811, p. 3

Died Aug. 7th at Nassau, New Providence, GEORGE WRIGHT, lately a merchant of Amelia
Co., Va.
VGWA 11 Oct. 1787, p. 3

Died, Dec. 31, 1811, in Fauquier Co., MAJ. JAMES WRIGHT, a soldier in the Revolution
VP 10 Jan. 1812, p. 3

Died, Nov. 20th, MRS. MARY WRIGHT, consort of Dr. Archibald Wright of Buckingham
Co., leaving husband & mother
RE 9 Dec. 1815, p. 3

Died on 13th Inst., at Hanover Town, CAPT. CARY WYATT
VGGA 22 Feb. 1792, p. 3

Died, JOHN J. WYATT, merchant, of this city, on Wed. last (May 24)
RE 30 May 1809, p. 3; VGGA 26 May, p. 3; Visitor 3 June, p. 70, says WIATT

COL. WYNKOOP was murdered in Hurley, Ulster Co., N.Y. on Dec. 3rd by a servant
VGRDA 31 Dec. 1792, p. 3

Died Jan. 2nd at house of Mr. Francis Butt, MISS ANN B. WYLD
VP 4 Jan. 1819, p. 2

Died, MR. WINNAH WYSE, who drowned on Nov. 5th, a native of Falkirk, Scotland,
age 65
VA 8 Dec. 1807, p. 3

Died on 18th Inst., MRS. ELIZABETH WYTHE, spouse of Hon. George Wyth, Esq. of
City of Williamsburg
VGWA 23 Aug. 1787, p. 2

Died, GEORGE WYTHE, Judge of the High Court of Chancery for the Richmond District,
on Sun. last (June 8)
VA 10 June 1806, p. 3; Imp. Obs. 14 June, p. 2; RE 10 June, p. 3; VGGA 11 June,
p. 3

Died on 2nd Inst. at Yanceyville in Louisa Co., age 22, MRS. ANNE YANCEY, wife of
David Yancey, Esq., Attorney at Law
RE 28 March 1806, p. 3

Died on 15th Oct., MRS. ANN YANCEY, widow of Rev. Robert Yancey, Minister of Trinity
Parish, Louisa Co., age 64, at res. of her son, Maj. Charles Yancey of Buckingham Co
RE 13 Dec. 1814, p. 3

Died on Nov. 22nd in King William, MR. CHARLES YARBROUGH, late of Phila.
VA 27 Nov. 1798, p. 3

Died, MRS. ANN YATES, wife of Capt. John Yates of Caroline Co., on 11th Inst.
VA 18 Dec. 1810, p. 3

Died about Nov. 14th at his seat in King & Queen Co., GEN. HENRY YOUNG, a Revolution
Soldier, age 76
VP 1 Dec. 1817, p. 3 and 2 Dec., p. 3

Died at Rocketts on Sun. (Aug. 1), MR. JAMES YOUNG
VP 3 Aug. 1819, p. 3

Died on 7th Inst., MR. JOHN YOUNG, of this city
VGRMA 9 April 1796, p. 3

Died lately in service of his country, LT. ISAAC YOUNGHUSBAND, of the army commanded by Gen. Wayne
VGRMA 12 Jan. 1795, p. 2

Died on Mon. last (April 27) CAPT. ISAAC YOUNGHUSBAND, near this city, at advanced age
VGGA 29 April, 1795, p. 3; VGRMA 30 April, p. 2

Died at Studley, seat of Hon. Peter Lyons, Esq. in Hanover Co., MRS. MARY YOUNGHUSBAND, consort of Mr. Pleasant Younghusband of this city. (No death date)
VGRMA 15 April 1793, p. 3

Died on Fri. last (Oct. 25) at Studley,seat of Hon. Peter Lyons, Esq., MASTER PETER YOUNGHUSBAND of this city
VGRMA 28 Oct. 1793, p. 3

Died on 15th Inst., at his seat near this city, PLEASANT YOUNGHUSBAND, Esq.
VA 20 Dec. 1808, p. 3

Married Dec. 24th by Rev. John D. Blair, MR. THOMAS H. ABNEY, to MISS ANN GOSDEN, both of Richmond
RE 30 Dec. 1817, p. 3

Married Nov. 11th, by Rev. Philip Courtney, JOHN ADAMS of Cumberland Co., to MISS MARY E. VAUGHN, daughter of Mr. John Vaughn of Richmond
VPRDMA 14 Nov. 1820, p. 3

Married at Scottsville, Powhatan Co. on 10th Inst., MR. JOSEPH ADAMS to MRS. JANE DUKE of that town
VGGA 14 Sept. 1791, p. 3

Married on 19th Inst. by Rev. James Dickerson, MR. SAMUEL ADAMS of Cumberland to MISS MARY HUDSON SAUNDERS, dau. of Rev. John S. Saunders of Powhatan
VGGA 25 Aug. 1801, p. 3

Married on Sat. last (Jan. 30) THOMAS B. ADAMS, Esq. of this city to MISS SALLY MORRISON of Chesterfield
VICGA 3 Feb. 1790, p. 3

Married on 13th Inst. in City of Phila, MR. ROBERT AITKIN, JR., printer to MISS NANCY PEARSON
VGWA 30 Aug. 1787, p. 3

Married on 30th Ult., in Charlotte Co., MR. PERRIN ALDEY, age 105, to MRS. ANN TANKESLEY, age 90. She is his third wife and he her third husband
VA 10 Aug. 1805, p. 3

Married on Sat. (Feb. 5) MR. JOHN ALLAN, merchant, to MISS FANNY VALENTINE, both of this city
VA 9 Feb. 1803, p. 3; VGGA 9 Feb., p. 3

Married on 8th Inst., by Rev. Drury Lace, MR. JOSIAH ALLEN of Buckingham, to MISS CAROLINE GORDON, dau. of Richard Gordon, Esq. of Cumberland
VA 16 Sept. 1813, p. 3

Married on 22nd Inst., WILSON ALLEN, Esq., Clerk of the General Court, to MISS SOPHIA HOOMES, dau. of James Hoomes, dec'd, of Bowling Green, Caroline Co.
VGGA 31 Jan. 1807, p. 3

Married Sept. 30th by Rev. Nathan Hoskinson, MR. WILLIAM ALLISON, merchant, of Richmond, Va., to MISS ANN WATERS of Montgomery Co., Md.
VP 11 Oct. 1819, p. 3

Married at Albany, N.Y. on 2nd Inst. by Rev. Mr. Johnston, JOSEPH ALSTON of S.C. to MISS THEODOSIA BURR, only child of Aaron Burr, Esq.
VA 24 Feb. 1801, p.3

Married, on Tues. last (July 9) by Rev. John Lindsay, MR. BALLARD AMMORY, to MISS FRANCES SHARPE, dau. of Mr. Peter Sharpe of Four Mile Creek
RE 12 July 1811, p. 3; VA 11 July, p. 3

Married on Sat. (Dec. 26) by Rev. Philip Courtney, MR. CHARLES B. ANDERSON of Prince Edward Co., TO MISS SAVANNAH S. NANCY of Henrico Co.
RE 31 Dec. 1818, p. 3; VP 29 Dec., p. 2

Married on Thurs. (Nov. 30) MR. FRANCIS ANDERSON of Amelia Co., to MISS MINERVA M. GREGORY, dau. of Richard Gregory of Chesterfield Co.
RE 7 Dec. 1820, p. 3

Married on Tues. last (Aug. 11) MR. RICHARD ANDERSON to MISS MARIA EGGLESTON, both of this city
VA 14 Aug. 1801, p. 3; VGGA 14 Aug., p. 3 (says Mr. Anderson "of Milton")

Married on 7th Inst., THOMAS ANDERSON, Esq., to MISS DOROTHEA COUCH, both of Buckingham
VA 26 Nov. 1799, p. 3

Married Thurs. last (Dec. 26) MR. WILLIAM ANDERSON, JR., merchant, to MISS BETSY MINOR, both of this city
VGRC 31 Dec. 1793, p. 3

Married on 24th Ult. in Williamsburg, ROBERT ANDREWS, Esq., to MISS MOLLY BLAIR, dau. of John Blair, Esq.
VGGA 1 April 1795, p. 2; VGRMA 30 March, p. 3

Married on 15th Ult. at Leesville, Westmoreland Co., MR. JAMES C. ANTHONY of this city to MISS MARY S. LEE, eldest dau. of Philip Lee, dec'd
RE 5 Aug. 1808, p. 3; VGGA 2 Aug., p. 3

Married on 7th Inst. by Rev. John D. Blair, WILLIAM ARCHER, Esq., a member of the General Assembly, from Powhatan Co., to MISS MARY ANNE CLARKE, eldest dau. of Maj. John Clarke of this city
RE 15 Sept. 1809, p. 3; Visitor 23 Sept., p. 135

Married on 9th Inst., MR. FREDERICK ARGYLE of this city, merchant, to MISS REBECCA WINSTON of Hanover
VA 19 Nov. 1799, p. 3; VGGA 15 Nov., p. 3

Married on 20th Inst., MR. THOMAS ARMISTEAD to MISS PRISCILLA ARMISTEAD of Norfolk
Visitor 31 March, 1810, p. 35

Married 25th last month, CAPT. WILLIAM ARMISTEAD of New Kent to MISS POLLY STITH ARMISTEAD of Elizabeth City
VGAA Sept. 13, 1783, p. 3

Married on Aug. 4th, by Rev. Rice, MR. HENRY J. ARNOLD, to MISS NANCY SOUTHWELL, both of Richmond
VP 10 Aug. 1814, p. 3; RC 9 Aug., p. 3

Married on Thurs. last (Dec. 18) at Powhatan, Henrico Co., seat of Col. Wm. Mayo, ROBERT ATKINSON, Esq. of Chesterfield, to MISS POLLY MAYO
VGRMA 22 Dec. 1794, p. 3

Married on Sat. last (Sept. 20) ROGER ATKINSON, JR. Esq. to MISS AGNES POYTHRESS of
Prince George, 6th dau. of late Col. Peter Poythress
IC 24 Sept. 1788, p. 3

Married in Buckingham Co., MR. ARCHIBALD AUSTIN, Attorney at Law, to MISS GRACE
BOWKER, granddaughter of Mr. Bernard Gains
VA 23 Sept. 1808, p. 3

Married Dec. 21st, MR. MORTON AUSTIN, to Miss FRANCES VALENTINE, both of Henrico Co.
RE 24 Dec. 1816, p. 3

Married Jan. 14th by Rev. John D. Blair, MR. ROBERT S. AUSTIN of Hanover Co., to
MISS MARIA MORRIS, daughter of Mr. Austin Morris, dec'd
RE 20 Jan. 1820, p. 3

Married on 29th April, WILLIAM AYLETT, Esq. of King William to MISS MARTHA POSLY
of New Kent
VA 8 May 1802, p. 2

Married on Sat. last (Dec. 24) MR. EDMUND BAILEY to MISS BETSEY TOMPKINS, both of
this city
VA 28 Dec. 1803, p. 3

Married on May 22nd by Rev. John Robertson, MAJ. WILLIAM BAILEY, to MISS MARY CLARK,
dau. of Col. John Clark, all of Halifax Co.
RE 10 June 1817, p. 3

Married, MR. JERMAN BAKER of Petersburg to MISS M.B. EPPES, dau. of Col. Francis
Eppes of Chesterfield. (No marriage date)
VA 30 Nov. 1798, p. 3

Married in Richmond on Thurs. (June 10) by Rev. John Buchanan, JOHN BAKER, attorney
at law, to MISS PRUDENTIA THWEATT
VP 12 June 1819, p. 3

Married, at Point of View, King & Queen Co., on 24 Dec. last by Rev. Robert Sample,
GEORGE BALL, Esq., attorney at law, of Gloucester Co., to MISS MARIA M. HOOMES,
dau. of Capt. Benjamin Hoomes, of that place
VA 5 Jan. 1808, p. 3

Married, COL. ROBERT BALLARD, formerly of Continental Army to MISS PLOWMAN of
Baltimore. (No marriage date)
VG Aug. 2, 1780, p. 2

Married on Sat. last (Nov. 5) at Norfolk, HENRY BANKS, Esq. of this city to MISS
PATSY READ, dau. of Dr. J. K. Read of Norfolk
VGGA 9 Nov. 1796, p. 6

Married Dec. 15th at res. of Dr. Cary Wilkinson in Charles City Co., by Rev. Dennis
MR. WILLIAM T. BANKS of Williamsburg, to MISS MARTHA ANN JACKSON
RE 29 Dec. 1818, p. 3

Married May 27th by Rev. Richard Dabbs, MR. EDWARD BAPTIST, formerly of Mecklenburg Co., to MISS ELIZA EGGLESTON, both of Powhatan Co.
RE 10 June 1817, p. 3

Married in Shelby Co., Ky, March 18th, by Rev. John S. Ravenscroft, MR. RICHARD H. BAPTIST, Attorney at Law, to MISS SARAH GOODE, dau. of Col. Samuel Goode, all of Mechkelburg Co.
RE 27 March 1818, p. 3; VP 26 March, p. 3

Married on Tues. (Nov. 21) JOHN S. BARBOUR of Culpeper Co., to MISS ELIZA BYRNE, eldest dau. of Col. James Byrne of Petersburg
RE 25 Nov. 1815, p. 3

Married on 30th Ult. by Rev. Mr. Buchanan, MR. DAVID BARCLAY, to MISS ANN GRETTER, all of this city
RE 13 July 1810, p. 3; VA 6 July, p. 3

Married on 1st Inst., MR. WILLIAM BARDENDALE of this city, to MISS MARY E. TABB of Amelia
RE 10 June 1815, p. 3

Married on Thurs. (Feb. 22) by Rev. John D. Blair, MR. A. BARRET to MISS R. SUTTON
Visitor 24 Feb. 1810, p. 15

Married on Sat. last (Sept. 28) MR. SAMUEL BARRETT to MISS CATHARINE BARKER, both of this city
VGGA 2 Oct. 1805, p. 2

Married in Fluvanna Co., by Rev. Joseph Logan, on 16th Ult., MR. WILLIAM F. BARRETT, to MRS. ELIZABETH M. ROSE
RE 4 Oct. 1815, p. 3

Married Dec. 26, 1816, by Rev. Charles Talley, MR. BARTLETT O. BARTON, to MISS ANN WHITE, dau. of Moses White, all of Hanover Co.
RE 7 Jan. 1817, p. 3

Married Nov. 26th by Rev. James Martin, MR. THOMAS R. BASS, to MISS MARGARET WILKINSON, dau. of Richard Wilkinson, all of Chesterfield
RE 8 Dec. 1818, p. 3

Married in Portsmouth, by Rev. Mr. Ballon, MR. THOMAS BATCHELDER, to MISS MARTHA MUCHMORE. (No marriage date)
VA 6 May 1811, p. 3

Married on 28th Ult. by Rev. Mr. Ford, CHARLES F. BATES, Esq., Attorney at Law, of Goochland, to MISS MARY HEATH MILLER, eldest dau. of Heath Jones Miller, Esq. of same co.
VA 6 June 1806, p. 3; RE 3 June, p. 3; VGGA 4 June, p. 3

Married, MR. JOHN BATTE of Prince George, to MISS POLLY POYTHRESS, dau. of Col. Peter Poythress of same co. (No marriage date)
VG June 28, 1780, p. 3

Married on 5th Inst., DAVID BATTESON, JR., Esq. of Mass., to MISS ELIZA CRUMP of Powhatan Co.
VA 15 Oct. 1799, p. 3

Married on 31st Dec. by Rev. Henry Hefferman, JAMES BAYLOR, Esq. of Gloucester to MISS CATHERINE YATES of Middlesex
RE 14 Jan. 1808, p. 3

Married, lately, MR. JOHN BAYLOR of King & Queen to MISS SALLY PRITCHET of Middlesex
VGAA April 13, 1782, p. 3

Married May 6th, JOHN BAYLOR to MISS MARIA ROY, both of Caroline Co.
RE 18 May 1819, p. 3

Married on 16th last, MR. WILLIAM BEASLEY, to MISS PATSEY M'CHAU, both of Amelia Co.
VA 28 Nov. 1806, p. 2

Married, on Thurs. last, MR. EDWIN BEATTEY, merchant, of Petersburg, to MISS SUSAN C. BURTON of Chesterfield
Visitor 10 March 1810, p. 23

Married May 11th, MR. JAMES BELL to MISS CATHARENE BROADDUS (in Caroline Co.?)
RE 9 June 1820, p. 3

Married on Sat. last (April 7) MR. THOMAS BENDLE to MISS BETSY COUTTS, both of this city
VA 14 April 1804, p. 2; VGGA 11 April, p. 3

Married on 15th Inst. by Rev. John Buchanan, CAPT. ISBON BENEDICT, of New York, to MISS FRANCES W. WEYMOUTH, eldest dau. of Capt. William W. Weymouth of this city
RE 25 Feb. 1812, p. 3

Married on 9th Inst., LEWIS BERKELEY, to MISS ELIZABETH DARRACOTT, both of Hanover C●
RE 29 March 1808, p. 3

Married on 27th. Ult. at Mount Airy, Richmond Co., the seat of John Taylor, Esq., ROBERT BEVERLEY, the younger, Esq. to MISS JANE TAYLOE, dau. of late Hon. John Tayloe, Esq.
VGGA 1 June 1791, p. 2

Married at Fort Barnwell, Craven Co., REV. WILLIAM P. BIDDLE of this state, to MISS MARY N. SIMPSON, only dau. of Gen. Samuel Simpson
Visitor 3 March 1810, p. 19

Married on Sat. last (Sept. 4) by Rev. John D. Blair, MR. JOSEPH BIGELOW, merchant, to MISS AGNES M. NISBET, both of Richmond
VA 8 Sept. 1813, p. 3

Married Nov. 18th, by Rev. John Courtney, MR. JESSE BLACKBURN of Henrico Co., to MISS URSULA EDDS of Richmond
RC 20 Nov. 1819, p. 3

Married on Tues. last (Sept. 20) JOHN BLAIR, Esq. to MISS MARGARET PAGE, dau. of
John Page, Esq., late Gov. of this Commonwealth, all of this city
VA 23 Sept. 1808, p. 3; RE 27 Sept., p. 3

Married, April 28th, MR. JOHN G. BLAIR to MISS SARAH HERON, all of Richmond
VP 1 May 1812, p. 3

Married Feb. 8th, by Rev. Turner, MR. SAMUEL J. BLAIR of Richmond, to MISS ELIZABETH
T. TRUEHEART, dau. of Col. William Trueheart of Hanover Co.
VPRDMA 12 Feb. 1820, p. 3

Married April 15th, MR. JOHN S. BLANTON, to MISS LUCY SOUTHWORTH (in Caroline Co.?)
RE 9 June 1820, p. 3

Married at Mendham, Mass., MR. WILLIAM BLAZER, age 16, to MISS CATHERINE YAYDEN,
age 11
VA 27 July 1803, p. 3

Married on Wed. last (Nov. 14) by Rev. Isaac H. Judah, MR. L. BLOCK of Yorktown, to
MISS CHARLOTTE WOLFE of this city
VA 16 Nov. 1810, p. 3

Married on Wed. last (March 30) by Rev. Isaac H. Judah, MR. SIMON BLOCK, merchant,
to MISS SUKY JACOBS, both of this city
VA 2 April 1803, p. 3

Married last evening, MR. JAMES BOCKIOUS, to MISS SUKEY PROSSER, both of this city
Observatory 14 June 1798, p. 3; VA 15 June, p. 3, says Jacob Bockius and Susannah
Prosser; VGGA 19 June, p. 3, says Bockius

Married on 1st Inst. by Rev. John D. Blair, MR. THOMAS BOHANNON to MISS MARIA FOX,
2nd dau. of Maj. Nathaniel Fox of King William
VA 13 Sept. 1808, p. 3

Married on 1st Inst. at Mount Pleasant, Prince George Co., MR. ROBERT BOLLING of
Petersburg to MISS SALLY WASHINGTON, dau. of Lawrence Washington, Sr., Esq.
VGRMA 17 Sept. 1796, p. 3

Married in Baltimore, Dec. 24th, by Rev. Bishop Carroll, MR. JEROME BONAPARTE,
youngest bro. of First Consul of the French Republic, and MISS ELIZABETH PATTERSON,
eldest dau. of Mr. Wm. Patterson of that city
VA 4 Jan. 1804, p. 3; VGGA 7 Jan., p. 3

Married on June 20th by Rev. Edward Baptist, MERRITT BOOKER of Cumberland Co., to
MISS MARTHA F. MOSBY, dau. of Gen. Littleberry Mosby of Powhatan Co.
RE 27 June 1820, p. 3; RC 27 June, p. 3

Married on May 29th, PARHAM BOOKER, Esq. to MISS ELIZABETH LEWIS OVERTON, both of
Amelia Co.
VA 6 June 1800, p. 3

Married on 26th Ult., MR. CHARLES BOSHER, to MISS MARIA LUMPKIN, both of this city
RE 8 Jan. 1811, p. 3

Married on Thurs. (Feb. 2) by Rev. Bryce, MR. JAMES BOSHER to MISS ANNE HOPKINS,
all of Richmond
VP 4 Feb. 1815, p. 3

Married Aug. 20th at New London, Campbell Co., by Rev. Alfred H. Dashiell, ALEXANDER
L. BOTTS of Richmond, to MISS SUSAN F. RANDOLPH of Warwick, Chesterfield Co.
RC 27 Aug. 1818, p. 3

Married Jan. 20th, DR. ROBERT C. BOULDIN to SARAH, daughter of Mr. William BRITTON,
all of Halifax Co.
RE 22 Feb. 1820, p. 3

Married at Norfolk, last Thurs. sen'night (Jan. 18), MR. JOHN BOUSH to MISS FRANCES
MOSELEY MUNFORD
VGWA 25 Jan. 1787, p. 3

Married on 17th Ult., DR. RICHARD C. BOWLES to MISS ELIZA W. PLEASANTS, dau. of
Philip Pleasants, Esq. all of Goochland
VA 5 July 1806, p. 3

Married in Williamsburg on July 23rd by Rev. John D. Blair, MR. WILLIAM J. BOYKIN
of Isle of Wight Co., to MISS DOREAS A. HAWKINS, 2nd dau. of William Hawkins
RC 29 July 1818, p. 3

Married Sept. 11th, by Rev. John Bryce, MR. WILSON BRACKETT, Merchant, to MISS MARY
H. BREEDEN, both of Richmond
RC 14 Sept. 1819, p. 3

Married on Thurs. last (June 1) MR. DAVIDSON BRADFUTE to MISS MARIA BYRD, both of
this city
RE 6 June 1809, p. 3; VGGA 6 June, p. 3; Visitor 3 June, p. 70

Married on Sat. last (June 15) MR. PLEASANT BRADLEY of Charles City Co., to MISS
MILDRED COLEMAN of this city
VA 22 June 1805, p. 3

Married on Tues. last (July 9) by Rev. John Lindsay, MR. ROBERT BRADLEY to MISS
SALLY SHARPE, dau. of Mr. Peter Sharpe of Four Mile Creek
RE 12 July 1811, p. 3; VA 11 July, p. 3

Married in Chesterfield Co., Feb. 20th, CAPT. BOLLING BRANCH of Buckingham to
MISS REBECCA GRAVES, dau. of Mr. Arthur Graves of Chesterfield
VA 25 March 1800, p. 3

Married April 30th at Philadelphia by Rev. Kenney, LT. R.H. BRANCH of Virginia, to
MISS GEORGEANNA EDWARDS of that city
RC 11 May 1820, p. 3

Married Jan. 21st by Rev. Bishop Moore, CARTER BRAXTON of Windsor, to MISS ANNA MATTILDA MUSE of Buckingham Lodge
RE 12 Feb. 1818, p. 3

Married April 5th, MR. CHARLES BRAY, a merchant, of Tappahannock, to MISS SUSAN CROXTON, all of Essex Co.
RE 14 April 1820, p. 3

Married on Thurs. last (Jan. 20) by Rev. John D. Blair, MR. JAMES BRAY, to MISS MARY STAPLES, both of this city
RE 22 Jan. 1814, p. 3

Married, Sat. last (Jan. 1) JAMES BRECKINRIDGE, Esq. of Botetourt Co., to MISS NANCY SELDEN of this city
VGGA 5 Jan. 1791, p. 2

Married on 22nd Inst. by Rev. Mr. Dunn, at Coton, seat of late Col. Thomas L. Lee, MR. WILLIAM BRENT of Stafford Co., to MISS WINIFRED B. LEE of Loudon Co.
RE 30 March 1810, p. 3; Visitor 31 Jay, p. 35

Married, MR. RICHARD BREWER of Westmoreland to MISS NANCY BLACKWELL of same county
VGIC 1 Nov. 1788, p. 2; IC of 29 Oct. 1788, says she is of Md.; VGNA 30 Oct., 1788

Married May 18th, MR. MORDECAI W. BROADDUS to MISS ELIZABETH DEJARNET (in Caroline Co.?)
RE 9 June 1820, p. 3

Married June 7th by Rev. David Jones, MR. THOMAS BROADWAY, age 65, to MISS MARIA BOWLER, age 15, both of Amelia Co.
RE 5 July 1817, p. 3

Married in Boston, GEORGE M. BROOKE of U.S. Army to MISS LUCY THOMAS
RE 16 Nov. 1819, p. 3

Married on Tues. last (Jan. 19) by Rev. John D. Blair, MR. RICHARD BROOKE to MISS SELINA POE, all of this city
VA 26 Jan. 1808, p. 3

Married on 22nd Ult. at Friends Meeting House, Montgomery Co., Md., MR. ROGER BROOKE to MISS MARIA PLEASANT YOUNGHUSBAND, both of said county
VA 8 Sept. 1804, p. 3

Married on 22nd Ult., MR. ZACHARIAH BROOKS of Manchester, to MISS MARGARET M'RAE of Powhatan
VGGA 11 Oct. 1808, p. 3

Married on Dec. 18, 1816, by Rev. Robert B. Semple, MR. ARCHIBALD BROWN, merchant, of King William Co., to MISS ANN SAUNDERS of King & Queen Co.
RE 7 Jan. 1816, p. 3

Married on 22nd Inst., MR. BASIL BROWN of King William to MISS FANNY R. DANDRIDGE, dau. of Capt. John Dandridge of Henrico Co.
VGGA 28 Dec. 1803, p. 3

Married April 25th by Rev. John Buchanan, MR. EDMUND BROWN, to MISS ANN H. GOOSELEY, all of Richmond
VP 30 April 1817, p. 3; RC 30 April, p. 2

Married on 28th Aug. by Rev. Christopher McRae, MR. JOHN BROWN of Caroline, to MISS MARY C. MOSELEY of Powhatan
VA 19 Sept. 1807, p. 2

Married on 25th last month, MR. JOHN BROWN, JR., to MISS MARIA COPLAND, both of this city
RE 10 Oct. 1806, p. 3

Married on Mon. last (Aug. 10) MR. WILLIAM BROWN of James City, to MRS. MARIA PLEASA, relict of Col. John Pleasants, dec'd, of Four Mile Creek
RC 18 Aug. 1795, p. 2; VGGA 26 Aug., says married Monday, 17th Inst.; VGRMA 15 Aug., p. 3

Married Nov. 11th by Rev. Wm. Tude, MR. ANDREW C. BROWNE, to MISS LUCY GARNETT all of King & Queen Co.
RE 27 Nov. 1818, p. 3

Married Sept. 17th by Rev. Mr. Matthews, MR. J. B. BRUNET of Richmond, to MISS ELIZA LABILLE of Georgetown, D.C.
RC 22 Dec. 1818, p. 3

Married Nov. 10th by Rev. John Courtney, REV. JOHN BRYCE to MISS MARY F. DANIEL, bot of Richmond
RC 11 Nov. 1819, p. 3

Married June 29th by Rev. William H. Hart, MR. PHILIP BUDLONG, to MISS MARY D. WILLS dau. of Capt. Charles Wills, all of Richmond
RC 7 July 1820, p. 3

Married on Thurs. last (March 20) at Locust Hill, Caroline Co. by Rev. Mr. Boggs, DAVID BULLOCK, Esq. of Richmond, Attorney at Law, to MISS CATHERINE W. ROY, eldest dau. of Mungo Roy, Esq.
VA 25 March 1806, p. 3; RE 25 March, p. 3; VGGA 26 March, p. 3

Married Sept. 24th by Rev. William Y. Hyter, MR. LEO BULLOCK of Louisa C.H. to MISS ANN WRIGHT, dau. of Mr. Charles Wright, of same county
RE 17 Oct. 1820, p. 3

Married, CHARLES B. BURGESS, to MISS ELIZABETH OWEN, dau. of Joel Owen of Powhatan Co., on August 12th
VA 6 Sept. 1813, p. 3

Married on 23rd Ult., at Osbornes in Chesterfield, MR. WILLIAM BURCH, to MISS ANN HOLLIDGE
VA 2 April 1799, p.3

Married Jan. 21st by Rev. Wm. H. Hart, CAPT. WILLIAM BURK, to MISS MARY ANN WEYMOUTH, dau. of late Capt. William W. Weymouth, all of Richmond
RC 23 Jan. 1819, p. 3

Married in Fredericksburg Sept. 22nd by Rev. Mr. Low, DR. LEWIS BURRELL of Frederick Co., to MISS MARIA M. PAGE, dau. of late Mann Page, Esq. of Mannsfield
RE 30 Sept. 1808, p. 3

Married on 1st Inst., MR. SAMUEL BURRUSS to MISS JANE GRAHAM, both of Caroline Co.
VGGA 7 July 1802, p. 3

Married Aug. 20th by Rev. Baptist, DR. AARON BURTON of Henrico Co., to MISS MARIA ANN TRUEHEART, eldest dau. of Mr. Bartholomew Trueheart of Powhatan Co.
RE 28 Aug. 1816, p. 3

Married, MR. ALLEN BURTON to MISS SALLY GOODIN, both of Amelia (No marriage date)
VGRMA 1 Aug. 1795, p. 3

Married on Fri. last (Dec. 4) MR. ROBERT BURTON, merchant, of this city, to MISS ANNA P. BRADDOCK, late of London
VGGA 8 Dec. 1801, p. 3

Married Thurs. last (Sept. 19) MR. THOMAS BURTON to MISS CLEMENTINA PLEASANTS, both of Henrico
VGRMA 23 Sept. 1793, p. 3

Married in Greensville Co. at house of Thomas Turner by Rev. William Coman, on Thurs. (Sept. 25) MR. WILLIAM M. BURTON of Richmond, to MISS LUCY S. BINFORD, dau. of Col. John Binford of Northampton Co., N.C.
RE 30 Sept. 1817, p. 3

Married Wed. last (Nov. 30) MR. WILLIAM BURTON, JR. to MISS ELIZABETH MOSBY, both of Henrico Co.
VA 7 Dec. 1803, p. 3

Married Nov. 22nd by Rev. John D. Blair, MR. BLAIR BURWELL to MISS SARAH HATCHER, dau. of Benjamin Hatcher, all of Manchester
RE 29 Nov. 1815, p. 3

Married in Gloucester Co. by Rev. Wm. H. Hart, on Tuesday (March 28) MR. GEORGE H. BURWELL of Frederick Co., to MISS ISABELLA S. DIXON, dau. of John Dixon of Gloucester Co.
RE 4 April 1820, p. 3

Married on Sat. last (May 30), LEWIS BURWELL, Esq. of Gloucester Co., to MISS JUDITH CANNON of this city
VGWA 4 June 1789, p. 3

Married at Mannsfield, near Fredericksburg, COL. NATHANIEL BURWELL to MRS. LUCY BAYLOR. (No marriage date)
VGWA 26 Feb. 1789, p. 3

Married, near Baltimore, WILLIAM A. BURWELL, Esq., a Congressman from Va. to MISS LETITIA McCREERY. (No marriage date)
RE 14 Jan. 1809, p. 3; Visitor, p. 7, 11 Feb.

Married on 18th Inst., MR. JAMES BUTLER of Cartersville to MISS MARIA OVERTON, dau. of Gen. Thomas Overton of Tenn.
RE 31 Dec. 1805, p. 3; VA 31 Dec., p. 3

Married on 1st Inst., MR. JOSEPH BUTLER, age 76 of Bladen, to MRS. ELIZABETH THAMES of Cumberland, age 60
Visitor 24 Feb. 1810, p. 15

Married on 21st Inst. (Ult.), MR. REUBEN BUTLER to MISS ELIZABETH RUFFIN, both of Surry Co.
VA 13 Nov. 1805, p. 3

Married on Thurs. (Jan. 4) by Rev. Blair, MR. JAMES CABANISS, merchant, of Petersburg to MISS ANN MATILDA HENING, dau. of William W. Hening of Richmond City
VA 6 Jan. 1816, p. 3

Married on Jan. 1st by Rev. Bishop Madison, at house of Hon. St. George Tucker in Williamsburg, MR. JOSEPH C. CABELL to MISS MARY CARTER
RE 8 Jan. 1807, p. 3; VGGA 10 Jan., p. 3

Married in this city on 11sth Inst., WILLIAM H. CABELL, Esq. of Amherst, to MISS AGNE SARAH BELL GAMBLE, dau. of Col. Robert Gamble
RE 19 March 1805, p. 3; VA 20 March, p. 3

Married on Thurs. (Nov. 25) at Fredericksburg, JAMES H. CALDWELL, Manager of Petersbu Fredericksburg and New Orleans Theatres, to MRS. MARIA CARTER WORMELEY, widow of late Warner Wormeley of Rosegill
RC 1 Dec. 1819, p. 3

Married by Rev. James Tompkins on 10th Inst., WILLIAM CALLOWAY, Jr. of Bedford Co., to MISS ELIZABETH CALLAND, dau. of Samuel Calland of Pittsylvania Co.
RE 25 Jan. 1805, p. 3

Married Thurs. last (Sept. 12), ALEXANDER CAMPBELL, Esq., Attorney at Law, to MISS HETTY HYLTON, eldest dau. of Wm. Hylton, Esq.
VGGA 18 Sept. 1793, p. 3

Married at Norfolk, MR. ARCHIBALD B. CAMPBELL to MISS MARY C. SMITH. (No marriage date)
Visitor 30 Dec. 1809, p. 190

Married Dec. 10, 1816, by Rev. Philip Montague, MR. PETER CAMPBELL of King & Queen Co., to MISS MARY HENLEY of Essex Co.
RE 7 Jan. 1817, p. 3

Married on Thurs. last (Dec. 18) MR. ROBERT CAMPBELL, merchant, to MISS NANCY ALLISON, both of this city
VGRMA 22 Dec. 1794, p. 3

Married Tues. (Sept. 22) by Rev. Montague, MR. WILLIAM CAMPBELL to MISS PRISCILLA COURTNEY, 2nd dau. of Capt. Robert Courtney, all of King & Queen Co.
RE 29 Sept. 1818, p. 3

Married at Wilmington, N.C., COLOMON CANADA, to MISS SUSANNAH BRITAIN. (No marriage date). We never supposed that Britain would Britain would be taken by Canada, but it is a voluntary surrender and we shall be very much deceived if, after the capitulation and matters are adjusted, Canada does not keep ossession.
RC 22 Oct. 1816, p. 3

Married, JOHN CARLISLE of Calf Pasture in Augusta Co. to MRS. WANLESS of same place. (No marriage date)
VGAA Nov. 22, 1783, p. 3

Married on Sat. (Sept. 16) by Rev. John H. Rice, MR. ASHBEL A. CARRINGTON, merchant, to MISS MARY GREEN, dau. of Mrs. Sarah Taylor, all of Richmond
RE 22 Sept. 1820, p. 3; RC 20 Sept., p. 3

Married on Sat. last (Dec. 8) COL. EDWARD CARRINGTON to MRS. ELIZABETH BRENT of this city
VGGA 12 Dec. 1792, p.3

Married on 25th Ult. WILSON J. CAREY of Williamsburg to MRS. VIRGINIA RANDOLPH of Albemarle
RE 3 Sept. 1805, p. 3; VA 4 Sept., p. 3 (says MISS); VGGA 4 Sept., p. 2

Married Aug. 24th by Rev. John D. Blair, HENRY L. CARTER of Richmond, to MISS NANCY WORTHAM of Chesterfield Co.
VPRDMA 30 Aug. 1820, p. 3

Married on Sat. (Feb. 14) MR. JOHN CARTER to MISS MATILDA WRAY
VGGA 18 Feb. 1795, p. 3

Married on 4th Inst., JOSEPH CARTER, Esq. to MISS NANCY ROBERTSON, dau. of Mr. Christopher Robertson, all of Pittsylvania Co.
VA 19 Dec. 1806, p. 3

Married on Sat. last (Sept. 19) by Rev. John D. Blair, MR. RICHARD CARTER to MISS SUSANNA PRICE, both of Henrico
VA 23 Sept. 1807, p. 3

Married in St. Johns, New Brunswick, MR. SAMUEL CARTER to LUCY, widow of Mr. Isaac Woodward. (No marriage date)
RE 12 May 1818, p. 3

Married Sat. last (Aug. 6) DR. THOMAS CARTER of this city to MISS BROADNAX of
Petersburg
VGWA 13 Aug. 1785, p. 3

Married, last Sat. (March 31) by Rev. Mr. Buchanan, MR. WILLIAM CARTER to MISS
CHARLOTTE FOUSHEE, 2nd dau. of Dr. William Foushee of this city
RE 3 April 1810, p. 3

Married on Tues. (June 25) CAPT. WILLIAM CARTER, USN, to MISS MARIA GIBBON, younge
dau. of Maj. James Gibbon of Richmond
VP 29 June 1816, p. 3

Married Nov. 18th at the Poor House of Richmond, by Rev. John Courtney, DR. WILLI
CARTER, to MRS. KESIAH WHITE, both residents of the Poor House
RC 23 Nov. 1819, p. 3

Married at Fredericksburg May 23rd, by Rev. Wilson, SAMUEL CARY of Richmond, to
MISS WILLIE M. CARTER, dau. of John Carter of Fredericksburg
VPRDMA 29 May 1820, p. 3

Married on Thurs. 18th (19th) JOHN CATLETT of King William Co., to MISS MARTHA BAI'
of Gloucester Co.
RE 28 Feb. 1818, p. 3

Married on Thurs. last (July 7) MR. DAVID CHAMBER of MISS AGNES CRUTCHFIELD, both (
this city
VGGA 13 July 1803, p. 3

Married at Suffolk on Tues. (Feb. 11) by Rev. George Vatterson, CAPT. EDWARD
CHAMBERLAIN of Norfolk, to MISS MARY ANN PRENTISS, youngest dau. of Hon. Joseph
Prentiss, dec'd
RC 13 March 1817, p. 3

Married on April 11th at Mt. Prospect, New Kent Co., the res. of Col. W. H. Macom,
by Rt. Rev. R.C. Moore, DR. LEWIS W. CHAMBERLAYNE of Richmond, to MISS MARTHA B.
DABNEY
RC 14 April 1820, p. 3

Married lately MR. WILLIAM CHAMBERLAYNE of New Kent Co., TO MISS PEGGY WILKINSON oi
Henrico
VGAA 7 Aug. 1784, p. 2

Married, at Athens, Vt., MR. SILAS CHAPLIN, 15, to MISS SUSANNA POWERS, 13
VA 21 Jan. 1804, p. 3

Married May 18th, MR. PHILIP CHAPMAN to MRS. JUDITH STIFF
RE 9 June 1820, p. 3

Married on 25th Ult., MR. NATHANIEL CHARTER to MISS WINNEFRED JOHNSON, both of thi
city
Visitor 3 June 1809, p. 70

Married on Dec. 22nd by Rev. John D. Blair, MR. JOHN W. CHEADLE, to MISS ELENEA P. SHIELDS, dau. of Mr. John P. Shields, all of Richmond
RC   27 Dec. 1814, p. 3

Married, MR. JOHN A. CHEVALLIE to MISS SALLY MAGEE. (No marriage date)
VICGA 6 Jan. 1790, p. 3

Married at Studley, seat of Hon. Peter Lyons in Hanover, on Thurs. last (May 15) JOHN A. CHEVALLIE, Esq. of this city to MISS KITTY LYONS
VGGA 21 May 1794, p. 3; VGRMA 19 May

Married lately in Elizabeth Town, MR. FRANCIS CHILDS, Editor of the Daily Advertiser of Ner York City, to MISS SARAH BLANCHARD, dau. of Mr. John Blanchard, Merchant, of Elizabeth Town
VGWA 23 Aug. 1787, p. 2

Married Sept. 30th by Rev. Robert B. Semple, CHARLES S. CHILTON, to MISS LEVINIA FOX, all of King & Queen Co.
RE   8 Oct. 1819, p. 3

Married Oct. 21st by Rev. John D. Blair, DR. JOHN FLEMING CHRISTIAN of New Kent Co., to MISS SARAH ANN, dau. of late Samuel PLEASANTS of Richmond
RC   25 Oct. 1819, p. 3

Married on 28th Ult. at Col. Heath J. Miller's in Goochland by Rev. Reuben Ford, MAJ. JOHN H. CHRISTIAN of New Kent, and MRS. MARY H. BATES
RE   15 March 1811, p. 3; VA 18 March, p. 3; VP 15 March, p. 3

Married at Albany, N.Y. on Wed. (No marriage date given) by Rev. Crawford, MR. ANTHONY CIVELL, to MISS FANNY WOLF, both of that city
RC   22 May 1820, p. 3

Married on 8th Inst., BATHURST CLAIBORNE of Windsor in Sussex to MISS POLLY CLAIBORNE of Manchester
VGRMA 17 Sept. 1796, p. 3

Married on 19th Ult. at White Apple Village, near Natchez, Miss, Terr., CAPT. FERDINAND LEIGH CLAIBORNE, late of 1st U.S. Regt. to MISS MAGDALINE HUTCHENS, dau. of Col. Hutchens of that territory. On the day after the wedding, Col. Hutchens placed Capt. Claiborne in the lap of ease by giving him a considerable fortune
VA 29 Sept. 1802, p. 3; VGGA 29 Sept., p. 3

Married by Rev. Rob. Hurt, MR. LEONARD CLAIBORNE, to MISS LETITIA W. CLARK, dau. of Col. William Clark, all of Pittsylvania Co.
RE   16 Jan. 1819, p. 3

Married by Rev. J. D. Blair, MR. JAMES CLARK, Jr. of Manchester, to MISS MARTHA MURCHIE of Chesterfield on 29th Ult.
VA   9 Nov. 1805, p. 3

Married Oct. 2nd by Rev. John Jenkins, MR. JAMES H. CLARK of Cabarus Co., N.C., to MISS NANCY W. COLEMAN, dau. of Capt. Stephen Coleman of Pittsylvania Co.
RE 10 Oct. 1817, p. 3

Married Dec. 29th, by Rev. John Bryce, DR. MICAJAH CLARK, to MISS CAROLINE VIRGINIA, dau. of Benjamin James Harris of Richmond
RC 31 Dec. 1819, p. 3

Married Sat. last (June 4) MR. SAMUEL CLARK, merchant, to MISS KITTY ROWLAND, both of this city
VA 8 June 1803, p. 3; VGGA 8 June, p. 3

Married on 25th Inst., MR. WILLIAM CLARK of Chesterfield, to MISS NANCY ROWLETT of Petersburg
Visitor 31 March 1810, p. 35

Married April 16th by Rev. John Kirkpatrick, COLIN CLARKE, of Powhatan Co., to MISS MARY G. LYLE of Manchester
RE 1 May 1818, p. 3

Married on Thurs. (Oct. 1) by Rev. John D. Blair, MR. FREDERICK CLARKE, merchant, of this city, to MISS MARIA E. BOTT, eldest dau. of Mr. Miles Bott of Manchester
RE 6 Oct. 1812, p. 3

Married Oct. 22nd, by Rev. John D. Blair, MR. JOTHAM CLARKE, to MISS MARY H. ALCOCK, all of Richmond
RC 24 Oct. 1818, p. 3

Married on Tues. (Nov. 10) by Rev. John D. Blair, MAJ. WILLIAM CLARKE, of Campbell Co., to MISS ELIZABETH H. WINSTON, dau. of Mr. George Winston of Richmond
RE 13 Nov. 1818, p. 3; RC 12 Nov., p. 3; VP 13 Nov., p. 3

Married on 18th Inst., MATTHEW CLAY, Esq., Member of Congress from this state to MISS NANCY SAUNDERS of Buckingham Co.
VA 25 June 1803, p. 3

Married 31 May, DR. MACE CLEMENTS to MISS PURKINS, dau. of Mr. Wm. Purkins, all of Essex Co.
RE 16 June 1804, p. 3

Married May 3rd at house of Benjamin Prescott, Colesville, N.Y., by Rev. Butler, MR. LAURENT CLERC of LaBalme, France, to MISS ELIZA C. BOARDMAN of Whitesborough, N.Y., both deaf and dumb. He is instructor at school for deaf and dumb at Hartford. She is his pupil.
VP 15 May 1819, p. 3

Married on 8th Inst., HOWELL COBB, Esq. Congressman from Georgia, to MISS MARTHA J. ROOTES, dau. of Thomas R. Rootes, Esq. of Fredericksburg, Va.
VA 18 May 1810, p. 3

Married Aug. 10th in Richmond, by Rev. McAdden, GEORGE COCHRANE, printer, to MISS SARAH BRICKEN
VPRDMA 14 Aug. 1820, p. 3

Married on 30th Ult. at Avonhill, in Jefferson Co., by Rev. Mr. Hill, DR. CHARLES COCKE of Amelia, to MISS SARAH W. TAYLOR of Southampton Co.
RE 17 July 1810, p. 3

Married on 3rd Inst., by Rev. Rhane Chastean, JAMES CODY, merchant, of Caira, to MISS ELIZA ANDERSON, dau. of Capt. Richard Anderson of Buckingham
VA 26 Jan. 1805, p. 3

Married on June 10th at Norfolk by Rev. Mr. Grigsby, REUBEN COFFIN to MISS POLLY BUTT
Impartial Observer 12 July 1806, p. 2

Married on 31st Oct. MR. THOMAS COHEN to MISS HEATH
Visitor 16 Dec. 1809, p. 182

Married in Europe, REV. THOMAS COKE, L.L.D., one of the Bishops of the Methodist Episcopal Church, U.S.A.
VA 17 July, 1805, p. 3

Married Feb. 4th at Woodberry, King William Co., late res. of Isaac Quarles, dec'd, CAPT. ARMISTEAD COLEMAN of Amelia Co., to MISS BETSY S. QUARLES
RE 14 Feb. 1818, p. 3

Married, on 18th Inst. by Rev. Simon Morgan, MR. ARCHER COLEMAN of Amelia Co., to MISS MARGARET QUARLES, dau. of Isaac Quarles, Esq. of King William Co.
VA 2 June 1809, p. 3; VGGA 30 May, p. 3; Visitor 3 June, p. 70

Married last evening, MR. ROBERT COLEMAN of Petersburg to MISS BETSEY HOLT of Williamsburg
VGWA 24 Dec. 1785, p. 3

Married on 29th April, by Rev. John Courtney, MR. LEONARD COLES of New York, to MISS MARY OMBERSON of this city
VA 3 May 1813, p. 3

Married on 11th Inst., WALTER COLES, ESQ. of Albermarle to MISS ELIZA FAUNTLEROY COCKE, eldest dau. of Bowler Cocke, Esq. of Turkey Island
VA 14 Nov. 1797, p. 2; VGGA 14 Nov., p. 2

Married on Sat. last (Feb. 13) MR. EDWARD COLLIER to MISS ELIZABETH HUTCHESON, both of this city
RC 16 Feb. 1796, p. 3; VGRMA 17 Feb., p. 3

Married May 25th by Rev. Buchanan, THOMAS M. COLSTON of Berkeley Co., Va. to MISS ELIZA J. FISHER, dau. of George Fisher of Richmond
RC 27 May 1820, p. 3; VPRDMA 27 May 1820, p. 3

Married on Sat. (April 19) by Rev. John H. Rice, MR. JOSEPHUS B. COLTON, of house of Colton & Reed, to MISS ABIGAIL CLARK, all of Richmond
VP 22 April 1817, p. 3; RC 22 April, p. 2

Married at Savannah, Ga., MR. SAMUEL COMB to MISS SARAH RUFFHEAD
VA 8 Dec. 1802, p. 3 (Put in paper for humor)

Married, MR. JOHN CONLIFFE to MISS ESTHER HUGHES, both of this city. (No marriage date)
VGWA 15 Oct. 1789, p. 3

Married in Amelia Co., Nov. 6th, by Rev. Logan, DR. JAMES H. CONWAY to MISS AUGUSTA GILES, eldest dau. of William B. Giles
RC 12 Nov. 1816, p. 3

Married on March 30th by Rev. Samuel Bishop, MR. JOHN COOK, to MISS MARY GWYN, all of Gloucester Co.
RE 14 April 1820, p. 3

Married on Sat. last (Nov. 15) by Rev. John Buchanan, MR. JOHN L. COOK, to MISS ELIZA DARROUS
RE 18 Nov. 1806, p. 3

Married in Northampton Co., N.C., on 28th Sept., MR. WILLIAM COOK of this city, to MISS ELIZABETH BENFORD of that place
RE 15 Oct. 1813, p. 3

Married at Urbanna on 16th Ult. by Mr. Hefferman, THOMAS COOKE, Esq. of Gloucester to MISS CATHERINE B. DIDLAKE
VGGA 1 Feb. 1806, p. 3

Married, FRANCIS CORBIN, Esq. of the Reeds, Caroline Co., to MISS BEVERLEY of Essex (No marriage date)
VGGA 6 Jan. 1796, p. 3

Married a few days since at Norfolk, MR. JOHN B. CORDIS of Boston to MISS ELIZA RANDOLPH, late of this city
VA 31 July 1801, p. 3

Married May 15th by Rev. James Logan, MR. PETER COTTOM of Richmond, to MISS MARTHA DANDRIDGE FLEMING of Goochland Co.
VP 21 May, 1817, p. 3

Married in Baltimore on 29th Ult., by Rt. Rev. Bishop Kemp, RICHARD COTTOM, Esq., of Petersburg, to MISS CHARLOTTE M. COCHRAN of that city
RE 10 June 1815, p. 3; VA 7 June, p. 3

Married on 29th Ult., MR. DANIEL COUCH of Little Creek, Goochland Co., to MISS SALL RICHARDSON, dau. of late John Richardson, Esq. of Westonville, in Hanover
VA 3 Feb. 1807, p. 2

Married on 21st Ult., DR. THOMAS COULTER, to MISS MARIA BARCLAY, both of Buckingham Co.
RE 2 June 1809, p. 3

Married lately in King & Queen Co., MR. DANDRIDGE P. COURTNEY and MISS SALLY COLEMAN
LUMPKIN
RE 8 March 1808, p. 3

Married in this city on Thurs. last (May 8) MR. JOHN COURTNEY, printer, of Staunton,
to MISS SALLY BARKER of this city
VA 13 May, 1800, p. 3

Married, on 9th Inst., by Rev. Robert Semple, MR. ROBERT COURTNEY, of this city, to
MISS SARAH CAMPBELL of King & Queen Co.
VA 16 April 1812, p. 3; VP 17 April, p. 3

Married on March 30th, by Rev. John Jones, CAPT. WILLIAM H. COUSINS of Dinwiddie Co.,
to MISS MARTHA ROBINSON, dau. of late Rev. Peter Robinson of Nottoway Co.
RE 23 April 1819, p. 3

Married May 13th by Rev. John D. Blair, CAPT. JOHN COWLEY, to MISS MARTHA, eldest
dau. of Capt. Richard CURD, of Henrico Co.
RC 15 May 1819, p. 3

Married on Thurs. (Feb. 12) MR. WILLIAM COX to MISS ELIZABETH WHITE, both of Powhatan
Co.
VGGA 18 Feb. 1795, p. 3; VGRMA 16 Feb., p. 3

Married, MR. ADAM CRAIG, of City of Richmond, to MISS POLLY MALLORY of Warwick Co.
(No marriage date)
VGWA 12 July 1787, p. 3

Married, on Sat. last (Sept. 4) at house of Mr. Nathaniel Charter, by the Rev. John
H. Rice, MR. EDWARD V. CRANDALL, to MISS CLORINDA CHARTER, all of this town
VA 6 Sept. 1813, p. 3

Married on 22nd Inst. (Ult.) by Rev. Armistead Smith, SAMUEL CRAWFORD, Esq. of
State of Georgia to MISS ROSY L. ROGERS, dau. of Capt. William Rogers of Gloucester
Co.
RE 9 Nov. 1810, p. 3

Married in Goochland Co. on 4th Inst., by Rev. Conrad Speece, MR. ASBURY CRENSHAW,
to MISS ANN PEMBERTON, dau. of Capt. Thomas Pemberton
RE 10 April 1810, p. 3

Married Dec. 23rd by Rev. John Bryce, MR. A.M. CREW to MISS MARGARET WAIDE, all
of Richmond
RC 30 Dec. 1819, p. 3

Married (No marriage date) to Rt. Rev. Bishop Hobart, LT-COL. CROGHAN, to MISS SERENA
LIVINGTON, dau. of John R. Livingston of New York
RC 16 May 1817, p. 3

Married Nov. 25th by Rev. J. D. Blair, MR. THOMAS CROUCH, merchant, of Richmond, to
MISS MARY, eldest dau. of Mr. Robert TEMPLE of Ampthill
RC 30 Nov. 1819, p. 3

Married on Thurs. (Dec. 19) by Rev. John D. Blair, MR. BENEDICT CRUMP to MISS MARY A
ROSE both of Richmond
RE 24 Dec. 1816, p. 3

Married on 27th March last, at Old Town, New Kent Co., by Rev. John Saunders,
DR. EDMUND P. CRUMP, to MISS JUDITH WILKINSON, both of that County
RE 22 April 1806, p. 3

Married Nov. 24th by Rev. Anderson, to CAPT. JOHN C. CRUMP of Surry Co., to
MISS ELIZABETH EMELINE JEFFERSON HINSON of Nansemond Co.
RE 4 Dec. 1818, p. 3

Married on 14th Inst., by Rev. John D. Blair, MR. JOSHUA CRUMP, to MISS ELIZABETH
MURPHY, both of this city
VA 21 Nov. 1811, p. 3

Married by Rev. C. Speice on 3rd Inst., MR. OTWAY CRUMP of Cumberland Co., to
MISS MARIA CLARKE, dau. of William Clark, Esq., of Powhatan Co.
RE 8 Feb. 1810, p. 3

Married on Thurs. last (June 2) by Rev. Mr. Willis, MR. THOMAS CRUMP to MISS REBECCA
FRAYSER, both of New Kent Co.
VA 7 June 1808, p. 3

Married on 5th Inst., at Mr. Robert Greenhow's in this city by the Rev. Mr. Buchanan
DR. WILLIAM CRUMP of Powhatan, to MISS MARIA MOODY of Williamsburg
RE 6 Nov. 1812, p. 3; VP 10 Nov., p. 3

Married on 15th Inst., by Rev. Mr. Willis, MR. WILLIAM B. CRUMPTON, to MISS AGNES
REDFORD, both of this county
VA 17 Oct. 1811, p. 3

Married on 18th Ult., MR. EDWARD CUNNINGHAM, merchant, of Cumberland Co., to MISS
ARIANA MACARTNEY of this city
VGRMA 3 Sept. 1796, p. 3

Married June 10th by Rev. John D. Blair, DR. EDWARD CURD, to MISS SARAH E. CLOPTON,
youngest dau. of David Clopton, Sr. of Henrico Co.
RC 15 June 1819, p. 3

Married on Oct. 31st by Rev. Logan, DR. THOMAS CURD, to MISS CAROLINE R. PLEASANTS,
dau. of James Pleasants, all of Goochland Co.
RE 8 Nov. 1815, p. 3

Married, DR. JAMES CURRIE of this city, to MRS. INGLES of Princess Anne Co. (No
marriage date)
VIC 25 Nov. 1789, p. 3

Married on Wed. (Oct. 14) MR. JAMES CURRIE to MISS CAROLINE PICKETT, dau. of George
Pickett, all of this city
RE 16 Oct. 1807, p. 3

Married in Gloucester on 27th Ult., DR. HENRY CURTIS of Hanover to MISS CHRISTIANA
B. TYLER, youngest dau. of late Judge Tyler of Charles City
RE 20 July 1813, p. 3

Married June 6th by Rev. J. D. Blair, THOMAS S. DABNEY to MISS MARY A. TYLER, all
of Williamsburg
RE 23 June 1820, p. 3; RC 13 June, p. 3

Married on Tues. last (Feb. 10), MR. WILLIAM DABNEY of this city, merchant, to
MISS HETTY HYLTON
VGGA 18 Feb. 1795, p. 3; VGRMA 16 Feb., p. 3

Married on 4th Inst., CAPT. LAWRENCE T. DADE of Orange, to MISS ANN MAYO, dau. of
Mr. William Mayo of Henrico
RE 10 May 1815, p. 3

Married Aug. 3rd by Rev. Bridgewater, MR. JOHN W. DANCE of Richmond, to MISS ELIZA
CARTER of Powhatan Co.
RC 12 Aug. 1820, p. 3

Married on Sat. last (Feb. 23) CAPT. JOHN DANDRIDGE to MISS BETSY BOOTH of Westham,
Henrico
VGAA 2 March, 1782, p. 3; VGWA 2 March

Married Nov. 30th, MR. JOHN DANGERFIELD, to MISS JUDITH BRAXTON, all of Essex Co.
RE 7 Dec. 1819, p. 3

Married on Sat. last (April 21) PETER V. DANIEL, Esq. to MISS LUCY RANDOLPH, youngest
dau. of Edmund Randolph, Esq., all of this city
RE 24 April, 1810, p. 3; VA 27 April, p. 3

Married on Mon. (before Feb. 10) WILLIAM DANIEL, Esq. to MISS PEGGY BALDWIN, dau.
of Dr. Cornelius Baldwin of Winchester
VA 19 Feb. 1802, p. 2

Married Aug. 16th by Rev. Isaac B. Sexias, MR. S. DANIELS, merchant, to MISS RACHEL
MARKS, youngest dau. of Mr. Myer Marks, all of Richmond
RC 23 Aug. 1820, p. 3

Married in Hanover Co., April 14th by Rev. Wydown, MR. DAVID DAVENPORT to MISS SUSAN
VALENTINE. Mr. Davenport is 67 and a patriot who served under Patrick Henry in the
"gunpowder expedition" at beginning of Revolutionary War
RE 9 May 1820, p. 3

Married on 15th Inst. by Rev. Henry Hefferman, JOHN DARBY, Esq. of Richmond Co., to
MRS. LUCY BURWELL CHURCHILL, widow of late Thomas Churchill, widow of late Thomas
Churchill of Wilton
RE 31 Dec. 1807, p. 3

196

Married on Sat. last (July 8) by Rev. Mr. Blair, MR. ISAAC DAVIS to MISS CATHARINE
FOX, both of this city
VA 11 July 1809, p. 3; VGGA 11 July, p. 3; Visitor 15 July, p. 94

Married on 19th Ult., MR. JOHN W. DAVIS of Petersburg to MISS MARTHA ANN DAVIES of
Chesterfield Co.
Visitor 4 Nov. 1809, p. 158

Married on Thurs. last (June 28) by Rev. Boggs, MR. LEWIS DAVIS to MISS CAROLINE
GRANTFIELD, both of Hanover Co.
VGGA 4 July 1804, p. 2

Married at Norfolk on 5th Inst. by Rev. Mr. Grigsby, the gallant CAPT. SHEPHEN
DECATUR, JR. of U.S. Navy to MISS SUSAN WHEELER only dau. of Luke Wheeler, Esq.,
Mayor of that Borough
RE 18 March 1806, p. 3

Married in Richmond Feb. 27th by Rev. Bishop Moore, J. M. DelCAMPO, merchant, to
widow V.C. WRECK, both of this city
RC 4 March 1817, p. 3

Married Aug. 7th by Rev. John D. Blair, MR. PETER DEMOVILLE of Charles City Co., to
MISS MARY ANN WINSTON, dau. of Mr. John P. Winston, dec'd, of Hanover Co.
RE 12 Aug. 1817, p. 3

Married Sept. 24th by Rev. John D. Blair, MR. RICHARD DENNY, JR., to MISS MATILDA
WALKER both of Richmond
RC 26 Sept. 1818, p. 3

Married on Sat. last (Dec. 24) by Rev. John D. Blair, MR. WILLIAM DEPRIEST to
MISS ELIZA LEWIS, both of Henrico Co.
VA 30 Dec. 1808, p. 2

Married at Natchez, Miss., Jan. 10th, JOHN DICK of New Orleans, La., at Attorney of
the U.S. for La. District, TO MISS MARY FARAR, daughter of Benjamin Farar of Laurel
Hill
RE 5 Feb. 1820, p. 3

Married May 25th, MR. JOHN DICKINSON to MISS JANE H. DICKINSON
RE 9 June 1820, p. 3

Married in Springfield, Mass., by Rev. Osgood, T. DICKMAN, Editor of Hampden, Mass.
Federalist, to Miss SARAH BREWER, dau. of Dr. Chauncey Brewer
RE 1 April 1817, p. 3

Married on Thurs. last (Oct. 8) in Petersburg, MR. JOHN DICKSON, Editor of The
Intelligencer to MISS ANN ROSE, both of that town
VA 14 Oct. 1807, p. 3; RE 20 Oct., p. 3

Married Thurs. last sen'night (Dec. 22) DUDLEY DIGGES, JR., Esq. to MISS POLLY
DIGGES, all of Williamsburg
VGAA 31 Dec. 1785, p. 2

Married on 13th Inst., CAPT. EDWARD DILLARD, of 5th U.S. Regt., TO MISS MINERVA RUFFIN of Rockingham Co.
RE 21 May 1811, p. 3

Married on 6th Inst., MR. THOMAS DILLON, merchant of Cumberland Co., to MISS BETSY KEELING of same county
VGWA 15 March 1787, p. 2

Married March 17th by Rev. Peter Davis, MR. WALTER DIX, to MISS JUDITH BOUGHTON, all of Essex Co.
RE 31 March 1820, p. 3

Married on Sat. last (Dec. 22), MR. GEORGE W. DIXON to MISS ELIZABETH BIRMINGHAM, both of this city
VA 29 Dec. 1804, p. 3; VGGA 25 Dec., p. 3

Married July 14th by Rev. James Lucas, MR. WILLIAM DONNALLY, to MISS ELEANOR TURNER, both of Williamsburg
RE 24 July 1818, p. 3

Married July 2nd by Rev. R. Baxter, MR. WILLIAM DORNIN to MISS MARY BOUNOR, both of Richmond
RC 7 July 1818, p. 3

Married Dec. 5th by Rev. Hatchet, MR. PAUL G. DOSWELL of Hanover Co., to MISS FRANCES GWATHMEY of King & Queen Co.
RE 17 Dec. 1816, p. 3

Married Thurs. (Feb. 11) by Rev. Hart, ROBERT DOUTHAT, Attorney at Law, of Richmond, to MISS ELEANOR WARNER LEWIS, daughter of Fielding Lewis of Charles City Co.
RE 16 Feb. 1819, p. 3; VP 16 Feb., p. 3

Married on 2nd. Inst., THOMAS DOUTHAT, Esq. of Staunton to MISS JANE PRICE of Henrico
VGRMA 24 June 1793, p. 3

Married on Mon. last (Nov. 28) by Rev. John Buchanan, DR. JOHN DOVE, to MISS ANN ELIZA EGE, both of Richmond
RC 1 Dec. 1814, p. 3

Married on 14th Inst., by Rev. J. D. Blair, MR. JACOB S. DOYLE, to MISS HANNAH WOOD, late of Philadelphia
VA 23 May, 1809, p. 3

Married last Sat. (April 13) by Rev. Blair, MR. CARTER H. DREW, to MISS JULIET SHORE, eldest dau. of Henry S. Shore, all of Richmond
VP 17 April 1816, p. 3

Married Dec. 22nd by Rev. John Massie, MR. JAMES DUKE, to MISS ELIZA SHARP, dau. of Mr. Martin Sharp, all of Louisa Co.
RE 29 Dec. 1819, p. 3; RC 29 Dec., p. 3

Married Nov. 9th in Phila, MR. JOHN DUNLAP of Doylestown, age 67, to MISS ELIZABETH CARR of Phila, age 69
RC 2 Dec. 1819, p. 2

Married on 6th Inst., by Rev. James Stevenson, the REV. JOHN DUNN, to MISS ELIZABETH MARYE, dau. of Rev. James Marye of Spotsylvania
VGGA 18 Nov. 1800, p. 3

Married on Thurs. (Feb. 4) MR. WILLIAM DUNN, merchant, to MISS MARTHA CRAWFORD, both of this city
VA 9 Feb. 1802, p. 3

Married on 22nd Ult., DR. DANIEL DUVAL, of Greenville, N.C., formerly of Gloucester Co., Va. to MRS. MARGARET EDWARDS of the same place
VA 30 April 1812, p. 3

Married on 29th Ult., MR. FRANCIS DUVAL of Tarborough, N.C., to MISS LUCY DuVAL, dau. of William DuVal, Esq., of Gloucester Co., Va.
RE 24 Jan. 1809, p. 3

Married in Dumfries on Dec. 20th (1815) by Rev. Norris of Alexandria, CAPT. JOHN P. DUVAL, late of U.S. Army, to MISS ANN F. TEBBS of Dumfries
RE 2 Jan. 1816, p. 3

Married Nov. 4th by Rev. Robert B. Semple, DR. JOHN DUVAL to MISS MARY ANN PENDLETON all of King & Queen Co.
VP 13 Nov. 1819, p. 3

Married on Thurs. last (May 8) by Rev. Ralph, MR. MAREEN H. DUVALL of Prince George Co., age 17, to MRS. DOROTHY ALLEN, age 50, widow of late Zachariah Allen, Esq. of this city
VA 19 May 1801, p. 3

Married at Williamsburg on 17th Ult., by Rev. Bracken, DR. PHILIP DUVAL of Richmond, to MISS MARY RANDOLPH of York
RE 9 March 1814, p. 3

Married on Sat. last (Feb. 7) in Buckingham Co., MAJ. WILLIAM DUVAL of this city to MISS CHRISTIAN of that co.
VA 10 Feb. 1807, p. 3; VGGA 11 Feb., p. 3

Married on Thurs. last (Oct. 8), MR. SAMUEL DYER, JR. merchant, of Albemarle, to MISS MARTHA T. WATKINS of Goochland
RE 16 Oct. 1812, p. 3

Married Sept. 14th by Rev. Davis Roper, MR. JOHN EATON, merchant, of Richmond, formerly of Mass., to MISS ELIZABETH JOHNSON, formerly of Newmark, N.J.
RC 16 Sept. 1820, p. 3

Married in Woodstock, Conn., DR. JOHN E. EATON, to MISS URSUM PAINE. (No marriage date)
Visitor 2 Dec. 1809, p. 174

Married on 15th Inst. at Pipsco, CAPT. JAMES DAVIES EDMUNDS, to MISS PHEBE BELL, both of Surry Co.
RE 23 April 1811, p. 3

Married Dec. 19, 1816, by Rev. John Mill, MR. AMBROSE EDWARDS, Jr., to MISS JANET EDWARDS, all of King William Co.
RE 7 Jan. 1817, p. 3

Married on Thurs. last (May 24) MR. RICHARD EDWARDS to MISS SARAH WILLIAMS both of Henrico Co.
VGGA 30 May 1804, p. 2

Married at the Glebe in Powhatan Co., by Rt. Rev. Bishop Moore, the REV. EGAN, to MRS. MARY H. PHINEZY, relict of Maj. Phinezy of Ga.
VP 21 Sept. 1819, p. 3

Married Thurs. last (March 11) MR. JACOB EGE of MISS BETSY STUBBLEFIELD
VGWA 13 March 1784, p. 3

Married Tues. last (Dec. 30, 1800) MR. JACOB GALT EGE and MISS JANE MORGAN, both of this city
VGGA 1 Jan. 1801, p. 3

Married, CITIZEN EDMUND EGGLETON to MISS JANE S. LANGHORNE, both of Amelia Co. (No marriage date)
VGRMA 21 Nov. 1795, p. 3

Married on Wed. last (Aug. 13) MR. MARCUS ELCAN, merchant, of Richmond, to MISS PHILY MICHAELS late of Boston
VA 19 Aug. 1800, p. 3; VGGA 19 Aug., p. 3

Married on 15th Inst., ROLFE ELDRIDGE, Jr., Esq., to MISS MARY MOSELEY, both of Buckingham
VA 23 Dec. 1808, p. 3

Married, The REV. MR. ELLIOTT to MISS BROCKENBROUGH, both of Westmoreland. (No marriage date)
VGWA 4 Jan. 1793, p. 3

Married on Sat. (Nov. 20) in Princess Anne by Rev. Mr. Symes, CHARLES ELLIS, Esq. of house of Ellis & Allen, merchants in this city, to MISS MARGARET NIMMO, eldest dau. of James Nimmo of Norfolk
RE 26 Nov. 1813, p. 3; VA 18 Nov., p. 3, says married Sat. last (Nov. 13); VP 23 Nov., p. 3

Married on 17th Inst., MR. WILLIAM EMMINS of Petersburg, to MISS PATSEY BURROW of
Dinwiddie
Visitor 31 March 1810, p. 35

Married on March 5th, by Rev. John Buchanan, MR. JOHN ENDERS to MISS SARAH EGE, both
of Richmond
RC 8 March 1814, p. 3

Married on 17th Ult., MR. JOHN EPPERSON, merchant, of Buckingham, to MISS BETSY ANN
WOODSON of Prince Edward
VA 22 March 1799, p. 3

Married in Halifax, N.C. on 15th Inst., JOHN W. EPPES, Esq., Member of Congress, to
MISS MARTHA JONES, dau. of late Willie Jones, Esq.
RE 25 April 1809, p. 3; VA 28 April, p. 3; Visitor 6 May, p. 54

Married on 31st Ult. in Currituck, N.C., MR. C. ETHERBRIDGE, to MISS HULDA FEREBEE
Visitor 2 Dec. 1809, p. 174

Married on 6th Inst. by Rev. Willis Hopwood, MR. GEORGE FACKLOR, partner of Johnson
Facklor & Hinton, merchants, of Pittsylvania C.H., to MISS POLLY WHITE, dau. of
Maj. Jeremiah White of Pittsylvania
VA 21 Sept. 1810, p. 3

Married on 20th Ult. at Evelington, seat of Mr. Alexander Moore in Charles City,
MR. THOMAS FAIRFAX of Fairfax Co., to MISS MARY AYLETT, dau. of Col. Wm. Aylett
of King William Co., dec'd
VGGA 4 Nov. 1795, p. 3; VGRMA 5 Nov., p. 3

Married on Sat. (Sept. 20) MR. WILLIAM FENWICK, merchant, to MRS. RONALD, both of
this city
VGGA 23 Sept. 1800, p. 3

Married on 27th Ult., CAPT. CHARLES GRANDISON FIELD of Mecklenburg, Va., to MISS
HARRIOTT EATON of Warren Co., N.C.
RE 9 April 1811, p. 3

Married Sept. 26th by Rev. Robert B. Semple, DR. CHRISTOPHER B. FLEET of King &
Queen Co., to MISS MARY ANN McKIM, only dau. of late Andrew McKim of Richmond
RE 29 Sept. 1820, p. 3; RC   28 Sept, p. 3

Married on Tues. last (Nov. 2) JORDAN FLOURNOY, Esq. of Powhatan Co., to MRS. WOODS
of this city
VA 4 Nov. 1813, p. 3

Married Oct. 24th by Rev. R. Ford, MR. DANIEL FORD of Richmond, to MRS. MILDRED B.
JONES of New Kent Co.
RC 4 Nov. 1816, p. 3

Married on Thurs. (March 14) by Rev. John D. Blair, MR. HENRY FORE to MISS MARY
DAVENPORT, both of Richmond
VP 16 March 1816, p. 3

Married Sun. last (Aug. 7) MR. FORSTER to MRS. KING of Petersburg
VGWA 13 Aug. 1785, p. 3

Married in New Kent Co., Feb. 27th by Rev. Richard Smith, MR. JAMES MONTAGUE FOSTER,
youngest son of John Foster, merchant, of Richmond, to MISS GENETY CHRISTIAN of New
Kent Co.
RE 4 March 1817, p. 3

Married on Sat. last (Dec. 15) by Rev. John D. Blair, CAPT. PETER FOSTER, to MRS.
ANN SHELTON, both of Hanover Co.
VA 19 Dec. 1804, p. 3

Married on 27th Aug. by Rev. John D. Blair, MAJ. NATHANIEL FOX of King William Co.,
to MRS. SUSAN BOCKIUS of this city
VA 13 Sept. 1808, p. 3

Married on 10th Inst. by Rev. J. D. Blair, MR. JOHN FOX, to MISS MARIA SMOCK, both
of this city
RE 12 Jan. 1811, p. 3

Married a few days ago, MR. THOMAS B. FOX of Gloucester to MISS COURTENAY ORANGE
BAYLOR, dau. of John Baylor, Esq. to New Market, Caroline Co.
VGGA 6 April 1803, p. 3

Married on 17th Inst., MR. ARCHIBALD FREELAND, merchant, of Manchester, to MRS. GRACE
MACON of Powhatan, relict of Mr. John Macon
VGRMA 31 Aug. 1796, p. 3

Married on Mon. last (Sept. 17) MR. WILLIAM FRENCH of Richmond to MISS MARIA B. DUVAL
of Henrico Co., only dau. of late Col. Daniel Duval
VA 19 Sept. 1804, p. 3

Married on 26th Ult. in this city, MR. WILLIAM FRIEND of Osbornes to MISS KITTY
CRAIG, dau. of Mr. James Craig of Williamsburg
VGGA 7 March 1792, p. 3

Married Nov. 30th, MR. WILLIAM FRITH, to MISS MARY PATRAM of Chesterfield Co.
RE 14 Dec. 1820, p. 3

Married on Sat. last (April 11) by Rev. John D. Blair, MR. WILLIAM FROST, to MISS
MARY L. COUTTS, both of Richmond
VA 14 April 1807, p. 3

Married Nov. 16th by Rev. John Bryce, MR. WILLIAM FULCHER, SR., to MISS MARY WOODFIN,
all of Richmond
RC 20 Nov. 1819, p. 3

Married Sun. last (Sept. 25) by Rev. John Blair, MR. FULTON of Baltimore to MISS
ELIZA MAYO, 2nd dau. of Col. William May of Henrico Co.
VA 1 Oct. 1803, p. 3

Married at Woodville, near Winchester Va., on 14th Inst., by Rev. A. Balmain, MR. JOSEPH GALES, Jr., one of the editors of the National Intelligencer, to MISS JULIANNA M. LEE, dau. of Theodorick Lee, Esq.
VA 23 Dec. 1813, p. 3

Married on 8th Inst., by Rev. John Buchanan, DR. ALEXANDER D. GALT of Williamsburg, to MISS MARY GALT of this palce
VA 15 July 1813, p. 3

Married at Petersburg on Mon. last (March 4) MR. JOHN GAMBLE of Richmond to MISS CHARLES SMITH DUNCAN of Petersburg
RE 8 March 1805, p. 3; VA 9 March, p. 3, days ELIZA SMITH DUNCAN)

Married on 11th Inst. by Rev. John D. Blair, at house of Thos. Wilson, Esq., MR. JOHN G. GAMBLE of this city, to MISS NANCY PEYTON GREENUP, eldest dau. of Christophe Greenup, Esq. late Gov. of Ky.
RE 19 March 1813, p. 3

Married on 2nd Ult., MR. ROBERT GAMBLE, Jun., Merchant of City of Richmond to MISS LETITIA BRECKENRIDGE, eldest dau. of Col. James Breckenridge of Botetourt Co.
VA 5 July, 1808, p. 3; RE 5 July, p. 3; VGGA 5 July, p. 3; Virginian 5 July, p. 2

Married in Phila, on 12th Inst., MR. GABRIEL GARESCHE, merchant, to MISS LOUISA DuPONCEAU, dau. of Peter S. DuPonceau, Esq., Counsellor of Law, also of that city
Visitor 21 Oct. 1809, p. 150

Married, on Sat. last (Nov. 9), JOHN GARLAND, Esq. of Hanover (VGWA says Henrico), to MISS FANNY TAYLOR of Chesterfield, dau. of late Wm. Black, Esq.
VGAA Nov. 16, 1782, p. 3; VGWA Nov. 16 (most complete of 2)

Married, on 19th Inst., MR. CAMM GARLICK to Miss MARY TALIAFERRO, both of King Willi Co.
RE 30 Jan. 1810, p. 3

Married on 21st Ult., MR. JOHN J. GARNETT of Essex Co., to MISS LUCY L. CARTER, gra daughter of late Col. Wm. Lyne of King & Queen Co.
RE 3 Oct. 1809, p. 3; Visitor 7 Oct., p. 142

Married on 6th Inst. by Rev. Robert S. Semple, LEWIS GARNETT, Esq. to MISS FRANCES B. BANKS of King William Co.
VA 14 Feb. 1806, p. 3

Married in Phila, Dec. 30th by Rt. Rev. Bishop White, ROBERT S. GARNETT, Esq., to MISS LeGOUGE, dau. of late French General LeGouge
RE 16 Jan. 1813, p. 3

Married Oct. 25th by Rev. William Duncan, MR. JOHN GARTH, to MISS MATILDA GILBERT, youngest dau. of Dr. E. Gilbert, all of Amherst Co.
RE 19 Nov. 1819, p. 3

Married on 18th Inst., by Rev. John Lindsey, MR. SAMUEL GARTHRIGHT, to MISS ELIZABETH
M. FRAYSER, both of this county
VA 25 June 1812, p. 3

Married on 5th Inst., MR. PHILIP GATEWOOD to MISS MARY M. PENDLETON, both of King
& Queen Co.
VA 11 April 1804, p. 3; VGGA 14 April, p. 3

Married May 18th, MR. THOMAS J. GATEWOOD to MISS ELIZABETH J. FREEMAN
RE 9 June 1820, p. 3

Married in Petersburg on Thurs. last (Nov. 17) MR. WILLIAM W. GEADY to MISS BETSY
PRENTIS, both of that place
VGGA 23 Nov. 1796, p. 2

Married, MR. JAMES GEDDY to MISS EUPHAN ARMISTEAD, both of Petersburg. (No marriage
date)
VGWA 21 May 1789, p. 3

Married on 11th Inst., MR. BASSET GENTRY, to MISS SUSAN FULCHER, both of this city
RE 19 April, 1811, p. 3

Married on Thurs. last (Jan. 7) by Rev. Mr. Blair, MR. HENRY GENTRY to MISS MARTHA
TIMBERLAKE, both of Hanover Co.
VGGA 12 Jan. 1808, p. 3

Married on Thurs. last (Oct. 23) by the Rev. John Linsay, MR. ALEXANDER GEORGE to
MISS POLLEY GARTHRIGHT, borh of Henrico Co.
RE 28 Oct. 1806, p. 3

Married on 8th Inst., CAPT. BYRD GEORGE of Henrico Co., to MISS WILSON of Caroline
Visitor 17 March 1810, p. 27

Married in N.Y. on 7th Inst., by Rev. Dr. West, CAPT. PETER GEYER, age 62, to MISS
POLLY SANCRY, 17
VA 11 Jan. 1804, p. 3

Married in Baltimore at res. of Walton Gray on 18th Inst., MR. JOHN W. GIBBONS of
firm of Owen & Gibbons of Norfolk, to MISS ADELINE GRAY of Baltimore
RE 24 Dec. 1818, p. 3

Married on Sat. last (May 4) MR. LAWRENCE GIBBONS of York to MISS PEGGY NICHOLSON
of Williamsburg
VGRMA 9 May 1793, p. 3

Married on 8th Inst., by Rev. John D. Blair, CHARLES GIBBS, to MISS MARY G. TRUEHEART
of Hanover Co.
RE 11 Feb. 1815, p. 3; RC 11 Feb., p. 3

Married on Sat. (Feb. 27) PATRICK GIBSON to MISS MARY ANN ELIZABETH MACMURDO, eldest dau. of Charles J. Macmurdo
VP   2 March 1813, p. 3

Married at Brookfield, Mass., MR. CALVIN GILBERT, age 17, to MISS THEODOCIA BARRETT, 15
VA   26 Jan. 1802, p. 3

Married on Thurs. last (May 26) MR. ALEXANDER GILCHRIST, merchant, to MISS POLLY WISE, both of this city
RC   31 May 1796, p. 2

Married at Mr. Ph. Duval's in Henrico Co., on May 18th by Rev. Hart, MR. FRANCIS GILDART of Miss., to MISS ELEANOR W. BEVERLEY, eldest dau. of Carter Beverley
RE   2 June 1820, p. 3; RC   22 May, p. 3

Married on Sat. last (May 24) CAPT. WILLIAM GILES of Richmond to MISS POLLY CLARKE of Hanover
VA   27 May 1800, p. 3

Married in Georgetown on 22 Feb. by Rev. Dr. Gant the HON. WILLIAM B. GILES, Senator from Va., to MISS FRANCES ANN GWYNN, eldest dau. of the late Thomas Peyton Gwynn of Va.
RE   9 March 1810, p. 3; Visitor 10 March, p. 23

Married at Hingham, Mass., MR. ISAAC GILKA 10, to MISS POLLY KING, age 16
VA   28 Aug. 1802, p. 3

Married a few days ago in Richmond by Rev. Mahoney, MR. GILLARD to MRS. DEVLIN, widow of Late Peter Devlin, for many years Hearth-money Collector of Dublin, Ireland, both of Petersburg
RC   7 Aug. 1820, p. 3

Married on Sat. (Aug. 12) by Rev. John Buchanan, the celebrated SIMON GILLIAT, age 80, to MISS FRANCES WHITE of Williamsburg, age 20. (People of color)
RC   15 Aug. 1820, p. 3

Married on 15th Inst. by Rev. John D. Blair, MR. RICHARD C. GILLUM of MISS FRANCES PATTESON, dau. of Col. David Patteson, all of Chesterfield
RE   27 Feb. 1810, p. 3; Visitor 24 Feb., p. 15, says GILLIAM

Married on 15th, MR. WILLIAM GILMORE of Halifax, N.C., to MISS POLLY PARSONS of Prince George
Visitor   24 March 1810, p. 31

Married Feb. 22nd by Rev. J. D. Blair, CAPT. GEORGE GLASCOCK of Westmoreland Co., to MISS MARGARET DUNLOP, dau. of James Dunlop of firm of James & Alexander Dunlop, formerly of Richmond
RC   25 Feb. 1820, p. 3

Married at New York, MR. JAMES GLASS, age 17, to MISS SALLY RALSON of Mendham, age 14
VA   28 Aug. 1802, p. 3

Married at Smithfield, Isle of Wight Co., May 6th, by Rev. Jacob Keeling, MR. WILSON
H. GODWIN, of Nansemond Co., to MISS GEORGIANA W. SOUTHALL, eldest dau. of Dr. James
B. Southall of Smithfield
RC 18 May 1819, p. 3

Married in Jay, Me., MR. SOLOMON GOODALE, to MRS. ELIZABETH COLE, each age 72
Visitor 23 Sept. 1809, p. 135

Married on 26th Oct., by Rev. John Bracken, MR. JOHN GOODALL to MISS MARTHA BURWELL
DIGGES, both of Williamsburg
RE 4 Nov. 1808, p. 3

Married on 28th Ult., MR. FRANCIS GOODE of Chesterfield Co., to MISS MARTHA HUGHES
of Powhatan Co.
VGGA 11 Nov. 1795, p. 3; VGRMA 12 Nov., p. 3

Married on Sat. last (Dec. 10) RICHARD E. GOODE, Esq., Attorney at Law, to MISS
SALLY H. WOODSON, both of Chesterfield
VA 12 Dec. 1796, p. 3

Married on 31st Ult., in Camden Co., N.C., JETHRO D. GOODMAN, Esq., Attorney at Law
of Pasquotank, to MISS ELIZABETH BURGES
Visitor 2 Dec. 1809, p. 174

Married at Dover, Goochland Co., Va., at house of Joseph S. Watkins on Jan. 23rd by
Rev. Wm. H. Hart, WILLIAM G. GOODE of Mecklenburg Co., to MISS S.W. TAZEWELL of
Williamsburg
RE 5 Feb. 1820, p. 3

Married on 5th Inst., MR. JOHN B. GOODRICH, merchant, of Cumberland, to MISS REBECCA
PEARCE of Chesterfield
VA 23 Oct. 1802, p. 3

Married June 12th at Willis Tavern in Fluvanna Co., by Rev. W. Timberlake, MR. JAMES
GORDON to MRS. MARIA RICHARDSON, both of Goochland Co.
RE 4 Aug. 1820, p. 3

Married on Thurs. (Feb. 2) by Rev. Mr. Blair, MR. NICHOLAS GORDON of Manchester, to
MISS ELIZABETH LYNCH of Richmond
VP 4 Feb. 1815, p. 3

Married on Sat. last (Dec. 21) MR. ROBERT GORDON, merchant, to MISS J. CURRIE, both
of this city
VA 27 Dec. 1799, p. 2; VGGA 24 Dec., p. 3

Married on Thurs. last (May 14) MR. JAMES GOSDEN of the Eastern Shore to MRS. MARY
TUCKER of Richmond
VA 16 May 1807, p. 3

Married in Washington City by Rev. Hawley, SAMUEL LAWRENCE GOUVERNEUR of New York, to MISS MARIA HESTER MONROE, youngest dau. of James Monroe, President of U.S.
RE 17 March 1820, p. 3

Married on 25th Ult., MR. JAMES GOVAN, merchant at Aylett's Warehouse to MISS ELIZABETH GARLICK
VGWA 4 Dec. 1788, p. 3; VIC 3 Dec.

Married on April 27th, MR. SAMPSON GRANTHAM, 65, to MRS. ELIZABETH WILLFORD, 74, bot of Surry Co.
RE 9 May 1817, p. 3; VP 7 May, p. 3

Married on Sun. (Oct. 4) by Rev. J. D. Blair, MR. SEATON GRANTLAND, formerly of Va., now of Milledgeville, Ga., to MISS ANNE TINSLEY, youngest dau. of Col. Thomas Tinsle of Hanover Co., Va.
RE 6 Oct. 1818, p. 3

Married on 6th Inst., DR. CHARLES H. GRAVES to MISS PATSY BROWNE, eldest dau. of Maj. Benjamin Edward Browne, all of Surry Co.
VA 19 June 1805, p. 3

Married on 28th Ult. by Rev. Mr. Buchanan, MR. WILLIAM P. GRAVES to MISS ELIZABETH HAYS, all of this city
VA 3 June 1808, p. 3

Married on Sat. last (Nov. 9) MR. WILLIAM GRAY, merchant of this city, to MISS JANE GUERRANT, dau. of Mr. John Guerrant, Sr. of Goochland Co.
VA 15 Nov. 1799, p. 3; VGGA 15 Nov., p. 3

Married at Newark on 19th Ult., WILLIAM R. GRAY, Esq. of Boston, to MISS MARY CLAY, dau. of Judge Clay of Ga.
Visitor 18 Nov. 1809, p. 166

Married on Thurs. (Jan. 25) by Rev. Bryce, MR. WILLIAM W. GRAY, printer, of Lynchb to MISS MARY _____, of Richmond
RE 30 Jan. 1816, p. 3

Married on Sat. last (July 18) MR. GEORGE GREENHOW, merchant, of Richmond to MISS ELIZA LEWIS of Louisa Co.
VA 24 July 1801, p. 3

Married, MR. JOHN GREENHOW to MISS KETTY VOSS, both of this city. (No marriage dat
VICGA 6 Jan. 1790, p. 3

Married Tues. last (April 10) MR. JOHN GREENHOW of this city to MISS ELIZABETH DuVA dau. of Mr. Wm. DuVal of Gloucester
VGGA 18 April 1792, p. 3

Married on Monday se'nnight (July 6) RICHARD GREGORY, Esq. of Petersburg to MISS ELIZABETH WILKINSON, 2nd dau. of Col. Nathaniel Wilkinson of Henrico Co.
VGWA 16 July 1789, p. 3; VIC 15 July

Married Oct. 31st by Rev. Eleazar Clay, MR. THOMAS GREGORY to MISS ELIZABETH CHEATHAM, all of Chesterfield Co.
RE 14 Dec. 1820, p. 3

Married Dec. 17, 1816, by Rev. Philip Montague, MR. HENRY GRESHAM, to MISS ELIZABETH OLIVER, both of King & Queen Co.
RE 14 Jan. 1817, p. 3

Married Nov. 20th by Kalorama, near Washington City, res. of Henry Middleton, by Rev. Matthews, HIS EXCELLENCY, T. FREDERICK GREUHK, His Prussian Majesty's Minister of the U.S. to MLLE, VIRGINIE BRIDON of Paris, France
RE 23 Nov. 1819, p. 3

Married on 25th Inst. MR. ANDERSON GRUBBS of Amelia to MISS SUSAN WINSTON of Hanover
VGGA 29 Sept. 1802, p. 3

Married on 13th Ult., HON. PHILIP GRYMES, Member of Executive Council of this state, to MISS SARAH STEPTOE of Middlesex Co.
VA 6 June 1804, p. 3; VGGA 2 June, p. 2

Married on 4th Inst. at Flat Creek, TEMPLE GUATHMEY, Esq., merchant, of Richmond (this man's name is probably Gwathmey- Ed.) to MISS NANCY WATTS, 5th dau. of late William Watts, Esq. of Campbell Co.
VP 20 Sept. 1811, p. 3

Married on 28th Ult. by Rev. Mr. Mitchell, DR. GEORGE GWATHMEY of King & Queen Co., to MISS ANN IRVINE, dau. of Capt. William Irvine of Locust Grove, Bedford Co.
RE 10 Dec. 1811, p. 3

Married on Thurs. last (June 1) MR. JAMES GWATHMEY to MISS MARY GILES, both of Henrico Co.
Visitor 3 June 1809, p. 70

Married on 9th Inst. by Rev. John Courtney, MR. PHILIP GULLEY, to MISS JANE CAMPBELL WILLIAMSON, youngest dau. of George Williamson, Esq. of this city
RE 20 July 1814, p. 3; RC 15 July, p. 3

Married on 18th Inst. by Rev. John D. Blair, MR. JOHN GUNN of MISS ANN ELIZA McCRAW, eldest dau. of Samuel McCraw, all of this city
RE 24 Nov. 1809, p. 3; VA 24 Nov., p. 3; Visitor 2 Dec., p. 174

Married on 27th May, MR. THOMAS GUY, merchant, of Richmond, to MISS LUCY PENN HUNT, 2nd dau. of Col. William Hunt of N.C.
RE 1 June 1813, p. 3; VA 3 June, p. 3; VP 1 June, p. 3

Married on 19th Ult. at Chilowee, seat of Wm. Randolph, Esq., RICHARD S. HACKLEY of New York, to MISS HARRIOTT RANDOLPH, dau. of late Thos. M. Randolph of Tuckahoe
RE 18 Jan. 1806, p. 3

Married June (   ) in Md., MR. JOHN N. HADEN, Jr. to MISS ELIZA WOODSON, both of Goochland Co.
RE 4 Aug. 1820, p. 3

Married on 31st May, JOHN HAILE, Esq. Collector of Tappahannock, to MISS SARAH
ALDRIDGE
RE 7 June 1811, p. 3

Married July 25th by Rev. John H. Rice, MR. CHARLES R. HALL of Fredericksburg, to
MISS LOUISA ANN QUARLES, only dau. of Col. Robert Quarles of Richmond
RE 31 July 1816, p. 3; VP 27 July, p. 3

Married Oct. 26th by Rev. Philip Courtney, MR. GREEN HALL of Manchester, to MISS
PAMELA S. BRIDGEWATER, dau. of Rev. Henry Bridgewater of Chesterfield Co.
RE 14 Dec. 1820, p. 3; RC 28 Oct., p. 3

Married at South Amboy, N.J. on 15th Ult. MR. JOSEPH HALL, age 96, to MISS PATIENCE
GULICK, age 60
VA 19 June 1801, p. 3

Married Feb. 17th by Rev. Ford, MR. WILLIAM V.M. HAMBLETON of Louisa Co., to MISS
MARY R., dau. of Mr. Nathaniel ANTHONY of Hanover Co.
RE 29 Feb. 1820, p. 3; RC 28 Feb., p. 3, says William Vans Murray Hambleton

Married last Sat. (April 23) MR. MICHAEL HANCOCK to MISS SOPHIA SCOTT, both of this
city (erroneously called John in paper of 26 April)
RE 29 April 1808, p. 3

Married Nov. 15th by Rev. John H. Byrd, CAPT. JOHN H. HANKINS of Chesterfield Co.,
to MISS MATLDA M. SUBLETT, dau. of Arthur Sublett of Powhatan Co.
RE 14 Dec. 1820, p. 3

Married on 1st Inst., MR. EDWIN HARVIE to MISS HARDAWAY of Amelia
RE 1 March 1808, p. 3

Married on June 24th, MR. ALEXANDER HARE to MISS SARAH MARTIN, both of Richmond
Examiner 26 Nov. 1803, p. 3

Married on 11th Inst., DR. WILLIAM B. HARE of Amherst Co., to MISS ELIZA CABELL,
dau. of Nicholas Cabell of same co.
VGGA 24 July 1793, p. 3

Married Nov. 9th at Friends Meeting House, Charles City Co., THOMAS HARGROVE, to
MISS SARAH H. HUBBARD, eldest dau. of George Hubbard, all of that county
RE 10 Nov. 1820, p. 3

Married on 21st Ult., MR. BENJAMIN JAMES HARRIS of this city, to MISS SARAH ELLYSON
of Patrick Co.
VA 4 May 1803, p. 3; Examiner 30 April, p.3

Married on Tues. (July 20) by Rev. John Bruce, MR. BENJAMIN JAMES HARRIS, to
MRS. FLORA WIATT, all of Richmond
RE 23 July 1819, p. 2; RC 22 July, p. 3, says last evening

Married, in Elizabeth Town, N.H. on 5th Inst. by Rev. Dr. Kollock, EDWARD HARRIS, Esq. of New Bern, N.C. to MISS SARAH H. KOLLOCK of former place
Visitor 29 July 1809, p. 102

Married on 24th Ult. CAPT. JOHN HARRIS of Powhatan Co. to MISS REBECCA BRITTON of Chesterfield
VGRMA 5 June 1794, p. 3

Married July 22nd by Rev. Samuel Davidson, COL. JOHN HARRIS of Buckingham Co., to MRS. JANE S. PATTESON of Clover Hill, Prince Edward Co.
RE 27 July 1819, p. 3

Married 24 Dec. MR. THOMAS HARRIS of this city to MISS FANNY MEAUX of New Kent Co.
VA 6 Jan. 1801, p. 3

Married on 7th of last, at Friends Meeting House at White Oak Swamp, DR. THOMAS HARRIS of Hanover, age 60, to UNITY LADD, dau. of John Ladd of Charles City Co., age 20
RE 5 Feb. 1805, p. 3; VA 6 Feb., p. 3

Married on 27th March by Rev. James Madison, MR. WILLIAM P. HARRIS, merchant in Williamsburg, to MISS LUCY TALIAFERRO of James City Co.
VA 8 April 1800, p. 3

Married Feb. 27th by Black Heath, by Rev. Blair, MR. ARCHIBALD HENRY HARRISON, to MISS KITTY HETH, eldest dau. of Capt. Harry Heth
RE 4 March 1817, p. 3; VP 4 March, p. 3; RC 4 March, p. 3

Married Jan. 16th by Rev. John Buchanan, MR. CARTER H. HARRISON of Cumberland Co., to MISS JANETTA R. FISHER, dau. of Mr. George Fisher of Richmond
RE 23 Jan. 1819, p. 3

Married on 22nd Ult. at Eppington in Chesterfield Co., MR. EDMUND HARRISON of Amelia to MISS SKIPWITH of Williamsburg
VA 2 Dec. 1806, p. 2

Married on Thurs. last (Feb. 23) MR. HENRY R. HARRISON of Sussex, to MISS ANNA BLAND of Prince George
Visitor 11 Feb. 1809, p. 14

Married on 31st Ult., MR. JACOB HARRISON to MISS PATSEY PROSSER, both of this city
VGGA 6 Jan. 1796, p. 3

Married on Sat. last (Oct. 15) by Rev. John D. Blair, MR. JACOB HARRISON to MISS ELIZABETH ROYSTER, eldest dau. of Mr. John Royster, all of this city
VA 18 Oct. 1808, p. 3; RE 18 Oct., p. 3

Married Dec. 19, 1816, by Rev. Robert B. Semple, CAPT. WILLIAM HARRISON of Caroline Co., to MISS MARTHA GATEWOOD of King & Queen Co.
RE 7 Jan. 1817, p. 3

Married in Staunton on 31st Ult., MR. JOHN HARRO, to MISS CHARLOTTE TAPP
Visitor 18 Nov. 1809, p. 166

Married on 21st Ult., MR. JOHN HASKINS to Powhatan to MISS SALLY WILEY, eldest dau.
of John Wiley of Amelia
RE 10 March 1809, p. 3; Visitor 11 March, p. 23

Married MR. BENJAMIN HATCHER of Manchester to MISS POLLY CRUMP of Powhatan. (No
marriage date)
VGGA 27 June 1792, p. 2

Married July 4th at Monumental Church by Rev. John Buchanan, GEORGE HAWKINS, merchant,
of Philadelphia, TO MISS GERTRUDE PARKER MOORE, dau. of Rt. Rev. Bishop Moore
RE 10 July 1816, p. 3; RC 6 July, p. 3

Married, GEORGE HAY, Esq. to MISS MONROE, dau. of James Monroe, all of this city
VA 7 Oct. 1808, p. 3; RE 7 Oct., p. 3 (says: Eliza Monroe); VGGA 11 Oct. (says
married on 28th), p. 3

Married at Carter Hall June 17th, JAMES HAY, formerly of Richmond, to MISS ELIZA G.
BURWELL, dau. of late Col. Nathaniel Burwell of Frederick Co.
RE 4 July 1817, p. 3

Married on Sat. last (May 1) MR. JAMES HAYES of this city to MRS. HARDYMAN, relict
of late Wm. Hardyman, Esq.
VGWA 8 May 1784, p. 3

Married at Fairfield, Hanover Co., Sept. 21st, by Rt. Rev. Bishop Moore, JAMES E. HEATH
Auditor of Public Accounts, to MISS ELIZABETH ANN MACON, dau. of Col. William H. Macon
of New Kent Co.
RE 26 Sept. 1820, p. 3; RC 25 Sept., p. 3; VPRDMA 26 Sept., p. 3

Married at Bladensburg (md.) JOHN P. HEATH, late Captain of U.S.M.C., to MISS ELIZABETH
dau. of Col. DEAKINS. (No marriage date)
VP 3 April 1819, p. 3

Married, DR. JAMES HENDERSON of Scottsville, Powhatan Co., to MISS POLLY OGILBY of
Amelia. (no marriage date)
VGGA 27 June 1792, p. 2

Married on 14th Inst., MR. JAMES HENDERSON, merchant of Williamsburg, to MRS. ELIZABETH
HORSBURG
Visitor 30 Dec. 1809, p. 190

Married on 19th Ult. by Rev. Mr. Alexander, MR. ELIJAH HENDRICK, merchant, of Buckingha
to MISS KITTY G. BAKER of Prince Edward Co.
VA 7 April 1801, p. 3

Married at Bacons Castle, Surry Co., on Feb. 27th by Rev. Merryman, BARTHOLOMEW D.
HENLEY, to MISS MARTHA ANN COCKE, dau. of Richard Cocke, all of that county
RC 13 March 1817, p.3

Married in Chesterfield Co., on Sat. (June 17) by Rev. Bridgwater, MR. JOHN HENRY,
to MISS MARY ANN WHITE, both of Richmond
RC 21 June 1820, p. 3

Married on 26th last month by Rev. J. Saunders, LAFAYETTE HENRY, Esq., to MISS ANN
ELCAN, both of Buckingham Co.
RE 3 April 1807, p. 3

Married, in Amherest Co., on 9th Inst., MR. PATRICK HENRY, son of the late sage
of Va., and MISS ELVIRA CABELL, dau. of late Col. Wm. Cabell of this place
VA 22 Feb. 1804, p. 3

Married Sat. last (Nov. 10) MR. HENRY HETH to MISS NANCY BLAIR, both of this city
VGWA 15 Nov. 1787, p. 2

Married on Sat. last (Feb. 15) by Rev. John Buchanan, JOHN W. HIGGINBOTHAM, Esq.,
Attorney at Law, of Mecklenburg Co., to MRS. LUCY RANDOLPH of Warwick
RE 21 Feb. 1806, p. 3

Married on Nov. 30th, MR. WOOD HIGHTOWER, to MISS FANNY THOMAS, both of Nottoway Co.
Visitor 16 Dec. 1809, p. 182

Married on 20th Ult., by Rev. J. D. Blair, BROOK HILL, Esq. of King & Queen Co.,
to MISS SARAH GAINES, dau. of Capt. William F. Gaines of King William Co.
RE 8 Jan. 1811, p. 3; VP 8 Jan., p. 3, gives grooms name as Brooke Hill

Married June 20th by Rev. John C. Fraylor, MR. JOHN W. HILL, to MISS JUDITH HILL,
both of Henry Co.
RE 13 July 1816, p. 3

Married on Thurs. last (Jan. 14) by Rev. J. Bryce, MR. PARK HILL of New Kent Co.,
to MRS. MILDRED RAWLEIGH of this city
RE 21 Jan. 1813, p. 3

Married on 15th Inst., MR. ROBERT B. HILL, Esq. of King & Queen, to MISS CATHARINE
POLLARD, dau. of Mr. Robert Pollard of King William
RE 20 March 1810, p. 3; Visitor 17 March, p. 27

Married on Wed. (Feb. 19) by Rev. John D. Blair, MR. BENJAMIN F. HILLARD to MISS
NANCY SMITHERS of Richmond
VP 21 Feb. 1817, p. 3; RC 20 Feb., p. 3

Married at Machias, Me., MR. JOHN B. HILLARD, merchant, of this city, to MISS
REBECCA A. STILLMAN, eldest dau. of late Gen. Geo. Stillman
VA 23 Sept. 1811, p. 3; VP 24 Sept., p. 2

Married in King William Co., Oct. 28th, MR. JOHN H. HILLIARD to MISS CATHARINE DABNEY
both of King William Co.
VP 2 Nov. 1814, p. 3

Married in George Town on 19th Inst. by Rev. Mr. Balch, DR. NICHOLAS HINGSTON,
merchant and botanist, of Alexandria, Va., to MISS ELIZABETH BLOOMFIELD, sister
to author of "Farmers Boy"
VA 31 Jan. 1806, p. 3

Married, lately, MR. SAMUEL HINTON, merchant of Petersburg, to MISS POLLY BATTE of Prince George Co.
Visitor 16 Dec. 1809, p. 182

Married Thurs. last (March 26) by the Rev. John Lindsay, MR. WILLIAM HOBSON, to MRS. CATHARINE BINFORD, all of this county
VA 30 March 1812, p. 3

Married Aug. 24th at Mr. Barret Smith's, Louisa Co., by Rev. William T. Hiter, MR. WALLER HOLLADAY, to MISS SARAH KIMBROUGH
RE 12 Sept. 1820, p. 3

Married on the 13th, JOHN HOLLAND, Esq., to MISS ELIZABETH BROWN, dau. of Mr. Clemen Brown, both of Cumberland Co.
VGRMA 20 Aug. 1796, p. 3

Married on Thurs. last (Nov. 14), MR. DAVID HOLLOWAY to MISS JULIA LEE DOVE, both of this city
VA 19 Nov. 1799, p. 3

Married on 6th Inst., CAPT. GEORGE HOLMAN of Goochland Co., to MRS. POLLY I. COCKE of Fluvanna
VA 18 Aug. 1804, p. 3; VGGA 15 Aug., p. 3

Married May 25th by Rev. Philip Courtney, MR. NATHANIEL W. HOLMAN, to MISS CAROLINE G. WINFREE, all of Richmond
RC 27 May 1820, p. 3

Married on Thurs. (Nov. 21) by Rev. Rob. B. Semple, MR. BENJAMIN P. HOOMES of Dunkirk, King & Queen Co., to MISS ELENOR DABNEY, dau. of Maj.-Gen. Dabney of King William Co.
RE 26 Nov. 1816, p. 3; VP 26 Nov., p. 3, says dau. of Maj. George Dabney

Married on Tues. (Dec. 16) by Rev. Robert B. Semple, MR. THOMAS C. HOOMES to MISS BETSY POLLARD, dau. of Robert Pollard, all of King & Queen Co.
RE 23 Dec. 1817, p. 3

Married on 28th Ult., MR. STEPHEN HOOPER of Buckingham to MISS HANNAH SCOTT of Cumberland
VA 13 Dec. 1799, p. 3

Married, JOHN HOPKINS, Esq., Receiver-General of Continental Loan Office in this state, to MISS LUCY LYONS, dau. of Hon. Peter Lyons, Esq. of Hanover Co. (No marriage date)
VGWA 15 Oct. 1789, p. 3

Married on March 24 at Page Brook, Frederick Co., by Rev. Meade, JOHN HOPKINS, JR. to MISS ABBY B.N. PAGE, dau. of John Page, all of Frederick Co.
RE 14 April 1820, p. 3

Married on 27 April last, DR. DABNEY M. HORTON, to MISS ANN SWAN, both of Powhatan Co.
RE 16 May 1809, p. 3; Visitor 20 May, p. 62, says Dabney Wharton

Married on 17th Ult. by Rev. Mr. McRae, MR. AARON HOSKINS to MISS ANN BRACKETT, both of Powhatan Co.
VA 19 Jan. 1802, p. 3; VGGA 15 Jan., p. 3

Married on 18th Inst., DR. JOHN HOSKINS of King & Queen Co., to MISS LUCY RUFFIN of King William Co.
RE 30 May 1809, p. 3

Married, on 14th Inst. at seat of Mrs. Mason in Loudon Co., BENJAMIN HOWARD, Esq., Gov. of La. Terr., to MISS MARY THOMPSON MASON, dau. of Stephen Thompson Mason, Esq., dec'd
RE 1 March 1811, p. 3

Married on Sat. last (Feb. 28) MR. FRANCIS HOWARD to MISS PEGGY T. SCHERER, both of this city
VA 3 March 1807, p. 3

Married on Sat. (Nov. 12) by Rev. J. D. Blair, MR. JAMES HOWARD, to MISS ANN GRANT, dau. of Mr. James Grant, all of Richmond
RC 15 Nov. 1814, p. 3

Married, on Friday last (March 10) at Chiltern Farm, Hanover Co., by Rev. Mr. Blair, THOMAS C. HOWARD, Esq., of this city, to MISS ELIZA POPE, eldest dau. of Nathaniel Pope, Esq.
VGGA 17 March 1809, p. 3

Married Aug. 2nd by Rev. Lewis Chardoin, MR. JAMES HOY, to MISS NANCY WITT, all of Goochland Co.
RE 29 Aug. 1820, p. 3

Married on the 8th Inst., DR. JAMES T. HUBARD of Petersburg, to MISS SUSAN WILLCOX of Buckingham Co.
RE 24 May 1805, p. 3; VA 18 May, p. 3

Married on June 29th, by the Rev. Mr. Mills, DR. CHRISTOPHER HUBBARD of this city, to MISS CATHERINE COTTRELL of King William
VA 15 July 1813, p. 3

Married on 17th Inst., MR. WILLIAM HUDSON to MISS ELIZABETH WOODSON, both of Campbell Co.
VGGA 25 May 1803, p. 3

Married on 29th May, MR. ARCHELAUS HUGHES to MISS NANCY J. CLOPTON, both of Richmond
VA 5 June 1802, p. 3; VGGA 5 June, p. 2

Married Sat. last (March 2) in this town, COL. JOHN HULL of Northumberland to MISS NANCY STRACHAN, dau. of Dr. Peter Strachan
VGWA March 9, 1782, p. 3

Married at Goshen, MAJ. OZIAS HUMPHREYS, age 60, to MISS MARGARET LISH, age 23, being the Major's 5th wife
RE 1 April 1817, p. 3

Married by Rev. Robert Hurt, MR. EUSTACE HUNT of Pittsylvania Co., to MISS ELIZA A. GLENN, 2nd dau. of MRS. GUNN of Halifax Co. (No marriage date)
RE 27 Nov. 1818, p. 3

Married Oct. 24th by Rev. Reynolds, JAMES HUNTER to MISS APPHIA B. ROUZEE, all of Essex Co.
RE 12 Nov. 1819, p. 3

Married yesterday by Rev. John Bryce, MR. CHARLES H. HYDE, to MISS ELIZA S. FISHER, both of Fredericksburg
RE 21 Dec. 1820, p. 3; RC 21 Dec., p. 3, says he is son of Robert Hyde and she dau. of Mrs. C. Fisher, and all of Richmond; VPRDMA 21 Dec., p. 3, says both of Richmond

Married Thurs. last (Jan. 28) RALPH HYLTON, Esq. to MISS POLLY WARD of Chesterfield Co.
VICGA 3 Feb. 1790, p. 3

Married on 10th Inst., by Rev. John D. Blair, MR. THOMAS R. INGHAM, merchant, of Norfolk, to MISS NANCY BLAKEY, dau. of Rev. Blakey of Henrico Co.
RE 13 May 1815, p. 3

Married at Danville, Ky., on 9th Feb., THE HON. HARRY INNES, Esq. to MRS. SHIELDS, by Rev. John Hurt, Chaplain in U.S. Army
VGGA 21 March 1792, p. 3

Married June 15th, MR. ZACHARIAH ISBELL, to MISS VIRGINIA DAVENPORT, both of Goochland Co.
RE 4 Aug. 1820, p. 3

Married on Thurs. last (May 7) ISAIAH ISAACS to Miss HETTY HAYES, both of this city, by Rev. Isaac H. Judah
VGRMA 9 May 1795, p. 2; VGRC 9 May, p. 2

Married, at Marietta, Hon. JOHN G. JACKSON of Clarksburgh, Va., to MISS MARY MEIGS, dau. of Col. R. J. Meigs of Marietta. (No marriage date)
RE 14 Aug. 1810, p. 3

Married Sept. 28th by Rev. John Buchanan, MR. JOSEPH JACKSON to MISS JANE ELIZA FOSTER, youngest dau. of John Foster, all of Richmond
RE 6 Oct. 1820, p. 3

Married in Lynchburg Nov. 9th, MR. PHILIP W. K. JACKSON, merchant, to MISS ABBY W. BYRD, all of that place
RE 29 Nov. 1815, p. 3

Married on Sat. (Oct. 16th) by Rev. Low, LT. WILLIAM JAMESON of U.S. Navy, to MISS CATHARINE M. ROSE, eldest dau. of Mrs. Mary Rose of Norfolk
RC 21 Oct. 1819, p. 3

Married Nov. 16th by Rev. William Todd, MR. WILLIAM JEFFRIES, to MISS LUCY GRAHAM, all of King & Queen Co.
RE   24 Nov. 1820, p. 3

Married in Powhatan Co., on 7th Inst., by Rev. Conrad Speece, MR. JAMES JENNINGS, merchant, of Cartersville, to MISS NANCY MONTAGUE, dau. of Capt. Mickleberry Montague of Powhatan Co.
VA 15 Sept. 1809, p. 3

Married on Thurs. last (Nov. 14) BATHURST JONES to MRS. BARBARA O. THILMAN, both of Hanover Co.
RE 19 Nov. 1805, p. 3; VA 23 Nov., p. 3

Married at Wilmington on June 27th, MR. SAMUEL R. JOCELYN, merchant, to MISS MARY ANN SAMPSON, dau. of Michael Sampson, Esq. of Sampson Co.
Visitor 29 July 1809, p. 102

Married Dec. 26, 1816, by Rev. John Mill, MR. AMMON JOHNSON to MISS ANN LITTLEPAGE all of King William Co.
RE   7 Jan. 1817, p. 3

Married on 27th Ult., CHAPMAN JOHNSON, Esq. of Staunton, to MISS MARYANNE NICHOLSON of this city
RE 10 Oct. 1806, p. 3

Married on Thurs. last (Sept. 12) by Rev. John D. Blair, MR. DAVID JOHNSON, merchant, of Yanceyville, Louisa Co., to MISS MARY TINSLEY, eldest dau. of Col. T. Tinsley of Hanover
RE 17 Sept. 1805, p. 3; VA 21 Sept., p. 3

Married July 27th by Rev. Reuben Ford, MR. FLEMING JOHNSON, to MISS ELIZABETH J. WATKINS of Goochland Co.
RE 29 Aug. 1820, p. 3

Married on June 12th by Rev. Churchill Gordon, MR. ROBERT C. JOHNSON to MRS. SUSAN BOLIN, all of Orange Co.
RE 23 June 1820, p. 3

Married June 15th, MR. RODERICK JOHNSON of Goochland Co., to MISS EVELINA PERKINS
RE   4 Aug. 1820, p. 3

Married on Thurs. last (Feb. 17) at Columbia on James River, MR. THOMAS JOHNSON of Louisa Co., to MISS HARRIET WASHINGTON, dau. of Harry Washington, dec'd
VGGA 23 Feb. 1803, p. 3

Married on 8th Inst., MR. WILLIAM JOHNSON, merchant, of Petersburg, to MISS MARY EVANS, dau. of Dr. George Evans of Chesterfield Co.
VA 17 Sept. 1803, p. 3

Married on 1st Inst., CHARLES JOHNSTON, Esq. to MISS BETSY STEPTOE, eldest dau. of James Steptoe, Esq., of New London, Bedford Co.
VGGA 17 Jan. 1807, p. 3

Married on 28th Ult., MR. CALEB JONES to MISS POLLY SOUTHALL of Hanover
VGRMA 15 April 1793, p. 3

Married on 10th Inst., near the Red House, Caswell Co., N.C., EDWARD D. JONES,
Esq., Attorney at Law, to MISS ELIZABETH H. RAINEY, dau. of William Rainey, Esq.,
all of that county
VA 21 Oct. 1811, p. 3

Married Tues. (April 21) by Rev. Bishop Moore, MR. JOHN JONES to MISS SARAH BROOKS,
dau. of Zachariah Brooks, all of Richmond
RE 24 April 1818, p. 3

Married on 13th Inst. by Rev. John D. Blair, CAPT. JOHN H. JONES, to MISS MARY G.
McCRAW, dau. of Samuel McCraw, Esq., all of Richmond
RE 19 Nov. 1814, p. 3; RC 19 Nov., p. 3

Married on 7th Inst., MR. LEOPOLD JONES, merchant, to MISS MARY HOLTON, eldest dau.
of Mr. Thomas Holton, all of this place
RE 9 Nov. 1810, p. 3

Married, MERIWETHER JONES, Esq. of Spring Garden, Hanover, to MISS LUCY FRANKLIN
READ, eldest dau. of Dr. Read of Hanover Town. (No marriage date)
VGWA 12 Feb. 1789, p. 3

Married on 2nd Inst., by Rev. John Buchanan, DR. W. P. JONES, to MISS HARRIET McRAE,
eldest dau. of Alexander McRae, all of this city
RE 11 Jan. 1815, p. 3; VA 11 Jan., p. 3

Married on Sat. (Jan. 24) ROBERT JOUETT, Esq., of Charlottesville, to MISS ALICE
LEWIS of Henrico
VGGA 28 Jan. 1795, p. 3; VGRMA 29 Jan., p. 3

Married on 20th Inst., FRANCIS JOURDAN, Esq., of Louisa to MISS POLLY BYARS of
Hanover
VA 25 June 1799, p. 3

Married last evening, MR. B.H. JUDAH, merchant, to MRS. MOSES, dau. of Mr. Delyon
of this city
VA 2 Dec. 1796, p. 3

Married on Wed. (Feb. 1) by Rev. Isaac H. Judah, MR. MANUEL JUDAH, to MISS GRACE
SEIXAS, dau. of Rev. Gershom Seixas of New York
VP 4 Feb. 1815, p. 3; RC 3 Feb., p. 3

Married on Thurs. (July 30) by Rev. John D. Blair, MR. FREDERICK JUDE, to MISS
ELIZA ANN BAKER, both of Richmond
RC 1 Aug. 1818, p. 3

Married on Sat. last (Aug. 11) by the Rev. A. Foster, MR. SWEN JUSTICE, to MISS
SARAH PARTEN, both of this city
VA 14 Aug. 1810, p. 3

Married May 25th, MR. JAMES KAY to MISS FANNY SPINDLE
RE 9 June 1820

Married in Charles City Co., Nov. 6th, by Rev. Foulkes, MR. THOMAS KEESEE, age 24,
to MRS. NANCY F. SHARP, age 50, both of Henrico Co.
RC 19 Nov. 1819, p. 3

Married on 31 Oct. in Bedford Co., REV. DANIEL KELLEAY to MISS NANCY BURTON of
said Co.
Visitor 16 Dec. 1809, p. 182

Married Nov. 30th by Rev. Simon Burton, MR. MATHEW W. KEMP to MISS CATHARINE YATES
both of Gloucester Co.
RE 7 Dec. 1820, p. 3

Married on Tues. (Nov. 10) by Rev. Philip Courtney, MR. CHARLES KENDALL, printer,
formerly of Vermont, to MISS MARGARET RAMSAY, late of Baltimore
RE 13 Nov. 1818, p. 3; RC 11 Nov., p. 3; VP 11 Nov., p. 3

Married on 16th Ult, COL. CUSTIS KENDALL to MISS SUSANNAH GORE, both of Northampton
Co.
VGWA 17 April 1784, p. 3

Married on 23rd Inst., MR. JOHN KENNEDY of this city to MISS MARTHA ANN RICHARDSON
of James City Co.
RE 24 Nov. 1809, p. 3; Visitor 2 Dec., p. 174

Married on July 4 by Rev. Charles Grimby, MR. RODHAM KENNER, to MRS. PRISCILLA
MATHEWS both of Westmoreland Co.
RE 15 July 1817, p. 3

Married Sept. 2nd, by Rev. Buchanan, THOMAS KERBY, to MISS ELIZA YARRINGTON, all
of Richmond
VPRDMA 9 Sept. 1820, p. 3

Married, MR. KINCAID of Manchester to MISS BETSEY CARY, dau. of late Archibald Cary,
Esq., Speaker of the Senate. (No marrage date)
VGWA 12 July 1787, p. 3

Married June 11th by Rev. G. Morris, MR. ROBERT KING of Orange Co., to Mrs. ELIZABETH
QUARLES of Louisa Co.
RE 23 June 1820, p. 3

Married, MRS. MARTHA RAGLAND to WILLIAM KING, Esq. both of Hanover Co., on Feb. 1st.
He is 89, and she 75.
VA 6 Feb. 1812, p. 3

Married on Sat. (Sept. 13) MR. JAMES KIRBY, merchant, to MISS ELIZABETH SCOTT,
both of this city
VGGA 16 Sept. 1800, p. 3

Married, on Thurs. last (Nov. 3) MR. JOSHUA KNIGHT of this city, to MISS MARY HART
of Hanover Co.
VGGA 8 Nov. 1808, p. 3

Married Mon. (Feb. 14) by Rev. William Willis, of Henrico Co., MR. HENRY KUNSMAN, to
MISS SARAH ANN ELIZABETH WILKINSON, both of Richmond
RC 16 Feb. 1820, p. 3

Married on Wed. (Jan.5) by Rev. Wm. H. Hart, MR. HAZLETT KYLE of House of Hazlett
& Robert Kyle, to MISS LUCY ANN WINSTON, dau. of George Winston, all of Richmond
City
RE 8 Jan. 1820, p. 3; RC 7 Jan., p. 3

Married on Thurs. (May 6) by Rev. Rice, MR. M.C. LACKLAND, merchant, of Richmond,
to MARY C., dau. of Samuel WHITE, dec'd
RC 11 May 1819, p. 3

Married on Wed. last (Aug. 7) at the Friends Meeting House in this city, THOMAS LADD
merchant, to ANN BELL, dau. of Nathan Bell of Hanover
VA 9 Aug. 1799, p. 3

Married on Wed. last (March 8) by Rev. John D. Blair, MR. AUBIN LaFOREST, to MRS.
JANE C. CLARKE, both of this city
RE 10 March 1809, p. 3; Visitor 11 March, p. 23

Married on Sat. last (Feb. 8) MR. JAMES G. LAIDLEY, Attorney at Law of Wood Co.,
to MISS HARRIET QUARRIER, eldest dau. of Col. Alexander Quarrier of this city
VA 14 Feb. 1806, p. 3; RE 11 Feb., p. 3; VGGA 12 Feb., p. 3

Married Oct. 28th by Rev. Carr, at res. of Stephen Girard, GEN. HENRY LALLEMAND,
to MISS HARRIET GIRARD, niece of Stephen Girard
RE 11 Nov. 1817, p. 3; VP 11 & 12 Nov., p. 3

Married on 2nd Inst., by Rev. Samuel K. Jennings, DR. JOHN F. LAMB to MISS SUSANNAH
TAYLOR, all of Lynchburg
RE 14 Jan. 1812, p. 3

Married lately, MR. DAVID LAMBERT, merchant, to MISS SALLY EGE, both of this city
VGAA Oct. 5, 1782, p. 3

Married on 17th Inst., MR. WILLIAM LAMBERT, to MISS MARY PICKETT, 2nd dau. of
George Pickett, Esq. all of this city
RE 21 Oct. 1815, p. 3; VA 18 Oct., p. 3

Married Dec. 2nd by Rev. William H. Hart, MR. JOHN A. LANCASTER, merchant to
MISS ADELAIDE DERRIEUX, all of Richmond
RC 7 Dec. 1819, p. 3

Married on 5th Inst., MR. MAURICE M. LANGHORNE of Buckingham, to MISS ANN ANDERSON,
dau. of Samuel Anderson, Esq. of Cumberland
VA 19 Jan. 1802, p. 3

Married on 26th Feb., MR. WILLIAM LANGHORNE of Cumberland, to MISS CATHARINE CALLAWAY
of Bedford
VA 4 April, 1811, p. 3

Married on 26th Ult., DR. PHILIP LARUS of this city to MISS MARY FRAYSER, eldest dau.
of Mr. Thomas Frayser of New Kent Co.
VA 4 Dec. 1805, p. 3; VGGA 4 Dec., p. 3, (says Polly Francis)

Married yesterday by Rev. John Courtney, MR. PHILIP LAWSON to MISS MARY ANN RANDOLPH,
both of Richmond
RC 19 May 1820, p. 3

Married at Powhatan, the res. of Mr. William Mayo, on Thurs. (Aug. 24) by Rev. Bishop
Moore, MR. JOHN O. LAY, merchant, of Richmond, to MISS LUCY MAY, dau. of Mr. John May
of Petersburg
RE 29 Aug. 1820, p. 3; VPRDMA 30 Aug., p. 3

Married in Person Co., Pa., on 11th Inst., JOHN LEA, Esq., age 60, to MISS PEGGY
SATERFIELD, age 55
Visitor 29 July 1809, p. 102

Married on 23rd Inst., MR. JOSIAH LEAKE, Attorney at Law, to MISS ELIZABETH HATCHER,
both of Goochland
VA 29 March 1799, p. 3

Married on Wed. last (Nov. 30) DANIEL LEE, Esq. of Shenandoah, to MISS BETSEY NICHOLSON
of this city
VA 7 Dec. 1803, p. 3

Married on 18th Inst. at Shirley, GOV. LEE TO MISS ANN CARTER, dau. of Charles Carter,
Esq.
VGGA 26 June 1793, p. 3; VGRMA 20 June

Married at Popes Creek, Westmoreland Co., on Tues. (April 1) by Rev. Norris, MAJ.
HENRY LEE, late of U.S. Army, to MISS ANN R. M'CARTY, all of same county
VP 7 April 1817, p. 3

Married at Williamsburg, Dec. 21st, by Rev. Mr. Bracken, RICHARD H. LEE, Esq. Attorney
at Law, to MISS ELIZA FINNIE
VGGA 7 Jan. 1804, p. 3

Married, THOMAS LEE, Esq. of the Senate to MISS MILDRED WASHINGTON, youngest dau.
of Col. John Augustine Washington and niece of Gen. Washington. (No marriage date)
VGIC 1 Nov. 1788, p. 2; IC 29 Oct., 1788, says eldest son, Richard Henry Lee, Esq.;
VGWA 30 Oct. 1788

Married on Thurs. (Nov. 5) by Rev. John D. Blair, MR. THOMAS LEE to MISS ANN OSMOND,
both of Richmond
RC 7 Nov. 1818, p. 3

Married on 26th Nov. by the Rev. John Wooldridge, MR. JEPTHA LEET of Powhatan, to MISS ELIZA BASS of Chesterfield
RE 5 Dec. 1812, p. 3

Married in Caroline Co., April 27th, MR. NORBORNE J. LEFONG to MISS ELIZABETH NEWTON
RE 9 June 1820, p. 3

Married last Friday (March 23) at Wilton, JOSEPH LEHILL (Or LETTILL), Esq. to MISS LUCY RANDOLPH
VGWA 29 March 1787, p. 2

Married on Sun. last (April 27) DR. ANDREW LEIPER to MISS FANNY TRENT, both of this city
VGGA 30 April 1794, p. 3; VGRMA 28 April

Married Sat. last (May 3) MISS LUCY LEIPER, niece of Dr. Andrew Leiper of this city to BERNARD MOORE, Esq. of King William
VGWA 8 May 1788, p. 3

Married on Sat. last, MR. JOHN LESLIE to MRS. MYERS (Sat. last was Feb. 5)
VGGA 9 Feb. 1803, p. 3

Married Nov. 21st by Rev. William H. Hart, MR. JOHN LESTER, to MISS JANE MILLER, dau. of Mr. Peter Miller, all of Richmond
RC 28 Nov. 1820, p. 3

Married Nov. 23rd by Rev. Jordan Martin, MR. JOHN LESTER, to MISS ANN LABARIER, all of Chesterfield Co.
RE 14 Dec. 1820, p. 3

Married on Sat. last (April 1) DR. PETER LeTELLIER, to MISS SUSANNA STAPLES
RE 8 April 1815, p. 3

Married on 16th Inst., MR. HOWEL LEWIS to MISS NANCY BOLLING, both of Goochland Co.
VGIC 24 April 1784, p. 3

Married on Sat. (Sept. 26) MR. HOWELL LEWIS of Fredericksburg to MISS NELLY POLLARD of this city
VGRMA 1 Oct. 1795, p. 3

Married May 11th, MR. JOSEPH LEWIS to MISS SUSAN JAMES (in Caroline Co. ?)
RE 9 June 1820, p. 3

Married on 15th Inst. at Elsing Green, King William Co., MR. ROBERT LEWIS, nephew and Aide de camp to Pres. of U.S., to MISS JUDITH WALKER BROWN, dau. of Wm. Burnet Brown, Esq.
VGGA 30 March 1791, p. 3

Married on 12th Inst. by Rev. Mr. Irvin, MR. FRANCIS LIGHTFOOT of Charles City Co., to MISS ELIZABETH VIRGINIA NICHOLAS of Albemarle
VA 20 Feb. 1805, p. 3

Married on 12th Inst., WILLIAM LIGHTFOOT, Esq. of Charles City to MISS NANCY ELLISON
of Hanover
VA 17 March 1807, p. 3; RE 17 March, p. 3, says Mr. Lightfoot is of "Sandy Point"
and calls bride, Ann C. Ellison

Married June 12th by Rev. Wm. Armstrong, MR. WILLIAM LINDSAY to MRS. (   )
HUNTON, all of Albemarle
RE 23 June 1820, p. 3

Married on May 13th by Rev. John Mill, MR. STIRLING LIPSCOMB, to MISS ELIZABETH
JOHNSON, youngest dau. of James Johnson, Esq. of Oldtown, King William Co.
VA 3 June 1813, p. 3

Married on June 20th by Rt. Rev. Bishop Moore, MR. ALEXANDER LITHGOW, to MISS MARY
BRANCH, dau. of Col. Thomas Branch of Chesterfield Co.
RC 21 June 1816, p. 3

Married Aug. 1st, MR. LEWIS B. LITTLEPAGE, to MISS ANN H. HOWARD, dau. of Mr.
Joseph Howard, all of Powhatan Co.
RC 5 Aug. 1818, p. 3

Married, MR. WILLIAM LITTLEPAGE to MISS SUKEY SMITH of Hanover. (No marriage date)
VGWA Aug. 17, 1782, p. 3

Married on 15th Ult. at Petersburg, MR. JAMES F. LOCKHEAD, merchant, to MISS LUCY
ANN JONES, dau. of Gen. Joseph Jones of that place
Visitor 1 July, 1809, p. 86

Married last Sun. (Dec. 18) MR. WILLIAM LOGWOOD of Chesterfield Co. to MISS JENNY
WALKER of Baltimore
VGWA Dec. 31, 1785, p. 3; VGWA Jan. 7,

Married July 25th at Mannsfield, seat of Mann Page, Esq., near Fredericksburg, by
Rev. Abner Waugh, JOHN TAYLOR LOMAX, Esq., Attorney at Law, and MISS CHARLOTTE
THORNTON, dau. of Presly Thornton, Esq. of Tennessee
RE 30 July 1805, p. 3

Married on 7th Inst. by Rev. John Courtney, MR. NICHOLAS LONG to MISS ELIZABETH
WILLIAMSON, dau. of G. Williamson, Esq. of this city
VA 17 May 1808, p. 3

Married Dec. 5th by Rev. William Todd, MR. RICHARD LONGEST, to MISS MARTHA CLAYTON,
all of King & Queen Co.
RE 17 Dec. 1816, p. 3

Married on 14th Inst. by Rev. Mr. Buchanan, MR. WILLIAM LOWNES to MISS ARIANNA WORMLEY
GLYNN, both of Richmond
RE 22 April 1808, p. 3; VGGA 22 April, p. 3

Married May 13th at res. of Mr. Edward Baugh in Powhatan Co., by Rev. Woodfin, MR. FRANCIS C. LOWRY, to MISS ANN E.R. GOODE of same county
RE 26 May 1820, p. 3; RC 22 May, p. 3, says, ANNE ELIZABETH REBECCA GOODE

Married on 18th Inst., MISS REBECCA TYLER, dau. of Chancellor Tyler of Williamsburg, to GEORGE LOYAL, Esq. of Norfolk
RE 29 March 1811, p. 3

Married at Middletown, Mass. a few weeks ago, JOHN LUCAS to his half aunt, CATHARINE CLINTON, dau. of Thomas Tilton
VA 4 April 1800, p. 3

Married, JOHN LUCUS, brother of Mary Lucus, to KATHY CLINTON, dau. of Thomas Tilton. (No marriage date)
RC 5 Jan. 1819, p. 3

Married on Sat. (July 25) MR. GUSTAVUS LUCKE, to MISS SALLY HUNTER, all of this city
VP 28 July 1812, p. 3

Married on Thurs. (June 20) by Rev. John Bryce, MR. CROXTON LUMPKIN, to MISS MARTHA P. PARSONS, all of Richmond
RC 22 June 1816, p. 3; RC 25 June, p. 3, corrects above to read, MARGARET P. PARSO

Married by Rev. Gabriel Walker Sept. 10th, MR. MOORE LUMPKIN, to MRS. WALKER of Tenn dau. of Mr. David Anderson of Buckingham Co.
VP 21 Oct. 1816, p. 3

Married on Sat. last (June 18) MR. JAMES LYLE, Jr. of Manchester to MISS SALLY GOODE of Chesterfield
VGRMA 22 June 1796, p. 2

Married on Mon. last (March 5), MR. JAMES HEAD LYNCH to MISS POLLY PERLEY, both of t city
VGGA 7 March 1804, p. 3

Married Tues. (Nov. 28) by Rev. John Courtney, MR. ROBERT LYNN, to MISS MATILDA CONY all of Richmond
RC 1 Dec. 1820, p. 3

Married in S.C. Feb. 1st, MR. STEPHEN LYON to MISS REBECCA LAMB
VP 12 Feb. 1817, p. 3

Married at Rutland, Vt., MR. THOMAS LYON to MISS BETSY LAMB. (No death date)
VA 20 Feb. 1805, p. 3

Married on 24th Ult., JOHN LYONS, Esq. of Hanover Co., to MISS ANNE (of Cleve) CART of King William
VIC 12 Aug. 1789, p. 3

Married Oct. 10th by Rev. John Courtney, MR. EMANUEL JOSEPH LYONS of the Richmond Theatre, to MISS ELEANOR BRYAN of Richmond
RC 13 Oct. 1820, p. 3

Married in Amelia Co., on 25th Ult. by Rev. John Skurry, DAVID MABEN, Jr., Esq. merchant, of Petersburg, to MISS ANN ELIZA T. PERKINSON, dau. of Col. Thos. Perkinson of Amelia
RE 5 Nov. 1813, p. 3

Married in New York Nov. 18th by Rev. Kuypers, DANIEL MACAULEY, merchant, of Charleston, to MISS MARY LEAYCRAFT HENDERSON, dau. of late Capt. John Henderson of Richmond
RC 25 Nov. 1820, p. 3

Married on Tues. last (Oct. 10) by Rev. Dr. Wilson, MR. JAMES M. MACON, to MISS LUCILLE T. NEWMAN, both of Orange
RE 14 Oct. 1815, p. 3

Married lately in Frederick Co., JAMES MADISON, Esq., Member of Congress from this state, to MRS. D. TOD of Phila.
VGRMA 6 Oct. 1794, p. 3

Married on July 10th by Rev. Symes, ROBERT L. MADISON of Madison Co., to MISS ELIZA STRACHAN of Petersburg
RE 17 July 1816, p. 3

Married on 9th Inst., MR. WILLIAM MANN, Deputy Marshal, to MISS FRANCES GATEWOOD, dau. of Chany Gatewood of King & Queen Co.
RE 17 March 1809, p. 3; Visitor 25 March, p. 31

Married in Richmond Feb. 5th by Rev. Rice, MR. OTIS MANSON of Boston, to MISS SARAH D. FARRILL of Petersburg
RE 10 Feb. 1818, p. 3

Married on Sat. last (April 9) MR. THOMAS P. MANSON to MISS PATSY BASS, both of this city
VA 13 April 1803, p. 3; Examiner 16 April, p. 3

Married on 8th Inst., MR. GEORGE MARKHAM to MISS ELIZA EVANS, dau. of Dr. Evans, all of Chesterfield
VA 18 May 1805, p. 3

Married on Thurs. last (March 3) by Rev. Bracken, MR. FRANCIS MARSHALL to MISS ELIZA HOWLE, both of New Kent Co.
RE 9 March 1814, p. 3

Married last Sat. (Jan. 4) JOHN MARSHALL, Esq., Member of Hon. Privy Council to MISS POLLY AMBLER of this city
VGAA 11 Jan. 1783, p. 3

Married in Baltimore, Feb. 3rd, by Rev., Kemp, MR. JOHN MARSHALL of Va., son of the Chief Justice of the U.S., to ELIZABETH MARIA, dau. of Dr. Ashton ALEXANDER of that city
RE 15 Feb. 1820, p. 3; VPRDMA 9 Feb., p. 20

Married, MR. THOMAS MARSHALL, eldest son of the Chief Justice, to MISS MARGARET LEWIS, eldest dau. of Mr. F. Lewis of Charles City Co. (No marriage date)
RE 31 Oct. 1809, p. 3; VGGA 24 Oct., p. 3; Visitor 4 Nov. 1809, p. 158, says married on 19th Ult.

Married on 20th Ult., MR. WILLIAM MARSHALL to MISS ALICE ADAMS, youngest dau. of Richard Adams, Esq. of this city
IC 9 July 1788, p. 3; VGWA 10 July

Married on 10th Inst., WILLIAM MARSHALL, Esq. of this city to MISS POLLY MACON, of Hanover
VA 21 Dec. 1803, p. 3; VGGA 14 Dec. 1803, p. 3

Married on Thurs. (May 4) by Rev. Isaac H. Judah, MR. HYMAN MARKS to MRS. GRACE MYERS all of this city
Visitor 6 May 1809, p. 54

Married on Wed. (Dec. 30, 1812) MR. MORDECAI MARKS, to MISS ESTHER RAPHAEL, both of Richmond
VP 1 Jan. 1813, p. 3

Married Wed. last (Dec. 9) by Rev. Isaac H. Judah, MR. MARX to MISS ZEPORAH REUBEN of this city
VA 11 Dec. 1801, p. 3

Married Wed. (Dec. 20) by Rev. Blair, MR. JOHN B. MARTIN, to MISS ELIZABETH ANN WINFREE, all of Richmond
RC 22 Dec. 1820, p. 3

Married on Dec. 22nd by Rev. John Courtney, MR. ROBERT MARTIN, to MISS CATHARINE PYNES, late of King & Queen Co.
RC 24 Dec. 1814, p. 3

Married on May 1st at Dr. Charles Cocke's in Albemarle, by Rev. Dunn of London, GEN. ARMISTEAD T. MASON, to MISS CHARLOTTE ELIZA TAYLOR, youngest dau. of late John Taylor of Southampton
RE 20 May 1817, p. 3

Married March 5th by Rev. John D. Blair, MR. CONWAY C. MASON of Orange Co., to MISS AGNES MAYO, dau. of Mr. William Mayo of Henrico Co.
RE 9 March 1816, p. 3

Married on 1st Inst., MR. STEPHEN THOMSON MASON, Member of General Assembly, to MISS POLLY ARMISTEAD of Louisa Co.
VGAA 17 May, 1783, p. 3

Married at Norfolk, Aug. 30th, MR. RICHARD MASON, merchant, of Williamsburg, to MISS MARY HODGE COCHRAN, late from St. Martins, West Indies
VA 10 Sept. 1803, p. 3

Married last week, HON. SAMPSON MATTHEWS to MRS. CATHERINE PARK
VGAA 14 June, 1783, p. 2

Married, MR. BENJAMIN MAYER, Editor of the German Aurora, a Harrisburg paper, to MISS ELIZABETH WETZEL. (No marriage date)
Visitor 9 Sept. 1809, p. 127

Married on 8th Inst. in Cumberland Co., by Rev. Abner Watkins, DANIEL W. MAYES, Esq., age 18, to MISS SURITTA CHRISTOPHER of Mecklenburg Co., age 45
VA   22 Aug. 1809, p. 3

Married on 19th Inst. by Rev. C. McRae, DR. EDWARD MAYO to SALLY PLEASANTS, eldest dau. of Samuel Pleasants, all of Powhatan Co.
VA   30 Nov. 1805, p. 3

Married on 28th Ult., MR. JOSEPH MAYO of Powhatan, to MISS ELIZABETH BLAIR, dau. of Rev. J. Blair of this city
Virginian   6 May 1808, p. 3

Married on 9th Inst. at Jonesborough, Tenn., PETER MAYO, Esq., Attorney at Law, of Abingdon, to MISS ELZA HELMES, dau. of Gen. Helmes of that state, though lately from Jersey
RE   18 Oct. 1811, p. 3; VA   21 Oct., p. 3

Married Oct. 7th at Rose Hill, Orange Co., by Rt. Rev. Bishop Moore, MR. ROBERT A. MAYO, youngest son of Col. William Mayo of Powhatan, to MISS SARAH, youngest dau. of Hay TALIAFERRO
RC   14 Oct. 1819, p. 3

Married on Thurs. (Nov. 12) by Rev. P. Courtney, MR. JOSEPH M'CALEB, formerly of Nelson Co., to MISS CATHARINE HARTGROVE of Manchester
RC   14 Nov. 1818, p. 3

Married Dec. 12, 1816, by Rev. John Mill, MR. JOHN M'CARTY, to MRS. POLLY MOORE, all of King William Co.
RE   7 Jan. 1817, p. 3

Married at Carrs Hill in Goochland Co., on Jan. 21st, by Rev. Reuben Ford, STOKES M'CAUL, JR., to MISS MARY D____DY
RE   30 Jan. 1817, p. 3

Married on Sat. (Nov. 20) by Rev. J. D. Blair, DR. WILLIAM R. McCAW, to MISS ELIZA, dau. of William RANDOLPH of Wilton
RC   23 Nov. 1819, p. 3

Married on 1st Inst., MR. NEILL M'COULL of Richmond, merchant, to MISS JULIA LOGAN, dau. of late Charles Logan, Esq. of Belle Meade
VA   6 June 1806, p. 3; RE   6 June, p. 3, (says Rill Meade); VGGA   7 June, p. 3

Married on Sat. last (May 8) MR. MILLER W. M'CRAW, merchant, to MISS PEGGY TOLER, both of this city
VA   12 May 1802, p. 3; Recorder   12 May, p. 2

Married on Sat. last (Nov. 2) SAMUEL McCRAW, attorney at law, to MRS. WHITLOCK, 2nd dau. of Col. John Harvie of this city
VA   9 Nov. 1805, p. 3; VGGA   6 Nov., p. 3

Married on Thurs. last (April 6) by Rev. John D. Blair, SAMUEL McCRAW, Esq., to MRS. SARAH GUNN, all of this city
RE   14 April 1809, p. 3; VA   14 April, p. 3; VGGA   18 April, p. 3, says 12th April; Visitor   6 May, p. 54

Married on Sat. last (May 14) MR. JOHN McCREEDY, merchant, to MRS. BYRDIE, both of this city
VGGA 21 May 1803, p. 3

Married, at Pelham, Mass., MR. WILLIAM M'FALL, age 100, to widow JUDITH PERKINS, age 79, both paupers
VA 23 May 1809, p. 3; VGGA 19 May, p. 3; Visitor 3 June, p. 70

Married in Fauquier Co., on 15th Inst., JAMES L. McKENNA, Esq., Cashier of Bank of Alexandria, to MISS ANN F. RANDOLPH, dau. of Col. Robert Randolph of that county
RE 22 Oct. 1813, p. 3

Married on Sat. last (Jan. 9) MR. WILLIAM MacKENZIE, merchant, to MISS JANE SCOTT, both of this city
VA 12 Jan. 1802, p. 3; VGGA 15 Jan., p. 3

Married Thurs. last (Dec. 26) MR. WILLIAM M'KIM to MISS BETSY ELLIOTT, both of this city
VGRC 31 Dec. 1793, p. 3

Married on Thurs. (Jan. 22) MR. DONALD M'KINZIE of Petersburg, merchant, to MISS SALLY HARRISON of this city
VGGA 28 Jan. 1795, p. 3; VGRMA 29 Jan., p. 3, says M'KENZIE

Married July 19th by Rev. William Talley, MR. GEORGE M'LAUGHLIN of Richmond, to MRS. SARAH OLIVER of Hanover Co.
VP 22 July 1817, p. 3

Married yesterday MR. JOSEPH M'LAURINE of Chesterfield to MISS SUKEY ELLIS of Hanover
VGRC 12 July 1793, p. 3

Married on Tues. last (Sept. 22), ALEXANDER M'RAE, Esq., Lt-.Gov. of this Commonwealth, to MISS NANCY HAYES of this city
VA 26 Sept. 1807, p. 3; RE 26 Sept., p. 3, says Ann Dent Hayes

Married on Wed. last (May 2) MR. COLIN M'RAE of Manchester, Merchant, to MISS ANN GRAVES, dau. of Mr. Charles Graves of Chesterfield Co.
VA 9 May 1804, p. 3

Married in Washington, Oct. 16th, by Rev. M'Cormick, MR. COLIN M'RAE, merchant of Manchester, to MISS JUDITH, dau. of late Maj. John HARRIS of Chesterfield Co.
RC 21 Oct. 1818, p. 3

Married on March 28th by Rev. Kirkpatrick, MR. COLIN M'RAE, merchant, of Manchester, to MISS HYPATIA HARRIS, dau. of late Maj. John Harris of Chesterfield Co.
RE 6 April, 1816, p. 3

Married on Wed. (Jan. 11) by Rev. Mr. Blair, MR. HODIJAH MEADE of Amelia Co., to MISS JANE RUTHERFORD of Richmond
VP 18 Jan. 1815, p. 3

Married on 14th Inst., MR. ELISHA MEREDITH of Hanover Co., to MISS SALLY B. CABELL of Buckingham Co.
RE 26 Nov. 1805, p. 3

Married on Thurs. (July 4), by Rev. John D. Blair, MR. REUBEN MEREDITH, to MISS ELIZABETH ANDERSON, dau. of Alexander Anderson, all of Hanover Co.
RC 9 July 1816, p. 3

Married May 1st, by Rev. William H. Hart, MR. RICHARD MESSITER, a native of England, to MISS MARY ROWZEE BOULWARE of Richmond
RC 11 May 1820, p. 3

Married, MR. MEUX of New Kent to MISS OLIVER of Hanover Co.
VGWA 21 May 1789, p. 3

Married Oct. 12th by Rev. Robert B. Semple, MR. JOHN H. MICOU, 2nd son of Col. Paul Micou, to MISS CATHARINE C. WOOD, youngest dau. of late Carter Wood, both of Essex Co.
RE 1 Nov. 1815, p. 3

Married on 28th Ult., DR. JAMES MIENOR to MISS MARY WATSON, all of Loudon Co.
RE 6 Aug. 1813, p. 3

Married at Lynchburg Dec. 23, 1819, by Rev. William Duncan, MR. BENJAMIN MILES, age 70, to MISS SALLY WILSON, all of Amherst Co.
RE 22 Jan. 1820, p. 3; VPRDMA 18 Jan., p. 3, says Miss Wilson is age 15

Married on 7th Inst., at seat of Gen. Brown, near Wilmington, N.C., MAJ. ALEXANDER C. MILLER, to MISS MARY BROWN
RE 26 July 1811, p. 3

Married on 4th Inst., JOHN MILLER, Esq., of Cumberland, to MISS MARTHA T. MACON of Powhatan
VP 12 Jan. 1811, p. 3

Married, MAURICE L. MILLER of Petersburg, to MISS ELIZA PLEASANTS of Charles City Co. (No marriage date)
RE 25 May 1810, p. 3

Married on 4th Ult., THOMAS MILLER, Esq., to MISS CATHERINE MACON, both of Powhatan Co.
VA 7 April 1801, p. 3

Married in Manchester on Sat. last (Aug. 10) MR. NICHOLAS MILLS to MISS SARAH RONALD, dau. of Andrew Ronald, dec'd
VGGA 17 Aug. 1805, p. 3

Married on Fri. last (June 26) by Rev. Richard Broaddus, MR. ARCHIBALD MINOR to MISS NANCY RAWLINGS, dau. of Mr. Jeremiah Rawlins, all of Caroline Co.
VA 1 July 1807, p. 3

Married, MR. HENRY MINOR of Clarksville, Tenn. to MISS FRANCES BARBOUR of Petersburg.
(No marriage date)
Visitor 23 Sept. 1809, p. 135

Married on 13th Ult. by Rev. Mr. Chastain, ALEXANDER MITCHELL, Esq., age 101 to
MISS JANE HAMMOND, age 16, both of Buckingham Co.
VGGA 20 Dec. 1797, p. 3

Married, on Dec. 15th by Rev. Mr. Ford, CAPT. CARY MITCHELL, merchant, of Cartersville
to MISS SALLY POWERS of Goochland Co.
VA 10 Feb. 1809, p. 3

Married June 17th, MR. SAMUEL C. MITCHELL, to MISS MARTHA COCKE, both of Goochland
RE 4 Aug. 1820, p. 3

Married Tues. last (July 17) by Rev. John Buchanan, MR. WILLIAM MITCHELL to MISS
ANN SMITH ARMISTEAD, 2nd dau. of Maj. Thomas Armistead, both of this city
VA 21 July 1804, p. 3; VGGA 21 July, p. 2 (says Mitchell is only son of Robert
Mitchell, Esq.)

Married 19th March in Albemarle Co. JOSEPH JONES MONROE to MISS ELIZABETH KERR,
dau. of James Kerr, Esq. of that co.
VGGA 30 March 1791, p. 3

Married Dec. 18 by Rev. John D. Blair, MR. HENRY B. MONTAGUE, merchant, of Cartersville to MISS MARY ANN MOODY, only dau. of Capt. John Moody of Richmond
RE 23 Dec. 1817, p. 3

Married Nov. 24th by Rev. Henry Bridgwater, MR. GEORGE B. MOODY, to MISS ANN SCOTT,
all of Chesterfield Co.
RE 14 Dec. 1820, p. 3

Married on Sat. last (Dec. 24) MR. JOHN MOODY, merchant, of this city, to MISS
ELIZABETH PRICE of Fluvanna
VA 30 Dec. 1796, p. 2

Married on Sat. last (May 28) MR. PHILIP MOODY, JR. of James City Co., to MISS
KITTY MOODY, eldest dau. of Mr. Matthew Moody of this city
VGGA 1 April 1795, p. 2

Married, in Caswell Co., N.C., CHARLES MOORE, Esq., age 63, to MISS GEYLLAR DUNNAVANT
Visitor 18 Nov. 1809, p. 166

Married on 25th Ult. MR. CHRISTOPHER MOON, son of Jacob Moon, dec'd, of Bedford Co.,
to MISS PATSY JOHNSON, 1st dau. of James Johnson, Esq., of King William Co.
VA 6 Jan. 1801, p. 3

Married on Tues. last (June 4) by Rev. Mr. Buchanan, MR. CURTIS R. MOORE, to MISS
PAMELA ANN COX
RE 7 June 1811, p. 3

Married lately in Buckingham Co., MR. ROBERT MOORE of Mason Co., Town of Warminster, to MISS JANE MOSELEY, dau. of Mr. Arthur Moseley
VA 23 Sept. 1808, p. 3

Married on Thurs. (Oct. 22?) by Rev.John D. Blair, DR. CHARLES MORRIS, to MISS EMILY TAYLOR, both of Hanover Co.
RE 23 Oct. 1812, p. 3; VP 23 Oct., p. 3, says married Oct. 15th

Married on Christmas Day, GOVERNEUR MORRIS, Esq. of Morrisania, to MISS ANN CARY RANDOLPH, dau. of late Thos. M. Randolph, Esq., of Va.
VA 9 Jan. 1810, p. 3; Visitor 13 Jan., p. 200

Married on 2nd Inst., MOSES MORRIS, SR. to MISS MASEY DICKINS, both of Amelia Co.
VGRMA 20 Aug. 1796, p. 3

Married on Mon. last (March 27) MR. BENJAMIN MOSBY to MISS POLLY CROUCH
VA 31 March 1797, p. 2; VGGA 29 March, p. 3

Married in Staunton 27th Sept. by Rev. William Wilson, MR. BENJAMIN MOSBY of this city to MISS MARY EDMONDSON of that town
VA 8 Oct. 1803, p. 3

Married on 14th Inst. MR. JOHN G. MOSBY of Powhatan Co., to MISS MARY W. PLEASANTS of Henrico
RE 20 Feb. 1810, p. 3

Married MR. WADE MOSBY of Powhatan to MISS SUKEY TRUEHEART of Hanover
VGAA 23 April 1785, p. 2

Married on Christmas Eve, 1807, MR. HEZEKIA MOSEBY of Powhatan to MISS ELIZABETH MERRYMAN, youngest dau. of Mr. Jesse Merryman of Cumberland Co.
RE 1 March 1808, p. 3

Married in Williamsburg Sat. last (June 9) MISS SOUTHALL, youngest dau. of Col. James Southall to MR. MOUTER, of N.C.
VGGA 13 June 1792, p. 2

Married on Tues. (Oct. 28) by Rev. Baptist, EDWARD MUMFORD to MISS SALLY MOSBY, dau. of Gen. Littleberry Mosby, all of Powhatan Co.
RE 4 Nov. 1817, p. 3; VP 4 Nov., p. 3

Married on Sat. last (Feb. 27) WILLIAM MUNFORD, Esq. of Mecklenburg Co., to MISS SARAH RADFORD, dau. of William Radford, Esq., of this city
VA 2 March 1802, p. 3

Married Dec. 30th last, HUDSON MUSE, Esq., to MISS AGNES NELSON, both of Urbanna
VGGA 19 Jan. 1791, p. 3

Married at Tappahannock, by Rev. R. B. Semple, on 5th Inst., MR. JAMES MUSE, JR., to MISS MARY W. COLEMAN
RE 24 March 1812, p. 3

Married on 1st Inst. at Urbanna, MR. LAWRENCE MUSE of Tappahannock to MISS JANE
SOUTHALL
VGGA 19 June 1793, p. 3; VGRMA 24 June

Married on Wed. last (June 8) by Rev. Isaac H. Judah, MR. ABRAHAM MYERS, merchant,
of New York, to MISS GRACE JUDAH of this city
VA 11 June 1803, p. 3

Married on 1st Inst.by Rev. Dr. Hopkins, JACOB MYERS, Esq. of Baltimore to MISS
ELIZA ROSS, eldest dau. of David Ross, Esq. of Cobham
VGGA 10 May 1797, p. 2

Married on Thurs. (May 16) SAMUEL MYERS of Norfolk to LOUISA, daughter of Joseph
MARX of Richmond
RE 18 May 1816, p. 3; VP 18 May, p. 3, says MARKS

Married on 12th Ult., ABNER NASH, Esq. of Prince Edward Co., to MISS MATILDA PENN,
dau. of Col. Gabriel Penn, of Amherst
VGGA 1 Aug. 1792, p. 3

Married on Dec. 21, 1815, by Rev. Seward, AUGUSTINE NEALE, to MISS JULIET McCarty,
both of Richmond Co.
RE 4 Jan. 1816, p. 3

Married on 10th Inst. by Rev. Micklejohn, MR. ROBERT NELSON of Mecklenburg Co., to
MISS ISABELLA H. WILSON, only dau. of John Wilson, Esq. of Halifax Co.
RE 21 Jan. 1809, p. 3; VA 20 Jan., p. 3; VGGA 20 Jan., p. 3

Married Oct. 18th in Albemarle Co., by Rev. Hatch, THOMAS NELSON of Frederick Co.,
to MISS MILDRED WALKER NELSON, dau. of Hugh Nelson
RE 20 Oct. 1820, p. 3

Married on Mon. last (date?) by Rev. Mr. Stephens, after a courtship of 6 hours,
MR. CHRISTOPHER NEUNHOFLER of Ludwigsburg, Swabia, Germany, age 60, to MISS BETSY
MARKS of New York, age 70
Visitor 9 Sept. 1809, p. 127

Married on 20th Ult., MR. WILLIAM NEWBURN of Chesterfield, to MISS SARAH RANDOLPH
of Powhatan
RE 19 Feb. 1814, p. 3

Married on Thurs. last (Aug. 7) MR. WILLIAM NICE of this city, to MISS NANCY COLEMA
of Henrico
VGRMA 11 Aug. 1794, p. 3

Married on 29th Ult., GEORGE NICOLSON, Esq. of this city to MISS WALLER of York Co.
VGGA 8 April 1800, p. 3

Married at Rosegill, Middlesex Co., on 4th Inst., DR. GEORGE D. NICOLSON, to MISS
SARAH TAYLOE WORMLEY, 2nd dau. of late Ralph Wormley of that place
RE 12 Dec. 1811, p. 3

Married last Thurs. in Williamsburg (July 31), JOHN NICHOLAS, Esq. of Albemarle Co., to MISS LOUISA CARTER of Williamsburg
VGWA 7 Aug. 1788, p.3

Married on 11th Inst. in Baltimore, PHILIP NORBORNE NICHOLAS, Esq. of this city to MISS MARY SPEAR of Balt.
VA 26 Feb. 1799, p. 3

Married on Thurs. last (Jan. 19) by Rev. John D. Blair, MR. GEORGE NICHOLSON, to MISS SARAH C. SHEPARD, dau. of Mr. Nathaniel Shepard, all of this city
VA 21 Jan. 1815, p. 3

Married on 1st Inst., MR. THOMAS NORTH of Charlotte, to MISS NANCY COX, age 14, of Campbell Co.
Visitor 17 March 1810, p. 27

Married in North Carolina on 23rd Sept., MR. JOHN C. NORTS of Charlotte Co., Va. to MISS ELIZABETH SMITH, dau. of Maj. Robert Smith of Lunenburg Co., Va.
VA 23 Oct. 1810, p. 3

Married on Wed. (June 24) by Rev. John Bryce, MR. EDMUND B. NORVELL of Lynchburg, to MISS SALUDA MORRISS, eldest dau. of Daniel Morriss, merchant of Richmond
RE 30 June 1818, p. 3

Married on Sat. last (Sept. 28) THOMAS NORVELL, Esq. of this city, to MISS NANCY MOSBY of Hanover
VGGA 2 Oct. 1805, p. 2

Married March 21st, by the Rev. Reuben Ford, MR. NELSON NUCKOLDS of Goochland Co., to MISS POLLY READY of Louisa Co.
VP 2 April 1811, p. 3

Married on 20th Inst., MR. JAMES OGILVE of this city to MISS SALLY WILKINSON of New Kent
VGGA 28 Dec. 1803, p. 3

Married on Sat. last (May 9) by Rev. Mr. Courtney, MR. JOSEPH OLIVER of Charlotte Co., to MRS. ANN AGNES ELLIOTT of this city
VA 13 May 1807, p. 3

Married on 25th Ult. at Romney, MR. DANIEL O'HARA, merchant, to MISS SUSAN HEISKILL
Visitor 9 Sept. 1809, p. 127

Married on 12th Inst., REV. SAMUEL O'HENDREN of Frederick Co., to MISS ANN M. FRENCH of Goochland
RE 24 Dec. 1811, p. 3

Married on Thurs. last (Dec. 5) MR. JOHN O'LYNCH, printer, to MISS MARGARET QUARRIER, both of this city
RE 10 Dec. 1811, p. 3; VP 10 Dec., p. 3

Married, on 27th Inst., MR. ROBERT O'REILEY, teacher, to MISS SARAH WHITE CHANDLER, Governess of the Female Academy in Manchester
Va. Patriot 30 Dec. 1809, p. 3; VA 2 Jan. 1810, p. 3, says 27th of last month; Visitor 13 Jan., p. 200, says 27th of last month

Married on 21st Ult., by Rev. John H. Saunders, MR. HUGH OWEN to MISS SARAH WOODSON, sole dau. of Mr. Hugh Woodson, dec'd, all of Powhatan Co.
VA 16 Aug. 1806, p. 3

Married on 8th Inst. by Rev. John D. Blair, MR. MATTHEW OWEN to MISS MARY BURTON, both of Henrico Co.
VA 14 Oct. 1807, p. 3

Married Nov. 6th, MR. POWELL OWNSBY to MISS MATILDA LEFTWICH, dau. of Mr. Peyton Leftwich, all of Bedford Co.
VP 18 Nov. 1817, p. 3

Married JOHN PAGE, Esq. of Hanover to MISS MARIA BYRD, dau. of Col. Wm. Byrd, dec'd of Charles City
VGWA 29 May 1784, p. 3

Married, ROBERT PAGE, Esq., Attorney at Law, to MISS SALLY PAGE of Hanover. (No marriage date)
VGWA 24 Jan. 1788, p. 3

Married on 19th Inst. by Rev. Mr. Buchanan, MR. WILLIAM BYRD PAGE to MISS JANE WISEHAM
RE 24 Nov. 1807, p. 3; VGGA 24 Nov., p. 3

Married in King William Co., on Oct. 28th, by Rev. Robert Semple, MR. WILLIAM B. PAGE, JR. of Richmond to MISS LUCY A. SEGAR of King William Co.
VP 2 Nov. 1814, p. 3

Married June 15th by Rev. Mills, DR. AMERICUS W. PAINE of Goochland Co., to MISS JANE BEVERLEY DUDLEY of King William Co.
RE 27 June 1820, p. 3

Married near Milledgeville, Ga., Oct. 16th, DR. CHARLES J. PAINE, late of Fredericks burg, to MRS. ANN J. McINTOSH, dau. of Judge David
RE 31 Oct. 1820, p. 3

Married on Sat. (Oct. 5) by Rev. Buchanan, ORRIS PAINE, to MISS CATHERINE E. WISEHAM
RC 9 Oct. 1816, p. 3

Married on Thurs. (Nov. 2) by Rev. John D. Blair, MR. CHARLES PALMER, merchant, to MISS MARY JANE LEWIS, all of Richmond
RC 4 Nov. 1820, p. 3

Married in Hertford, N.C. by Rev. Ross, June 8th, ELIAS T. PARKER of Chowan, N.C. to MISS MARGARET TOWNSEND, dau. of Josiah Townsend of Hertford
VPRDMA 24 June 1820, p. 3

Married on Thurs. last (June 2) by Rev. Mr. Buchanan, MR. RICHARD E. PARKER of
Westmoreland, to MISS ELIZABETH FOUSHEE, eldest dau. of Dr. Foushee of this city
VA 7 June 1808, p. 3; RE 3 June, p. 3; VGGA 10 June, p. 3

Married on Tues. (Jan. 31) MR. JOHN PARKHILL, merchant, to MISS ELIZABETH COPLAND,
dau. of Charles Copland, all of Richmond
VP 4 Feb. 1815, p. 3

Married on Thurs. (Oct. 23) by Rev. John H. Rice, MR. SAMUEL PARKHILL, merchant, of
Richmond, to MISS MARTHA ANN BOTT, dau. of Miles Bott of Manchester
VP 29 Oct. 1817, p. 3

Married MR. SAMUEL P. PARSONS of this city to MISS ELIZABETH LADD of Charles City
VA 17 Oct. 1804, p. 3

Married on 17th Inst. in Amherst Co., by Rev. Charles Crawford, MR. PATTEN, merchant,
of Boston, to MISS SARAH CRAWFORD
RE 6 Sept. 1815, p. 3

Married at Warren, Va. on 31 May, MR. JOHN PATTERSON of Baltimore, to MISS POLLY
NICHOLAS, dau. of Wilson Cary Nicholas, Esq.
VA 17 June 1806, p. 3

Married on Dec. 18th by the Rev. John D. Blair, MR. WILLIAM PATTERSON, merchant,
of Richmond, to MISS ANN P. ATKINSON of Mannsfield, near Petersburg
RC 23 Dec. 1814, p. 3

Married in Washington City by Rt. Rev. Bishop Hobart, JAMES K. PAULDING, Sec. of
Bd. of Navy Commissioners, to GERTRUDE, eldest dau. of Peter KEMBLE of New York.
(No marriage date)
RE 27 Nov. 1818, p. 3

Married, at Stafford, MR. CHESTER PEALE, age 20, to MISS LOTTE BEAN, age 47,   (No
marriage date)
VGGA 19 May 1809, p. 3

Married Sept. 5th by Rev. Wm. H. Hart, MR. WILLIAM PEARSON of firm of Walford &
Pearson, to MISS MARY ANNA WELSH, all of Richmond
RC 8 Sept. 1820, p. 3

Married Mon. last (March 19) MR. DAVID PEARCE, to MISS MARGARET M. MARTIN, eldest
dau. of Mr. Andrew Martin, all of Norfolk
Visitor 24 March 1810, p. 31

Married on Sat. (Feb. 11) by Rev. Courtney, MR. CHARLES PEERS, to MISS MARY OLIVER,
all of Richmond
RC 14 Feb. 1815, p. 3

Married on 6th Inst., MR. BENJAMIN PENDLETON to MISS CATHARINE GATEWOOD, both of King & Queen Co.
VA 11 April 1804, p. 3; VGGA 14 April, p. 3

Married Sunday last (Sept. 20) in Williamsburg, MR. JOHN PENDLETON of Caroline Co., to MISS NANCY LEWIS to Richmond
VGWA 24 Sept. 1789, p. 3

Married May 26th, MR. JOHN L. PENDLETON to MISS ELIZA B. MAGRUDER
RE 9 June 1820, p. 3

Married March 6, by Rev. John D. Blair, MR. GEORGE PERKINS of Cumberland, to MISS ELIZA S. RICHARDSON, dau. of Capt. John A. Richardson of Hanover Co.
RE 9 March 1816, p. 3

Married, at Petersburg, on Thurs. last (April 16) MR. EDWARD PESCUD, Editor of The Republican, to MISS ELIZA PEARCE, both of Petersburg
RE 24 April 1807, p. 3

Married Jan. 18th by Rev. J. Saunders, MAJ. EDWARD PESCUD, Editor of the Petersburg Republican, to MISS SUSAN BROOKE FRANCISCO, dau. of Peter Francisco of Summerville, Buckingham Co.
VPRDMA 26 Jan. 1820, p. 3

Married in Port Royal June 20th, by Rev. Samuel B. Wilson, VALENTINE PEYTON, to MISS ELIZA F. BROCKENBROUGH
VPRDMA 26 June 1820, p. 3

Married on Feb. 27th by Rev. Wm. Hart, at Capt. A. Turner's, MR. SAMUEL W. PHILIPS, to MISS SARAH ANN TURNER, all of Richmond
RC 5 March 1817, p. 3

Married March 30th by Rev. John D. Blair, MR. CHARLES PICKETT, to MISS MARGARET, dau. of Mr. John ADAMS of Richmond
RC 1 April 1819, p. 3

Married, MR. GEORGE PICKETT of this city to MRS. MARGARET FLINT, late of Baltimore, (No marriage date)
VGWA 22 Oct. 1789, p. 3; VIC 21 Oct.

Married July 2 by Rev. John Buchanan, GEORGE B. PICKETT of Fauquier Co., to MISS COURTNEY HERON of Richmond
RC 4 July 1818, p. 3

Married on Tues. last (Feb. 2) MR. CHARLES PINKNEY to MISS CLARA MOODY, both of this city
RC 5 Feb. 1796, p. 3

Married May 13th by Rev. Thomas M. Henley, of Essex Co., REV. HIPKINS PITMAN of
Caroline Co., age 74, to MRS. PHOEBE ADAMS, age 72, of King & Queen Co. Her
mother is still living, having married Mr. James Bates about 1725.
RE 8 June 1819, p. 3

Married on 19th Ult., MR. ARCHIBALD PLEASANTS, of house of Ralston & Pleasants, to
MISS MARY BREND
RE 5 Dec. 1812, p. 3

Married Wed. (Sept. 15) in Richmond by Rev. John Bryce, MR. BASIL B. PLEASANTS of
Goochland Co., to MISS PHOEBE RING, late of New York
RC 18 Sept. 1819, p. 3

Married on 8th Ult., MR. FREDERICK PLEASANTS of house of Moncure, Robinson & Pleasants,
to MISS SARAH MARIA EUSTACE of Woodford, Stafford Co.
RE 5 Dec. 1812, p. 3

Married on Sat. last (May 16) by Rev. John D. Blair, MR. JOHN W. PLEASANTS, to
MISS ELIZABETH W. COLEMAN, dau. of Maj. Samuel Coleman, all of this city
VA 20 May 1807, p. 3

Married at Friends Meeting House, Hanover Co., Oct. 9th, JOSEPH I. PLEASANTS of
Goochland Co., to MARTHA BATES, 2nd dau. of late Benjamin Bates
RE 12 Oct. 1819, p. 3

Married on 10th Inst. at Bell Meade in Powhatan Co., MR. ROBERT CARY PLEASANTS
to MRS. MARY LOGAN, widow of Mr. Charles Logan
VGRMA 16 Dec. 1795, p. 3

Married Aug. 1st by Rev. Edward Baptist, MR. ROBERT W. PLEASANTS, to MISS MARY P.
HARRIS, eldest dau. of John L. Harris, all of Goochland Co.
RE 29 Aug. 1820, p. 3

Married in Goochland Co., Aug. 1st by Rev. Edward Baptist, ROBERT W. PLEASANTS
to MISS MARGARET PLEASANTS
VPRDMA 30 Aug. 1820, p. 3

Married Aug. 23rd by Rev. Fife, MR. TARLTON W. PLEASANTS, to MISS MARGARET PLEASANTS,
all of Goochland
RE 29 Aug. 1820, p. 3

Married Sat. last (June 20), MR. SAMUEL PLEASANTS, printer, to MISS DEBORAH LOWNES,
both of this city
RC 23 July 1795, p. 3; VGGA 22 July

Married, on Mon. last (Oct. 1) by Rev. J. D. Blair, SAMUEL PLEASANTS of Powhatan to
MISS MARGARET T.J. HETH of Curls, Henrico Co.
RE 5 Oct. 1810, p. 3

Married July 18th by Rev. Courtney, MR. FRANCIS PLEDGE of Richmond, to MISS KITTY
HUGHES of Hanover Co.
RE 25 July 1820, p. 3; RC 21 July, p. 3

Married Nov. 23rd by Rev. Henry Bridgewater, MR. EDWARD W. POINDEXTER, to MISS
MARTHA F. WINFREE, all of Chesterfield Co.
RE 14 Dec. 1820, p. 3

Married on 16th Inst. MR. JAMES POINDEXTER, Clerk of the County Court of Powhatan,
to MISS NANCY WILLIAMSON of Janetto
VA 27 Nov. 1802, p. 3

Married on Sat. last (July 3) MR. SAMUEL POINTER to MISS POLLY WATSON, both of this
city
VGGA 7 July 1802, p. 3

Married in Richmond on Tues. (Feb. 4) by Rt. Rev. R. C. Moore, BENJAMIN POLLARD, to
MISS ELIZA LOYALL, both of Norfolk
RE 6 Feb. 1817, p. 3

Married on Thurs. last (Jan. 19 or 26) by Rev. John D. Blair, MR. ROBERT POLLARD, JF
of King William, to MISS EVELINE CHAMBERLAYNE of Henrico
VA 27 Jan. 1809, p. 3; Visitor 11 Feb., p. 7

Married, WILLIAM POPE, Esq. of Goochland to MISS ANN WOODSON of Powhatan. (No
marriage date)
VGGA 6 June 1792, p. 3

Married at Sempronius, N.Y., WILLIAM POTTER, age 16, to MISS MINDWELL FORBUSH,
age 13, after courtship of 10 evenings
RC 7 Nov. 1820, p. 3

Married on 12th Inst., by Rev. John D. Blair, MR. WILLIAM G. POVALL, to MISS ROSINA
MOSELEY, both of Richmond
RE 20 Sept. 1815, p. 3

Married on 19th Ult., MR. GEORGE POWELL, to MISS SOPHIA PENDLETON, 2nd dau. of
Reuben Pendleton, Esq. of Amherst
Visitor 16 Dec. 1809, p. 182

Married on 13th Inst., MR. THOMAS POWELL to MISS REBECCA MARKHAM, dau. of Capt.
George Markham, dec'd, both of Amelia Co.
VA 29 Jan. 1803, p. 3

Married on Thurs. (May 12) by Rev. Taylor, MR. JOHN B. PRENTIS, to MISS CATHARINE
DABNEY, all of Richmond
VP 14 May 1814, p. 3

Married, MR. WILLIAM PRENTIS, Printer,to MISS POLLY GEDDY, both of Petersburg.
(No marriage date)
VGWA 12 March 1789, p. 2

Married on 10th Jan. FRANCIS PRESTON, ESQ. of Montgomery Co., Attorney at Law, to MISS SALLY B. CAMPBELL, only dau. of late Gen. Wm. Campbell, dec'd, of Washington Co.
VGGA 30 Jan. 1793, p. 3

Married on Mon. last (June 11) COL. JOHN PRESTON of Botetourt Co., to MISS POLLY RADFORD, eldest dau. of William Radford, Esq. of this city
Observatory 14 June 1798, p. 3; VA 15 June, p. 3; VGGA 19 June, p. 3

Married on Sat. last (March 30) GEN. JOHN PRESTON, Treas. of this Commonwealth, to MRS. MAYO of this city
RE 2 April 1811, p. 3; VA 4 April, p. 3; VP 2 April, p. 3

Married on Thurs. last (June 12) THOMAS PRESTON, Esq. of Montgomery, Attorney at Law, to MISS EDMONIA RANDOLPH, 2nd dau. of Edmund Randolph, Esq. of Richmond
VA 17 June 1806, p. 3; RE 17 June, p. 3 (says Preston is of Rockbridge Co.); VGGA 14 June, p. 3

Married Dec. 23, 1819, in Lynchburg, MR. WILLIAM R. PRESTON of Botetourt Co., to MISS ELIZABETH A. CABELL, dau. of Mr. Landon Cabell of that place
RE 8 Jan. 1820, p. 3; RC 7 Jan., p. 3

Married on Thurs. last (Oct. 13) by Rev. John D. Blair, JOHN F. PRICE, Esq. of this city to MISS MARIA O. WINSTON of Hanover Co.
VA 18 Oct. 1808, p. 3; RE 18 Oct., p. 3

Married, CAPT. JOSEPH PRICE to MISS LUCY BURTON, both of this county, on Mon. last (Dec. 8)
VGRMA 11 Dec. 1794, p. 3

Married on Thurs. last (June 25) MR. MARION PRICE to MISS PATSY DEPRIEST, both of Henrico Co.
VA 1 July 1807, p. 3

Married on last Thursday (Dec. 6) MR. WILLIAM PRICE of Fluvanna, to MISS SALLY LEWIS of Goochland
VGWA 13 Dec. 1787, p. 2

Married on Thurs. (Feb. 12) MR. WILLIAM PRICE to MISS LUCY DuVAL, both of this city
VGGA 18 Feb. 1795, p. 3; VGRMA 16 Feb., p. 3

Married May 26th, MR. GEORGE PRITCHETT TO MISS MARY E. KENNEDAY
RE 9 June 1820, p. 3

Married on Thurs. last (22 Feb.) MR. H. PRIDDY to MISS ANN HEWLET
Visitor 24 Feb. 1810, p. 15

Married in Powhatan Co., Oct. 1st, by Rev. John Rice, MAJ. FERDINAND PRINIZY, of Augusta, Ga., to MRS. MARY HUSTON ADAMS, dau. of Rev. John Hyde Saunders of Powhatan
RC 5 Oct. 1814, p. 3

Married on Thurs. (22 nov.) by Rev. John D. Blair, MR. PRITCHARD, Bookseller, to MISS
ANN WILKINSON of Hanover
VA 24 Nov. 1804, p. 3; VA 28 Nov., p. 3; VGGA 28 Nov., p. 3 (says Prichard)

Married on Thurs. last (June 26) MR. THOMAS H. PROSSER to MISS HYLTON, dau. of
Daniel Hylton, Esq., all of Henrico Co.
VA 30 June 1801, p. 3

Married, on 19th, MR. WILLIAM PROSSER of this city to MRS. LETITIA RING of Tuckomon,
King William Co.
VA 27 Jan. 1809, p. 3; Visitor 11 Feb., p. 7

Married on Thurs. last (Oct. 13), COL. JOHN PRYOR of this city to MISS NANCY WHITING
of Gloucester
VGGA 19 Oct. 1796, p. 3

Married April 27th, MR. RICHARD PUGH to MISS POLLY LORREL (In Caroline Co. ?)
RE 9 June 1820, p. 3

Married Dec. 19, 1815, by Rev. Andrew Broaddus, MR. HILARY QUARLES, to MISS POLLY
HICKELL, all of Caroline Co.
VA 13 Jan. 1816, p. 3

Married Sept. 4th at St. Louis, Missouri Terr. by Rev. Giddings, DR. PRYOR QUARLES,
to MISS JOANNA A. EASTON, dau. of Col. Rufus Easton
RE 10 Oct. 1817, p. 3

Married on 3rd Inst. by Rev. John Blair, WILLIAM RADFORD, Esq., Attorney at Law of
Lynchburg, to MISS ELIZABETH MOSELEY, dau. of late Treasurer of this state
Visitor 8 April 1809, p. 38

Married in Albemarle Co., Nov. 15th, by Rev. James C. Wilson, of Staunton, DANIEL
MAYO RAILEY, age 19, to MISS LUCY JANE WATSON, age 15, 2nd dau. of John Watson of
Milton
RE 7 Dec. 1816, p. 3

Married Sat. last (May 7) by Rev. John D. Blair, MR. PETER RALSTON to MRS. JANETT
GILCHRIST, both of this city
RE 10 May 1808, p. 3

Married, DR. JAMES RAMSAY of Norfolk to MRS. MARGARET BOUSH (No marriage date)
VGWA 12 July 1787, p. 3

Married in Williamsburg, PETER RANDOLPH, Esq. of Chatsworth to MISS ELIZABETH SOUTH,
2nd dau. of Col. James Southall of Williamsburg. (No marriage date)
VGWA 5 Feb. 1789, p. 3

Married on 17th Inst., PEYTON RANDOLPH, Esq., of Richmond, to MISS MARIA WARD of
Amelia
VA 25 March 1806, p. 3; RE 25 March, p. 3; VGGA 22 March, p. 3

Married, ROBERT B. RANDOLPH, Esq. of Fauquier, to MISS LAVINIA HETH, eldest dau.
of Capt. Harry Heth of Chesterfield Co. (No marriage date)
VGGA 22 Jan. 1808, p. 3

Married, MR. RYLAND RANDOLPH of Prince Edward to MISS BETSY FRASER of Petersburg
VGRMA 11 July 1795, p. 3

Married Nov. 18th by Rev. John D. Blair, MR. WILLIAM B. RANDOLPH of Henrico Co.,
to MISS SARAH RUTHERFORD of Richmond
RE 22 Nov. 1815, p. 3; VA 22 Nov., p. 3, says Randolph is of Chatsworth, Henrico
Co., says Sarah Rutherfoord, and dau. of Thomas Rutherfoord

Married on May 21st, WILLIAM BEVERLEY RANDOLPH, of Va., to MISS SARAH LINGAN, dau.
of late Gen. Lingan of Md.
VP 29 May 1816, p. 3

Married on Sun. last (May 21) by Rev. Isaac B. Seixas, MR. ISAAC RAPHAEL, to
MISS CLARISSA WOLFE, dau. of Maj. Benjamin Wolfe of Richmond
RE 27 May 1815, p. 3

Married at New Orleans on 25 March, BENJAMIN F. READ, Esq. U.S.N., to MISS CATHERINE
POLLOCK of that city
Visitor 6 May 1809, p. 54

Married Sat. last (June 25) in Norfolk, DR. J.K. READ to MRS. MAXWELL, relict of
Capt. James Maxwell, late of Norfolk
RC 2 July 1796, p. 2; VGRMA 2 July, p. 3

Married on Wed. last (Feb. 17) JOHN READ, Esq., Member House of Delegates last
session from Accomac, to MRS. S. POTTER of this city, relict of Capt. Edmund
Potter, dec'd
VA 19 Feb. 1808, p. 3

Married on 23rd Ult. by Rev. J. D. Blair, MR. JAMES REAT to MISS CATHERINE STROBIA,
both of this city
RE 4 Sept. 1810, p. 3; VA 4 Sept., p. 3

Married Dec. 29, 1816, by Rev. Peter Frans, WALLER REDD of Henry Co., to MISS
KEZIA C. STAPLES of Patrick Co.
RE 7 Jan. 1817, p. 3

Married on Sat. last (April 11) by Rev. John Lindsay, MR. BRAXTON REDFORD to MISS
SARAH ROYSTER, both of this county
VA 13 April 1812, p. 3

Married on Sun. (June 30) by Rev. John Buchanan, MR. FREDERICK J. REDFORD of Petersburg,
to MISS MARY GLYNN of Richmond
RC 4 July 1816, p. 3

Married MR. ZALMA REHINE, Merchant of Richmond, to MISS RACHEL JUDAH, late of New
York. (No marriage date)
VA 21 Jan. 1800, p. 3

Married at New York on 8th Ult. by Rev. Mr. Miller, MR. GEORGE EDWARD CHARLES
FREDERICK MEREDITH ROSE REYNOLDS, to MISS ALLEN HAGEMAN, dau. of Mr. Jacob
Hageman of Baltimore
VA 19 Jan. 1805, p. 3

Married on 2nd Inst., CAPT. WILLIAM REYNOLDS of Henrico to MISS BETSY WHITLOCK of
same
VGGA 13 Oct. 1790, p. 2

Married on 9th Inst., MR. CHARLES RICE, to MISS CATHARINE LEIGH, both of Prince
Edward Co.
VA 29 Feb. 1804, p. 3

Married Aug. 1st by Rev. John H. Rice, MR. MATHEW H. RICE, merchant, to MRS.
CATHARINE CLARKE, all of Richmond
RC 5 Aug. 1818, p. 3

Married on 12th Inst. at the seat of Holenby Dixon, Esq., in Hanover, JOHN RICHARDS
to MISS POLLY DIXON, dau. of late Col. John Dixon of this city
VGGA 23 July 1794, p. 3; VGRMA 17 July

Married on Thurs. (Oct. 8) by Rev. John D. Blair, MR. GEORGE P. RICHARDSON, of
Lynchburg to MISS ANN GOVAN, 3rd dau. of James Govan of Powhite, Hanover Co.
RE 13 Oct. 1818, p. 3

Married on Thurs. last (Feb. 17) at Columbia on James River, MR. SAMUEL RICHARDSON
of Fluvanna Co. to MISS MARIA WASHINGTON, dau. of Harry Washington, dec'd
VGGA 23 Feb. 1803, p. 3

Married Dec. 16th by Rev. John D. Blair, CAPT. WILLIAM H. RICHARDSON of Richmond,
to MISS MARY RANDOLPH of Prince George Co.
RC 19 Dec. 1816, p. 3

Married in Cumberland Co. on 6th Ult., PEYTON RIDDLE, Esq. merchant at Buckingham
C.H. to MISS PATSY WOODSON of Cumberland
VA 9 Sept. 1800, p. 3

Married on Thurs. last (Nov. 13) at seat of Mrs. Seabrook in Hanover Co., MR. JAMES
RIND to MISS SALLY SEABROOK
VGRMA 17 Nov. 1794, p. 3; VGRC 18 Nov.

Married on Sat. last (Feb. 7) MR. THOMAS RITCHIE, Editor of The Enquirer, to
MISS ISABELLA FOUSHEE, dau. of Dr. William Foushee, all of this city
VA 10 Feb. 1807, p. 3

Married on 14th Inst., MR. THOMAS RIVES to MISS FRANCES S. THWEATT, dau. of Mr.
Charles Thweatt, all of Dinwiddie Co.
Visitor 30 Dec. 1809, p. 190

Married March 24th by Rev. Wydown, WILLIAM C. RIVES, of Nelson Co., to MISS JUDITH P. WALKER, dau. of late Col. Francis Walker of Albemarle Co.
RE 27 April 1819, p. 3

Married in Williamsburg, May 20th, by Rev. Dennis, MR. NEWMAN B. ROANE of King William Co., to MISS MARIA G. HANKINS, eldest dau. of Mr. William Hankins of that city
RE 27 May 1817, p. 3

Married on 19th in King & Queen, SPENCER ROANE, Esq., one of Judges of Court of Appeals, to MISS ELIZA HOSKINS, dau. of Col. John Hoskins
VA 31 March 1801, p. 3

Married on Sat. last (May 6) MR. WILLIAM ROANE, eldest son of Hon. Judge Roane, to MISS MARTHA SELDEN, only dau. of Miles Selden, Esq., near this city
RE 9 May 1809, p. 3; VA 12 May, p. 3

Married on Dec. 4th, WILLIAM R. ROANE, Esq., Attorney at Law, of Charles City Co., to MISS MARY B. SMITH of Nottoway Co.
VA 17 Dec. 1812, p. 3

Married on 21st Ult., MR. JOHN ROBERTS, merchant, of Dinwiddie, to MISS JANE S. HORSLEY, eldest dau. of John Horsley, Esq., of Amherst
VA 2 Feb. 1802, p. 3

Married on Thurs. last (April 27) by Rev. Mr. Buchanan, MAJ. JOHN ROBERTS of Culpeper, to MISS LUCY ANNE POLLARD of this city
RE 2 May 1809, p. 3; VA 5 May, p. 3; VGGA 9 May, p. 3, says 3rd dau. of Robert Pollard, Esq. of this city; Visitor 6 May, p. 54

Married in Bath, Steuben Co., N.Y., June 25th, MR. SAMUEL ROBERTS to MISS POLLY CONKRIGHT, after a courtship of only 5 minutes
RC 26 July 1820, p. 3

Married on 25th Ult., MR. ARCHER ROBERTSON to MISS NANCY M.BOOKER of Amelia Co.
RE 2 Aug. 1805, p. 3

Married on 7th Inst., by Rev. Dr. Philips, EDWIN ROBERTSON, Esq., Attorney at Law, of Amelia Co., to MISS ANN BROOKE MENNIS of Liberty, Bedford Co.
RE 21 April 1812, p. 3

Married at Plain Dealing on 20th Inst., by Rev. Mr. Dawson, MR. GEORGE ROBERTSON, merchant, of Richmond, to MISS ANN DYER, dau. of Mr. Samuel Dyer of Albemarle
RE 30 Oct. 1812, p. 3; VA 2 Nov., p. 3

Married April 28th by Rev. Baptist, JOHN ROBERTSON, Attorney General of Va., to MISS ANNE TRENT, 2nd dau. of Mr. John Trent of Cumberland Co.
RE 4 May 1819, p. 3

Married on Thurs. last (March 10) at Hay Market Gardens, by Rev. John D. Blair, MR. JOHN H. ROBERTSON of Richmond to MISS MARTHA H. DAVENPORT
RE 12 March 1814, p. 3

Married on Oct. 19th, MR. WILLIAM ROBERTSON, Attorney at Law, to MISS CHRISTANNA WILLIAMS dau. of Mr. Frederick Williams, all of Petersburg
Visitor 4 Nov. 1809, p. 158

Married on 7th Ult., MR. WILLIAM ROBERTSON, merchant of this city, to MISS NANCY SPOTSWOOD of Petersburg
Visitor 16 Dec. 1809, p. 182

Married on Nov. 19th, MR. JOHN A. ROBERTSON of Amelia to MISS ELIZABETH ROYALL of Nottoway, dau. of John Royall
VGRMA 12 Dec. 1795, p. 3

Married, on April 2nd, MR. A. L. ROBINSON to MISS BETSY HALL, both of King William Co.
RE 10 April 1807, p. 3

Married Dec. 5th by Rev. Rob. B. Semple, MR. GREGORY ROBINSON of King William Co., to MISS LOUISA HILL of Essex Co.
RE 17 Dec. 1816, p. 3

Married on Sat. (July 25) THOMAS R. ROOTES, to MRS. PROSSER, widow of Mr. John Prosser
VP 28 July 1812, p. 3

Married on Tues. last (July 9) by Rev. John Lindsay, MR. GEORGE ROPER to MISS ANN SHARPE, dau. of Mr. Peter Sharpe of Four Mile Creek
RE 12 July 1811, p. 3; VA 11 July, p. 3

Married Aug. 27th in Norfolk, by Rev. Mr. Cowan, MR. GEORGE ROPER to MISS MARIA OVERTON MARSHALL, both of Richmond
RC 3 Aug. 1818, p. 3

Married on Wed. (Aug. 16) by Rev. Hart, MR. GEORGE ROPER, merchant, to MISS SUSAN EVANS all of Richmond
RC 23 Aug. 1820, p. 3

Married in Augusta Co. at Mr. Doolts, by Rev. Steavans, on June 8th, MR. WILLIAM ROPER of Richmond, to MISS CATHARINE TRIMPER, only dau. of Lorrance Trimper of Staunton
RC 13 June 1820, p. 3

Married at Norfolk, MR. STEPHEN P. ROSE, printer, to MISS SARAH A. GIBBONS. (No marriage date)
Visitor 30 Dec. 1809, p. 190

Married May 11th, MR. GEORGE ROTHROCK to MISS MARTHA H. TALIAFERRO
RE 9 June 1820, p. 3

Married on Tues. (May 13th) by Rev. John Mills, MR. FRANCIS ROW of King & Queen Co., to MISS LUCY ANN BUTLER of King William Co.
RE 20 May 1817, p. 3

Married Feb. 24th by Rev. Courtney, MAJ. JAMES G. ROWE of King & Queen Co., to MISS HARRIET HAWKINS of Richmond
RE 27 Feb. 1819, p. 3; RC 27 Feb., p. 3

Married on Wed. last (Dec. 4) MR. MUNGO ROY to MISS NANCY POPE, all of this city
VGGA 6 Dec. 1799, p.3

Married Oct. 21st by Rev. Andrus, WALKER ROY of Caroline Co., to MISS JANE N. MICOU of Essex Co.
RE 12 Nov. 1819, p. 3

Married Jan. 29th by Rev. John B. Hoge, MR. JOHN B. ROYALL, Attorney at Law, of Halifax Co., to MISS PAMELIA W. PRICE, only dau. of Pugh W. Price of Prince Edward Co.
RE 15 Feb. 1817, p. 3

Married on 10th Inst., MR. JAMES ROYSTER of this city, merchant, to MISS POLLY BOHANNON, dau. of Col. Joseph Bohannon of Essex
VA 19 Sept. 1807, p. 2

Married on 14th Inst. by Rev. Robert B. Semple, MR. ROBERT RUFFIN of N.C., to MISS DOLLY HOSKINS, youngest dau. of Col. John Hoskins of King & Queen Co.
RE 21 Dec. 1811, p. 3

Married Oct. 4th by Rev. Mills, WILLIAM RUFFIN, age 18, to MISS PEGGY G. WINFREY, age 15, all of King William Co.
RE 12 Oct. 1816, p. 3

Married Sat. last (Dec. 17) MR. WILLIAM RUSSELL of Williamsburg to MISS MOLLY CAMPBELL of said city
VGWA 24 Dec. 1785, p. 3

Married on 16th Inst. by Rev. John D. Blair, MR. JOHN RUTHERFOORD of Charlotte Co., to MISS ELIZA PRICE of Henrico Co.
VA 22 Aug. 1804, p. 3

Married on 29th Ult., MR. ROBERT RUTHERFORD, of Lynchburg, to MISS ELIZABETH ROYSTER of Goochland
RE 7 May 1811, p. 3

Married on Sat. last (Aug. 21), MR. THOMAS RUTHERORD, merchant of this city, to MISS SALLY WINSTON of Hanover
VGWA 26 Aug. 1790, p. 3

Married Aug. 24th at Mr. Barret Smith's Louisa Co., by Rev. William T. Hiter, MR. SAMUEL A. SALE, to MISS JANE KIMBROUGH
RE 12 Sept. 1820, p. 3

244

Married July 20th by Rev. Chardoin, MR. JOHN SATTERWHITE, to MISS ANN GRAVES, all of Goochland Co.
RE 4 Aug. 1820, p. 3

Married at res. of Maj. Thomas Starke, on Thurs. last (March 19) MR. THOMAS SATTERWHIT of King William Co., to MISS MARTHA T. TALLEY of Hanover
RE 24 March 1812, p. 3; VP 24 March, p. 3

Married in Charleston, Kanawha Co., Va. on May 25th by Rev. Chaddock, MR. ASA L. SAUNDERS, to MISS ANN WRIGHT, both formerly of Richmond
RC 4 July 1820, p. 3; VPRDMA 4 July 1820, p. 3

Married May 9th in North Carolina, LT. JAMES SAUNDERS of U.S. Navy, to MISS HARRIET DAVIS, dau. of Mr. William Davis, printer, of Norfolk
VP 14 May 1814, p. 3

Married at Norfolk, MR. JOHN C. SAUNDERS, merchant, to MISS MARY ANN CAMPBELL. (No marriage date)
Visitor 17 Feb. 1810, p. 11

Married on 1st Inst., by Rev. Mr. Ford, at Mr. John Trevilian's in Goochland, COL. ROBERT SAUNDERS to MISS LUCY MAYO, dau. of late Joseph Mayo, Esq. of Powhatan
RE 13 Feb. 1810, p. 3; VA 13 Feb., p. 3

Married on Thurs. last (Sept. 3) by Rev. Mr. Blair, MR. SAMUEL S. SAUNDERS of Chesterfield to MISS ELIZA Q. DAVIDSON, eldest dau. of Mr. Robert Davidson of this city
RE 11 Sept. 1812, p. 3

Married last evening, MR. GEORGE SAVAGE, printer, to MISS ELIZABETH GATHRIGHT of Henrico
VGGA 22 Nov. 1799, p. 3

Married on 12th Inst., MR. JOHN SAVAGE of Warminster, to MISS AGGY DOBBINS, eldest dau. of George Dobbins, Esq., of Amherst
The Observatory 31 Aug. 1797, p. 3

Married, THOMAS LITTLETON SAVAGE, Esq. of New Kent to MISS MARY BURTON SAVAGE, dau. of Col. Littleton Savage of Northampton Co. (No marriage date)
VGWA 18 June 1789, p. 3; VIC 17 June

Married 29th Nov. MR. WILLAIM SAVAGE of New Kent Co., to MISS SALLY WHITLOCK of Henrico Co.
VGRMA 8 Dec. 1794, p. 3

Married Dec. 18, 1816, in Buncombe Co., N.C., MR. LEWIS SAWYERS, SR., age 80, to MRS. HANNAH POSTON, age 90, both of Greene Co., Tenn.
VP 2 Jan. 1817, p.3

Married Dec. 9th by Rev. Willis, MR. ROBERT B. SAYRES, merchant, of Richmond, to
MISS FRANCES E. ALLEN, dau. of Christian Allen of Henrico Co.
RC 13 Dec. 1819, p. 3

Married, MR. SAMUEL SCHERER to MISS HANNAH TANKARD, both of this town, (No marriage
date)
VGWA 20 April, 1782, p. 3

Married on Thurs. last (July 26) MR. JAMES SCOTT, JR. of Manchester, Merchant, to
MISS PATSEY GOODE, 2nd dau. of Col. Robert Goode of Whitby
VGGA 1 Aug. 1804, p. 3

Married on 25th Ult., by Rev. J. D. Blair, MR. SAMUEL SCOTT to MISS ELIZABETH SEATON
RE 5 March 1813, p. 3; VA 8 March, p. 3, says married on 5th Ult.

Married on Sun. (Dec. 20) MR. WILLIAM SCOTT, son of Maj. Joseph Scott, Marshal of
Eastern District of Va., to MISS SALLY MITCHELL, only dau. of Robert Mitchell, Esq.
of this city
VGGA 22 Dec. 1801, p. 3

Married at Bellville on Tues. (March 11) MAJ-GEN. WINFIELD SCOTT to MISS MARIA MAYO,
eldest dau. of Col. John Mayo
VP 13 March 1817, p. 3; RC 13 March, p. 3

Married at Raleigh on 30th Ult., MR. WILLIAM W. SEATON, Printer, to MISS SARAH GALES,
dau. of Joseph Gales, Esq., Printer of the State of North Carolina
Visitor 8 April 1809, p. 38

Married in Urbanna on 16th Inst., by Rev. Henry Heffernan, MAJ. RICHARD M. SEGAR,
of Wood Green, to MISS MARY ROANE, dau. of late col. Thomas Roane of Roseberry, all
of Middlesex Co.
RE 25 Feb. 1812, p. 3

Married on Wed. last (May 31) by Rev. Isaac H. Judah, MR. I.B. SEXIAS, to MISS
REBECCA JUDAH, both of this city
Visitor 3 June 1809, p. 70.

Married Thurs. last (June 21) by Rev. James Whitehead, MR. CARY SELDEN to MISS
FRANCES LOYALL, eldest dau. of George Loyall of this borough (Norfolk)
VA 27 June 1804, p. 3

Married Sept. 24th at Mr. Brockenbrough's near Univ. of Va., by Rev. Hatch,
JOSEPH SELDEN, Judge of Arkansas Terr., to MISS HARRIET GRAY of Albemarle Co.
RE 17 Oct. 1820, p. 2; RC 17 Oct., p. 3

Married on 2nd Inst., MR. NATHANIEL SELDEN to MISS CATHERINE MASON, both of Powhatan
VA 7 Oct. 1800, p. 3

Married in Petersburg at res. of Mr. P. Lynch, on Wed. (Oct. 18) MR. MATTHEW SEMPLE, merchant, of Richmond, to MISS CATHARINE BROADY of Petersburg
RE   20 Oct. 1820, p. 3

Married on 30th Ult., DANIEL SHEFFEY, Esq., Congressman from Va., to MISS MARIA HANSON, dau. of Samuel Hanson, Esq. of this city
VA   10 Feb. 1812, p. 3

Married Feb. 2nd by Rev. Griffeth Dickenson, MR. ABRAHAM C. SHELTON of Pittsylvania Co., to MISS MARY CLAIBORNE of Franklin
RE   27 Feb. 1819, p. 3

Married on Sat. last (March 21) MR. JOHN SHELTON, Merchant, to MISS SARAH BOYCE, both of this city
VA   24 March 1807, p. 3; RE   24 March, p. 3

Married on Thurs. last (Nov. 21) MR. NATHANIEL SHEPARD to MISS POLLY PENDLETON, both of this city
VGGA   26 Nov. 1799, p. 3

Married Dec. 26th by Rev. John D. Blair, MR. SAMUEL SHEPHERD, to MISS MARIA, dau. of Augustine Davis of Richmond
RE   29 Dec. 1818, p. 3

Married on Sat. last (Dec. 22) DR. JOSEPH SHEPPARD to MISS JUDITH BROWN, eldest dau. of John Brown, Esq. of this city
VGGA   26 Dec. 1792, p. 2

Married on Thurs. last (March 17) MR. NATHANIEL SHEPPARD of this city to MISS NANCY BROWN, dau. of John Brown, Esq. of same
RC   22 March 1796, p. 3; VGGA   23 March, p. 3; VGRMA   19 March, p. 3

Married on Sat. last (March 25) MR. SAMUEL SHEPPARD to MISS POLLY MOSS, both of this city
VA   31 March 1797, p. 2; VGGA   29 March, p. 3

Married lately in New Kent Co., MICHAEL SHERMAN, age 97, to MISS ELIZA POINDEXTER, age 14
The Recorder   27 March 1802, p. 3

Married, MR. JAMES SHIELD, JR. of James City to MISS PATTY VAUGHAN of Goochland. (No marriage date)
VGWA 12 Jan. 1782, p. 2

Married Christmas 1818, by Rev. Paxton, HAMILTON SHIELDS, one of Editors of American Beacon, to MISS HARRIET ROGERS eldest dau. of Mr. William Rogers, all of Norfolk
RE   2 Jan. 1819, p. 3

Married at Norfolk on Sun. (Nov. 15) by Rev. Cornelius, MR. WILLIAM C. SHIELDS, one of editors of The American Beacon, to MISS ELIZABETH FINCH, dau. of Mr. George Finch of Norfolk
RE 20 Nov. 1818, p. 3; VP 19 Nov. p. 3

Married on Sat. (Jan. 24) MR. HENRY S. SHORE to MISS PATSEY WINSTON, both of this city
VGGA 28 Jan. 1795, p. 3; VGRMA 26 Jan., p. 3

Married on 2nd Inst., MR. HENRY S. SHORE of this city to MISS CATHARINE WINSTON, dau. of Col. William O. Winston of Hanover
VA 8 Aug. 1804, p. 3; VGGA 11 Aug., p. 2

Married at Norwich, Conn, CHARLES SIGOURNEY of Hartford, Conn, to MISS LYDIA HUNTLY, the elegant Conn. poetess. (No marriage date)
RC 21 Aug. 1819, p. 3

Married at Lebanon, BENJAMIN SILLIMAN, Esq., Prof. of Chem & Nat. Hist. at Yale, to MISS HARRIOT TRUMBULL, dau. of late Gov. Trumbull of Conn.
Visitor 21 Oct. 1809, p. 150

Married June 22nd at Mr. John Penn's in Amherst Co., by Rev. William Duncan, MR. JOHN SIMONTON from the bogs of Ireland, to MISS SARAH PEACOCK of Amherst Co.
RC 6 July 1820, p. 3

Married on 15th Inst., by Rev. Mr. Hurt, JOHN SIMS, Esq., to MARIA W. CLARK, eldest dau. of Col. John Clark of Halifax Co.
RE 28 Aug. 1810, p. 3

Married in Halifax Co., on 21st Ult., CAPT. ARTHUR SINCLAIR, U.S.N. to MISS SARAH S. KENNON, dau. of late Gen. Richard Kennon
RE 6 Feb. 1810, p. 3

Married on 9th Inst., CAPT. SINGLETON of this city to MRS. RANDOLPH of Wilton
IC 22 Oct. 1788, p. 3; VGWA 16 Oct., 1788

Married June 15th in Caroline Co., by Rev. A. Walke, MR. REUBEN M. SIZER, merchant, of Richmond, to MISS CATHARINE H. DICKINSON, youngest dau. of Thos. Dickinson of that county
RE 27 June 1820, p. 3; RC 23 June, p. 3

Married on Sat. last (Dec. 14) HENRY SKIPWITH, Esq. of Cumberland, to MRS. ELIZABETH HILL DUNBAR, all of City of Williamsburg
VGGA 17 Dec. 1799, p. 3

Married at Norfolk by Rev. Bishop Moore, HUMBERTSON SKIPWITH, of Mecklenburg Co., to MISS SARAH S. NIVISON, 2nd dau. of Col. John Nivison of Norfolk (No death date)
RE 17 Nov. 1818, p. 3

Married, SIR PEYTON SKIPWITH of Mill Farm, Mecklenburg Co., to MISS MILLER, lately arrived from Great Britain. (No marriage date)
IC 15 Oct. 1788, p. 3; VGWA 16 Oct., 1788

Married on 20th Ult. at Dungeness on Cumberland Ireland, St. Marys, Ga., PEYTON SKIPWITH, JUN'R, Esq., son of Sir Peyton Skipwith, Baronet of Va., to MISS CORNELIA LOTT GREENE, dau. of late Nathaniel Greene, Maj-Gen. U.S.
VGGA 26 May 1802, p. 3

Married at Passawunk, Maine, MR. SAMUEL SMART, to MISS SALLY PAYNE. (No marriage date)
VA 17 March 1807, p. 3

Married on 10th Inst. (Ult.) FRANCIS SMITH, Esq., Attorney at Law, to MISS ELIZA HENRY RUSSELL, dau. of late Gen. Wm. Russell, late of Washington Co.
VA 1 Feb. 1804, p. 3

Married on 7th Inst. by Rev. Stephen Bovell, CAPT. FRANCIS SMITH, to MRS. MARY KING, both of Abingdon
RE 29 March 1811, p. 3

Married on Thurs. last (June 9) by Rev. Mr. Ellis, GEORGE WILLIAM SMITH, Esq., Attorney at Law & Member of the Privy Council of this state, to MRS. JONES, relict of late Meriwether Jones, all of this city
VA 14 June 1808, p. 3

Married Oct. 5th by Rev. William H. Hart, GEORGE WILLIAM SMITH of Richmond, to MISS ANN B. CAMPBELL, dau. of John Campbell of Westmoreland Co.
RE 13 Oct. 1820, p. 3; RC 11 Oct., p. 2

Married on 27th Inst., by Rev. Mr. Logan, GRANVILLE SMITH, Esq., to MISS MARIANNA L. PLEASANTS, dau. of James Pleasants, Esq., of Goochland Co.
RE 30 Oct. 1812, p. 3; VA 2 Nov., p. 3

Married, MR. JOHN SMITH to MISS SALLY WALLER, youngest dau. of Benjamin Waller, Esq. late of Williamsburg
VGWA 24 Jan. 1788, p. 3

Married on Sat. last (Dec. 21) MR. JOHN SMITH to MISS CAROLINE CRUTCHFIELD
VGGA 25 Dec. 1804, p. 3

Married Nov. 18th by Rev. King in Staunton, MR. JOSEPH SMITH, merchant, to MISS ANN PRICE, formerly of Baltimore
RE 2 Dec. 1817, p. 3

Married on April 30th by Rev. John Bracken, DR. PHILLIP SMITH of Williamsburg, to MISS LOUISA C. CHRISTIAN, only dau. of late Col. John Christian of Charles City Co.
RC 4 May 1815, p. 3

Married, at Washington City, HON. SAMUEL SMITH, Member of Congress, from Pa., to MISS SUSAN GRAYSON of that city, dau. of late Richard Spencer Grayson of Va.
Visitor 27 Jan. 1810, p. 206

Married Thurs. last (March 20) MR. THOMAS SMITH of Louisa to MISS BETSY RUSSELL, dau. of Maj. John Russell of Hanover
VA 25 March 1800, p. 3

Married on Fri. last (Dec. 28, 1804) by Rev. James M'Conochie, MR. YEAMANS SMITH of Richmond to MISS NANCY MYREE of Spotsylvania Co.
RE 3 Jan. 1805, p. 3

Married Nov. 24th in Botetourt Co., CAPT. HAROLD SMYTHE, late of U.S. Army, to MISS ANN BOWYER, dau. of Col. Henry Bowyer of that county
VP 30 Nov. 1816, p. 3

Married Nov. 16th by Rev. Bernard Reynolds, CAPT. JESSE SNEED of Hanover, to MISS JANE MARIA JOHNSON, dau. of Mrs. Mary Johnson of Henrico
RE 19 Nov. 1819, p. 3

Married on May 1st, REV. JOHN SNIPES to MISS POLLY GILL, 2nd dau. of Col. David Gill, all of Charles City Co.
VA 10 May 1808, p. 3

Married Friday last (June 22) MISS FRANCES SOUTHALL, dau. of Col. James Southall of Williamsburg to MR. WILLIAM DAINGERFIELD of Spotsylvania Co.
VGWA 28 June 1787, p. 3

Married, PHILIP SOUTHALL, Esq. of this city to MISS JENNY NEILSON of Urbana. (No marriage date)
IC 6 Aug. 1788, p. 3; VGWA says Sun. Sen'night (Sept. 14)

Married on 27th Ult. MR. JOHN SPEARS to MISS ELIZABETH MILLER, both of Powhatan Co.
VA 4 Sept. 1801, p. 3

Married on 13th Ult., MR. JOHN JAMES SPEED, of Gennessee, N.Y., to MISS POLLY NICOLSON of Mecklenburg, Va.
VP 12 March 1811, p. 3

Married on Sat. (Sept. 26) MR. CHARLES SPENCER, merchant, to MISS ELIZABETH CARTER, both of this place
VGRMA 1 Oct. 1795, p. 3

Married Feb. 26th by Rev. William Todd, MR. ROBERT M. SPENCER, merchant, to MISS LOUISA, eldest dau. of John SOUTHGATE, all of King & Queen Co.
RE 14 March 1820, p. 3

Married on Thurs. last (Oct. 29) MR. JOHN SPOTSWOOD, Jr. of Fredericksburg to MISS POLLY GOODE, eldest dau. of Hon. Col. Robert Goode
VGGA 4 Nov. 1795, p. 3; VGRMA 5 Nov., p. 3

Married on 27th Nov. by Rev. Mr. Buchanan, MR. EDWARD CARTER STANARD of Albemarle
Co. to MISS REBECCA CARTER of this city
VA 2 Dec. 1806, p. 2; RE 28 Nov., p. 3

Married in Edgemont, N.H., MR. J. STANLEY, to ELLEN C. HILL, both of Society of
Shakers
RC 18 Jan. 1820, p. 3

Married March 25th by Rev. Woolfolk in Caroline Co., CAPT. BOWLING STARKE of
Hanover Co., to MISS ELIZA G. NEW, dau. of Col. Anthony New of Ky.
RE 30 March 1819, p. 3

Married on 17th Inst., at res. of Maj. Thos. Starke, CAPT. WILLIAM STARKE, to
MISS SUSAN L. TATE, both of Hanover Co.
RE 26 March 1813, p. 3

Married Dec. 23rd by Rev. Benj. Watkins, MR. JONAH STARR, formerly of Danbury, Conn.
to MISS CYNTHIA CARY, eldest dau. of Rev. Peter M. Cary of Chesterfield Co.
RE 29 Dec. 1818, p. 3

Married Jan. 31st by Rev. John Courtney, MR. GEORGE STEEL, to MISS ELIZABETH DORSETT
all of Richmond
RC 2 Feb. 1820, p. 3

Married July 19th, by Rev. J. Chardoin, MR. FRANCIS F. STEGER to MISS ANN P. CLEMENT
of Goochland Co.
RE 4 Aug. 1820, p. 3

Married on Sat. last by Rev. Mr. Blair (Sat. was March 30), MR. BENJAMIN STETSON,
merchant, to MISS NANCY LYLE, all of this place
RE 2 April 1805, p. 3; VA 3 April, p. 3

Married by Rev. Dawson in Albemarle Co., on Oct. 8th, ANDREW STEVENSON of Richmond,
to MISS SARAH COLES, dau. of Col. John Coles, dec'd
RE 19 Oct. 1816, p. 3; VP 18 Oct., p. 3; RC 18 Oct., p. 3

Married in Staunton on June 28th by Rev. Mr. Ring, JAMES STEVENSON, alias STAUNTON,
age 100, to ELIZABETH CUMMINS, age 62
Visitor 9 Sept. 1809, p. 127

Married Thurs. last (Feb. 26) MR. JOHN STEWART, merchant, to MISS KATEY HAIR, both
of this city
VGAA 28 Feb. 1784, p. 3

Married, BASSETT STITH, Esq. of this city, merchant, to MISS POLLY LONG of North
Carolina, a lady of large fortune.(No marriage date)

Married on Thurs. last (June 2) MR. JOHN ST. JOHN, to MISS HARRIETT LOGAN, both
of this city
VA 7 June 1808, p. 3; VGGA 10 June, p. 3

Married on Sat. last (June 18) MR. GERVAS STORRS of Henrico, to MISS PATSEY TRUEHEART
of Hanover
VGRMA 22 June 1796, p. 2

Married Sept. 30th by Rev. John D. Blair, MR. JOSHUA STORRS of Henrico Co., to MISS
MARY SEMPLE, dau. of Judge James Semple of Williamsburg
RE 5 Oct. 1819, p. 3; RC 4 Oct., p. 3

Married on 15th Ult. in Phila., MR. EBENEZER STOTT, merchant, of Petersburg, to MISS
ELIZA PHILE, dau. of Frederick Phile, Esq., Navel Officer for the Port of Phila.
VGWA 3 Sept. 1789, p. 3

Married at Poughkeepsie, N.Y., MASTER PETER I. STOUTENBURGH, 16, to MISS POLLY
BRIGGS, 14, both of Clinton
VA 18 April 1804, p. 3

Married in this city Fri. last (Nov. 22) GEORGE H. STRAS, Esq. to MRS. SOUTHALL,
widow of late Maj. Stephen Southall
VA 26 Nov. 1799, p. 3; VGGA 26 Nov., p. 3

Married on 23rd Inst. (Ult.) by Rev. John D. Blair, MR. ANTHONY STREET, to MISS
SUSAN GOODALL, both of Hanover Co.
RE 4 April 1809, p. 3; Visitor 8 April, p. 38

Married on 2nd Inst., by Rev. J. D. Blair, MR. JOHN HENRY STROBIA, to MISS ANN MARIA
LAMBERT, eldest dau. of Col. D. Lambert, all of this city
RE 8 June 1810, p. 3; VA 12 June, p. 2; VP 8 June, p. 2

Married at Lexington, Ky., MR. JOHN STRONG to MISS SALLY SHEAFORD. (No marriage
date)
VA 20 Feb. 1805, p. 3)

Married on 20th Ult. in Fairfax Co., DR. STUART of Town of Alexandria to MRS. CUSTIS,
relict of late John Parke Custis, Esq.
VGWA 6 Dec. 1783, p. 3

Married on 18th Inst., by Rev. A. Foster, MR. JOHN S. STUBBS, SR., by MRS. ISABELLA
C. JONES, lately of Gloucester Co.
RE 22 July 1815, p. 3

Married on 6th Inst., DR. JOHN T. SWANN of Goochland to MRS. JANE J. THOMPSON of
Rocky Mills
VA 7 Dec. 1803, p. 3

Married on 24th Inst., by Rev. John D. Blair, MR. FORTUNATUS SYDNOR of Lynchburg,
to MISS ELIZABETH MOSBY of this city
RE 29 Nov. 1814, p. 3

Married Feb. 24 by Rev. Galachot, MR. RICHARD AVERY TAYLOR of James City Co., but late of Richmond City, to MISS ANN ELLIOTT of Richmond
RE 31 March 1820, p. 3

Married on Sat. last (May 10) by Rev. Mr. Ellis, MR. RICHARDSON TAYLOR, to MISS LUCY CARTER, both of this city
VGGA 14 May 1806, p. 3

Married in Brunswick Co., on 14th Inst., MR. ROBERT A. TAYLOR, merchant, of Louisberg to MISS MARGARET SAUNDERS of Brunswick
Visitor 3 March 1810, p. 19

Married at Alexandria on 6th Inst., by Rev. Thomas Davis, ROBERT I. TAYLOR, Esq. to MISS MARIA M. ROSE, both of that place
VGGA 12 March 1806, p. 3

Married on Thurs. (June 8) MR. THOMAS TAYLOR to MRS. J. SHEPPARD, both of this city
VGGA 14 June 1797, p. 3

Married by Rev. Mr. Buchanan, on Sun. last (April 12) THOMAS TAYLOR, Esq. to MISS LUCY SINGLETON, both of this city
RE 17 April 1807, p. 3; VGGA 15 April, p. 3

Married on Thurs. last (Aug. 29) MR. WILLIAM D. TAYLOR of Hanover to MISS SALLY BURNLEY of Orange Co.
VGGA 4 Sept. 1805, p. 2

Married Sept. 20th at Mr. James Marshalls in Frederick Co., by Rev. Lemon, MR. WILLIA D. TAYLOR of Hanover Co., to MISS ELIZA A. MARSHALL of Fauquier Co.
RE 15 Oct. 1819, p. 3

Married on Tues. last (Aug. 7) DR. TAZEWELL of Williamsburg to MISS P. TANNER
RE 11 Aug. 1804, p. 3

Married Dec. 19th by Rev. Braggs, LT. WILLIAM T. TEMPLE, U.S.N., to MISS LUCY R. TOMPKINS of Caroline Co.
RE 28 Dec. 1820, p. 3

Married, MR. CHARLES TERRELL of this city, to MISS CORDELIA UPSHAW of Essex Co.
(No marriage date)
RE 25 May 1810, p. 3

Married at Friends Meeting House in this city Wed. last (May 7) MR. SAMUEL TERRELL, merchant, of Oxford, Caroline Co., to MISS ELIZABETH HARRIS of this city
VA 9 May 1800, p. 3

Married on 22nd Inst., PAUL THILMAN, Esq., to MISS BARBARA O. WINSTON, both of Hanover
VA 26 May 1797, p. 3

Married on 27th Ult., by Rev. Mr. Buchanan, MR. NORBORNE K. THOMAS, to MISS ELIZA
ANN BURWELL, dau. of Col. Lewis Burwell, all of this city
RE 6 March 1812, p. 3

Married, MR. URIAH THOMAS, 65, to MISS RACHEL JONES, 15. (No marriage date)
VA 21 April 1807, p. 3

Married MR. THOMPSON from Madeira to MISS NANCY PLEASANTS, dau. of Mr. Robert
Pleasants of Henrico Co.
VGIC 22 May 1784, p. 3

Married at Rocky Mills in Hanover Co., on 2nd Inst., THOMAS THOMPSON, Esq., of
this city to MISS JANE ISABELLA SYME, dau. of Col John Syme
VGGA 13 May 1795, p. 3; VGRMA 7 May, p. 2; VGRC 5 May, p. 2

Married on 1st Inst., CAPT. WILLIAM THOMSON of Hanover, age 81, to MRS. TATE OF
Richmond, age 66
VA 4 April 1800, p. 3

Married Tues. last (Feb. 8) in Petersburg, WILLIAM THOMSON, Esq., Attorney at Law,
of Manchester, to MISS HOLT, of that town
VA 12 Feb. 1803, p. 3; Recorder 9 Feb., p. 2 (says Thompson and of Mass. not
Manchester to Miss Elizabeth Holt)

Married on 25th Inst. by Rev. John Buchanan, DR. PHILIP THORNTON to MISS CAROLINE
R. HOMASSEL, all of this city
RE 28 April 1812, p. 3; VA 30 April, p. 3; VP 1 May, p. 3

Married May 21st, MR. PHILIP THORNTON to MISS ELIZABETH CANNON
RE 9 June 1820, p. 3

Married Sat. last (June 9) at seat of Col. James Innes near this city, PRESLEY
THORNTON, Esq. to MISS SALLY INNES, dau. of Harry Innes, Esq.
VGGA 13 June 1792, p. 3; *VGGA of 20 June says marriage was on 2nd June and
Sally married Francis Thornton (Henrico Co. records say Francis Thornton. Marriage
Bond dated June 1)

Married at Severn House, Gloucester Co., on April 29th, by Rev. Kisher, THOMAS
THROCKMORTON, Esq., to MISS JULIA LEWIS, youngest dau. of Col. Warner Lewis
of Warner Hall
RE 10 May 1815, p. 3

Married in Gloucester Co., Jan. 13th, by Rev. Wm. Tood, EMANUEL J. THRUSTON, to
MISS CATHERINE PENDLETON COOKE, both of that county
RE 20 Jan. 1820, p. 3

Married in Bradford, Mass., HON. NATHANIEL THRUSTON, one of Senators of Essex,
to MISS FLETCHER, his 7th wife
Visitor 12 Aug. 1809, p. 110

Married, at Capt. Thomas Holcombe's in Lynchburg, on Nov. 13th, by Rev. Wm. S. Reid,
FORTUNATUS SYDNOR, Cashier of Bank of Va. at Lynchburg, to MISS ELIZA ROYALL, dau.
of late Joseph Royall of Amelia Co.
RE 18 Nov. 1817, p. 3

Married, REV. ELKANA TALLEY to MRS. ANDERSON, relict of Col. John Anderson of Hanove
VGWA 12 Feb. 1789, p. 3

Married July 4th by the Rev. Blair, MR. JOHN TALLEY, eldest son of Mr. William Talle
of Hanover Co., to MISS SARAH B. WILLIAMSON, dau. of Mr. John Williamson, dec'd of
Henrico Co.
RE 10 July 1816, p. 3

Married on Sat. last (Nov. 30) by Rev. John D. Blair, MR. JAMES TALLIAFERRO, mercha
of this city, to MISS PATSEY PRICE of this county
VGGA 4 Dec. 1805, p. 3

Married on Tues. last (July 22) MR. BENJAMIN TATE of this city to MRS. ANNA POE of
Henrico
VGRMA 24 July 1794, p. 3

Married on Sat. (Nov. 21) BENNETT TAYLOR, Esq. Attorney at Law to MISS SUSAN RANDOL
eldest dau. of Edmund Randolph, Esq. all of this city
VA 27 Nov. 1801, p. 3; VGGA 24 Nov., p. 3

Married on Wed. (Nov. 20) by Rev. John D. Blair, MR. EDMUND TAYLOR of Richmond, to
MISS FRANCES ANN RICHARDSON of Hanover Co.
RE 23 Nov. 1816, p. 3; VP 25 Nov., p. 3; RC 23 Nov., p. 3, says she is dau. of
Capt. John Allen Richardson of Hanover Co.

Married Sept. 7th by Rev. Wills, MR. EDMUND TAYLOR of Osbornes, Chesterfield Co.
to MISS DAMARIS REDFORD, dau. of late Milner Redford of Henrico Co.
RC 11 Sept. 1820, p. 3

Married on 11th Ult,, GEORGE C. TAYLOR, Esq. of Orange Co., to MISS ELIZA DIXON
of Caroline
VA 13 June 1800, p. 3

Married on Sat. last (Dec. 21), GEORGE KEITH TAYLOR, Esq., representative from
Prince George Co., in the Gen. Assembly, to MISS JANE MARSHALL of this city
VA 27 Dec. 1799, p. 2; VGGA 24 Dec., p. 3

Married on Tues. last (April 28) MR. JAMES TAYLOR of this city, to MISS MARIA GORDO
of Occoquan
VA 1 May 1807, p. 3; RE 1 May, p. 3, says married by Rev. John Buchanan

Married at Suffolk, last Wed. (Dec. 30, 1812) REV. R. L. TAYLOR of Richmond, to MIS
MARY KRAUTH of Suffolk
VP 5 Jan. 1813, p. 3

Married, GEORGE T. TILTON, age 76, to MISS MARY LUCUS, age 18. (No marriage date)
Bride is daughter of his former wife.
RC 5 Jan. 1819, p. 3

Married at Middletown, Mass. on 5th Ult., MR. THOMAS TILTON, age 76, to MARY LUCAS,
age 13. She is granddaughter of Thomas Tilton's former wife.
VA 4 April 1800, p. 3

Married in N.C. on Mon. last (Jan. 26) MR. DAVID TIMBERLAKE to MISS SARAH HILL,
only dau. of James Hill of Hanover Co.
RE 31 Jan. 1807, p. 3; VGGA 31 Jan., p. 3

Married on 14th Inst., by Rev. Reuben Ford, MR. GRANVILLE TIMBERLAKE, to MISS MARY
RICHARDSON, all of Hanover Co.
RE 29 May 1812, p. 3

Married on Sun. last (Nov. 30) MR. DANIEL TIMMINGS to MISS ELIZABETH RAILEY of this
city
VGRMA 4 Dec. 1794, p. 3

Married on Tues. last (July 12) PETER TINSLEY, Esq., to MISS MARIA BROWN, dau.
of John Brown, Esq., all of this city
VGGA 16 July 1803, p. 3

Married Nov. 27th at res. of Mrs. Bryan in York Co., by Rev. John D. Blair, MR.
THOMAS G. TINSLEY of Hanover Co., to MISS HARRIET W. BRYAN
RE 7 Dec. 1820, p. 3; RC 6 Dec., p. 2

Married on 28th Ult., MR. HENRY TOLER of this city, merchant, to MISS CYNTHIA
SOUTHALL
VGRMA 15 April 1793, p. 3

Married on Thurs. last (Feb. 8) by Rev. Mr. Blair, MR. JOHN TOMPKINS, merchant,
to MISS ELVIRA POE, all of this city
RE 13 Feb. 1810, p. 3; VA 9 Feb., p. 3; Visitor 10 Feb., p. 6

Married Nov. 16th by Rev. John D. Blair, MR. ROBERT TOMPKINS of Albemarle Co., to
MISS ELIZABETH T. STAPLES, dau. of Maj. John Staples of Richmond
RC 18 Nov. 1820, p. 3

Married at Mount Air on Aug. 6th, by Rev. Dawson, MR. WILLIAM TOMPKINS to MISS ANN
HUDSON, 2nd dau. of Col. Christopher Hudson, all of Albemarle Co.
RE 17 Aug. 1816, p. 3

Married on 15th Inst., MR. GEORGE TRANT, Attorney at Law, to MISS MARY E. WALKER,
both of King William Co.
RE 21 Dec. 1809, p. 3; Visitor 30 Dec., p. 190

Married on 17th Inst. by Rev. Christopher McRae, MR. ALEXANDER TRENT of Cumberland
Co., to MISS MARY WILSON, dau. of Mr. James Wilson of Buckingham
VA 26 Sept. 1807, p. 3

Married, DR. JOSEPH TRENT, of this city to MISS NANCY REYNOLDS of New Kent Co. (No marriage date)
RE 26 May 1809, p. 3; VA 23 May, p. 3, says married Thurs. last (May 18) says ANN REYNOLD; VGGA 23 May, p. 3, says REYNOLDS; Visitor 3 June, p. 70

Married on Wed. (13 Jan.) by Rev. Mr. Bryce, MR. JEFFERSON E. TRICE, to MISS CATHARINE, daughter of Mr. David ANDERSON, all of Richmond
RC 16 Jan. 1819, p. 3

Married on 7th Inst., by Rev. Mr. Blair, MR. MAXWELL TROKES, merchant, of New York, to MRS. SARAH H. GOODE of Manchester
RE 20 Aug. 1813, p. 3

Married on Thurs. last (Nov. 13) MR. BARTHOLOMEW TRUEHEART to MISS POLLY SEABROOK at seat of Mrs. Seabrook in Hanover
VGRMA 17 Nov. 1794, p. 3; VGRC 18 Nov.

Married on Thurs. (Dec. 22) by Rev. John D. Blair, MR. DANIEL TRUEHEART, printer, to MISS MARIA RIND, both of Richmond
VP 24 Dec. 1814, p. 3

Married at Marion Hill, Aug. 31st, by Rev. John D. Blair, MR. DANIEL TRUEHEART, one of proprietors of the Richmond Complier, to MISS ELIZABETH SEABROOKE, dau. of John Seabrooke
RE 1 Sept. 1820, p. 3; RC 2 Sept., p. 3; VPRDMA 2 Sept., p. 3

Married MR. GEORGE WASHINGTON TRUEHEART of Hanover to MISS FANNY OVERTON, dau. of Col. John Overton of Louisa (No marriage date)
VA 10 Feb. 1801, p. 3

Married on 23rd Ult, JAMES H. TUCKER, Esq. merchant, of Norfolk, to MISS ANNE R. TODD eldest dau. of Mr. Todd of Smithfield
Visitor 12 Aug. 1809, p. 110

Married Thurs. last (Jan. 28) CAPT. EDMUND TUNSTAL, one of Representatives from Pittsylvania Co., to MRS. ELIZABETH SMITH, widow of late Col. Wm. Smith of Chester-field
VA 2 Feb. 1802, p. 3

Married, MR. JOHN TURBERVILLE of Hickory Hill to Mrs. ANN BALLENDINE, both of Westmoreland Co. (No marriage date)
VGWA 4 Jan. 1793, p. 3

Married on 6th Inst., MR. JAMES TURNER, to MRS. MARY KING, all of King William Co.
RE 20 March 1810, p. 3; Visitor 17 March, p. 27, says Turner is of Bath Co.

Married on Tues. last (April 23) by Rev. John D. Blair, MR. JESSE H. TURNER to MISS HARRIETT BURR
RE 26 April 1811, p. 3; VA 29 April, p. 3

Married on 17th Inst., by Rev. Mr. Blair, MR. ARCHER TURPIN of Cumberland Co. to MISS REBECCA SMITH, only dau. of Samuel Smith, dec'd, of Chesterfield
VA 22 March 1808, p. 3

Married May 23rd by Rev. Louis Chardoin, MR. HENRY TURPIN to MISS LUCY SATTERWHITE of Goochland Co.
RE 4 Aug. 1820, p. 3

Married on Sat. last (May 10) by Rev. John D. Blair, MR. JOHN TURPIN to MISS HARRIET GUNN, both of Henrico Co.
VGGA 14 May 1806, p. 3

Married on 12th Inst., MR. JOHN TURPIN of Ga. to MISS SARAH FINNEY of this county
VA 22 March 1808, p. 3

Married on Sat. last (Dec. 10) DR. PHILIP TURPIN to MRS. McCALLUM, relict of Mr. Daniel McCallum of Osbornes
VA 12 Dec. 1796, p. 3

Married 29th last month, JOHN TYLER, Esq., Attorney at Law of Charles City Co., to MISS LETITIA CHRISTIAN, 3rd dau. of Robert Christian, Esq. of New Kent
RE 13 April 1813, p. 3; VA 12 April, p.3

Married, COL. THOMAS UNDERWOOD of Goochland to MISS JANE DANDRIDGE of Hanover, on 15th Inst.
VGRMA 26 Jan. 1795, p. 3

Married on 13th Inst. MR. THOMAS UNDERWOOD to MISS ELIZA SOUTHALL, both of this city
VA 15 May 1802, p. 3

Married on 25th Nov. by Rev. Boggs, JOHN HORACE UPSHAW, Esq., a member of Senate of Va., to MISS LUCY ELIZA T. BAYLOR, dau. of late John Baylor of New Market
RE 5 Dec. 1809, p. 3; VA 5 Dec., p. 3; Visitor 16 Dec., p. 182

Married Feb. 26th, ABEL P. UPSHUR of City of Richmond, to MISS E.W. DENNIS of Princess Anne, Md.
RE 25 March 1817, p. 3; VP 25 March, p. 3

Married on Sun. last (Dec. 23) by Rev. John D. Blair, LITTLETON UPSHUR, Esq. a senator from Northampton, to MISS MARY WILSON, 2nd dau. of Thomas Wilson, Esq. of this city
VP 25 Dec. 1810, p.3

Married on 11th Inst., MR. JACOB VALENTINE to MISS MARIA WILLIAMSON, both of this city
RE 23 April 1811, p. 3

Married on Thurs. (June 29) by Rev. John D. Blair, MR. MANN S. VALENTINE of Richmond to MISS ELIZABETH MOSBY, dau. of Benjamin Mosby of Henrico Co.
RC 3 July 1820, p. 3

Married at Vernon, N.J. Sept. 28th by Rev. Teasdale, MR. JOHN VANDEGRAFF, merchant, to MISS SARAH EDSALL, dau. of Col. Richard Edsall, all of that place
RC 8 Oct. 1816, p. 3

Married March 25th by Rev. Matthew P. Wallace, MR. WILLIAM VANDERGRIFF, merchant, of Hamilton, late of Richmond, to MISS MARGARET DOUGLASS, dau. of William Douglass, all of Butler Co., Ohio
RC 16 Aug. 1819, p. 3

Married, COL. MARKES VANDEWALL, Vendue Master of this city, to MISS SUSANNAH LEWIS, dau. of Mr. Charles Lewis of Henrico Co. (No marriage date)
VGWA 22 Oct. 1789, p. 3; VIC 21 Oct.

Married Dec. 31, 1803, CORNELIUS Van HOUTEN, merchant, of City of New York, to MISS SUSANNA DAVIS, eldest dau. of Micajah Davis, Merchant, of Richmond
RE 2 Jan. 1804, p. 3

Married Jan. 10th by Rev. William H. Hart, MR. JOHN VAN LEW of firm of Adams & VanLew to MISS ELIZA LOUISA BAKER of Richmond
RE 15 Jan. 1818, p. 3; VP 14 Jan., p. 3

Married Oct. 19th at Dr. E. W. Shelton's in Powhatan Co., by Rev. John Martin, MR. THOMAS VANNERSON, to ANN ALLEN, dau. of Jeremiah Allen of Fredericksburg
RE 31 Oct. 1820, p. 3

Married on Mon. last (March 30) by Rev. J. Buchanan, MR. NICHOLAS B. Van ZANDT of Washington City, to MISS MARIA WOOD SOUTHALL of this city
RE 3 April 1807, p. 3; VGGA 4 April, p. 3

Married on Thurs. (Aug. 8) MR. JOHN VARNER to MISS NANCY DESEAR, both of Chester-field Co.
RC 10 Aug. 1816, p. 3

Married on 13th Inst., DR. NICHOLAS M. VAUGHAN to MISS ANNA R. PLEASANTS, eldest dau. of Mr. Isaac W. Pleasants, all of Goochland
VA 23 June 1804, p. 3

Married on Thurs. (Aug. 1) by Rev. Charles Tally, MR. GIBSON VIA, to MISS MARY WHIT eldest dau. of Mr. John White, all of Hanover Co.
RC 7 Aug. 1816, p. 3

Married on 27th Ult. EDWARD WADE to ELIZABETH THURMON, of Hanover Co., having begun their courtship 50 or 60 years ago
VGWA 10 Sept. 1789, p. 3

Married Thurs. last (Feb. 14) in Williamsburg, by Rev. John Bracken, MISS BETSEY
BOOTH to DR. WADDRINGTON of George Town, Md.
VGWA 21 Feb. 1788, p. 3

Married in Charles City Co., on Wed. last (Dec. 24) by Rev. John D. Blair, MR.
THOMAS WAGAMAN of Baltimore, to MISS MARTHA TYLER, dau. of Hon. Judge Tyler
VGGA 31 Dec. 1806, p. 4

Married on Wed. last (Aug. 12) by Rev. Simon Morgan, DR. JOHN R. WALK, to MISS
MARTHA B. BRANCH, both of Chesterfield
RE 23 Aug. 1811, p. 3

Married Jan. 15th by Rev. John D. Blair, MR. BAYLOR WALKER to MISS SARAH D. CRADDOCK,
both of Richmond
RE 17 Jan. 1818, p. 3

Married Dec. 18th by Rev. Edward Folker, MR. HENRY WALKER, JR. to MRS. MARTHA CHANDLER,
all of Charles City Co.
RE 27 Dec. 1817, p. 3

Married at Cherry Hill, April 13th, by Rev. John Ayres, REV. LIVINGTON WALKER, to
MRS. LUCY DAVIS of Buckingham Co.
RE 23 April 1819, p. 3

Married on 1st Inst., MR. ROBERT WALKER of King & Queen Co., to MISS NANCY F. POWELL
of Amherst
VGGA 23 May 1792, p. 3

Married on 4th Inst., MR. WILLIAM WALKER of Goochland Co., age 75, to MISS JANE BURTON
of Louisa, age 17
VA 15 April 1800, p. 3

Married Tues. last (Dec. 30, 1800) CAPT. WILLIAM WALKER of Rocketts to MISS MARY S.
EGE, both of this city
VGGA 1 Jan. 1801, p. 3

Married on Sun. (Sept. 15?) at Philadelphia, MR. WILLIAM WALLACE, merchant, to MISS
KITTY LEEGY, both of that city
RC 19 Sept. 1816, p. 3

Married on June 10th by Rev. Mathew Wood, MR. EDMUND WALLER of James City Co., to
MISS MARY ANN JONES of Warwick Co.
RE 19 June 1818, p. 3

Married lately in Poquoson, York Co., ROBERT WALLER, Esq. of Williamsburg, to
MISS NANCY CAMM, dau. of late John Camm, Pres. of William & Mary
VGWA 19 March 1789, p. 3

Married June 29th by Rev. John Bracken, DR. ROBERT WALLER of Williamsburg, to MISS
ELIZA C. GRIFFIN, dau. of Maj. Thomas Griffin of York-town
VP 5 July 1815, p. 3

Married Feb. 23rd by Rev. John Bracken, WILLIAM WALLER of Williamsburg, to MRS. MARY B. GRIFFIN, eldest dau. of Maj. Thomas Griffin of York-town
VP   4 March 1815, p. 3

Married on Tues. last (Oct. 4) MR. JOHN B. WALTON to MRS. NANCY BAGNOIS, both of this city
VGRMA   8 Oct., 1796, p. 3

Married lately, MAJ. JOHN WARBURTON to MISS BETSEY HARRIS, both of James City Co.
VGAA   26 June 1784, p. 2

Married on 29th Ult. at Mr. J. Wharfe's in Baltimore by Rev. Dr. Rattoone, WILLIAM WARREN, Esq. to MRS. ANN WIGNELL, both of the Baltimore and Phila. Theatre
VA   6 Sept. 1806, p. 3

Married Jan. 21st by Rev. John D. Blair, MAJ. WILLIAM WARWICK of Amherst Co., to MRS. FRANCES A. REED of Henrico Co.
RE   27 Jan. 1818, p. 3

Married March 13th by Rev. Low, CAPT. LEWIS WASHINGTON, to MISS CAREY KING, dau. of late Miles King
RE   18 March 1817, p. 3

Married March 25th by Rev. Logan, MR. BENJAMIN H. WATKINS, Attorney at Law, of Buckingham Co., to MISS MARIA CARRINGTON of Cumberland Co.
RE   7 April 1818, p. 3

Married Sept. 21st at Johnson's Spring, by Rev. Ford, EDWARD OSBORNE WATKINS, to MISS HARRIOT TABB TREVILLIAN, dau. of Late John Trevillian, all of Goochland Co.
RE   26 Sept. 1820, p. 3

Married Dec. 21st by Rev. Edward Baptist, MR. FRANCIS WATKINS, to MISS SUSAN RANDOLPH, dau. of Mr. Brett Randolph, all of Powhatan Co.
RE   28 Dec. 1820, p. 3

Married on 16th Inst. at Mrs. Mary Watkins in Goochland by Rev. Reuben Ford, MR. JOHN E. WATKINS to MISS JUDITH EVELINA WATKINS, 3rd dau. of Mrs. Watkins
RE   8 May 1812, p. 3

Married in this city on 16th Inst., MR. MANSFIELD WATKINS of Manchester to MISS POLLY R. WILLIS
VA   23 Feb. 1805, p. 3

Married Sat. last (March 1) MR. ROBERT WATKINS, merchant of this city, to MISS POLLY OSBORNE of Nottoway
VGGA   7 March 1800, p. 3

Married on 11th Inst., MR. ALEXANDER WATSON, to MISS ELIZABETH PETTYJOHN of Amherst Co.
Visitor   24 Feb. 1810, p. 15

Married in Boston, BENJAMIN M. WATSON, Esq. to MISS ELIZA PARSONS, 3rd dau. of Chief Justice Parsons
Visitor 9 Sept. 1809, p. 127

Married on 19th Inst. (Ult.) DAVID WATSON, Esq., Attorney at Law of Louisa Co., to MISS SALLY MINOR, dau. of Col. Garrett Minor, dec'd
VA 6 March 1801, p. 3

Married on Tues. (May 16) by Rev. Blair, DR. GEORGE WATSON to MISS NANCY RIDDLE, eldest dau. of Joseph Riddle, all of Richmond
VP 20 May 1815, p. 3

Married on 7th May, EDWARD WATTS, Esq., Attorney at Law, of Campbell Co., to MISS ELIZABETH BRECKENRIDGE, 2nd dau. of James Breckenridge, Esq. of Botetourt Co.
VP 4 June 1811, p. 3

Married at Colchester, Conn., MR. LEVI WEBSTER, age 80, to MRS. MERCY ROBINSON, 86
Visitor 18 Nov. 1809, p. 166

Married on Sat. last (Nov. 12) by Rev. Mr. Blair, MR. EDMUND WEBSTER, to MISS PEGGY BEER, both of this city
VGGA 16 Nov. 1803, p. 3

Married on 15th Inst. at Phila., WILLIAM HENRY WEBSTER, comedian, to MISS REBECCA MERICKEN, of that city
Visitor 21 Oct. 1809, p. 150

Married in Richmond on Thurs. (Oct. 10) by Rev. Brice, MR. JOSEPH A. WEED, merchant, to MISS POLLY GEORGE, both of this city
RE 16 Oct. 1816, p. 3; RC 14 Oct., p. 3

Married on Sat. last (May 24) by Rev. Mr. Blair, MR. LOUIS WERCQ to MISS VICTORIA CELESTE CANY, both of Richmond
VA 27 May 1806, p. 3; RE 30 May, p. 3; VGGA 28 May, p. 3

Married Nov. 20, 1814, MR. GEORGE WEST, age 106, of Giles Co., to MRS. MARY GARDNER of Monroe Co., age 80
VP 23 March 1816, p. 3

Married at Norfolk on 22nd Inst., MR. J. WEST to MRS. BIGNALL, both of Va. Co. of Comedians
VGRMA 30 May 1795, p. 3

Married on 2nd Inst., MR. ROBERT WEST of Gloucester Co., to MISS MARY GRYMES of same place
RE 5 Dec. 1809, p. 3

Married in Norfolk, Sun. last (Nov.2) MR. THOMAS WEST of Norfolk to MISS PEGGY WILLOUGHBY
VGWA 6 Nov. 1788, p. 3

Married Sat. last (July 11), MR. THOMAS WHITE, merchant, to MRS. SALLY WELCH, both
of this city
VGRMA 16 July 1795, p. 3

Married, MR. WILLIAM WHITE of this city, merchant, to MRS. THILMAN of Hanover
VGAA 23 April 1785, p. 2

Married on 18th Inst., COL. WILLIAM WHITE of Louisa Co., to MRS. ELIZABETH WHITE
of Hanover
VGWA 26 July 1787, p. 3

Married on 5th Inst., CAPT. WILLIAM WHITE of Hanover to MISS MILDRED ELLIS of same
co.
VA 6 Sept. 1799, p. 3; VGGA 6 Sept., p. 3

Married Nov. 13th by Rev. Thrift, MR. CHRISTOPHER WHITING, to MISS ELIZABETH S. ROBI
dau. of William Robins, all of Gloucester Co.
RE 28 Nov. 1817, p. 3

Married on 6th Inst., FRANCIS WHITING, Esq., of Gloucester to MISS POLLY FOX of
said co.
VGWA 18 Dec. 1788, p. 3

Married on Thurs. (Jan. 14) by Rev. John Courtney, MR. NATHANIEL WHITLOW, to MISS
NANCY NEWMAN, both of Henrico Co.
VA 18 Jan. 1813, p. 3

Married in this city Thurs. last (March 20) JOHN WICKHAM, Esq., Attorney at Law, to
MISS ELIZABETH M'CLURG, dau. of Dr. James M'Clurg of this city
VA 25 March 1800, p. 3; VGGA 25 March, p. 3

Married Nov. 9th at Shirley in Charles City Co., by Rt. Rev. Bishop Moore, WILLIAM
F. WICKHAM, to MISS ANN B. CARTER
RE 14 Dec. 1819, p. 3; RC 11 Dec., p. 3

Married May 18th, MR. JOSEPH WIGGLESWORTH, to MISS EVALINA TURNER (in Caroline Co.?)
RE 9 June 1820, p. 3

Married May 4th in Middlesex Co., by Rev. Hart, MR. JAMES WIATT of Gloucester Co.,
to MISS ISABELLA FAUNTLEROY
RE 28 May 1819, p. 3

Married on 7th Inst., MR. JOHN WILKINS of Brunswick to MISS MARIA CLAIBORNE of
Dinwiddie
Visitor 17 March 1810, p. 27

Married on Thurs. (Aug. 26) by Rev. Wm. Ratcliffe, JAMES H. WILKINSON, to MISS
MARIA B. ARMISTEAD, all of New Kent Co.
RC 8 Sept. 1819, p. 3

Married on Thurs. (April 6) by Rev. John D. Blair, MR. JAMES WILLETT, to MISS
MARY B. CROUCH, 3rd dau. of James R. Crouch of King William Co.
RC 8 April 1820, p. 3; VPRDMA 8 April, p. 3

Married last Friday sen'night (Dec. 21) BARTLETT WILLIAMS, Esq., Attorney at Law,
to MISS SALLY CLOUGH of New Kent Co.
VG or AA 29 Dec. 1781, p. 3

Married at Greenwood Seminary on Feb. 19th by Rev. Samuel D. Hoge, MR. CHARLES
B. WILLIAMS, of Halifax Co., to MISS ANN MERCER HACKLEY
RE 2 March 1819, p. 3

Married on Tues. (Nov. 12) by Rev. John D. Blair, MR. JAMES WILLIAMS, of New Kent
Co., son of James Williams, to MISS ANN MARIA BROTHERHOOD, dau. of Joshua Brotherhood of Richmond
RE 14 Nov. 1816, p. 3; VP 14 Nov., p. 3, says bride was MISS ANN MARIA RUTHERFOORD,
dau. of James B. Rutherfoord; RC 14 Nov., p. 3, says BROTHERHOOD

Married on 19th Ult., MR. JOHN WILLIAMS of Prince George, to MISS MARY BAUGH of
same county
Visitor 4 Nov. 1809, p. 158

Married Oct. 10th by Rev. John Buchanan, MR. JOHN WILLIAMS, to MISS SIANNA A. DANDRIDGE,
both of Richmond
RC 14 Oct. 1820, p. 3

Married on Fri. last (March 14), WILLIAM C. WILLIAMS, Esq. of Culpeper to MISS ALICE
BURWELL of this city
VGGA 19 March 1794, p. 3

Married on Thurs. last (May 12) MR. DABNEY WILLIAMSON to MISS LUCY BURTON, both of
this county
VGRMA 18 May 1796, p. 3

Married, MR. JOHN WILLIAMSON of Amelia to MISS MOLLY ANDERSON of this town. (No
marriage date)
VGWA 27 April, 1782, p. 3

Married on Sat. last (Feb. 21) MR. JOHN WILLIAMSON of this city to MISS FANNY DUDLEY
of New Kent Co.
VA 27 Feb. 1807, p. 3; RE 27 Feb., p. 3, adds married by Rev. McBlair.

Married on Tues. (May 26) by Rev. John D. Blair, MR. ROBERT C. WILLIAMSON, merchant,
of Richmond, to MISS LUCY P. CHAMBERLAYNE of King William Co.
RE 2 June 1818, p. 3

Married on Sat. last (May 24) MR. THOMAS WILLIAMSON to MISS BETSY GALT, both of this
city
VA 27 May 1800, p. 3

Married on 6th Inst. by Rev. Mr. McRae, DR. DANIEL WILSON of this city to MISS HENRIETTA JOHNSON of Powhatan Co.
RE 19 April 1805, p. 3; VA 20 April, p. 3

Married on Mon. last (June 18) by Rev. Mr. Blair, MR. JAMES WILSON of Mecklenburg Co., Merchant, to MISS SUSAN PRICHARD, only dau. of William Prichard, merchant, of this city
VA 23 June 1804, p. 3

Married on Sept. 22nd by Rev. Hooe, MR. JOHN P. WILSON of Berkeley Co., to MISS MARIA W. WILSON, only dau. of Willis Wilson of Cumberland Co.
VP 5 Oct. 1814, p. 3

Married at Green Hill, Campbell Co., on Nov. 6th, CAPT. ROBERT WILSON of Pittsylvania Co. to MISS CATHARINE PANNILL, dau. of Samuel Pannill
VP 18 Nov. 1817, p. 3

Married on Sat. last (Nov. 30) MR. THOMAS WILSON to MISS LUCINDA POPE
VGGA 6 Dec. 1799, p. 3

Married on Sat. last (Sept. 10) MR. CHARLES WINGFIELD of Hanover Co., to MISS ELIZA WILSON, eldest dau. of Thomas Wilson, Esq. of this city
VA 13 Sept. 1808, p. 3; RE 16 Sept., p. 3; VGGA 13 Sept., p. 3

Married on March 9th by Rev. Martin Dawson, MISS CARY ANN NICHOLAS to MR. CHARLES WINGFIELD, JR. both of Albemarle Co.
RE 15 March 1815, p. 3

Married on 18th Ult., GEORGE D. WINSTON, Esq. of Chestnut Hill to MISS DOROTHEA SPOTSWOOD HENRY, 4th dau. of Hon. Patrick Henry of Long Islan
VGRMA 9 July 1795, p. 3

Married on Sun. last (Nov. 9) MR. JOHN WINSTON of this city to MISS RHODA PEATROSS o Caroline
VA 14 Nov. 1806, p. 3

Married on 20th Inst., MR. THOMAS WINSTON, merchant, to MISS ANNE A. TINSLEY, eldest dau. of Maj. John Tinsley, both of Town of Columbia
VA 25 Aug. 1804, p. 3; VGGA 25 Aug., p. 2

Married Jan. 19th by Rev. Parson Hobson, MR. VERE WIRT, to MRS. TABITHA TUCKER, both of this city
VP 22 Jan. 1818, p. 3

Married on Tues. last (Sept. 7) HON. WILLIAM WIRT, Esq., Judge of High Court of Chancery for Williamsburg District, to MISS ELIZABETH WASHINGTON GAMBLE, dau. of Col. Robert Gamble of this city
VGGA 11 Sept. 1802, p. 3

Married in Brunswick Co., May 29th, DR. WILLIAM WITHERS, to MISS ELIZA AUGUSTA STITH, dau. of Richard Stith of that county
RE 17 June 1817, p. 3

Married on Wed. last (July 29) MR. BENJAMIN WOLFE, merchant, to MISS SOPHIA SAMUEL, both of this city
RC 1 Aug. 1795, p. 3; VGRMA 30 July, p. 3

Married Sat. last (Jan. 15) MR. BASIL WOOD to MISS PEGGY RICHARDSON, both of this city
VGGA 19 Jan. 1791, p. 3

Married on Thurs. (Oct. 31) by Rev. John D. Blair, MR. JOHN W. WOOD, to MISS AMELIA HARRIS of Richmond
RE 6 Nov. 1816, p. 3

Married in this city on Sat. (May 17) MR. LEIGHTON WOOD to MISS POLLY YOUNGHUSBAND
VGGA 21 May 1794, p. 3; VGRMA 19 May

Married on Thurs. (Sept. 23) by Rev. John D. Blair, MR. GEORGE WOODFIN, to MISS SUSAN MILLS, both of Richmond
RC 27 Sept. 1813, p. 3

Married on 4th Inst., MR. THOMAS WOODS of Powhatan to MISS PATSY CLEMENS of Amelia Co.
RE 27 March 1807, p. 3

Married July 19th, MR. THOMAS A. WOODSON, to MISS CHRISTIAN JOHNSON, both of Goochland Co.
RE 4 Aug. 1820, p. 3

Married Nov. 2nd, MR. PICHEGRU WOOLFOLK of Holly Hill, Caroline Co., to MISS ANGELINA F. WINSTON, dau. of Mrs. Sarah Winston of Hanover Co.
RE 19 Nov. 1819, p. 3; RC 8 Nov., p. 3

Married on Sat. last (Dec. 22) MR. WILLIAM WORD of Richmond to MISS CYNTHIA CRUTCHFIELD of Hanover Co.
VGGA 25 Dec. 1804, p. 3

Married by Rev. Henry Heffernan, on 7th May, RALPH WORMELEY, son of Ralph Wormeley, Esq. of Rosegill, to MISS ELIZABETH BOSSWELL of Oakley Hill, Gloucester Co.
VGGA 22 May 1805, p. 3

Married on 20th Ult. at Westwood, by Rev. John D. Blair, MR. WILLIAM D. WREN of this city, to MISS THEODOCIA PRICE, youngest dau. of Capt. James Price, dec'd of Henrico
VGGA 3 Oct. 1804, p. 3

Married on 20th Ult., MR. JOHN WRIGHT of Dinwiddie, to MISS MARIA CLOUCH of Petersburg
Visitor 6 May 1809, p. 54

Married on 14th Sept., MR. LEVI WRIGHT, to MISS ELIZA FARGAS, both of Amelia Co.
RE 1 Oct. 1811, p. 3

Married April 15th, MR. MINOR WRIGHT, to MISS ELIZABETH ESTIS (in Caroline Co.?)
RE 9 June 1820, p. 3

Married, MR. JOHN WYATT, merchant, to MISS FLORA McDANIEL, both of this city, on
Sat. last (Oct. 12)
VA 16 Oct. 1805, p. 3

Married Dec. 18th, MAJ. JOHN WYATT of Fayette Co., Ky., to MISS PATSY HARRIS of
Hanover Co.
RE 30 Dec. 1817, p. 3

Married on 8th Inst., RICHARD WYATT, Esq. of Caroline, to MISS NANCY WARE, 4th dau.
of John Ware, Esq. of Goochland
VA 16 Dec. 1796, p. 3

Married by Rev. Low, CAPT. EDWARD L. YOUNG, Commander of steamboat "Richmond", to
MISS HARRIET COLLEY, 2nd dau. of late Capt. W. Colley
RE 17 Nov. 1818, p. 3

Married Wed. (Sept. 15th) MR. JOHN F. YOUNG, to MISS REBECCA BRYAN, dau. of Capt.
Wilson Bryan, all of Richmond
RC 18 Sept. 1819, p. 3

Married on 2nd Inst., by Rev. John D. Blair, MR. WILLIAM YOUNG, to MISS MARY R.
BROOKE, dau. of Col. John Brooke, all of this county
VA 7 Nov. 1811, p. 2

Married on Sat. last (March 20) PLEASANT YOUNGHUSBAND, Esq. of Henrico Co., to
MRS. ELIZA PLEASANTS of this city
VA 23 March 1802, p. 3

INDEX TO BRIDES

BROWN
Maria 255
Mary 227
Nancy 246
BROWNE
Patsy 206
BRYAN
Eleanor 222
Harriet W. 255
Rebecca 266
BYRDIE
Mrs. 226
BURGES
Elizabeth 205
BURNLEY
Sally 253
BURR
Harriett 256
Theodosia 176
BURROW
Patsey 200
BURTON
Jane 259
Lucy 237
Mary 232
Nancy 217
Susan C. 180
BUTLER
Lucy Ann 242
BUTT
Polly 191
BURWELL
Alice 263
Eliza Ann 254
Eliza G. 210
BURTON
Lucy 263
BYARS
Polly 216
BYRD
Abby W. 214
Maria 232
Maria 182
BYRNE
Eliza 179

CABELL
Eliza 208
Elizabeth A. 237
Elvira 211
Sally B. 227
CALLAND
Elizabeth 186
CALLAWAY
Catharine 219
CAMM
Nancy 259
CAMPBELL
Ann B. 248
Mary Ann 244
Molly 243
Sally B. 237
Sarah 193
CANNON
Elizabeth 254
Judith 185
CANY
Victoria Celeste 261
CARR
Elizabeth 198
CARRINGTON
Maria 260
CARTER
Anne 222
Ann 219
Ann B. 262
Eliza 195
Elizabeth 249
Louisa 231
Lucy 253
Lucy L. 202
Mary 186
Rebecca 250
Willie M. 188
CARY
Betsey 217
Cynthia 250
CHAMBERLAYNE
Eveline 236
Lucy P. 263
CHANDLER
Martha 259
Sarah White 232

CHARTER
  Clorinda 193
CHEATHAM
  Elizabeth 207
CHRISTIAN
  Genety 201
  Lelitia 257
  Louisa C. 248
  Miss 198
CHRISTOPHER
  Suritta 225
CHURCHILL
  Lucy Burwell 195
CLAIBORNE
  Maria 262
  Mary 246
  Polly 189
CLARK
  Abigail 192
  Letitia W. 189
  Maria W. 247
  Mary 178
CLARKE
  Catharine 240
  Jane C. 218
  Maria 194
  Mary Anne 177
  Polly 204
CLAY
  Mary 206
CLAYTON
  Martha 221
CLEMENS
  Patsy 265
CLEMENTS
  Ann P. 250
CLINTON
  Catharine 222
  Kathy 222
CLOPTON
  Nancy J. 213
  Sarah E. 194
CLOUGH
  Maria 265
  Sally 263
COCKE
  Eliza Fauntleroy 191
  Martha 228
  Martha Ann 210
  Polly I. 212

COCHRAN
  Charlotte M. 192
  Mary Hodge 224
COLE
  Elizabeth 205
COLEMAN
  Elizabeth W. 235
  Mary W. 229
  Mildred 182
  Nancy 230
  Nancy W. 190
COLES
  Sarah 250
COLLEY
  Harriet 266
CONKRIGHT
  Polly 241
CONWAY
  Matilda 222
COOKE
  Catherine Pendleton 254
COPLAND
  Elizabeth 233
  Maria 184
COTTRELL
  Catherine 213
COUCH
  Dorothea 177
COURTNEY
  Priscilla 187
COUTTS
  Betsy 180
  Mary L. 201
COX
  Nancy 231
  Pamela Ann 228
CRADDOCK
  Sarah D. 259
CRAIG
  Kitty 201
CRAWFORD
  Martha 198
  Sarah 233
CROUCH
  Mary B. 263
  Polly 229
CROXTON
  Susan 183
CRUMP
  Eliza 180

DuVAL
Elizabeth 206
Lucy 237
Lucy 198
Maria B. 201
DYER
Ann 241

EASTON
Joanna A. 238
EATON
Harriott 200
EDDS
Ursula 180
EDMONDSON
Mary 229
EDSALL
Sarah 258
EDWARDS
Georgeanna 182
Janet 199
Margaret 198
EGE
Ann Eliza 197
Mary S. 259
Sally 218
Sarah 200
EGGLESTON
Eliza 179
Maria 177
ELCAN
Ann 211
ELLIOTT
Ann 253
Ann Agnes 231
Betsy 226
ELLIS
Mildred 262
Sukey 226
ELLISON
Nancy 221
ELLYSON
Sarah 208
EPPES
M. B. 178
ESTIS
Elizabeth 266
EUSTACE
Sarah Maria 235

EVANS
Eliza 223
Mary 215
Susan 242

FARRAR
Mary 196
FARGAS
Eliza 265
FARRILL
Sarah D. 223
FAUNTLEROY
Isabella 262
FEREBEE
Hulda 200
FINCH
Elizabeth 247
FINNEY
Sarah 257
FINNIE
Eliza 219
FISHER
Eliza J. 191
Eliza S. 214
Janetta R. 209
FLEMING
Martha Dandridge 192
FLETCHER
Miss 254
FLINT
Margaret 234
FORBUSH
Mindwell 236
FOSTER
Jane Eliza 214
FOUSHEE
Charlotte 188
Elizabeth 233
Isabella 240
FOX
Catharine 196
Levina 189
Maria 181
Polly 262
FRANCIS
Polly 219
FRANCISCO
Susan Brooke 234
FRASER
Betsy 239

MALLOY
    Polly 193
MARKHAM
    Rebecca 236
MARKS
    Betsy 230
    Rachel 195
MARSHALL
    Eliza A. 253
    Jane 252
    Maria Overton 242
MARTIN
    Margaret M. 233
    Sarah 208
MARX
    Louisa 230
MARYE
    Elizabeth 198
MASON
    Catherine 245
    Mary Thompson 213
MATHEWS
    Priscilla 217
MAXWELL
    Mrs. 239
MAY
    Lucy 219
MAYO
    Agnes 224
    Ann 195
    Eliza 201
    Lucy 244
    Maria 245
    Mrs. 237
    Polly 177
McCALLUM
    Mrs. 257
M'CARTY
    Ann R. 219
McCARTY
    Juliet 230
M'CLURG
    Elizabeth 262
McCRAW
    Ann Eliza 207
    Mary G. 216
McCREERY
    Letitia 186
M'CHAU
    Patsey 180

McDANIEL
    Flora 266
McINTOSH
    Ann J. 232
McKIM
    Mary Ann 200
McRAE
    Harriet 216
M'RAE
    Margaret 183
MEAUX
    Fanny 209
MEIGGS
    Mary 214
MEIRCKEN
    Rebecca 261
MENNIS
    Ann Brooke 241
MERRYMAN
    Elizabeth 229
MICHAELS
    Phily 199
MICOU
    Jane N. 243
MILLER
    Elizabeth 249
    Jane 220
    Mary Heath 179
    Miss 248
MILLS
    Susan 265
MINOR
    Betsy 177
    Sally 261
MITCHELL
    Sally 245
MONROE
    Maria Hester 206
    Miss 210
MONTAGUE
    Nancy 215
MOODY
    Clara 234
    Kitty 228
    Maria 194
    Mary Ann 228
MOORE
    Gertrude Parker 210
    Polly 225

ADDITIONS AND CORRECTIONS

MARRIAGE NOTICE OMITTED:

Married on 1st Instant, MR. EDWIN HARVIE, to MISS HARDAWAY of Amelia
RE 1 March 1808, p. 3

GROOMS OUT OF ALPHABETICAL ORDER:

WILLIAM DAINGERFIELD is on p. 249
BATHURST JONES is on p. 215
BERNARD MOORE is on p. 220